SENTINEL

48 LIBERAL LIES ABOUT AMERICAN HISTORY

Larry Schweikart is the coauthor of *A Patriot's History of the United States* and the author of *America's Victories*. He is a regular guest on *Fox & Friends* where he discusses biases in American history textbooks. A professor of history at the University of Dayton, he has written more than twenty other books on national defense, business, and financial history. He lives in Centerville, Ohio.

48 Liberal Lies About American History

(That You Probably Learned in School)

Larry Schweikart

Sentinel

SENTINEL
Published by the Penguin Group
Penguin Group (USA) Inc., 375 Hudson Street, New York, New York 10014, U.S.A. • Penguin Group
(Canada), 90 Eglinton Avenue East, Suite 700, Toronto, Ontario, Canada M4P 2Y3 (a division of
Pearson Penguin Canada Inc.) • Penguin Books Ltd, 80 Strand, London WC2R 0RL, England • Penguin
Ireland, 25 St Stephen's Green, Dublin 2, Ireland (a division of Penguin Books Ltd) • Penguin Books
Australia Ltd, 250 Camberwell Road, Camberwell, Victoria 3124, Australia
(a division of Pearson Australia Group Pty Ltd) • Penguin Books India Pvt Ltd, 11 Community Centre,
Panchsheel Park, New Delhi – 110 017, India • Penguin Group (NZ), 67 Apollo Drive, Rosedale,
North Shore 0632, New Zealand (a division of Pearson New Zealand Ltd) • Penguin Books (South Africa)
(Pty) Ltd, 24 Sturdee Avenue, Rosebank, Johannesburg 2196, South Africa

Penguin Books Ltd, Registered Offices:
80 Strand, London WC2R 0RL, England

First published in the United States of America by Sentinel, a member of Penguin Group (USA) Inc. 2008
This paperback edition with a new chapter and revisions published 2009

1 3 5 7 9 10 8 6 4 2

Copyright © Larry Schweikart, 2008, 2009
All rights reserved

Illustration credits
pp. 3, 92: National Archives
p. 51: United States Navy
p. 140: Ronald Reagan Library
p. 168: Gary L. Friedman (www.Friedman/Archives.com)
p. 237: from *The American Pageant*, 9th edition, by Thomas A. Bailey and David M. Kennedy (Houghton
Mifflin)

LIBRARY OF CONGRESS CATALOGING-IN-PUBLICATION DATA
Schweikart, Larry.
48 liberal lies about American history : (that you probably learned in school) / Larry Schweikart.
p. cm.
Includes bibliographical references and index.
ISBN 978-1-59523-051-5 (hc.)
ISBN 978-1-59523-056-0 (pbk.)
1. United States—History—Miscellanea. I. Title. II. Title: Forty-eight liberal lies
about American history.
E179.S35 2008
973—dc22   2008007334

Printed in the United Stares of America
Designed by Spring Hoteling

To those honest and ethical scholars everywhere
who allow the evidence to determine their worldview, not the opposite.

ACKNOWLEDGMENTS

Conservatives frequently ask, "How is it for you on a college campus? Are you harassed? Is it hard to get along?" I am always pleased to respond that the University of Dayton has been extremely supportive of all my work since I arrived there in 1985. While certainly I do not speak for UD, nor does the university endorse most of my views—if any of them—nevertheless, UD has done what an institution of higher education is supposed to do: advance and foster the expansion of knowledge, no matter where it leads. Even though I tip my hat to UD in virtually every one of my books, I'd like to once again thank the administrators, department chairmen and chairwomen, and colleagues who have for two decades encouraged me and made possible yet another book. My chairman, Professor Julius Amin, has kept my other duties at a minimum, and located research support funds when I needed them. At UD, in particular, I want to thank Ron Acklin at Print and Design for once again providing excellent graphics, and Professor Yuguen (David) Yu, now at Wilberforce University, for lending me recent editions of U.S. history textbooks.

Burton Folsom, a historian at Hillsdale College, offered moral support and allowed me to look at parts of his unfinished manuscript on Franklin Roosevelt and the New Deal. Clayton Cramer shared material on early American history, as well as his superb work on guns in the early Republic. Richard Newby educated me on the Sacco-Vanzetti debate. My coauthor on *A Patriot's History of the United States,* Mike Allen, helped with timely information and a critical reading of key sections. Vicki Harlow was of immense assistance in acquiring photographs, and my son, Adam Schweikart, contributed research to almost every entry.

To be fair, this book was Adrian Zackheim's idea originally, and he got the project started. But it was Bernadette Malone Serton, my editor on *A Patriot's History of the United States* and *America's Victories,* who kept the process going and refined the focus. Brooke Carey stepped in to apply the final touches. Obviously, none of them are to blame for any errors, for which I take full responsibility. Finally, thanks again to my excellent agent, Ed Knappman.

Larry Schweikart
Centerville, Ohio

CONTENTS

48 Liberal Lies
About
American History

INTRODUCTION

If you surveyed ten of the most widely used American history survey textbooks looking at the twentieth century, what picture do you think you would find most commonly represented? The sailor kissing the woman in Times Square at the end of World War II? A smiling Franklin D. Roosevelt? The atomic bomb? It might surprise you to know that one of the most frequently appearing images depicting American life in the *1920s*—not Reconstruction—is that of the Ku Klux Klan.[1] Virtually all of these textbooks dedicate at least one page, often more, to the Klan in the twentieth century. George B. Tindall and David E. Shi's *America: A Narrative History* uses almost two pages to cover the Klan; Paul S. Boyer et al.'s *Enduring Vision* also gives the Klan the better part of two pages—about the same as it gives to the Clinton impeachment, despite the fact that Clinton's was only the second impeachment of a president in U.S. history.

According to these historians, the Klan, above all other groups, defined America. Mark C. Carnes and John Garraty's *American Destiny* provides the standard photo and claims that "the Klan remained influential for a number of years," but fails to mention that, as of 2007, U.S. senator Robert Byrd of West Virginia, a former Klan member himself, still sits in the Senate as a well-regarded Democrat.[2] This over-the-top coverage, meant to characterize the 1920s as an age of backwardness and bigotry, is common among almost all textbooks, despite the fact that the Klan's largest march numbered only forty thousand. The Klan, one of many white-supremacy and racist guerrilla-terror groups during the Reconstruction era, had made a comeback in the 1920s. Marches were the least violent of their activities—Klansmen, as a group or individually, were involved in the lynching of blacks and in shootings and firebombings. As a terror organization, however, the KKK was still fairly small, and no more representative of mainstream America than the Illuminati. A single Billy Graham crusade drew more; Woodstock pulled in more than twice as many; and a University of Michigan home football game had double the attendance—not even counting the "tailgaters." And *none* of these textbooks include images of *any* of the million-plus pro-life marches in Washington in the 1980s.[3]

Or consider this: In chapter-length treatments of the United States in World War II, what image (besides the obligatory atomic bomb) might one normally expect to find? Soldiers, right? Given that the military was unfortunately still segregated, and that whites did the overwhelming share of front-line fighting, one would expect to see at least a few pictures of average American soldiers fighting in Europe or in the South Pacific. One might . . . but one wouldn't. *The American Journey,* by David Goldfield et al., has only one distant shot of D-Day—but not a single close-up picture of American soldiers in combat. There is a picture of some soldiers—African Americans, but not in combat—under a discussion of "the black experience." Indeed, in *The American Journey,* for the entire twentieth and twenty-first centuries, the only non-black soldier is depicted fighting in Iraq. Despite the fact that four million Americans served in World War I alone—and over 53,000 were killed in that conflict—*The American Journey* does not bother to include a single photo of the war. Instead, police are shown beating strikers with their nightsticks under a discussion of the dislocations of the postwar economy.

Merely a photo/image study of major college history textbooks would reveal a great deal about their biases, but we have their words and content as well. With issue after issue—the Great Depression, slavery, World War I, the Far West, the Reagan years—modern textbooks are obvious in their leftward slant that America is a racist, sexist, imperialist regime. Even when trying to take conservatism seriously, historians show their true colors. In 1992, *The American Historical Review* published an article called "The Grass-Roots Right: New Histories of U.S. Conservatism in the Twentieth Century." The author, Michael Kazin, correctly noted that most historians were "overwhelmingly cosmopolitan in their cultural tastes and liberal or radical in their politics."[4] Then, Kazin proceeded to review five new books on American conservatism, including two histories of . . . the Ku Klux Klan! Edward Shapiro, reviewing Kazin's article in *Continuity,* observed, "Not only did Kazin identify conservatism with racism and nativism, he also drew attention to the similarities between the American Right and Nazism, Italian fascism, and the French nativist politician Jean-Marie Le Pen."[5]

Other than a photo of Franklin D. Roosevelt or the atomic bomb, the most commonly appearing picture in the twentieth-century section of U.S. history textbooks is some depiction of the Ku Klux Klan. The implication is that the "Roaring Twenties" were racist and that somehow the economic growth of the decade rested on nativism and intolerance.

What does the post-Vietnam wave of history books do with all the pages it does not dedicate to exposing the activities of the Ku Klux Klan? A sampling of major textbooks reveals a tendency to describe Franklin Roosevelt and his New Deal as the only possible salvation to a country wracked by the failures of "big business," or the Great Society as "remarkable" and "impressive," despite the fact that it created the massive rise in black family breakup and illegitimacy.[6] Native Americans—at least those Columbus didn't kill—are portrayed as wonderful environmentalists who "lived in harmony" with the buffalo; the Founders, on the other hand, are often represented as "moneyed interests" who sought to cement their position at the top of the heap through the Constitution. Early presidents avoided all international "entanglements" and were backward isolationists; Andrew Jackson was the forerunner of new liberal Democrats and the opponent of the "elites"; and the causes of the Civil War were complex, including disagreements over the tariff and a clash of cultures. Abraham Lincoln only issued the Emancipation Proclamation because he was running out of white troops to prosecute the war. The Scopes trial exposed "religious fundamentalism" as unintellectual and unpopular; Prohibition failed in all its objectives; and government successfully stepped in to control the rapacious "robber barons."

While most of these books correctly characterize World War II, the conclusion of the war brings immediate questions about whether the United States used "atomic diplomacy" to bully the poor, helpless Soviet Union. Little attention is paid to Soviet spies, such as Julius and Ethel Rosenberg—it is far more interesting to demagogue Senator Joseph McCarthy for his attempts to expose Communists in the U.S. government. Richard Nixon expanded the Vietnam War—but John F. Kennedy was going to "pull us out" if he had lived. The dense and lazy Ronald Reagan merely regurgitated policies developed by his staff and knew "Star Wars" would not work. While none of the texts I have surveyed go so far as to claim the United States "deserved" the 9/11 attacks, some of the more radical histories question whether the World Trade Center was actually hit by airplanes, and many perpetuate the notion that terrorists were merely poor, downtrodden, uneducated people who hated the United States because of our support for Israel.

The list of historical lies, distortions, and myths is extensive. How is it that this book is limited to exposing only forty-nine? In fact, while many had to be left out or combined, others were selected because they proved easier cases to clearly disprove, relying less on interpretation. Textbooks can be slanted in a number of ways, including labeling (using loaded terms to describe those positions liberals favor as "progressive," "forward-thinking," "liberating," while characterizing conservative or religious views as "fundamentalist," "backward," "nativist," or "prejudiced"). Labeling is a fairly easy tactic to identify and illuminate. More difficult to spot are forms of bias involving interpretation or coverage. Omitting "good news" is common. Chapters on the 1980s routinely leave out the incredible turnaround in employment and inflation, focusing obsessively on deficits (which are never treated as problems in Democratic administrations). A favorite tactic of historians (and the press) is to preface the historian's own views through deceptive terms such as "critics argued" or "many feared" or similar "fair"-sounding phrases. In fact, most of the time, the "critics" were leftists far outside the mainstream who had little credibility at all with the majority of Americans, but who are presented as an "equal" voice in the debate.

While there is nothing wrong with solid interpretation, the goal here is to identify clearly those examples of bias that seem to afflict the largest numbers of leftward-slanted books. But that does not mean interpretation is not a legitimate field upon which to challenge textbooks. In a 1992 issue of *Continuity*, Edward Shapiro provided one of the first comprehensive looks at liberalism in college textbooks.[7] Shapiro examined nuances and phrases in popular textbooks of the 1990s. For example, Alan Brinkley et al., in *American History: A Survey*, offered the innocent-appearing analysis that John F. Kennedy "inspired enthusiasm among relatively few liberals" in the 1960 election.[8] Unstated was the fact that if liberals disliked Kennedy, conservatives were likely attracted to him, and his strength in the South and elsewhere probably offset his liberal losses. But the implied message to students? Liberal support is more valuable than conservative support. Another popular book, Tindall and Shi's *America: A Narrative History*, described Michael Harrington's *The Other America* as a "powerful exposé" featuring "an impressive array of statistics as well as convincing theories of social psychology."[9] Given that the third edition of *America* was published in 1992, the authors should know that Harrington's "impressive array of statistics" was questionable, since no one could ever provide any reliable definition of poverty. Moreover, his "convincing theories of social psychology" became the basis of Great Society meddling that utterly destroyed the lives of millions of inner-city residents.

In his review of 1990s textbooks, Shapiro found that one of the more prominent, *The National Experience* by John Morton Blum et al., with chapters written by famous historians such as C. Vann Woodward and Arthur Schlesinger, typified the "interpretation" style of bias through long-winded harangues that led the student to the conclusion the professors wanted.[10] Grover Cleveland (arguably the last good Democratic president) is described as a "stubborn conservative . . . out of touch with the radical discontent of the country."[11] Oh really? This would be the same Grover Cleveland elected twice, and who was only narrowly defeated a third time? Apparently that "radical discontent" never actually reached the *voters*! As will be seen in the entry on the transcontinental railroads, it was an article of faith that "some form of public credit was essential" in building the railroads, although there is no mention of the fact that James J. Hill managed to build a transcontinental railroad without a dime of public support.[12] Similarly, in his section on the New Deal, Arthur Schlesinger praised Social Security, the tax laws of the

1930s, and the Agricultural Adjustment Administration, without bothering to mention a single negative impact of any of those pieces of legislation (and there were many). In a ridiculous claim, Schlesinger maintained that hiking the income tax rate to 79 percent for the top tier of income earners "had considerable, progressive impact."[13] Perhaps, as some liberal economists have argued, ludicrously high taxes had no effect on that 12.5 percent unemployment rate in 1937 . . . but it's doubtful any mainstream economist would acknowledge such a claim. *The National Experience,* predictably, described the Eisenhower years (of growth and remarkable change) as an era of "stagnation," and only the wonderful Kennedy presidency "broke the crust that had settled over the country in the 1950s."[14]

A priceless example of word bias in texts can be seen in *The National Experience*'s comments about Lyndon Johnson, who had become "more conservative" since the New Deal, but nevertheless "retained an authentic concern for the poor."[15] Obviously, the astute reader will see that "there was a negative correlation between conservatism and concern for the poor."[16] *The National Experience* then drifted from bias into fantasy by describing the Reagan economic boom as an "economic quagmire."[17] Most Americans, presented with a "quagmire" economy that added eight million net new jobs in seven years and utterly eliminated all inflation, would say, "Gimme that quagmire!"

Burton W. Folsom Jr. conducted a similar survey to Shapiro's of literature related to the "robber barons" of the nineteenth and early twentieth centuries, finding authors routinely ignored any positive comments about Cornelius Vanderbilt, John D. Rockefeller, Andrew Carnegie, or Andrew Mellon, choosing instead to focus on criticisms by failed business rivals or government officials. Folsom found that the impact of these titans on the price of shipping, kerosene, or steel was routinely ignored in favor of discussions about "monopolies" (which none of them ever achieved). Astoundingly, in the same breath, historians complained about "cutthroat competition," described as "a problem."[18] Of course, not one single consumer who experienced falling prices at the store or on train trips ever once referred to lower prices as a "problem." Low prices, it seems, were only "problems" for liberal historians who favor government control of business.

In the case of Rockefeller, his phenomenal church giving was never alluded to; nor was Mellon's stunning donation of his massive and priceless art collection to the people of the United States.[19] Yet virtually all textbooks refer to Matthew Josephson's original screed against the captains of industry (*The Robber Barons*, 1934) without bothering to correct the record with Folsom's research. I specifically expanded Folsom's analysis to business history textbooks and found similar disturbing trends.[20] Commenting on the 1980s, one author complained that American businesses were "so busy fighting [corporate] raiders [such as Carl Icahn and T. Boone Pickens] that they cannot fight Japanese competitors," without appreciating that it was precisely *because* of the discipline imposed by such "raiders" that many U.S. companies survived and the Japanese floundered.[21] Even in a "conservative" field such as American business history, college-level textbooks routinely praised government interference in the free market, ignored unintended consequences of such involvement, and downplayed the role of entrepreneurs in favor of coverage of large corporations, as though they, like Athena, sprang, full-bodied, from the head of Zeus.

If a field such as business history cannot "get it right," what hope is there for such leftist-dominated fields as "social" history? This leads us to another major source of bias, namely coverage and emphasis. When Thomas A. Bailey and David M. Kennedy's established standard text, *The American Pageant*, asserted that the feminist and civil rights revolutions "have fueled an explosion of scholarship about race, gender and class relations in the past," it completely begged the question about whether such an "explosion" was useful or even an accurate representation of our history.[22] Supposedly mainstream historians such as Gary B. Nash cheered the "flowering of social history," which "replaced the nationalist, white-centered, hero-driven, and male-dominated" narrative of the traditional history books.[23] Heroes, bad, nationalism, worse, as Nash implies. But the very focus on "everyday life" defeats the purpose of history, for *no* book can accurately reflect the daily experiences of even a few thousand people, let alone millions, even more so over hundreds of years. By its very definition, history must always deal with those events and people who affected the greatest number over time—and that means discussing George Washington and Robert E. Lee, not their slaves; Andrew Carnegie, not his steelworkers; and Dwight Eisenhower, not the suburban housewives of Levittown. Heroes, by definition, do what others cannot and do not do—they lift everyone up. Would Nash prefer we focus on life's unextraordinary figures?

Thus coverage insidiously erodes notions of heroism, significance, and great ideas in favor of sameness, insignificance, and the daily drudge. While it is absolutely true that Carnegie would have achieved little without *all* of his labor force, the cold fact is that he wouldn't have missed a beat had any *one* of them never been born. Certainly individuals represent ideas and movements—which is precisely why the Rosenbergs deserved coverage for their treason, but Sacco and Vanzetti's murder during a robbery is an overused crutch for leftists seeking to drum up a "red scare" when none existed.

Not surprisingly, the "New Left" historians were outraged at the biases in textbooks (of course, they are always outraged)—but the cause of their outrage was that the "counterculture" wasn't given its due! Writing in the once-prestigious (but now mundane) *Journal of American History,* Bruce Schulman complained that textbooks *insufficiently* covered the sixties protests, neglected to include extracts from the Port Huron Statement (1962), usually considered the first major "policy statement" of the protesting, counterculture crowd, and routinely mischaracterized the flower-waving, acid-tripping, half-naked, foul-mouthed sixties hippies as, well, hippies.[24] "The New Left," he whined, "receives scant attention largely because it does not fit the main story line—the rising tide of identity politics."[25] Well, not exactly. The New Left "receives scant attention," even from liberal textbooks, because it has been thoroughly discredited. Robert James Maddox's book *The New Left and the Origins of the Cold War,* among others, exposed the utter fabrication and distortion of evidence to make whatever point the New Left author wanted to make.[26] It seems that those who knew the Left best were ridiculed and demonized once they left the Left. A stream of books appeared, authored by former true believers and movement leaders, including Peter Collier and David Horowitz, or defectors from the Soviet bloc, such as Viktor Belenko and Vasili Mitrokhin.[27] Nevertheless, Schulman claimed that U.S. history texts "mistreat the New Left," when they almost uniformly ignored or excluded the evidence of these former "insiders."[28] Considering the New Left's credibility, that's almost impossible. Nevertheless, he maintained that texts "underestimate the political content of cultural rebellion and ignore the intimate links between New Left politics and countercultural experimentation."[29] Schulman writes that "the standard textbook accounts simply miss [the] fundamental connection" linking "personal liberation and political revolution."[30] Perhaps that was because the radicals themselves knew their objectives were self-defeating. As Jerry Rubin, one of the Yippie leaders, confessed, "All we want from these meetings [with authorities] are demands that the Establishment can never satisfy. . . . Goals are *irrelevant*."[31] The entire New Left ideology was one of nihilistic destruction, which the academics apparently realized after a few years away from the bong-filled communes. Everything about the "movement" was in contradiction to itself: "Get close to nature," but use twentieth-century pharmaceuticals to "drop out." "Get in touch with your inner self," preferably if that "inner self" was rude, obnoxious, angry, and hostile to bathing.

Indeed, the textbooks' treatment of the sixties radicals was completely defensive, portraying them as innocent and harmless, although well meaning and possessing "the right" fundamental values. Were these portrayals to be more honest, the writers well know that even naive students would blow off the Yippies and their ilk as "doofuses," "losers," and "clueless." While the current generation of college students may be cynical and less literate than previous generations, they disdain phoniness. The popular television program *South Park* routinely ridicules the hippie movement (as much as it does conservatives). Woodstock, the crowning event of the counterculture decade, is ridiculed by modern students, who find the images of nearly naked, mud-caked, frizzy-haired teens gyrating to sounds emanating from a stage they can barely see as anachronistic as a taffy pull. For all their depression and alienation, few of the "grunge" era, post-MTV music icons would be so pompous as to describe themselves as the "Lizard King," as the Doors' Jim Morrison once did. Where the radical academics rhapsodize about Woodstock, one of the participants correctly noted that its "peace and love" came primarily from the widespread use of drugs: what else would "a million kids on grass, acid, and hog tranquilizers be" except peaceful?[32] Instead of representing the "presence of the invisible time travelers from the future," as Grateful Dead guitarist Jerry Garcia (now deceased) called them, the Woodstockers were more often than not "kids freaking out from megadoses of acid or almost audibly buzzing from battery-acid crank like flies trapped in a soda can."[33] There is a good reason most textbooks avoid these kinds of honest evaluations.[34]

Another element of revisionism appeared in textbooks after the 1960s: a view that the United States needed to be punished for its success. As noted in the entry on Lee Harvey Oswald, one writer has traced this to a perverted analysis of the Kennedy assassination—that the deed was some cosmic wrath inflicted on all America for past sins. This "punishment revisionism" soon worked its way into the fabric of high school and middle school textbooks as well. Although not the focus of this book, the major textbooks offered to lower grades began to resemble their college-level models, suffering from overarching "inclusive-ism," political correctness, and old-fashioned factual errors. Mel Gabler has fought a campaign for years to force changes in the Texas school system's textbook adoptions. He has met with some success, but has not been able to halt a steady intrusion of politically correct terminology. Words such as "tribe" and "slave" have been banned, replaced by "group" and "enslaved person." Of course, American Indians (oops! Make that, according to the new textbook Nazis, "Native Americans") *never* referred to themselves as "groups" (although Indians would refer to themselves by *tribe*). Some high school textbooks have even insisted that American blacks be referred to as "Africans."[35] This must present some difficulties for passages dealing with recent African immigrants to America! Texas and California account for 20 percent of all textbooks sold in the United States, so Gabler's campaign is critical in shaping the nation's history curriculum.

Beyond the critical content issues, the lower-level textbooks are run through computer programs that excise words considered "too difficult" for ten- or eleven-year-olds. Publishers routinely test their books against a list of words and the frequencies with which they occur developed by Edward Lee Thorndike and against the Dale-Chall "readability" tests. Author James Michener, who worked as a textbook editor for Macmillan, described the "tyranny of that list," stating that it represented the first step in the "dumbing down of the curriculum."[36] Michener found that texts originally written for middle schoolers soon were adopted for high school students, and what was appropriate for high schools was soon used as the standard college text. A grandmother named Joy Hakim, disgusted by the crop of elementary/high school textbooks, wrote her own history book, *A History of the United States,* which restored some of the balance and perspective to the past.[37] At least Hakim, when dealing with the Lewis and Clark expedition, focuses on the exploration of North America and only when appropriate mentions William Clark's manservant, York, whereas most texts would have students believe that Meriwether Lewis and Clark were mere appendages to the "real" adventurer, York.

Few high school and middle school history teachers, however, have time to consult extensive secondary sources to develop their lesson plans and study guides, naturally relying in many cases on the flawed college history texts mentioned above. It was the oppressive bias of those college textbooks, under which Michael Allen and I labored for many years, that led us in the 1990s to begin work on *A Patriot's History of the United States*.[38] While the success of that book after its 2004 release initially surprised us, it shouldn't have. We quickly realized that homeschoolers, many high school teachers who indeed wanted the truth, and even "mainstream" academics were interested in an alternative to the left-dominated textbooks on the market. A dozen university courses have adopted *A Patriot's History*—sometimes requiring it alongside Howard Zinn's *A People's History* (a battle we are confident we will win, every time). *A Patriot's History* didn't just spackle over a gap, it filled a Grand Canyon–size hole in American history education.

Rather than reinvent the wheel with another comprehensive reinterpretation of American history, this book attempts to develop more fully many of the errors and myths perpetrated by the so-called mainstream texts. Arranged according to my own (admittedly biased) assessment of the significance of historical issues, *48 Liberal Lies About American History* documents in every entry the specific errors in these books by using the authors' own words. For the sake of brevity and convenience, some issues have been combined under one heading (the Great Crash, the Great Depression, and the New Deal); some, necessarily, have been omitted, as in the cases where an explanation of the textbooks' errors would nearly result in a textbook-long explanation. Unlike Edward Shapiro, who only examined in depth a few textbooks, I have sought to include as many major oft-used textbooks as I could, which carried with it a disadvantage, in that I did not frequently engage in long, passage-length phrase analysis as Shapiro did. While his method was entirely appropriate, I sought broader coverage so as to make the point that it is not "one or two" rogue textbooks engaging in consistently flawed presentations.

Lovers of freedom and genuine intellectual advancement can take solace in the trend among most college-level introductory history classes to depend increasingly on primary source writings and less on textbooks. Students, therefore, at least get to see the primary actors of history speak for themselves, although certainly instructors can (and usually do) "translate" what these figures from the past "really meant." If there is one desirable result of the sixties revolution, it is that the cult of individuality has produced a rebellion among college instructors against using any common textbook, lest they become one of the "organization men." Students are the beneficiaries of this trend. At the same time, the new obsession with "critical thinking" has all but destroyed the concept both of historical context and of significance.

And there is another new development that bodes ill for the liberal textbook industry. In 2007, Osman Rashid cofounded Chegg, a textbook rental business that operates much like the online DVD rental site Netflix. Chegg rents and delivers textbooks to college students at a 50–70 percent discount. A new $100 textbook could cost as little as $32 to rent so students are encouraged to rent textbooks instead of buying them. With fewer purchases, there will be far less interest by publishers to commission new books and even less interest in investing time and money into revising the books with every passing fad. It is through these efforts to keep books current that most of the leftist ideology seeps in: it's far too difficult for professors to rewrite hundreds of pages of earlier material, but it's easy to slip in a bit about global warming, to demonize George W. Bush, or fawn over Barack Obama. Thus, in a few pages of revisions, a writer can completely change the thrust of an even reliable book—this was to a large degree the case of both *The American Pageant* and *America: A Narrative History*, both of which drifted sharply to the left with newer revisions. Virtually all of the global warming nonsense has come in the most recent revisions.

What Chegg may do, in fact, is to force historians to actually put more effort into recording history rather than current events. How many readers think that in fifty years, global warming will have been a serious issue? Or, for a different example, just look at the scare-mongering over the "economic power" of Japan just fifteen years go, when Japan was going to "buy up" the United States. Yet today, Japan is drifting downward with massive financial and economic woes. By ending the tyranny of revisions, Chegg may in fact end revisionism![39]

Nowhere will this be tested more than in the case of the more ridiculous circulating assertions about the 9/11 attacks, which I originally decided to include in this book because, even though these theories have not yet been accepted as fact, it seemed to me that they were becoming more mainstream. I figured it was better to head them off at the pass by including them in my book. If Chegg has the impact I think it may have, then the profession may avoid the embarrassment it would suffer if these ridiculous leftist assertions found their way into their supposedly factual textbooks.

Some of the conclusions I have made in this book cut across traditional partisan lines, but I go where I think the evidence leads. Prohibition wasn't the flop it has been portrayed as being; LBJ didn't "off" John Kennedy; and

Franklin Roosevelt did not "set up" the U.S. 7th Fleet to be destroyed at Pearl Harbor. Facts are uncomfortable things. On the other hand, most of the falsehoods examined here do seem to originate on the left side of the political spectrum, and that fact, too, is an uncomfortable thing.

One reality is certain: if those who read history are grounded in truth, bias will reveal itself in no time. And once that happens, the market for politically correct, agenda-driven textbooks will dry up and blow away like the marijuana leaves at Woodstock.

LIE #1

THE FIRST PRESIDENTS INTENDED FOR THE UNITED STATES TO BE ISOLATIONIST

In his farewell address, [George] Washington urged that the United States stay out of European affairs and make no permanent alliances, a principle that would be a hallmark of American foreign policy for a century and a half.
—JAMES WEST DAVIDSON ET AL., NATION OF NATIONS

Thomas Jefferson, in his Inaugural Address of 1801, paraphrased the first principle of American foreign policy as "peace, commerce, and honest friendship with all nations, entangling alliances with none."
—JOHN MACK FARAGHER ET AL., OUT OF MANY

Jefferson's federalism reflected his posture as a "half-way pacifist," in, but not of, the world of power politics.
—PETER S. ONUF, "'THE STRONGEST GOVERNMENT ON EARTH': JEFFERSON'S REPUBLICANISM, THE EXPANSION OF THE UNION, AND THE NEW NATION'S DESTINY" (2003)

While few people have read much of what George Washington had to say, many readily cite his warning about avoiding entangling alliances as evidence that the United States should not be involved in foreign wars. As noted above, the actual phrase "entangling alliances with none" was used by Thomas Jefferson, not George Washington, although Washington uttered similar sentiments in his famous "Farewell Address." In neither case did the concept mean "isolationism" or even an absence of foreign military operations, or even a complete refusal to engage in alliances. Nevertheless, it is frequently invoked by both modern leftists and radical libertarians as an excuse to avoid fighting foreign enemies unless the landing craft are actually dropping troops on the New Jersey shore.

Not only did Washington's comments require context, but he personally had not followed his own advice on many occasions. Certainly he did not oppose aggressive, even unilateral military action. He enthusiastically led a small force to drive the French out of Fort Duquesne, but failed and had to surrender Fort Necessity, his own fortifications. Neither did his successors eschew foreign military action, including Thomas Jefferson, often held up as the epitome of a pacifist president, despite Reginald Stuart's description of him as a "half-way pacifist."[1]

Understanding Washington requires that the phrases in the "Farewell Address" be placed in the context of the full address. Washington urged his countrymen to "observe good faith and justice towards all nations; cultivate peace and harmony with all. Religion and morality enjoin this conduct. . . ." In achieving this "good faith and justice," Washington said, "nothing is more essential than that permanent, inveterate antipathies against particular nations, and passionate attachments for others, should be excluded; and that, in place of them, just and amicable feelings towards all should be cultivated." His concern was that an *unfounded* hatred—"permanent, inveterate antipathies against particular nations"—would draw the country into war "contrary to the best calculations of policy." Sympathy for the favorite nation, facilitating the illusion of an imaginary common interest in cases "where no real common interest exists . . . [risks] a participation in the quarrels and wars of the latter without adequate inducement or justification."[2] Having spent the first three-fourths of the address criticizing political parties, Washington warned that the "avenues of foreign influence" would shape American policy. Sounding much like a twentieth-century multinational corporate leader, Washington said, "The great rule of conduct for us in regard to foreign nations is in extending our commercial relations, to have with them as little political connection as possible."

Europe, Washington warned, "has a set of primary interests which to us have none; or a very remote relation." There were occasions on which alliances were acceptable. However, he urged Americans to "steer clear of permanent alliances with any portion of the foreign world; so far, I mean, as we are now at liberty to do it." Then Washington clarified: "Let me not be understood as capable of patronizing infidelity to existing engagements." Existing treaties were to be honored, and future treaties "for extraordinary emergencies" might be necessary. Indeed, much of Washington's second administration had been absorbed with securing new commercial treaties with England and Spain, working tirelessly to secure peace treaties with the "foreign nations" on America's immediate borders—the Indians.[3]

All this was not exactly a pacifist manifesto. As Washington stated in the "Farewell Address," "Our detached and distant situation" allowed the United States to "pursue a different course" from Europe. The "period is not far off," he foresaw, "when we may *defy material injury from external annoyance;* when we may take such an attitude as will cause the neutrality we may at any time resolve upon to be scrupulously respected . . . [and] *when we shall choose peace or war, as our interest guided by our justice shall Counsel* [emphasis mine]." Washington well knew that in 1796, the young Republic could not engage in a foreign conflict if it so chose. It had neither the army nor the navy—although John Adams's administration soon rectified the latter by building new, heavy frigates.

If the United States "is preserved in tranquility twenty years longer, it may bid defiance, in a just cause, to any power whatever, such, in that time will be its population, wealth, and resource."[4] The twenty-year span appeared again in a letter to Charles Carroll the following year: "Twenty years peace with such an increase in population and resources as we have a right to expect, added to our remote situation from the jarring power, will in all probability enable us in a just cause, to bid defiance to any power on earth."[5] Even in the draft comments for the "Farewell Address," which were not published in the final version, Washington wrote "that if this country can remain in peace 20 years longer: and I devoutly pray that it may do so to the end of time; such in all probability will be its population, riches, and resources, when combined with its peculiarly happy and remote Situation from the other quarters of the globe, as to bid defiance, in a just cause, to any earthly power whatsoever."[6]

In other words, Washington knew that practicality demanded a careful, noninterventionist foreign policy for at least twenty years. A nation that could "choose peace or war" had to be powerful enough to make such a choice, and Washington knew it. Just as he had as General Washington, President

Washington bought time for the nation to build up its material and martial resources. It should also be noted that Washington emphasized the need for national unity in military matters, to the point that he declared any who did not support such actions unpatriotic. Referring to the spirit that connected Americans during time of war, Washington observed in the "Farewell Address" that there will "always be reason to distrust the patriotism of those who in any quarter may endeavor to weaken its bands."

Washington was not alone. John Adams pushed for the construction of a "blue water" navy, in contrast to what Thomas Jefferson supported (a fleet of coastal gunboats). Adams clearly intended American warships to be capable of "power projection" on the high seas. Jefferson, often portrayed as an early small-government libertarian, took a decidedly internationalist view of foreign policy, particularly when it came to the Barbary pirates. Since the United States obtained independence, it had paid tribute to the North African terrorists known as the Barbary pirates. These Tripolitans, Algerians, and others not only demanded monetary tribute (Congress appropriated $80,000 as early as 1784 to pay them off), but often wanted lavish and ridiculous gifts, including in one instance a specially outfitted frigate.

Even though Jefferson, as one of the ministers to Europe, helped negotiate with the Barbary terrorists, he loathed them and in the 1780s wrote of fighting rather than paying their bribes. His famous line, roughly quoted as "millions for defense, not one cent for tribute," captured Jefferson's attitude toward dealing with hostage-takers. Those were hardly the words of a pacifist. In July 1785, Algerians captured two American vessels and held their crews for a ransom of $60,000. Immediately Jefferson sought to form an alliance with interested European powers—one might say, a "coalition of the willing." Jefferson plainly admitted he favored "peace thro' the medium of war [*sic*]." "The [Barbary] states must see the rod; perhaps it must be felt by some of them," he wrote to James Monroe in 1786.[7] The man who urged avoiding "entangling alliances" saw the prudence of building just such a coalition with Portugal, Naples, Venice, Malta, the Sicilies, and even England and France, but the two larger nations wanted to continue paying ransoms, and the proposal was scotched. Jefferson decided to go it alone, although he had preferred having help.

Funny thing about dealing with terrorists: the demands keep going up. By 1795, Americans were paying the Barbary states more than $1 million per year, and still had to ransom hundreds of sailors from Tunis, Morocco, Tripoli, and Algeria. As president, Jefferson acted upon his inclinations to "make war, not love." Indeed, the strike on the Tripolitan pirates can rightly be called "America's first preemptive war."[8] Jefferson, like George W. Bush two hundred years later, never received a declaration of war from Congress, and as one author put it, "the United States embarked on its first distant foreign war without Congress even being informed, much less consulted."[9] Like Bush, Jefferson operated on a set of joint resolutions that permitted the president to authorize acts "of precaution or hostility as the state of war will justify." When the bey of Tripoli cut down the U.S. flagpole (then viewed as an act of war), Jefferson dispatched the large ships built by the administration of his hated rival, John Adams, which paid immediate dividends in 1801 when the USS *Enterprise* blasted apart a Tripolitan corsair. Soon the *Enterprise* was joined by the *Constellation,* the *Intrepid,* the *Argus,* the *Chesapeake,* the *Philadelphia,* and "Old Ironsides," the *Constitution.* Under Commodore Edward Preble, the American fleet set up a blockade of the Barbary ports and began "hit and run" strikes on Tripolitan cities.

Morocco quit the fight in 1803, although the war against Tripoli literally hit a snag when the USS *Philadelphia* ran aground and was captured. Captain William Bainbridge and the entire crew became hostages.[10] Three months later, in February 1804, Lieutenant Stephen Decatur and a small force from the *Intrepid* managed to board the *Philadelphia* and burn her, denying the ship to the enemy. Preble's reinforcements soon arrived and in July he opened fire on Tripoli itself. The following year, ex-consul William Eaton and Lieutenant Presley O'Bannon, USMC, led a remarkable force of Greeks, Turks, English, French, Spanish, Arabs, Egyptians, plus eight U.S. Marines, across the desert in a stunning flanking attack on Tripoli, storming the city of Derna in May 1805.[11] A month later, the new ruler signed a treaty ending hostilities. Although the United States did agree in the treaty to pay a final "ransom" for Bainbridge and his crew, it was differentiated from "tribute," which was ended temporarily.[12]

American forces had to make their point one more time, in 1807, with Algiers. After that, temporarily absorbed with the War of 1812, the United States did not return to the region until 1815. At that point, now Commodore Stephen Decatur and the once captive and now Commodore William Bainbridge were sent back to the Mediterranean. Bainbridge's squadron departed a month and a half after Decatur's, and by the time he arrived, Decatur's forces had settled the matter.[13] After capturing a pair of Algerian ships, Decatur forced the dey of Algiers to return all captives and pay a $10,000 fine, in addition to guaranteeing the end of hostage-taking. (The practice of enslaving Christians continued, fanned by the good intentions of the Catholic Church and philanthropists who ransomed captives, giving the Barbary pirates an ongoing incentive to seize more hostages.)[14] Although a final end to all Barbary depredations did not come until British and Dutch fleets reinforced the American "message" sent by Decatur, Jefferson—and then James Madison—had shown that the United States was far from "isolationist."[15]

LIE #2

THE MEXICAN AND SPANISH-AMERICAN WARS WERE IMPERIALIST EFFORTS DRUMMED UP BY "CORPORATE INTERESTS"

Ordering troops to the Rio Grande, into territory inhabited by Mexicans, was clearly a provocation. . . . [The Mexican War] was a war of the American elite against the Mexican elite. . . .
— HOWARD ZINN, A PEOPLE'S HISTORY OF THE UNITED STATES

Beyond dominating domestic politics, the corporate elite influenced U.S. foreign policy . . . by contributing to surging expansionist pressures. . . . [E]lite calls for international assertiveness sparked a war between the United States and Spain in 1898.
— PAUL S. BOYER ET AL., THE ENDURING VISION

. . . in the end, the "splendid little war" [with Spain] came as a result of less lofty ambitions: empire, trade, glory.
— JAMES WEST DAVIDSON ET AL., NATION OF NATIONS

The Mexican War and the Spanish-American War allow sufficient wiggle room for liberal historians to have it both ways. On the one hand, there was strong opposition to each war, allowing critics to brandish quotations from antiwar sources as the "true" sentiment of America. In each case, no small amount of sentiment was racially based. In the case of the Mexican War, Northerners did not want to add new slave territories to the Union, and in the case of the Spanish-American War, many critics feared an influx of "brown people" from newly acquired territories, especially Cuba. These views, however, merely "proved" that Americans were racist and evil. Thus, when American forces pulled out of Mexico, it was because we "didn't like those people."

On the other hand, when the United States did hold on to conquered territories, it demonstrated our acquisitive, imperialistic intentions. It seems in the world of liberal historians, poor old Uncle Sam can't win. Predictably, Mark Carnes and John Garraty's *American Destiny* solves this conundrum with the subheading "Imperialism Without Colonies," which must be akin to alcoholism without booze.[1] Likewise, *Nation of Nations* indicts both pro- and antiwar advocates by insisting, "Racist ideas shaped both sides of the argument. Imperialists believed that the racial inferiority of nonwhites made occupation of the Philippines necessary . . . [while] Anti-imperialists . . . feared racial intermixing and the possibility that Asian workers would flood the American labor market."[2] Those evil Americans! If they captured territory in war, it was because they were racists, and if they gave it back to the native people, it was because . . . they were racists. Not to be outdone on the "race card," Jeanne Boydston et al. (*Making a Nation*) inform the reader that "[w]hite supremacists asked whether Filipinos would become citizens or be allowed to vote. . . ."[3]

All anyone needs to know about American "imperial" interests is this: even before war on Spain was declared, the U.S. House and Senate passed the Teller Amendment (April 19, 1898, and signed the next day by President William McKinley), which required the United States to hand sovereignty of Cuba over to its people once the hostilities were concluded.[4] (This was remarkably similar to the statements by George W. Bush that once Iraq was stabilized, the intention of the United States was to return sovereignty to the Iraqi people, which was done on June 28, 2004.) This declaration of withdrawal was novel in all of human history. No "empire" had ever voluntarily ceded control of territories back to the inhabitants—certainly not without a fight.

Fifty years prior to the Spanish-American War, American troops had held Mexico City and other key urban areas of central Mexico. Without a specific "Teller Amendment," the United States voluntarily withdrew from the conquered territory of a defeated foe. Nothing could have pushed the American forces out, and Mexico's tumultuous political history suggests more than a few citizens would have preferred we stay. Instead, the defeated power was presented with conditions that were, by nineteenth-century world standards, remarkably generous—ceding California and the New Mexico territories, acknowledging the Rio Grande as Texas's southern border, and in return receiving $15 million (or about $313 million in 2006 dollars) and an assumption of another $3.25 million ($68 million in 2006 dollars) of debts Mexico owed to U.S. citizens.[5]

Opposition to the Mexican War had come less from moral positions against violence in particular than from concerns about expansion benefiting slave states. Activists such as the jailed writer Henry David Thoreau and Whig legislator Abraham Lincoln saw the hands of the "slave power" in the conflict, while many American Catholics were hesitant to fight another Catholic nation. Lincoln, of course, demanded to know the exact spot where blood was shed in the incident leading to war.

In both cases, however, critics obsessed with American "imperialism" ignored the eagerness with which our foes entered the wars. In both cases, the enemy forces were expected to win handily. Even Boyer's *Enduring Vision* admits, "Most European observers expected Mexico to win the war. Its army was four times the size of the American forces, and it was fighting on home ground."[6] As I explained in *America's Victories: Why the U.S. Wins Wars,* virtually every foe U.S. forces have encountered has underestimated our military: in 1775, a British surgeon described the colonial militia as "a drunken, canty, lying, praying, hypocritical rabble without order, subjection, discipline, or cleanliness," and in 1812, another Englishman, watching regular U.S. infantry drill, portrayed their exercises as "loose and slovenly."[7] Mexican leaders' opinions of the American military were similarly low, promising their own troops that U.S. forces were "totally unfit to operate beyond their [own] borders."[8] After he was reinstated as president, dictator Antonio López de Santa Anna promised to capture Washington, D.C., and Mexican newspapers such as *La Voz del Pueblo* exclaimed, "We have more than enough strength to make war . . . victory will perch upon our banners."[9] The London *Times* predicted any American invasion of Mexico would fail, as U.S. troops could not "resist artillery and cavalry . . . [and were not] amenable to discipline."[10] Both the *Paris Globe* and England's *Britannia* prophesied ruin for any offensive action by the United States, with the latter claiming the American military was "fit for nothing but to fight Indians."[11] Fortunately for the British, they never had to deal with Geronimo or Crazy Horse, or they might have had a different assessment!

When it came to the Spanish-American War, Spain's diplomatic affronts were described as "blunders," not deliberate provocations: "The Spaniards seemed to be their own worst enemies," wrote Irwin Unger, no doubt much like the misunderstood German dictator some forty years later.[12]

Even when our enemies were hell-bent on fighting, it seems the historians have a hard time celebrating any kind of American victory. *Making a Nation* tells students that Spain, "rather than surrender to the Filipinos . . . surrendered to the Americans on August 13, 1898."[13] The authors do manage to record the critical battle of Manila Bay—two pages earlier, separating the cause and effect of Spanish defeat and surrender and making it appear that the Filipino rebels, not Commodore George Dewey's superior naval squadron, whipped the mighty empire of Spain. The authors treated Dewey's astounding feat (not losing a single man to enemy fire while utterly destroying the Spanish flotilla) as an accident, noting, "The country went wild with relief and triumph."[14] Perhaps Americans had been reading all those foreign papers that predicted the Spaniards would throttle the upstart U.S. fleet.

The belligerence of Mexico and Spain aside, the historians have all but concluded the United States was only after conquest. Boyer's textbook features a picture of the tall hat called the shako worn by U.S. troops, "adorned with decorative plates showing the eagle spreading its wings, *the symbol of Manifest Destiny*."[15] It couldn't be that the U.S. Army merely adopted for its hats the *national symbol,* the eagle? (One wonders what the textbook writers would have dreamed up had Benjamin Franklin's suggestion of the turkey as the national symbol been adopted.) The fact that the United States in two wars voluntarily gave up more territory than many empires ever possessed seems to be of no import to the proponents of the "American Empire" view.

Certainly, the United States did retain some territories—Hawaii, for example—but the Philippines were given independence, then the U.S. Navy acceded to the wishes of the government and withdrew altogether in the 1990s. Other areas occupied and held by American forces (often as the only source of order and, yes, civilization) were likewise returned to their native owners. All of this was done while the United States was in a position of strength, which was unprecedented in world history. Britain left India and her African colonies when she could no longer hold them. The Soviet Union released Latvia, Lithuania, the Ukraine, and other captive nations when communism imploded. There is a genuine story to celebrate when it comes to America's wars abroad, but the historians are too obsessed with "imperialism" to tell it.

LIE #3

FDR KNEW IN ADVANCE ABOUT THE JAPANESE ATTACK ON PEARL HARBOR

Immediately after December 7, 1941, military communications documents that disclose American foreknowledge of the Pearl Harbor disaster were locked in U.S. Navy vaults away from the prying eyes of congressional investigators, historians, and authors. Though the Freedom of Information Act freed the foreknowledge documents from the secretive vaults to the sunlight of the National Archives in 1995, a cottage industry continues to cover up America's foreknowledge of Pearl Harbor.

—ROBERT B. STINNETT, HONOLULU ADVERTISER, DECEMBER 7, 2000

The only "cottage industry" related to Pearl Harbor is the one churning out endless "FDR-knew-in-advance" books, such as Robert Stinnett's *Day of Deceit.* But you can pretty well be sure that when Wikipedia decides an entry is too insane to publish, it probably ranks alongside healing pyramids and alien bodies at Area 51. Such is the case with the decades-old claim that President Franklin Delano Roosevelt knew that the Japanese were planning to attack Pearl Harbor on December 7, 1941, and allowed it to happen to draw us into the European war against Hitler through the "back door." While it is true Roosevelt feared Hitler was about to defeat England in the fall of 1940 during the Battle of Britain, by late 1941 that prospect had faded. Germany lacked long-range bombers, air power sufficient to cover an invasion, and, above all, sufficient landing craft to threaten England directly. Logically and historically, then, the "back door to war" thesis was groundless. Nevertheless, each time this preposterous assertion appears to finally be dying, like Freddie and Jason put together, it suddenly finds new life through a new publication with "shocking" new "facts." Most recently, Stinnett, in *Day of Deceit,* claimed that "new" information showed that Japanese radio transmissions had been intercepted and passed on to George C. Marshall and, ultimately, Roosevelt.[1]

World War II had barely ended when the "back door to war" thesis surfaced in the publications of Charles Tansill and Walter Millis.[2] In his famous book *Back Door to War,* Tansill accused Roosevelt of allowing a Japanese attack at Pearl Harbor to provide the United States with the motivation and justification to enter the war against Hitler in Europe. A number of historians and writers added to the Tansill thesis over the years, but little new evidence was produced until the 1980s, when renowned author John Toland published his book *Infamy: Pearl Harbor and Its Aftermath.*[3] Toland claimed to have located a Navy witness who, while on duty in San Francisco, received transmissions that identified the location of the Japanese carriers, which the sailor's superior forwarded to Washington. Were that true, the information that a Japanese carrier task force was located north of Pearl Harbor—if passed on to Washington—would have implicated American leadership in allowing the attack to occur.

Adding to Toland's revelations, a "notes and documents" piece in the prestigious *American Historical Review* of 1982 made public new material gained through the Freedom of Information Act.[4] Those documents disclosed that the FBI had acquired information from an Axis double agent named Dusko Popov, code-named "Tricycle."[5] Popov's information, contained on a microdot, consisted of extensive German-acquired intelligence on the facilities at Pearl Harbor. Although Toland and others maintained that Popov's documents included a "detailed plan" of the Japanese air attack, they did no such thing. Tricycle's data dealt almost exclusively with buildings and installations, but had nothing on ships, aircraft, scouting patterns, or any of the rather important items that one would expect from a "detailed plan." More important, it contained numerous errors of locations and names, which, taken together, cast doubt on the entire body of information. Thus, although Popov met FBI director J. Edgar Hoover, the director thoroughly distrusted Tricycle and his information. Hoover did, however, pass along microdot information to one of FDR's advisers, but nothing involving Hawaii. This has led many to condemn Hoover for shortsightedness. In the director's defense, however, declassified documents have shown that he worked with the Office of Naval Intelligence to pass material back through Popov that would suggest to the Japanese that Pearl Harbor was better defended than it really was.

In 1981, historian Gordon Prange of the University of Maryland prepared to publish *At Dawn We Slept*, his massive multivolume history of the war in the Pacific. Just before it appeared, Prange died, and his graduate students, Donald M. Goldstein and Katherine V. Dillon, completed the books and shepherded them into publication.[6] Although Prange and his students dealt with some of the controversy, the new Toland and *AHR* revelations had surfaced too late to be dealt with in *At Dawn We Slept*. Therefore, Goldstein and Dillon organized Prange's material around the old and new Pearl Harbor claims, under the title *Pearl Harbor: The Verdict of History*.[7] The authors searched out Toland's mystery sailor, "seaman Z" (whose real name was Robert Ogg). He emphatically rejected Toland's assertion that he said he had intercepted any massive Japanese radio traffic, maintaining only that he was told by a superior that the communications unit had intercepted Japanese radio traffic. He never asked how it was established that the signals came from warships: he assumed his superiors knew what they were doing. Documents acquired from the Japanese archives, however, showed that the Japanese fleet was under strict radio silence during the voyage to attack Pearl Harbor.

The road to Pearl Harbor ran through England as well, with a 1992 book that claimed a November 1941 radio signal was intercepted (again, since none were ever sent, that was a problem) by British and Dutch code breakers, which revealed the position and destination of the Japanese strike force.[8] This information was deliberately withheld from Roosevelt by Winston Churchill so he could draw us into the European war. This "new information" has likewise been debunked.[9] According to the recently released minutes of the Joint Intelligence Committee (JIC) of 1941, there is no evidence for such assertions.

Then came Stinnett's broadside, *Day of Deceit*. Filled with ostensibly important "new" information on American code-breaking activities, Stinnett never produced a single piece of genuine evidence that Roosevelt knew about the attack—in fact, quite the contrary.[10] Wildly interchanging intelligence terms with precise meanings—code breaking, interception, translation, analysis—Stinnett repeatedly assumed that "intercepted" documents were decrypted, translated, analyzed, then forwarded to Washington, all in time to stop the attack. Some of the intercepts in November 1941 were indeed broken, but not translated or analyzed until . . . 1945! Many of his wild claims actually prove the opposite of his thesis. One "gotcha" involves a December 2, 1941, decryption that had Naval Intelligence telling Pearl Harbor commander Admiral Husband Kimmel that the fleet actions implied "a move from Japan proper to the south." On any Rand McNally map, Hawaii is still east of Japan. New Guinea is due south.

If anything, the successes in breaking the "Purple" diplomatic code played no part in alerting the United States to military movements.[11] American code breakers *had* broken two key Japanese codes, including the "Purple" diplomatic code, which signaled potential changes in Japanese foreign policy (which was of no use in determining when or if Japan was going to war; that announcement was made in the open, although after the Pearl Harbor attack was nearly over); and the JN-25B code, which was a naval code. The difficulty, though, in using the JN-25B code to *predict* an attack was that only a handful of transmissions were decrypted and translated (which took time). Those had to be analyzed, then the results forwarded to the appropriate civilian or military commanders. The volume was so great that *most of the November–December JN-25B codes were not even analyzed until 1944.* According to the U.S. Navy's own history of code breaking, "The lack of confidence in [the diplomatic transmissions] made traffic intelligence from the Pacific during the last half of 1941 more an elaborate rumor than trustworthy source material."[12] If the Navy lacked confidence in the diplomatic transmissions, it did have confidence in the JN-25B decryptions, but as the World War II cryptanalysts unanimously agree, they were overwhelmed by the sheer number and conflicting information of decrypts they received. An argument using the information from the JN-25B codes could have better been made for predicting a Japanese attack in the Dutch East Indies. Moreover, at each step of the way, code breakers had to second-guess themselves and ensure that the Japanese hadn't already caught on to the fact that they had been compromised and thus change their codes. A failure to do so could have caused an American fleet to sail straight into a deep-sea ambush.

Similar egregious errors, such as Stinnett's misunderstanding of code-breaking work, are found in Timothy Wilford's *Pearl Harbor Redefined* (better entitled "Pearl Harbor Reimagined").[13] Entire histories of code breaking have been declassified as late as 1998, of which Stinnett seemed unaware. Nor did he seem to comprehend that no more than five—and usually two—code breakers were at work on the Japanese OP-20-G naval codes at any given time.[14] The Japanese changed their code keys every day, and merely acquiring the keys from the previous day required a "huge cryptanalytic effort" before the first document could be read.[15]

Stinnett's assertions cast such a broad net that hundreds of U.S. Navy code breakers, translators, analysts, and communications personnel would have been involved in the "conspiracy" to allow thousands of their fellow sailors to be killed. Such an astonishing claim provoked dozens of surviving World War II–era Navy cryptanalysts to launch a massive effort to debunk Stinnett's unsupported claims.[16] As one debunker, Commander Philip Jacobsen, observed, "It is sad that revisionists do not seem to consider the implications allegations of foreknowledge of the Japanese attack on Pearl Harbor necessarily have on the reputations of dead intelligence personnel who are unable to defend themselves."[17]

Jacobsen, for example, has shredded various conspiracy theorists with his working knowledge of the differences between translating, analyzing, decrypting, and so on. He has debunked the radio silence issue, the "foreknowledge" issue, and the "breaking" of the JN-25B code.[18] Indeed, as Stephen Budiansky, another code expert, notes, a conspiracy required that Roosevelt and his "henchmen" begin altering documents long *before* the attack—Budiansky estimates the officers would have had to begin concealing their work on Japanese codes in *January 1940.* Yet the actual documents on Japanese operating systems show that "nothing has been removed, redacted, expurgated, or censored," which in turn means that for the FDR conspiracy to work, the Navy would have had to selectively remove thousands of pieces of paper and *also* comprehensively examine and redact existing documents. Of course, the evidence shows no such effort.[19] Quite the contrary: "On December 1, 1941, only 3,800 of the 30,000-plus code groups and 2,500 of the 50,000 additive had been recovered from . . . the code book that had gone into effect December 1, 1940" by the Japanese. "This was simply not enough," Budiansky notes, "to render any messages comprehensible."[20]

Another of Stinnett's key assertions is that American listening stations picked up Japanese radio traffic from the strike force while it was at sea. Yet his own notes show that the *only* confirmed intercepted radio transmissions occurred *before* the fleet declared radio silence and while it was still in port. Intercepting any codes would have been a supernatural occurrence because all radio transmitters aboard the Japanese ships were physically disabled prior to departure from Japan specifically to prevent any accidental transmissions, and

Japanese officers to a man stated that no radio traffic occurred. Jacobsen exposes the incredible basic mistakes and misunderstandings in which Stinnett and others did not even have the correct operating frequencies for the Japanese navy. Even the infamous SS *Lurline,* heading from San Francisco to Hawaii, which claimed to have heard unusual radio traffic, had its location finally plotted by a report given by her radio operator, Leslie Grogan, and it does not support the broadcasting thesis.[21]

The revisionists' claims hinge on the notion that FDR "couldn't get into the war with Germany" without a pretext. Of course, the United States already had ample cause for war. Nazi U-boats had sunk American ships, killed American sailors, and in all ways shown themselves hostile—equaling the offenses that justified the U.S. involvement in World War I. Germany had long since crossed the line needed for a declaration of war. Even with the isolationist sentiment in Congress, it is entirely possible that FDR could have asked for a declaration of war after the *Reuben James* was sunk. Pearl Harbor was a tragedy, but not a conspiracy.

LIE #4

HARRY TRUMAN ORDERED THE ATOMIC BOMBING OF JAPAN TO INTIMIDATE THE SOVIETS WITH "ATOMIC DIPLOMACY"

[Truman] felt that because of the weapon, he did not need (or want) the Soviets to invade Manchuria or Japan.

—WALTER LAFEBER, THE AMERICAN AGE

Truman agreed with [James] *Byrnes that use of the bomb would permit them to "out maneuver* [sic] *Stalin on China," that is, negate the Yalta concessions in Manchuria and guarantee that Russia would "not get in so much on the kill" of Japan or its occupation.*

—ARNOLD OFFNER, "ANOTHER SUCH VICTORY: PRESIDENT TRUMAN, AMERICAN FOREIGN POLICY, AND THE COLD WAR" (1999)

In the 1960s, a group of historians concocted a view that only an academic could come up with: the atomic bomb, America's greatest weapon, was used almost exclusively to intimidate an ally—Russia—not to crush an unrepentant Japan.[1] Typically, most of the New Left revisionists looked favorably on the Soviet Union and blamed America for the world's ills, and therefore they treated any evidence to recast the use of the bomb as "anti-Soviet" as desirable. An analysis of their works by Robert James Maddox later revealed that they had literally concocted "evidence" by patching together different speeches by Truman, *even on different topics,* made at different times![2] Three decades later, Maddox, reviewing new articles and books, found that despite new evidence from Soviet archives rejecting such a view, many New Left historians are as determined as ever to make the Cold War about "atomic diplomacy."[3] Some recent books, such as Robert Jay Lifton and Greg Mitchell's *Hiroshima in America,* have sought to portray the dropping of the bombs in terms of the long-term damage they did to the *American* psyche. Americans, it seems, were obsessed with Hiroshima and just didn't know it.[4]

Atomic debates came to a head in 1994 when the Smithsonian Institution prepared an exhibit to commemorate the atomic bombing of Japan by . . . blaming America! A firestorm of protest ensued from veterans' groups and patriots of every type, until the Smithsonian produced a simple exhibit with no explanation of Japanese atrocities, projected casualty numbers, or even the attack on Pearl Harbor. To summarize one *New York Times* analysis, Americans apparently just woke up and decided to drop an atomic bomb on Japan for no reason![5]

More recently, the historical discussion shifted from what was in Truman's mind—since it was clear he was *not, in any way,* concerned with "impressing the Soviets"—to what he was being briefed on the casualty numbers expected in an invasion of Japan. A generally accepted number that military planners relied on came from "Operations Against Japan Subsequent to Formosa," a poorly named document produced in the spring of 1945 that used Okinawa as a measuring rod to determine that it would take one American killed (and, therefore, eight wounded) to kill seven Japanese. Extrapolated forward, this led to the "Saipan ratio," which produced the infamous "half million" deaths for a Japanese invasion. These estimates, critics claimed, were vastly inflated.

The "casualty myth," as the revisionists called it, gained recent attention in works such as Barton Bernstein's "The Atomic Bombings Reconsidered" and John Ray Skates's *The Invasion of Japan: Alternative to the Bomb,* which argued that the casualty estimates for invading Japan were unduly high, and that Japan would have surrendered anyway.[6]

Historical reality has, of course, intruded on the leftist scenarios and resulted in the obvious conclusion: Truman dropped the bombs because Japan was still fighting and had no intention of surrendering. And the estimates of invasion casualties were unbelievably low.

During the summer of 1945, with Germany defeated, the United States turned its attention to the final stages of the war with Japan. Gen. Curtis LeMay, who directed the XX Bomber Command in China, then the XXI

Bomber Command in the Pacific, in January 1945 was given command of all strategic air operations against Japan. He began a massive bombing campaign to bring Japan to surrender, but the first raids, staged from China, had to overcome phenomenal logistics and delivery problems. When the United States conquered the Marianas Islands, LeMay had the opportunity to launch the large-scale raids he envisioned, including the March 9–10, 1945, firebombing of Tokyo, the most destructive air raid in human history. To secure an emergency landing field for the B-29s, Iwo Jima was captured at great cost (6,825 Allied soldiers, sailors, and Marines killed).

Later that month, American forces invaded Okinawa to obtain a staging area for the final invasion of Japan. Iwo Jima and Okinawa—where the U.S. Navy encountered swarms of kamikaze, or "divine wind," suicide planes—convinced American planners that a full-scale invasion of Japan would be incredibly bloody. The armed services produced updated casualty estimates in the summer of 1945 for the invasion, with the low casualty estimate of 100,000 and a high estimate of one million briefed to President Truman, although selective service numbers had already been ratcheted upward dramatically in line with casualties of more than one million. (The U.S. Army alone in the spring of 1945 had increased its requirement to 100,000 per month, and was increasing the number of training regiments *after* Germany fell.) Virtually all the evidence now available suggests even those estimates were too low. Richard Frank, researching Japanese archives, found that at least two Japanese divisions had been moved to the Kyushu region, where Operation Olympic was to occur.[7] American intelligence was unaware of the presence of those divisions. Moreover, figures provided to President Truman only included ground-battle casualties, not air and naval losses, and, as D. M. Giangreco showed, every estimate was a short-run estimate with little consideration of extended operations or even the second invasion, Operation Coronet. Furthermore, none of the battle projections included the consideration that Gen. Douglas MacArthur's staff was prepared to hold the island.[8] Gen. Dwight D. Eisenhower, Supreme Allied Commander in Europe, when told of the "half million" estimate, thought it "a tremendous error in calculation."[9] By June of 1945—still three months out from the planned invasion—estimates were rising at a shocking rate, and at a meeting with President Truman on June 18, Gen. George Marshall used a phrase that has misled nonmilitary historians. Referring to a table of casualties from Leyte, Luzon, Iwo Jima, Okinawa, and

Normandy, Marshall presented both a ratio and a total casualty number. He told Truman that the "first 30 days in Kyushu should not exceed the price we paid for Luzon."[10] But Marshall referred to a *ratio* of Americans to Japanese killed, *not* a total number, and again, it was based on the low number of eight Japanese divisions, or 350,000 troops on the island, not the actual number, which was higher by as much as 80,000 men! A June 1945 study by advisers to Secretary of War Henry Stimson, Edward Bowles and William Shockley, based on the desperation of nations in Japan's situation, produced an even more sobering picture: "We shall probably have to kill at least 5 to 10 million Japanese [and] this might cost us between 1.7 and 4 million casualties, including 400,000 and 800,000 killed."[11]

Moreover, none of this took into account the fact that almost all of Japan's remaining air power was being reserved for kamikaze attacks; the population was being trained in suicide attacks on beaches. Divers were taught to wait under the water with explosives until landing craft came over them, then become human bombs. Children were trained in throwing themselves under tank treads as live munitions. Women and the elderly underwent training with bamboo spears. Truman was not naive in his expectations. He "hoped" to prevent "an Okinawa from one end of Japan to the other."[12] Stimson "was informed that [the invasion] might be expected to cost over a million casualties."[13] It bears repeating yet again: these estimates were *too low*.

Most of the Japanese preparations went undiscovered by American intelligence, as did the fact that the Japanese had moved their units closer to the intended invasion points. Their response would be deadlier than American planners ever dreamed. All that made for American casualties (let alone Japanese losses, conservatively pegged at between one and ten million) that would have been far higher than original estimates—contrary to the nonsensical claims by John Ray Skates that the casualties would have been closer to 20,000![14] D. M. Giangreco, for example, has meticulously noted the weather patterns in Japan that likely would have flooded the plains on which American planners hoped to build airstrips and would have left U.S. forces "fighting in terrain similar to that later encountered in Vietnam, less the helicopters."[15] Furthermore, there were no bridges capable of taking vehicles larger than twelve tons, forcing American engineers to build every new river crossing that would have been needed.

Moreover, the isolation of Japan by sea was complete. Virtually no war materials were reaching the island by early 1945. Bombers flew at will, so much so that in preparation for the bomb, American B-29s began flying over cities in groups of two and three. Neither naval nor conventional aerial warfare could have accomplished much more.

Based on the calculations he had, thankfully President Truman decided to use the atomic bomb at the first available opportunity if Japan had not surrendered. Historian Sadao Asada discovered internal Japanese government documents which showed that *only* the atomic bomb persuaded the warlords to surrender. The deputy chief of staff of the Japanese Army General Staff wrote in his memoirs, "There is nothing we can do about the . . . atomic bomb. That nullifies everything."[16] The bombs made it possible for competing groups inside the Japanese government to agree on surrender. One source of continuing interest in the "atomic diplomacy" interpretations—aside from anti-American scholars—is Japanese historians who have sought "victimization" status for a brutal regime. The cult of victimization in Japan remains so strong that only a few Japanese historians have accurately depicted *any* of the events of World War II; few have acknowledged the atrocities in China and elsewhere in the Pacific; and only a handful have pointed out that the bombs fulfilled their purpose of forcing Japan's surrender. One of them—the aforementioned Asada—has been called, astoundingly, a "Japanese revisionist" by the *New York Times!*[17]

Oddly, the New Left historians and modern antibomb critics never bother to examine the Japanese side of the decision to surrender—something Asada and Richard B. Frank, among others, have done extensively. Prime Minister Kantaro Suzuki, after the war, admitted that the atomic bomb "provided an additional reason for surrender . . . [one not afforded] by the B-29 bombings alone."[18] Moreover, the suspicious timing of the Soviet Union in attacking Japanese troops in Manchuria, namely *two days after* the bombing of Hiroshima, meant that Truman could in no way count on the Soviets to help. Quite the contrary, based on their previous broken promises, he fully expected that they would not join until the last minute. On August 9, before the second atomic attack was publicly disclosed, Truman had written Senator Richard Russell of Georgia—who urged that he annihilate Japan—saying that he regretted the necessity of "wiping out whole populations because of the 'pigheadedness' of the leaders . . . and, for your information, I am not going to do it unless it is absolutely necessary. . . . My object is to save as many American lives as possible but I also have a humane feeling for the women and children of Japan."[19]

Truman's "obsession" with intimidating the Soviets in this and other letters and actions is utterly underwhelming. Indeed, as Richard Frank put it, the numbers alone—and the impact such losses would have on public morale—dictated the use of the bombs: "[O]nce American leaders learned of the odds facing Olympic, there is no prospect that any other consideration could have stayed the use of atomic weapons." Simply put, the Japanese had not left Harry Truman any other choice but to drop both atomic bombs, or even more, had Japan not come to its senses.

LIE #5

JOHN F. KENNEDY WAS KILLED BY LBJ AND A
SECRET TEAM TO KEEP HIM FROM GETTING US OUT OF VIETNAM

There was a secret election in 1963....
—DAVID LIFTON, BEST EVIDENCE: THE VIDEO

Book title: Blood, Money & Power: How L.B.J. Killed J. F. K., *by Barr McClellan*

Compared to some of the other humdingers featured in this book, this particular lie probably doesn't have much currency with too many Americans, but because it has been immortalized in the movie *JFK* by Oliver Stone, it requires addressing. Needless to say, Stone didn't come up with this idea on his own, but relied instead on a slew of conspiracy books about the Kennedy assassination. The most prominent of these is L. Fletcher Prouty's *Secret Team* (1973). Prouty ("X," played by Donald Sutherland in *JFK*) claimed that "big business," the military, and the CIA, with Lyndon Johnson's blessing, "whacked" the president of the United States on November 22, 1963, because Kennedy planned to "get us out of Vietnam" as soon as the election was over.[1]

The "Jackobite" mythology—as some Kennedy scribes have called the legend—evolved as a form of Camelot spin control the instant the president died. Writer William Manchester was given full access to develop his *Death of a President,* while historian Arthur Schlesinger Jr. turned out an ode to JFK's administration, *A Thousand Days,* where Kennedy was portrayed as a tough anti-Communist.[2] However, by the late 1960s, the mood of the liberal parts of the United States had shifted strongly against the Vietnam War, requiring revisions of the Kennedy mythology. Specifically, Kennedy had to be turned from a "hawk" into a "dove" to maintain continuity with his by then left-leaning brother Bobby. Moreover, there was no passion play if virtually no policy differences existed between JFK, Lyndon Johnson, and Republican Richard Nixon. A frontal assault on Johnson and Nixon coincided with a radical makeover of the Kennedy "hawk" image, which in turn meant coming up with some plausible story that Kennedy planned to withdraw all U.S. troops from Vietnam "right after" the election.

A few basic facts are in order when it comes to the Prouty/Stone fantasy. First, the notion that the "military-industrial complex" wanted into Vietnam because Bell Helicopter (based in Texas) would get work is nearly beyond comment. Despite the perennial fear of the military-industrial complex that the Left lives under, all the top military contractors *put together* couldn't equal the revenues of a major car company or McDonald's. A single one, even in Texas, was almost irrelevant, in terms of both votes and political clout; and a single *division* of a single company is barely worth making a campaign stop for, let alone expanding a war over. More to the point, what Stone and other conspiracy nuts completely miss is that helicopters were not used in the context of troop delivery systems for offensive military actions *until late 1965*. This was *two years* after Kennedy's assassination: no one had even conceived of choppers as the "new cavalry" until Col. Hal Moore's Seventh Cavalry experimented with them at the battle of the Ia Drang Valley.[3]

As to the Kennedy assassination itself, the problem is that the evidence against Lee Harvey Oswald is both "too good" and yet "not good enough." Had he lived, Oswald certainly would have been convicted on the available evidence and procedures of the day (which, of course, would not be applicable in 2008). Although a 1992 American Bar Association mock trial of Oswald resulted in a hung jury, a 1986 mock trial with famous attorneys Vincent Bugliosi for the prosecution and Gerry Spence for Oswald resulted in a guilty verdict for Oswald, and a majority "no" on the question of a conspiracy. Regardless, modern "jurors" cannot escape the thirty years of questions raised by the conspiracy camp and certainly have been tainted. No one knows if the palm print on the Mannlicher-Carcano rifle—Oswald's print—plus his order form for the gun, the ballistics linking the bullets to the gun, and the photo of him with the gun would have provided proof "beyond a reasonable doubt" to convict Oswald in any modern court. In 1964 or 1965, the outcome would have been virtually certain. But Jack Ruby, thinking he was doing the nation a favor by exacting vigilante justice on JFK's killer, in fact condemned the United States to at least another fifty years of debate over what various people said, saw, or did on November 22, 1963.

In addition to the "LBJ did it" school, there are other conspiracy interpretations, the most prominent of which are:

1. *The Mafia did it.* This theory maintains that in retribution for JFK's failure to "get Bobby off their back," the Mafia dons had the president assassinated. Most of the mob theories originate from Kennedy's "love/hate" relationship with organized crime, using Mafia hit men—via the CIA—to try to eliminate Castro. These efforts were unsuccessful, but the mob expected payment anyway, and its terms (supposedly discussed at the outset) involved having Attorney General Robert Kennedy stop his effective campaign against organized crime bosses. When he did not, the mob retaliated. Oswald, in these views, is either a willing or unsuspecting accomplice who was indeed the "patsy" for the syndicate. Evidence supporting these views comes from comments made by Sam Giancana, head of the Chicago mob; wiretap comments of New Orleans mobster Carlos Marcello; and the well-known "deal" struck by the Kennedys and the Mafia that was directed through mail folder dropoffs when Judy Exner would sexually service the president at regular meetings with him. Further variations on this theme involve the television "revelations" that a squad of Corsican hit men performed the deed, or that a Texan named Ricky White was the "real shooter."[4]

2. *The Cubans (either pro- or anti-Castro) did it.* In this view, members of the Cuban exile community, angry over the Bay of Pigs, or Cuban secret police, angry over the Bay of Pigs, assassinated Kennedy and set up Oswald. There is less evidence for this view, although the motive was probably more credible than that of the "mob" theory. The Secret Service had already investigated a reliable report of an assassination threat coming from Miami in the days prior to Dallas.[5]

3. *The government did it, Part Deux:* A second government tack is more credible than the LBJ-did-it argument. This view holds that Johnson had nothing to do with the assassination, but that a rogue team of disaffected CIA agents, military malcontents, and other administration "loose cannons"

pulled off a "silent coup" from within. Again, aside from the substantial problems of lack of evidence—which are vastly greater for advocates of either variant of the government-did-it positions—the obvious question is, "What was to be gained from substituting Johnson for Kennedy?" It was JFK who ordered the invasion of Cuba, who nearly went to war over the Soviet missiles, and who had increased American troop strength in Vietnam from 600 to 16,000 in a three-year period.[6]

4. *The body was altered.* A subtheme of the last explanation comes from David Lifton's book, *Best Evidence.*[7] He subscribed to the LBJ-did-it view, but his book is important because he actually uncovered evidence—or, more accurately, he brought to the public's attention material already *in evidence*—that Kennedy's body might have been altered between the procedures at Dallas and the autopsy at Bethesda, Maryland. Lifton provided impressive interviews with the personnel who put Kennedy into a fancy bronze ceremonial coffin at Parkland Hospital in Dallas, contrasted with interviews of U.S. Navy personnel who took the body out of a gray shipping casket. The dressings of the body, the condition of the head wound, and many other characteristics of the body were dramatically different in the two sets of eyewitness accounts. This led Lifton to the conclusion that the body had been altered after the assassination to cover up the crime. Whether anyone could have gained access to the body or not is the issue. David Wrone has produced an excellent Web site with each argument, including the body alteration argument, dissected.[8] In the case of Lifton's thesis, Wrone deals effectively with virtually all of the evidence except the eyewitness statements Lifton has caught on the video version of his book.[9]

But even if it is somehow true that the body underwent a "pre-autopsy" at Walter Reed Army Hospital prior to its rather late arrival at Bethesda, it might be due to a genuine concern that the government was determining whether there were multiple shooters (especially Soviet assassins), so as to prepare a responsible policy response to the likelihood that foreign nationals besides Oswald had been involved. In other words, one might accept some of Lifton's evidence without reaching the same conclusions as he did about its meaning.

Needless to say, whichever theory one subscribes to, the proponents of one—or all four—of the other interpretations will come after you hammer and tong. Although they all benefit from each other's work, the "researchers" are a competitive and ideologically diverse group, each of whom is convinced of the rightness of his or her own view.[10] Although Michael Kurtz, a professional historian, has argued a case for conspiracy, the large majority of historians have agreed with the government's conclusion that Oswald acted alone. But other victims of the Kennedy-Oswald shootings were journalism and the media. Virtually all the "majors" got the coverage secondhand, and none had any role in uncovering any of the evidence on Oswald or anyone else. After the Warren Commission, the mainstream media accepted the "lone gunman" story whole hog, leaving nonprofessionals to uncover all the rather shocking and perhaps important details that surfaced later. The media blew it badly with the JFK assassination, and spent the next decade attempting to reestablish its credibility, even if it meant swinging in the other direction with full-scale assaults on Johnson, Richard Nixon, and the military during Vietnam.

As to Oswald's guilt, while the 1993 best seller *Case Closed* by attorney Gerald Posner has some flaws, his convincing evidence concerning the so-called magic bullet—which turns out to be not so magic at all when the seats in the presidential limousine were aligned as they were in 1963—indeed closes the case. While a number of strange loose ends remain, the absence of *any* other gunshot sounds at the scene in 1963 (the event was caught on tape), the inability of a single conspiracy theorist to produce one bullet tied to the crime other than Oswald's (or, indeed, any forensic evidence at all), and the fact that the *only* actual fraud exposed over the years has been on the part of the conspiracy camp, leaves us with a verdict of "guilty" for Lee Harvey Oswald, not Lyndon Baines Johnson.

LIE #6

RICHARD NIXON EXPANDED THE VIETNAM WAR

[I]n April 1970, Nixon sent American forces on a sweep through Cambodia. . . . A seeming escalation of fighting, this move electrified the anti-war movement.
—IRWIN UNGER, THESE UNITED STATES

"You've got to electrify the people," [Nixon] told the Joint Chiefs of Staff. "Let's go blow the hell out of [the Viet Cong/NorthVietnamese]."
—MARK C. CARNES AND JOHN A. GARRATY, AMERICAN DESTINY

No matter how patently absurd something is, if you repeat it often enough, many people will eventually believe it. Researchers have, in fact, discovered that in a given population, up to one-third of a subject group's opinions can be made to change if other members of the group (who are, in fact, plants) "change" their opinion. Given this malleability, no wonder so many Americans believe that Richard Nixon somehow was increasing U.S. involvement in the Vietnam War—when it is abundantly obvious he ended the American presence in Vietnam.

Cross-reference this with Lie #5, whereby the conspiracy theorists had John Kennedy getting whacked by "dark forces" that may have included Lyndon Johnson in order to "keep him from pulling us out" of Vietnam. This was the underpinning of David Lifton's best seller, *Best Evidence* (1980), which subtly argued that Lyndon Johnson had ordered a "hit" on Kennedy because the president was about to pull out of Vietnam after the election. (Lifton, of course, was not alone in this theory, made famous in the Oliver Stone movie

JFK, which was based on Jim Garrison's 1988 book *On the Trail of the Assassins.*) John Newman (*JFK and Vietnam*, 1992) and David Kaiser (*American Tragedy*, 2000) likewise perpetuated the "JFK-would-have-gotten-us-out" mythology developed by the "Jackobites," as JFK official John Roche called them.[1] Roche recalled "odd stories" that surfaced whereby Kennedy told speechwriter and friend Kenny O'Donnell that "once he was re-elected . . . he'd get out of Vietnam," and that Johnson had somehow "betrayed the Kennedy trust" by plunging the United States into a war JFK would have disapproved of.[2]

Then there are the facts. When John Kennedy promised to "pay any price" and "bear any burden," there were far fewer than 1,000 U.S. advisers in all of southeast Asia (many put the number at around 600). The new president had already received a briefing from Dwight Eisenhower's Joint Chiefs of Staff that told him 40,000 American soldiers would be needed to combat about 17,000 Viet Cong guerrillas—and more than 120,000 if the North Vietnamese got involved. Kennedy developed the famed Green Berets especially for Vietnam, and shipped off the first 500 graduates.

They were only the tip of the iceberg: under JFK, some 17,000 troops arrived in South Vietnam.[3] In one unguarded moment, Kennedy actually referred to the "25,000 American troops" in southeast Asia, although it's not clear if he included Thailand and other areas near Vietnam. (The 25,000 figure was ironically used to further the Jackobite myth by John McCone, former director of the CIA.) The U.S. Army's own history of Vietnam notes that there were "almost 24,000 by the end of 1964. Of these, 15,000 were Army. . . ."[4] Kennedy himself said at Billings, Montana, in September 1963 that in Vietnam, "over 25,000 of your sons and brothers [are] bearing arms."[5] When Kennedy did remove 1,000 troops in 1963, the national security adviser, McGeorge Bundy, issued a memo that ordered "no formal announcement be made of the implementation of plans to withdraw 1,000 military personnel."[6] Indeed, the 1,000 troops consisted mostly of an engineering battalion whose work was completed.

Without question, Kennedy inserted the United States into Vietnam, and Lyndon Johnson expanded the number of troops to 553,000 by 1969, when Richard Nixon became president. Nixon promised "peace with honor," or, in other words, withdrawal after making sure South Vietnam was secure. While remaining vague during the campaign of 1968, Nixon privately intended to "Vietnamize" the war through increased training of Vietnamese troops and heavy bombing of the North, while secretly he also planned to negotiate with the North Vietnamese. By 1971, he had reduced the number of U.S. troops in Vietnam to under 200,000, and by February 1972, the number fell by another 45,000.

Ironically, Nixon's troop reductions benefited from Johnson's greatest public relations disaster, the Tet offensive, which utterly annihilated the Viet Cong as a fighting force. Gen. Tran Van Tra, a top Communist official, said of Tet: "We suffered large sacrifices and losses with regard to manpower and material."[7] American military historian Robert Leckie called Tet "the most appalling defeat in the history of the war," and an "unmitigated disaster" for Hanoi.[8] American forces killed so many Communists that North Vietnamese leaders quipped they could only stand a few more such "victories." Thus, by the time Nixon entered the White House, he was dealing with a war that was very nearly won on the battlefield, if lost in newsrooms and homes.

Nixon's "carrot and stick" approach included the first ever efforts to pursue North Vietnamese soldiers across the Cambodian border and to sever the Ho Chi Minh Trail. The United States also increased bombing of North Vietnam under Operation Linebacker II (December 1972), which, according to witnesses inside Hanoi (including some U.S. prisoners of war), badly staggered the North Vietnamese government. Although early in Linebacker the Air Force took severe losses, the Americans adapted to enemy tactics and soon had extremely light losses while wreaking havoc with the Communists. Polls showed Nixon had a 65 percent approval rating in 1972 for his handling of the war.[9] Nixon had been successful, in the short run, in going over the heads of the media straight to the American public.

Nixon sent Henry Kissinger to Paris to meet with Le Duc Tho, and they hammered out an agreement in January 1973. Before he resigned over Watergate, Nixon had withdrawn all but 50,000 American troops, and South Vietnam temporarily remained free. Nixon's "stick"—American air power— nevertheless remained a powerful incentive for the Communists to behave. All of that depended on South Vietnam having an ally in the Oval Office, namely Nixon, and when Watergate spiraled into a near-impeachment, South Vietnam's best friend resigned. Almost immediately, Congress pulled the plug on further U.S. aid to South Vietnam, and in January 1975, it was overrun. The Democrat-controlled Congress ignored President Gerald Ford's appeals to help the Vietnamese, leading not only to the tragedy of up to a million deaths in Vietnam and countless "boat people" who fled, but also to the million deaths in nearby Cambodia, which fell exactly as predicted by the domino theory so derided by liberals.

Nixon's resignation, accompanied by the rise of a predominantly liberal media and abetted by entrenched liberal academics, ensured that only Nixon's role in Watergate would define his presidency, not his successful conclusion of the war. It remains one of the great ironies of American history that the man who got us into the war—Kennedy—receives almost no blame or criticism for his actions, while the man who extracted us—in line with, supposedly, the wishes of liberals—is routinely portrayed as though he had started, rather than ended, the conflict.

LIE #7

THE "PEACE MOVEMENT" ACTIVISTS WERE NOT DUPES OF THE KGB

[Reagan's tough talk], coupled with the military buildup and the faltering of arms control, sparked a grass-roots reaction as millions of Americans felt a growing threat of nuclear war. Concerned citizens campaigned for a freeze on the manufacture and deployment of nuclear weapons. In June 1982, eight hundred thousand anti-nuclear protestors rallied in New York's Central Park.
— PAUL S. BOYER ET AL., THE ENDURING VISION

[Caption to a photo]: *A nuclear freeze rally in New York City in 1982. For a time, the movement to halt the introduction of new nuclear weapons challenged President Reagan's plans for an arms buildup.*
— JEANNE BOYDSTON ET AL., MAKING A NATION

During 1983, the antiwar and nuclear disarmament movements, in eclipse since the end of the Vietnam War, revived explosively. . . . [T]here were demonstrations in major cities to protest the arms race and demand a "nuclear freeze."
— IRWIN UNGER, THESE UNITED STATES

Viewing such comments, certainly one must conclude these antinuke protesters were merely concerned people—average Americans who "felt a growing fear," as Boyer's *Enduring Vision* claims. Or perhaps, as Unger's *These United States* suggests, "public jitters were amplified by Jonathan Schell's best-selling book, *The Fate of the Earth*."[1] Of course, it should be kept in mind that public jitters were also amplified by Orson Welles's 1938 radio broadcast,

The War of the Worlds. It doesn't necessarily mean the jitters had any grounds for their "amplification."

When it comes to admitting that antiwar activists were, in fact, "useful idiots" of the Communists for almost forty years, the sound of mea culpas from the leaders of the American Left is deafening. Deafeningly silent, that is. Now, with access to the former Soviet Union's archives, the influence of Soviet/KGB/East German agents in the European and American antiwar/ antinuclear/freeze movements is provable. The KGB ramped up its activities as never before against the man it considered to be "far more anti-Soviet" than any recent president—Ronald Reagan.[2] Agents floated stories in foreign presses that Reagan's health had been "affected by his father's alcoholism," and Yuri Andropov, chairman of the KGB, ordered all his agents to make their first priority the defeat of Reagan in the 1984 election.[3] They failed. They infiltrated the European and American freeze movements to stop deployment of the "Euromissiles" and the Strategic Defense Initiative. They failed there, too.

Long before the KGB infiltrated the "peace" movement, however, the Soviets had engaged in remarkable—occasionally loony—antics that mirrored the CIA's attempts to rig Fidel Castro's cigars to explode. Vasili Mitrokhin, an archivist for the KGB who smuggled out enormous numbers of files, documented a front publisher who originated the Oliver Stone–themed notion that Lee Harvey Oswald was an FBI/CIA agent who worked for "the military-industrial complex."[4] The KGB also conceived the notion that the AIDS virus had been made by U.S. biological experts at Fort Detrick, Maryland, and spread into the Third World.[5] Even the Communists themselves were shocked at how easily some of their lies spread, and were equally perturbed that others had no effect—for example, their attempts to make a dent in Reagan's reelection effort.

What is obvious from Mitrokhin's data and other materials now available to Western researchers is that the KGB desperately attempted to shape American domestic politics. Soviet subsidies to the Communist Party USA reached $2 million a year in the 1970s. Every embassy and consulate was an active outpost of KGB activity. Often, for their own survival within the Soviet system, KGB officers overstated their effectiveness, but frequently the reason they were not more successful, as the agents noted, was precisely because sometimes the Western peace movements did their bidding without being told. For example, the Politburo, in 1976, "extolled the value of encouraging the peace movement [as a means to weaken] Western resolve," and Moscow funded protest groups that opposed the neutron bomb in 1977.[6] When Germans Petra Kelly and her boyfriend, former general Gert Bastian, came to the United States in 1981 to oppose Reagan's policies, the media tour was arranged by the American antimilitary activist group SANE. Whether SANE leadership knew—or cared—that Bastian was on the payroll of the East German Stasi (secret police) is not known, but perhaps not surprisingly, Bastian's groups organized mass protests against both Secretary of State Alexander Haig and Secretary of Defense Caspar Weinberger when they visited Germany, but were noticeably absent when Leonid Brezhnev came to Bonn in November 1981. The German Peace Union received five million deutsche marks annually from the Stasi, while Sergei Grigoriev, a top official in the USSR's "International Department," funded peace groups through "public organizations and a number of communist parties. Millions of dollars were injected into the creation of all sorts of ad-hoc groups and coalitions."[7] Needless to say, not a single one of these "peace" groups ever had the slightest problem with any Soviet policy, anywhere.

In 1976, Yuri Andropov told the Politburo of the value of the Western "peace movement": "We have to open up a wider network to win public opinion, to mobilize public opinion of the Western countries of Europe and America against the location of the nuclear weapons in Europe. . . ."[8] One "peace commission" started by former Swedish prime minister Olof Palme named as the Soviet representative Georgi Arbatov, a secret agent for the KGB. Ted Turner, founder of CNN, asked Arbatov to join the board of directors of his Better World Society, presumably under the assumption that having the KGB represented made it a better world.

Then there was the World Peace Council, supposedly committed to global disarmament (which, of course, never meant *Soviet* disarmament). The Politburo funded the World Peace Council to the tune of $50 million a year, under the strict control of the Central Committee of the USSR. Certainly the KGB took credit for "stirring up the anti-military movement in countries of the west."[9] Twenty-five members of the Bundestag who opposed the installation of the Euromissiles were "outed" in the 1990s as paid agents of the German Democratic Republic.[10]

It wasn't just the infiltration of peace organizations in the West: the Soviets had so completely buffaloed American liberal politicians that they might as well have been on the payroll of the Central Committee. Senator George McGovern called Yuri Andropov a "reasonable guy and somewhat restrained." He was "thankful" that Andropov ran the Kremlin, because he could save the world from the war that McGovern was sure Reagan wanted.[11] McGovern was typical of well-meaning Soviet dupes. Ronald Reagan once met Dr. Helen Caldicott, one of the leaders of the freeze movement, in the Oval Office, and wrote, "she seems like a nice, caring person but . . . knows an awful lot of things that aren't true."[12] Similarly, he wrote in 1981, "Sometimes I think (forgive me) the [National Council of Churches] believes God can be reached through Moscow."[13]

Without question, however, the confluence of Soviet KGB activities in the peace movement reached its apex in the 1982–1984 battles over deployment of the Pershing and cruise missiles in western Europe to counter the SS-20s the Soviets had already put in place west of the Urals. One KGB agent bragged to his embassy counselor to London in July 1982 that "it was us, the KGB residency, who brought a quarter of a million people out onto the streets."[14] Evidence shows, however, that the KGB participated in the London demonstration, but did not organize it. Indeed, one center created by the KGB in London to direct such operations found that they did not need to: the Western peace movements were their dupes, enthusiastically and reliably mounting anti-U.S. campaigns at the drop of a hat.

After it failed to prevent the deployment of the western Euromissiles, the KGB countermeasures directorate actively sought the defeat of Ronald Reagan in the 1984 election. Agents were immediately sent off to dig up dirt on Reagan and were instructed to popularize the slogan among the peace crowd, "Reagan *eto voina!*" ("Reagan means war!").[15]

Reagan's "Star Wars" (see Lie #8) defense shield buried the freeze movement once and for all, as the Soviets made abundantly clear they knew the system would work. Far from being, as historians claimed, "unsettling . . . not possible technically," it not only has proven possible, but is now deployed![16] Historians who brushed off Soviet involvement in "peace" efforts, to quote Ricky Ricardo, "have some 'splainin' to do."

LIE #8

RONALD REAGAN KNEW "STAR WARS" WOULDN'T WORK BUT WANTED TO PROVOKE A WAR WITH THE USSR

Although funded by Congress, SDI was a long way from reality in 1983. Critics, convinced SDI was science fiction, called the plan Star Wars.
—JEANNE BOYDSTON ET AL., MAKING A NATION

But even as the Pentagon launched an SDI research program, critics pointed out not only the project's prohibitive cost and technological implausibility but also the likelihood that it would further escalate the arms race.
—PAUL S. BOYER ET AL., THE ENDURING VISION

Nicknamed "Star Wars" after a popular science fiction film, it spent billions of dollars trying to establish a space-based defense system. Most scientists contended that the project was as fantastic as the movie.
—JAMES WEST DAVIDSON ET AL., NATION OF NATIONS

Probably no lie is taken for granted more in college textbooks than the notion that "Star Wars won't work." Both the Soviet Union and the United States had early antimissile systems in place in the late 1960s, but these were virtually eliminated with the Anti-Ballistic Missile Treaty of 1969. Still, as early as the 1970s, the Soviet Union was engaged in serious experimentation with laser beams and particle beam weapons for the purposes of use in space. Throughout the decade, both U.S. Air Force special investigations teams and the Central Intelligence Agency tracked Soviet experiments with beam technologies. What was holding them back, however, was a severe dearth of computer technology—the kind of technology provided by the American private sector in the form of Steve Jobs and Steve Wozniak's Apple personal computer, introduced in 1976. Computing technology in the 1970s underwent a transformation from giant CRAY-type supercomputers used in the Pentagon to the possibility of thousands of personal workstations spread across the nation.

At the same time, advances in military radars, tracking, and targeting meant that intercontinental ballistic missiles (ICBMs) could be identified and tracked from space and, if necessary, destroyed. While none of this necessarily required laser beams (*l*ight *a*mplification by the *s*timulated *e*mission of *r*adiation) or charged particle beams, both worked exceptionally well in space without the diffusion effects of earth's atmosphere, and therefore seemed perfectly tailored to destroying ICBMs in flight. By 1983, when President Ronald Reagan made his renowned speech, most of the technologies were in place to destroy at least some incoming missiles in the event of an enemy attack.

Reagan had always searched for a way to circumvent "MAD"—Mutual Assured Destruction. "Almost as long as I have known him . . . [Reagan] was very interested in some sort of defense against missiles—ballistic missiles—and nuclear warfare," recalled former chief of staff Edwin Meese.[1] Even as governor of California, Reagan discussed defenses against missiles with Caspar Weinberger, who would later be his secretary of defense. MAD was ridiculous, in Reagan's mind, and needed to be countered. Martin Anderson, a policy adviser to Reagan, recalled that his "main concern [was] the threat of nuclear weapons, and what we're going to do about it, and how we're going to solve it." Reagan, Anderson noted, was determined to do "something about what he used to call 'Armageddon'—the threat of nuclear war."[2] The president even commented to one adviser, Fred Iklé, that an automatic retaliatory missile launch upon the detection of Soviet missiles being fired at the United States would be wrong, and some advisers questioned whether he would order a retaliatory launch under any circumstances.[3]

When George Keyworth, Reagan's science adviser, and former director of the Defense Intelligence Agency Daniel Graham began to investigate possibilities in the early 1980s, they concluded that "off-the-shelf" technologies alone could provide a measure of defense. All of this played out within Reagan's broader objectives in the Cold War, outlined in a National Security Council April 1982 paper (released in 1996) that, for the first time, stated the

U.S. goal was not just to "contain" the USSR but to "reverse" its expansion. Among the numerous strategies to do this was to restrain or weaken Soviet military spending. In 1981, Reagan told a reporter that for the first time the Soviets were "going to be faced with [the fact] that we could go forward with an arms race and they can't keep up."[4] The 1982 paper again emphasized the U.S. advantage in technology, and cited other internal studies showing (rightly) that the Soviet economy had slowed dramatically.

These realities congealed in Reagan's mind as he ushered in a "top-down" initiative on strategic defense. As Reagan himself wrote, "SDI wasn't conceived by scientists." Indeed, it was only at Reagan's insistence that strategic defense started to become a routine part of military studies done by the Joint Chiefs. National Security Adviser Robert MacFarlane appreciated Reagan's direction, arguing that "the Russians had such a high regard for American technology that you leverage their perceptions dramatically by an investment in high technology. . . . [You] create expectations of discovery. . . ."[5]

Reagan made no outlandish promises, did not use the term "laser beams," "space weapons," and certainly not "Star Wars," and in his diaries he noted, "I made no optimistic forecasts—said it might take 20 yrs. Or more but we had to do it. I felt good."[6] But he did understand, as he wrote in his diary in October 1986, that "the Soviets if faced with an arms race would have to negotiate—they can't squeeze their people any more to try & stay even with us."[7]

In 1985, Reagan introduced the Strategic Defense Initiative (SDI). Contrary to the claims of most textbooks, it was not scientists who labeled the system "Star Wars," but the press, in a deliberate attempt to ridicule it. But the Soviets took it quite seriously. Why—if it was so "fantastic" or just "science fiction"? The obvious answer was, it was fantastic only in the sense that it very well might work, and it was far from science fiction. They knew, as did our own engineers, that the key to SDI was computers. We had 'em, the Soviets didn't.

Soviet general secretary Mikhail Gorbachev said, "Even now, due to computer technology, one side could get ahead in space."[8] Although he pretended he "did not know what lay at the bottom of the U.S. position" on SDI, Gorbachev acted very much like a man who knew exactly what American technology could do. Although he labeled it "an illusion," Gorbachev—according to Reagan's secretary of state George Schultz—made clear that his primary focus was to "stop the SDI program."[9] At every meeting, Gorbachev was obsessed with SDI. At Reykjavík in 1985, Reagan employed his acting skills regarding

It was the astounding precision of American technology, represented by this Tomahawk cruise missile about to hit a target of a few inches in diameter after a flight of nearly one thousand miles, that terrified Mikhail Gorbachev. He knew that "Star Wars" could indeed work, and would produce the capability to destroy Soviet ICBMs in flight.

"Star Wars": when Gorbachev wanted language to kill SDI, Reagan refused. Gorbachev "tried to act jovial but I acted mad and it showed."[10] The administration even added to the Soviets' paranoia by rigging an SDI test in 1984 to show "success."[11]

Inside the Kremlin, the top Soviet generals were terrified. They knew SDI had the potential to work. Nikolai Leonov said that "it underlined still more our technological backwardness."[12] Gen. Makhmud Gareev, the deputy chief of the Soviet General Staff, agreed, saying it was "beyond our power" to compete with the Americans technologically.[13] In 1981, a Soviet arms negotiator said, "Oh, you Americans! . . . You are going to make us spend and spend to keep up and our lousy standard of living will go down and down and in the end you will win."[14] At a meeting in Munich in 1990 with former Hungarian Communist officials, I was repeatedly told that "Star Wars" in particular pushed the Soviets over the cliff. Foreign Minister Andrei Gromyko warned the "system would be used to blackmail the USSR."[15]

The question then has answered itself. Why would the Soviets worry in the least about a system that "wouldn't work"? Indeed, why would you not *urge* your enemy to build such a system and divert (or waste) his money? The answer was, it would work, and the Soviets knew it. As Andrew Busch put it,

SDI threatened the Soviets "with the choice of an unacceptable strategic defeat or an unacceptable technological and economic burden."[16]

By the late 1980s, the U.S. Air Force's "Flying Laser Laboratory" showed it could shoot down four missiles in flight simultaneously, and in the Gulf War, modified Patriot antiaircraft missiles demonstrated the capability to shoot down so-called terminal-phase ICBMs by killing several of Iraq's Scud missiles. While the record of the earliest Patriot batteries was debated, the more recent (PAC-2) antimissile variants have proven extremely effective. An even more advanced (PAC-3) version went operational in 2003. In 1992, space-based interceptors were successfully tested. As early as 1991, the Air Force (which had by then taken over most of the Office of Strategic Defense Initiative work) destroyed an ICBM using an interceptor missile launched almost five thousand miles away in the Pacific Ocean; another in 2007 shot down a Scud-type missile in the final stages of flight.

In 2007, numerous successful tests underscored the practicality of missile defense: new ground-based interceptors were demonstrated; an interceptor fired by a destroyer killed a target missile; and the Aegis ballistic missile defense system went three-for-three in its tests to destroy incoming warheads.[17] The new "Peace Through Light" flying "raygun" 747 airborne laser, capable of zapping enemy missiles during boost phase, was battling for its budget life, but it was a budgetary issue, not a technological question.[18] By July 2007, the modified jet completed a key test that "demonstrated most of the steps needed for the Airborne Laser to engage a threat missile."[19] In September 2007, yet another successful test led Gen. Victor E. Renuart Jr., commander of the North American Aerospace Defense Command, U.S. Northern Command, to state that the Star Wars system was ready to be used at any time. "I'm fully confident that we have all the pieces in place that, if the nation needed to, we could respond [to an incoming ballistic missile threat]."[20] Finally, in the spring of 2008 a "Star Wars" antimissile missile shot down a satellite, which was falling out of orbit and posing a threat to the U.S. population. Do you think any of the textbooks bothered to go back and revise their stunningly stupid predictions about Star Wars? Don't hold your breath.

The technological questions had been answered: Star Wars worked, and right on time. Reagan's twenty-year estimate for the technology to mature was on target after all. As Jean-François Revel observed, "Translating communism's economic disaster into political disaster required translators."[21] Ronald Reagan was an excellent translator, and his language was "Star Wars"!

LIE #9

MIKHAIL GORBACHEV, NOT RONALD REAGAN, WAS RESPONSIBLE FOR ENDING THE COLD WAR

Gorbachev's reform policies led not only to the collapse of the Soviet empire but also to the breakup of the Soviet Union itself.
—JAMES WEST DAVIDSON ET AL., NATION OF NATIONS

Gorbachev also backed off Soviet imperial ambitions.
—GEORGE BROWN TINDALL AND DAVID EMORI SHI, AMERICA:
A NARRATIVE HISTORY

Perhaps more important [than Reagan], under a new, younger leadership, the Kremlin allowed long-dormant forces of change to emerge and drive the U.S.S.R. toward democracy and a market economy.
—DAVID E. HARRELL ET AL., UNTO A GOOD LAND

An oft-repeated position in many major U.S. history textbooks is the notion that Mikhail Gorbachev ended the Cold War with his liberal reforms of *perestroika* ("restructuring") and *glasnost* ("openness in government"). According to this view, Gorbachev wanted to move the government of the Soviet Union more toward a market economy, but by doing so, he unwittingly unleashed a revolution he could not control. Moreover, Gorbachev was not an "imperialist" in the tradition of his Stalinist predecessors. In short, according to this line of thinking, Gorbachev was a benign monarch whose changes made possible negotiations with the West.

Even if such assessments were accurate—never mind that this great liberal kept a Soviet army in Afghanistan until high casualties forced him to withdraw, or that he supported the Cuban takeover of Grenada—they would still miss the essential point: Gorbachev was motivated by the new pressures put on him by Ronald Reagan. Even before he became president, Reagan intuitively knew that a Communist system cannot sustain itself or provide for the basic necessities of its population. Once he entered the White House, Reagan received intelligence estimates that confirmed his instincts. "The Soviet economy was being held together with bailing wire; it was a basket case," he said.[1] Less than two weeks after taking the oath of office, Reagan wrote in his diary, "Trade was supposed to make [the] Soviets moderate, instead it has allowed them to build armaments.... Their socialism is an ec[onomic] failure. Wouldn't we be doing more for their people if we let their system fail instead of constantly bailing it out?"[2] He told a reporter that for the first time the Soviets were "going to be faced with [the fact] that we could go forward with an arms race and they can't keep up."[3]

Time and again, intelligence showed that the Soviet Union was on the brink of economic collapse—all it needed was a push, and Reagan intended to give it a shove. In early 1982, the Reagan administration issued a series of National Security Decision Directives (NSDDs) that spelled out in detail how the United States would bankrupt the Soviet Union. One line of attack was to reverse Soviet expansion throughout the world—the first time since 1946 that any president made it official U.S. policy to roll back the Soviet empire, not contain it.[4] Another emphasis was stopping the new Soviet gas and oil pipeline to western Europe, thereby depriving the USSR of hard cash. It didn't take the Soviets long to figure out this new threat: "You have declared war on us, economic war," said General Secretary Leonid Brezhnev, Gorbachev's predecessor.[5] Putting high-tech items such as computers, software, and testing equipment on the restricted lists, Reagan made it impossible for the USSR to stay abreast of the United States in advanced technologies.

Reagan also authorized a remarkable strategy, which even recently was not well known. While blocking the sales of high-tech equipment, Reagan approved CIA director William Casey's plan to allow certain products to slip through the U.S. high-tech blockade. An initiative begun by a National Security Council staffer named Gus Weiss, called the "Farewell Dossier," leveraged the Soviets' organized effort to steal American technology by providing "enticing new technologies" that would appear genuine but which would later prove destructive.[6] One of these involved pipeline technology, which the Soviets swallowed hook, line, and sinker. Later the technology passed its tests, only to fail when it actually came online, severely retarding the Soviets' pipeline effort. Software to run the Soviet pumps, built to pass its tests, was secretly programmed to produce pressures that would burst the pipeline's tolerances. In 1982, a section of the pipeline failed, but it took twenty years for Weiss or anyone else in the CIA to admit the secret embedding.[7]

By 1983, Soviet high-tech imports from the United States had fallen sevenfold, while customs agents dashed efforts to steal the technology by seizing more than 1,400 illegal shipments totaling $200 million.[8] Without American technology, the Soviet economy fell further behind, at the very time it needed to surge ahead. Combined with the constricting impact on the cash flow from the slowed pipeline, the USSR was rapidly becoming a Third World country. All of this presumed that Gorbachev would not cut back his military spending to support improvements in the lives of ordinary citizens, and the presumption proved correct. While the numbers are hotly debated, a general consensus is that the Soviets spent between 25 percent and 40 percent of their gross domestic product on their military (the United States spent 5 percent). The "great dynamic success of capitalism has given us a powerful weapon in our battle against Communism— money," Reagan wrote.[9] Then, so to speak, Reagan dropped "the bomb."

Having already secured an overall expansion of American weapons systems, including construction of the B-1 bomber, deployment of cruise and Pershing missiles, installation of fifty MX ICBMs, and construction of numerous new warships, Reagan stunned the Soviet leaders in 1983 with his "Star Wars" speech. The Gipper never wavered in his belief that the Strategic Defense Initiative could—and eventually would—really work, writing in his diary after the speech, "I made no optimistic forecasts [but] said it might take 20 yrs. or more but we had to do it."[10] In the short term, however, the impact would be unmistakable: the Soviets would have to capitulate or drastically ramp up their military spending to counter "Star Wars." Like a high-stakes poker player, Reagan worked every angle, approving a faked SDI test in June 1984 to further convince the Soviets that Star Wars was ahead of schedule.[11] It worked. SDI was the Soviets' "number-one preoccupation," and Foreign Minister Alexander Bessmertnykh said they were "enormously frightened by SDI."[12]

It is well documented that the KGB tried, with little impact, to affect the 1984 U.S. presidential election in Walter Mondale's favor. At the same time, however, the Reagan administration exerted subtle pressure on the Kremlin to replace the deceased Soviet dictator Konstantin Chernenko with someone more sensible and—to use a buzzword of our day—"moderate." More than a few observers have argued that Reagan's policies drove the Soviets to install a "less dangerous Soviet leader" (as Secretary of the Interior William Clark wrote).[13] It's unarguable that Gorbachev was already working his way up the ranks of the Communist leadership in the USSR, being named to the Politburo in 1980, before Reagan was even elected. But Yuri Andropov, who headed the KGB and who recognized that the hard-liners were getting nowhere, supported Gorbachev as a better counterpart to Reagan than other existing candidates. Left-wing historian John Lewis Gaddis saw SDI as one of the factors that "contributed to the rise of Gorbachev."[14]

Reagan's NSDDs also devised a strategy to bog down the Soviets in Afghanistan. Sending Stinger antiaircraft missiles to the Afghan mujahideen, Reagan evened the odds for the resistance and eventually forced the Soviet withdrawal. In NSDD-166, U.S. policy officially became to "keep maximum pressure on Moscow for withdrawal" and to "ensure that the Soviets' political, military, and other costs remain high while the occupation continues."[15] Peter Rodman, a State Department official, said the United States had a "clear policy of seeking to defeat the Soviet Union . . . and force a Soviet withdrawal."[16]

In 1980, candidate Reagan said that an arms race was the "last thing" the Soviets wanted to see from the United States: "They know that if we turned our full industrial might into an arms race, they cannot keep pace with us. Why haven't we played that card?"[17] As president, the Gipper played that card. Across the board, using American banks and bullets, money and missiles, technology and diplomacy, the United States put a full-court press on the Soviet Union. The best that can be said for Gorbachev was that he was open to defeat. In 1989, historian John Lewis Gaddis—once a stalwart of the New Left historians—conceded, "The time has come to acknowledge an astonishing development: . . . Ronald Reagan has presided over the most dramatic improvement in U.S.-Soviet relations—and the most solid progress in arms control—since the Cold War began."[18]

SEPTEMBER 11 WAS NOT THE WORK OF TERRORISTS:
IT WAS A GOVERNMENT CONSPIRACY

[D]id it sorta look like those buildings came down in a controlled demolition?
—CHARLIE SHEEN (2006)

Don't ask me to tell you what happened on 9/11. All I know is that the official account of the buildings' collapse is improbable.
—PAUL CRAIG ROBERTS, "GULLIBLE AMERICANS," AUGUST 14, 2006

Perhaps we shouldn't be surprised that it was a Frenchman, Thierry Meyssan, who first concocted the ridiculous mantra that the United States destroyed the Twin Towers and hit the Pentagon.[1] Nor should it be surprising that his publisher specializes in titles such as *Moon Landings: Did NASA Lie?* or *The Greatest Illusion: The Death? of Adolf Hitler*. It probably didn't even raise many eyebrows when *The View*'s Rosie O'Donnell—one of the angriest of angry women—claimed that 9/11 was the "first time in history that fire has ever melted steel," and that "we don't know that it imploded," and that it "was an implosion and a demolition."[2] While O'Donnell has appeared unbalanced on many an occasion, some were surprised when actor Charlie Sheen (son of left-wing activist/actor Martin Sheen) on *The Alex Jones Show* said: "It seems to me like 19 amateurs with box cutters taking over four commercial airliners and hitting 75% of their targets, that feels like a conspiracy theory. It raises a lot of questions."[3] Sheen, a reasonably solid actor, must have been driven mad by overexposure to the canned laugh tracks of *Two and a Half Men*.

Shortly after 9/11, seeing that President George W. Bush had responded magnificently to a terrorist attack on the nation, the Democratic Party sought to diminish the credit going to the president. In May 2002, on the floor of the U.S. Senate, Hillary Clinton waved a copy of that day's edition of the *New York Post* with its headline, BUSH KNEW. The story claimed the president had been given a briefing warning of impending terrorist attacks. "The president knew what?" she asked. "My constituents would like to know the answer to that and many other questions. . . ."[4] All that remained unsaid was that Mrs. Clinton's constituents wanted to know how fire could "melt" steel.

The editors of the blue-collar magazine *Popular Mechanics* joined the fray by reviewing some of the conspiracy books before publishing *Debunking 9/11 Myths* in 2006.[5] The airplanes carried some ten thousand gallons of jet fuel each. Jet fuel burns at 1,100 to 1,200 degrees Celsius, and steel doesn't melt until it reaches 1,510 degrees Celsius. But it loses strength at 400 degrees Celsius, and at 980 degrees, it possesses less than 10 percent of its strength. Load-bearing columns and beams did not need to melt: they only had to be weakened and bent sufficiently. The National Institute of Science and Technology (NIST) conducted a study of the buildings' collapse and found that the impact had stripped "fireproofing insulation from trusses that supported 80,000 square feet of floor space."[6] As floors began to sag, they put additional stress on the 90 percent weakened steel columns, pulling them inward and adding to the stress on surviving columns. None of this even begins to take into consideration the phenomenal impact stresses of a jetliner striking the buildings at over 150 miles per hour, or the "hollowing out" of the load-bearing elevator shafts by the fuel and fire that shot down them. Brigham Young University's Steven Jones, in a paper called "Why Indeed Did the World Trade Center Buildings Completely Collapse on 9-11-01?," argued that the World Trade Center steel did not perform as models say it should.[7] Jones and some others claim that thousands of pounds of high explosives placed inside the World Trade Center brought it down. Yet not a single witness reported any unusual movements of people, let alone dozens of people in black suits marching into the 80th to 105th floors of the buildings with thousands of pounds of explosives.

More unbelievable are the absurd claims about the hundreds of people on board the airplanes, who are, according to Peter Meyer and other conspiracy theorists, being detained at a government facility so they can't "spill the beans." Another theory postulates that the passengers aren't listed as dead since the planes could have off-loaded them at any of a number of military bases. Odd that there is no record of any of those jets being seen again, let alone landing.[8] Of course, the families who heard from their loved ones, including the solicitor general of the United States, Ted Olson, who heard from his wife Barbara before her plane hit the Pentagon, know what happened to the passengers.

Others have claimed that missiles, not airplanes, brought down the towers, but this is easily refuted by the identification of aircraft parts that exited the buildings. Airplane parts carry identifying marks. Landing gear and engine parts specifically tied to the planes that hit the towers were recovered. "Well," say the conspiracy theorists, "the planes were real, but they weren't passenger planes—they were special military airplanes." From the "military pod" to the "absence of windows" on one or all of the airplanes, the entire argument is preposterous. It denies (a) the eyewitnesses who saw the planes take off and the crews that boarded them; (b) the radar data that tracked them; (c) the dozens of passengers who called *from* all the airplanes (not only on cell phones—which indeed can operate at the altitudes the planes flew—but also the air phones that were on the aircraft; and (d) the eyewitnesses who saw the planes hit, including many who saw the impact at the Pentagon. Barbara Olson called her husband twice to alert him to Flight 77's path and its intended target. Twelve people made calls from Flight 93, including Tom Burnett, who called his wife three times. Allowing for the time in which radar and the "black boxes" could track the aircraft, there was no time to land even one of them and deplane people (who had to then be whisked off mysteriously without ever again contacting anyone—an operation that, according to the conspiracists, had to be carried out with absolutely no flaws or leaks), take off again and then acquire the target. The fact that the airplanes are clearly the same ones that took off less than an hour earlier, and can be identified as such not only by wreckage but by (in some cases) photos taken just before impact, has not been explained by the kook lobby. Moreover, no one can explain why the very same hijackers who had trained to conduct exactly such an operation would have mysteriously boarded four planes that just "happened" to hit the targets they trained to strike, nor why Osama bin Laden would take credit for an operation that he and Khalid Sheikh Mohammed both admitted to planning. Neither Charlie Sheen nor Rosie O'Donnell can explain why there was a struggle on Flight 93 with the very Muslims who were identified as boarding earlier.

In short, there is a good reason we have terms like "kook," "wacko," and "tinfoil hat crowd." The fact that some conspiracists actually hold respectable jobs or appear normal under other circumstances should not conceal the fact that they are on one side, and the American Society of Civil Engineers, the National Fire Protection Association, Underwriters Laboratories, several prominent universities, the 9/11 Commission, plus virtually every agency within the government that has in any way examined the evidence, are on the other side. It's also not surprising that many of the same conspiracy theorists are still searching for the alien bodies at Roswell.

LIE #11

No Terrorists or Weapons of Mass Destruction Were Hiding in Iraq

The web of half-truths and falsehoods used to sell the war did not happen by accident; it was woven by design and . . . foisted on the public by a P.R. operation built expressly for that purpose.
— Frank Rich, New York Times, November 27, 2005

A systematic search found no active production facilities or stockpiles for chemical, nuclear, or biological weapons of mass destruction, refuting one of the basic justifications for the war.
— David Goldfield et al., The American Journey

Yet another administration claim was laid to rest in September 2004 when the national commission appointed to investigate 9/11 reported that it had found "no credible evidence that Iraq and Al Qaeda [had] cooperated on attacks" against the United States.
— Irwin Unger, These United States

Repeat a fib often enough and it becomes accepted truth. Hitler called it the "big lie." In this case, the lie is that Saddam Hussein's Iraq was no threat to anyone prior to the U.S. invasion in March 2003. In October 2002, President George W. Bush laid out the case for deposing Iraqi dictator Saddam Hussein at the Cincinnati Union Terminal. His case rested on three main stated premises: (1) there were "weapons of mass destruction" (WMDs) in Iraq, which could fall into the hands of terrorists; (2) there were terrorists in Iraq for those weapons to be given to; and (3) the Iraqi people, if offered a chance at democracy, would provide an important buffer in the Middle East against further terrorism. Five years later, presidential candidate John Edwards referred to the "War on Terror" as a "bumper sticker," and virtually all politicians in Washington—including many of the president's staunchest allies—have repudiated the claim that there were WMDs in Iraq.

The forgotten question in all this is, "If there were no weapons of mass destruction in Iraq, why did everyone and his brother say that there were prior to the election of George W. Bush?" The French, British, Spanish, Australian, Japanese, German, Israeli, and NATO intelligence services all confirmed the existence of such weapons, as did Iran. Egypt's president and the king of Jordan both told Gen. Tommy Franks in 2002 that the WMDs were in Iraq.[1] Russia's Vladimir Putin not only reaffirmed that the WMDs were there, but warned President Bush that his country's intelligence services had received information about an impending strike against the United States specifically using these weapons. The United Nations, in more than a dozen Security Council resolutions, claimed Iraq had WMDs—and demanded that Saddam disarm. (He ignored the UN.)

Physical evidence from the gassing of the Kurds in 1988 and from the use of chemical and biological ("chem/bio") weapons in the Iran-Iraq War of the 1980s established that Saddam had WMDs—WMDs that the United Nations never could account for, including 6,500 chemical weapons, according to Hans Blix.[2] Deserters and defectors from Iraq's military affirmed he had WMDs, and some *four tons* of biological agents were never found.[3] Among those in the American leadership who stated without question that Saddam had WMDs were President Bill Clinton, who said (1998), "We want to seriously diminish the threat posed by Iraq's weapons of mass destruction program"; now-Senator Hillary Clinton; presidential candidate John Kerry, Senator Tom Daschle, and Senator Carl Levin, who in a letter to President Bill Clinton (1998) urged him to "take necessary actions (including, if appropriate, air and missile strikes . . .) to respond effectively to the threat posed by Iraq's refusal to end its weapons of mass destruction programs"; Secretary of State Madeleine Albright, who said (1999), "Hussein has . . . chosen to spend his money building weapons of mass destruction"; Senator Ted Kennedy, who claimed that (2002) "Saddam Hussein is seeking and developing weapons of mass destruction"; and Vice President (and later presidential candidate)

Al Gore, who asserted (2002), "We know that he has stored secret supplies of biological and chemical weapons throughout his country." Despite some after-the-fact backtracking, the former CIA director under both Clinton and Bush, George Tenet, admitted to assuring President Bush that the case for Saddam having WMDs was a "slam dunk."

Did Saddam Hussein have a biological weapons expert on his staff known as "Dr. Germ" so that he could dispose of his current WMDs, or develop new ones? Did he employ a chemical weapons expert dubbed "Chemical Ali" for similar reasons? Prior to the 2003 invasion, two of Saddam's sons-in-law defected and testified about the Iraqi programs before they were kidnapped and returned to Iraq for execution. In the translations of the Saddam tapes, repeated references to nuclear power research and ongoing attempts to purchase materials related to making nuclear weapons and facilities can be heard.[4]

Around 2002, Iraq began transferring its permanent WMD sites underground and into mobile units.[5] Dissidents reported that year and after the invasion that weapons were also being moved to mosques, since Coalition forces refrained from searching mosques. A full listing of all the reputed sites given by sources who collaborated with the Coalition lists more than a dozen locations.[6] More than one hundred cases of "mysterious" illnesses reported by soldiers doing cleanup activities suggests that these were examples of missed WMD traces.[7] British troops in Basra reported being fired at with 82mm mortar rounds containing chemical weapons.[8] In 2003, a UN weapons inspector confidently stated that Iraq had an ongoing nuclear program, and that he knew personally of uranium reprocessing at a facility six miles from Tarmiya.[9] A twenty-gallon barrel found in northern Iraq tested positive for sarin, and another tested positive for mustard gas.[10]

The infamous "looting" appears to have been orchestrated to remove evidence of WMDs, as confirmed by the Kay interim report. David Kay told a House committee on October 2, 2003, that "significant elements of this looting were carried out in a systematic and deliberate manner, with the clear aim of concealing pre-OIF [Operation Iraqi Freedom] activities of Saddam's regime."[11] Perhaps the most credible evidence comes from ex–Iraqi general Georges Sada, who published his evidence in *Saddam's Secrets* (2006), providing firsthand observation of these programs.[12] Sada, an air vice marshal in the Iraqi Air Force, had ordered a sarin gas attack on Israel in 1990 that was called off because it would have required Iraqi jets to fly over Syrian and Jordanian airspace. In 2006, Sada revealed that he knew those "who were involved in smuggling the WMDs out of Iraq in 2002 and 2003. . . . I know how and when they were transported and shipped out of Iraq [including] how many aircraft were actually used and what types of planes they were."[13]

Then there were the tapes and documents that came out of postinvasion Iraq: more than three thousand hours of Saddam meeting with his war cabinet and millions of pages relating to Saddam's WMDs. *These documents included orders to transport the WMDs out of the country in the event of a pending invasion or UN weapons inspection.* In these tapes, Saddam can be heard discussing Iraq's WMD and nuclear programs and how he fooled the weapons inspectors. In September 2002, Jon Wolfsthal, an analyst then with the Carnegie Endowment for International Peace—hardly a right-wing think tank!—stated flatly, "Iraq continues to possess several tons of chemical weapons agents, enough to kill thousands and thousands of civilians or soldiers."[14] Further, Sada noted that the term "special weapons," which always denoted WMDs, was used by Saddam on numerous occasions. Eventually, realizing he was about to be invaded, Saddam "called a meeting of all the top scientists, researchers, and technicians involved in developing weapons systems, and told them to memorize their plans," then ordered all schematics, plans, and data related to WMDs destroyed.[15] When a Syrian dam broke in 2002, and Syrian president Bashar al-Assad asked Saddam for help, interspersed in the "relief" effort were the main elements of the WMD program. Some fifty-six sorties of commercial jetliners, with their seats and other equipment removed to make room for the WMDs, took the weapons to Syria. Demetrius Perricos, president of the United Nations Monitoring, Verification and Inspection Commission (UNMOVIC), confirmed in June 2004 that Saddam had indeed smuggled the WMDs out of Iraq before the war. Clearly Syria was implicated (other sources also suggest the Russians supplied trucks to assist this move), and no one in the UN or in the U.S. government wanted to "go there." So the WMD issue was dropped. The Jordanians, however, knew the real story, and broke up a plot by Abu Musab al-Zarqawi to explode "a large chemical weapon in the center of Amman, Jordan."[16] If the weapons inspectors and Iraq Study Group had looked half as hard for the WMDs as Nixon's tormentors looked for evidence of his involvement in Watergate, they'd be awash in chemical and biological weapons right now.

It is also a sleight of hand to claim that President Bush made Saddam's possession of WMDs the *only* issue that triggered Operation Iraqi Freedom.

While he primarily focused on WMDs in the famous 2002 State of the Union "Axis of Evil" speech, in his Cincinnati address leading up to the war nine months later, he listed three main casus belli, namely WMDs, the presence of terrorists (including, but *not limited to,* al-Qaeda) in Iraq, and the prospect that a free and democratic Iraq would further reduce the conditions that supported and nourished terrorism.[17]

Subsequently, most commentators focused solely on the comments about WMDs. The misdirection was also present, but not as pronounced, in the press coverage of the "Axis of Evil" speech itself, whereby the media glossed over the president's statement that North Korea, Iraq, and Iran were merely *examples.* By zeroing in on the three, the media left "them in possession of the field of evil."[18] As media historian Jim Kuypers showed, virtually none of the media picked up on the larger concept relayed by Bush, even as they recoiled against the term "evil."[19] Even then, however, the *CBS Morning News* noted that "the CIA believes [Iraq has] been trying to develop nuclear weapons and already have chemical and probably biological weapons."[20] As Kuypers concludes about the press coverage that followed, "In a definitive shift from the previous chapters, opinion essays and editorials [following the State of the Union] took a decidedly negative shape."[21]

Then there were the "deniers," people such as Richard Clarke, former Clinton and Bush counterterrorism official, who made the ridiculous claim, "There's absolutely no evidence that Iraq was supporting al Qaeda, ever."[22] As Stephen Hayes, who has studied the al-Qaeda/Iraq links, noted, there were "literally hundreds of intelligence reports detailing links between Iraq and al-Qaeda's worldwide operations."[23] The Web site "Regime of Terror" lists dozens of specific terrorists in Iraq prior to Operation Iraqi Freedom.[24] President Bush went out of his way to state that there was not any *evidence* ruling out any Iraqi involvement in the 9/11 attacks, but no one has ruled it out, and some "circumstantial and speculative" evidence suggests such a connection may exist.[25] Even more obvious was the fact that there were terrorists in Iraq prior to Operation Iraqi Freedom. In 2007, former CIA director George Tenet published his book *At the Center of the Storm,* in which he claimed the al-Qaeda/ Iraq links were minimal.[26] Almost immediately, however, one of his own analysts, Christina Shelton, completely disavowed Tenet's claims that there was "no further analysis required" of the relationship.[27] Shelton told the director that the accumulated sources "reflected a pattern of Iraqi support for al-Qaeda, including high-level contacts between Iraqi senior officials and al-Qaeda, training in bomb making, Iraqi offers of safe haven, and a nonaggression agreement to cooperate on unspecified areas."[28] Earlier, she noted, Tenet told the U.S. Senate, "We have solid reporting of senior level contacts between Iraq and al-Qa'ida going back a decade."[29] The famous "Feith memo," presented to the Senate Intelligence Committee in October 2003, concluded that "the substantial body of intelligence reporting—for over a decade—from a variety of sources—reflects a pattern of Iraqi support for al Qaeda's activities."[30]

Although a Pentagon report released in March 2008 found no "operational links" with al-Qaeda, operational links are different from aid, assistance, and support. Operational links imply direct contact in planning and carrying out terrorist attacks. But the list of Saddam/al-Qaeda *connections* is overwhelming, and goes back to the 1990s:

* October 1998 (as reported in the January 10, 1999, edition of *Al-Majallah*), an Iraqi intelligence official met with the Taliban leader Mullah Omar, "Osama bin Ladin [*sic*], and Dr. Ayman al-Zawahiri, leader of Egypt's Jihad movement" (and bin Laden's number two officer). "On December 21, a high-ranking Iraqi diplomat visited Taleban [*sic*] leader Mullah Omar's residence [then] he met with bin Ladin and al-Zawahiri. . . . [He] affirmed to his Afghan and Arab audience *Iraq's willingness to provide financial, logistic, political and informational support* for the Taleban and the Afghan Arabs [emphasis mine]."[31]
* November 4, 1998, U.S. Attorney Mary Jo White indicted Osama bin Laden and several others in the African embassy bombings. That indictment contained this stunning phrase: "On particular projects, specifically including weapons development, al Qaeda would work cooperatively with the Government of Iraq."[32]
* 1998, the CIA reported from a "regular and reliable source" about meetings between al-Qaeda and Iraqi intelligence.[33]
* January 15, 1999, Cynthia McFadden of ABC News reported that bin Laden was "in secret meetings with Saddam Hussein's top men."
* February 6, 1999, the *Guardian* reported, "The Western Nightmare: Saddam and Bin Laden versus the World."
* December 2000, two al-Qaeda operatives were sent to Iraq for training in chemical and biological weapons.
* The highly regarded *Jane's* reported in September 2001, just a week after

the World Trade Center attacks, that "for the past two years Iraqi intelligence officers were shuttling between Baghdad and Afghanistan, meeting with Ayman Al Zawahiri."[34]

- November 11, 2001, the London *Observer* reported an active camp called Salman Pak where students practiced hijacking techniques on a Boeing 707. What is notable about this is that it was in what was called the "foreigners' camp." A defector told the FBI and CIA that the "foreigners" (i.e., what the Iraqis called al-Qaeda and other Arabs) were trained "to use small knives" to take over airplanes. The defector stated flatly that Saddam controlled the camps.

- November 2001, Ibn al-Sheikh al-Libi was captured by Pakistanis. A member of bin Laden's inner circle, he "spoke openly" about the collaboration between al-Qaeda and Iraq on WMDs.

- 2002, Qassem Hussein Muhammed, interviewed by a *New Yorker* reporter, said he was one of seventeen Iraqi bodyguards who escorted al-Qaeda's number two man, Ayman al-Zawahiri, during a 1992 trip, and Iraqi premier Iyad Allawi confirmed a second visit to Iraq in 1999, and was aware that the "Iraqi secret service had documents detailing the [Saddam/al-Qaeda] relationship."[35]

- May 31, 2002, CBS reported that Abdul Rahman Yasin, a participant in the first attempt to blow up the World Trade Center in 1993, escaped and fled to . . . Iraq.

- July 14, 2002, a former colonel in Saddam's Fedayeen claimed that he trained with al-Qaeda terrorists in camps near Baghdad.[36] (A man known as "The Ghost" trained terrorists at Salman Pak and other locations and told interrogators that there were "foreigners" at those camps and that they were trained separately from Iraqis.)[37]

- September 5, 2002, CBS News reported that more than a thousand victims of the 9/11 attacks sued Iraq for its involvement in the conspiracy with Osama bin Laden to attack the United States. The suit claimed that Iraqi officials were aware of the plan before 9/11, and one of the lawyers bringing the suit said, "We have evidence Iraq knew and approved of the Sept. 11 attacks."[38]

- October 2002, House Minority Leader Richard Gephardt (D-Mo.) said on ABC's *This Week* that he had seen "lots of intelligence" that Saddam had ties to al-Qaeda.

- February 7, 2003, *The Independent* in Britain identified Abu Musab al-Zarqawi as the "head of an Iraqi-based al-Qa'ida [*sic*] cell."[40] Note that this was *more than a month before the U.S. invasion!*
- March 16, 2003, Spain indicted Yusuf Galan, who was photographed at an al-Qaeda camp, for being "directly involved with the preparation and carrying out of the attacks . . . by the suicide pilots on 11 September."[39]
- In 2007, questions still remain as to Saddam's connections to the first World Trade Center bombing and the Oklahoma City bombing.[41]

Note that none of this evidence gets to some of the most damning material, produced by the Czech Republic, which alleges that the foreign minister of Iraq met with Mohammed Atta in Prague just months before the 9/11 attacks. Czech intelligence to this day stands by that claim, and a security camera clearly shows Ahmed Samir al-Ani casing a U.S. government building in Prague with a man who looked remarkably like Atta. George Tenet, former CIA director, said that while he did not have clear evidence, he thought the meeting took place.[42]

We won't even bother with the *non-al-Qaeda terrorists,* such as the late Abu Nidal, or Abd-al-Rahman Isa, his second in command, who were harbored by Saddam for years, or the uncomfortable evidence raised by Laurie Mylroie—a Clinton adviser on Iraq—that the main perpetrator of the 1993 WTC bombing, Ramzi Yousef, was known as "Rashid the Iraqi," and that one of his conspirators, Mohammed Salameh, made forty-six phone calls to Iraq prior to the bombing![43] Yet another of the 1993 bombers, Abdul Rahman Yasin, traveled to the United States from Baghdad and then escaped after the bombing to Baghdad, where his presence was well known to Iraqi secret police. Even a *Newsweek* reporter found him in Baghdad—but, of course, there were no terrorists in Iraq![44]

Instead, it's better to let Ayman al-Zawahiri state the case himself as in July 2007 when he said Iraq was the centerpiece of al-Qaeda's terror efforts and urged Muslims to "rush to the fields of jihad" in Iraq.[45] According to *USA Today,* Rita Katz, director of the now-defunct SITE Institute, which monitored terrorist-related activity around the world, "said she didn't have 'any doubt' that al-Qaeda in Iraq is linked to bin Laden's network."[46] The best news contained in the July 2007 video is that Zawahiri displayed concern that al-Qaeda was losing in Iraq. George Bush's original claims of both WMDs and terrorists in Iraq were not only valid, they were overwhelming.

UPDATE: Since the first edition of *48 Liberal Lies* went into production, news surfaced of an ongoing secret program by the United States and its allies to process an astonishing 500 *tons* of uranium and to transfer it out of Iraq. On July 7, 2008, CNN reported that the U.S. had transported 500 metric tons of "yellowcake" uranium from Iraq to Canada—precisely the same "yellowcake" that Joe Wilson claimed the Iraqis were *not* trying to acquire from Niger. The original claim by President Bush—that Iraq was seeking to acquire such yellowcake—had in turn led to a massive investigation about the leak of the supposed covert status of Wilson's wife, Valerie Plame, and then to a witch-hunt by the Left to implicate Karl Rove for leaking her identity. The sordid affair ended when the prosecutor refused to name the real leaker, State Department official Richard Armitage, and instead indicted Rove aide Scooter Libby for perjury in what is called a "process crime"—the same sort of crime Clinton committed but the Left excused.

Known as "Operation McCall," the transfer of 500 tons of uranium from a nation that had no operating nuclear plants should have raised eyebrows among even the staunchest "no-WMDs-in-Iraq" Bush-haters. As the *American Thinker* correctly stated, no one ever asked what 500 tons of yellowcake uranium were still doing at the nuclear research center of Al-Tuwaitha in Iraq when American tanks rolled into Bagdhad?[47] This buildup occurred under the very noses of the International Atomic Energy Agency (IAEA)—the United Nations bureaucrats in charge of making sure Saddam didn't have WMDs! Both the Butler Review in England and a Senate Select Committee stated without equivocation that Saddam had attempted to purchase yellowcake. Whether this was in addition to the massive stockpile he already had—and, I repeat a second time, for a nation with *no* nuclear plants—is not clear.

What is abundantly clear is that the "No WMDs" crowd was horribly wrong, but that Bush was still badly hurt by the secrecy surrounding the mission to clear the uranium—and almost certainly other deadly toxins and materials—out of the country safely.

LIE #12

THE FOUNDERS ENVISIONED A "WALL OF SEPARATION" BETWEEN CHURCH AND STATE, KEEPING RELIGIOUS INFLUENCE OUT OF GOVERNMENT

The Founding Fathers did not intend to establish the United States of America as a Christian nation [and] the assertion that the United States . . . was founded as a "Christian nation" is itself a myth.
—MARK WELDON WHITTEN, THE MYTH OF CHRISTIAN AMERICA

How many times have you heard that there is a "wall of separation" between church and state and that the Constitution prohibits any kind of "state religion"?[1] No one would be more surprised—and aghast—at such an interpretation than the Founders and their forefathers, the ones who set up the state constitutions on which the U.S. Constitution was based. As late as 1833, Justice Joseph Story (who after Chief Justice John Marshall was perhaps our greatest legal mind in the antebellum era) wrote: "The whole power over the subject of religion is *left exclusively to the State governments,* to be acted upon according to their own sense of justice and State Constitutions" (emphasis mine).[2] John Bouvier's *Law Dictionary* noted in its definition of religion, "The Christian religion is, of course, recognized by the government, yet . . . the preservation of religious liberty is *left to the states.*"[3] When Ronald Reagan told the Republican National Convention in 1984 that "politics and morality are inseparable [and] religion and politics are necessarily related," he observed that "government needs the church because only those humble enough to admit they're sinners can bring to democracy the tolerance it requires."[4] The Founders would have said, "Amen."

Virginia's first charter (1606) stated, "We, greatly commending, and graciously accepting of, their Desires for the Furtherance of so noble a Work . . . in propagating of Christian Religion to such People [i.e., Indians] as yet live in Darkness and miserable Ignorance of the true Knowledge and Worship of God," establish the colony of Virginia.[5] Three years later, the second charter of Virginia asserted the "principal Effect" of establishing the colony "is the Conversion . . . of the People in those Parts unto the true Worship of God and Christian Religion."[6] In 1624, the Virginia assembly established a law that on every plantation there be a place "where the people use to meet for the worship of God," and that "there be an uniformity in our Church as near as may be to the Canons in England." Delaware added a statement at its constitutional convention that required all members of the state House of Representatives to make the following profession of faith: "And I do acknowledge the Holy Scriptures of the Old and New Testament to be given by divine Inspiration."[7] Maryland was established to extend the Christian religion and to ensure that "no Interpretation thereof be made whereby God's Holy and true Christian Religion" would be changed.[8] Maryland's constitution, in Article 35, required as the only qualification to serve in a state office "a declaration of a belief in the Christian religion."[9]

The Continental Congress in 1777 ordered a day of thanksgiving and praise that the people "join the penitent confession of their manifold sins . . . [that the day, through] their humble and earnest supplication . . . may please God, through the merits of Jesus Christ. . . ."[10] Even the supposed Deist Benjamin Franklin urged the members of the Constitutional Convention to pray, saying,

> I have lived, sir, a long time, and, the longer I live, the more convincing proofs I see of this truth—that God governs in the affairs of men. And if a sparrow cannot fall to the ground without his notice, is it probable that an empire can rise without his aid? We have been assured, sir, in the sacred writings, that "except the Lord build the house, they labor in vain that build it."[11]

Another Founder whose faith is frequently challenged, George Washington, in his "Thanksgiving Proclamation," said that November 26 should be devoted to "the service of that great and glorious Being, who is the beneficent Author of all the good that was, that is, or that will be."[12]

By 1632, there were statutes in some colonies requiring attendance at church every Sunday. Absence was punished by a shilling per offense, and by 1656, there were laws exempting ministers from paying taxes in Virginia. Just two years before the U.S. Constitution was adopted, the Virginia Assembly debated a bill for the support of the Christian religion. James Madison objected to the bill because he feared it would put civil judges into the position of deciding what constituted Christianity. Yet Madison reasoned the bill was "adverse to the diffusion . . . of Christianity," and was concerned that the bill would discourage those followers of "false religions" from "coming into the regions of [the light of truth, i.e., Christianity]."[13] Thomas Jefferson's own draft bill on freedom of religion reasoned that God's very nature led Him to choose "not to propagate His religion by coercion" but to "extend it by its influence on reason alone."[14]

Similarly, the Charter of New England (1620) announced that the main objective of the colony was "the enlargement of Christian religion, to the Glory of God Almighty."[15] It repeated the objective of "the Conversion and reduction of the People in those Parts unto the true Worship of God and the Christian Religion."[16] The Mayflower Compact stated that the purpose of the colony was the "Advancement of the Christian Faith."[17] Massachusetts Bay's charter directed the colony's inhabitants to "the Knowledge and Obedience of the only true God and Savior of Mankind, and the Christian Faith."[18] The first book printed in North America was the *Bay Psalm Book*. Maine, which was part of Massachusetts, stated in its Grant of the Province a desire that "the Religion now professed in the Church of England and Ecclesiastical Government now used in the same shall be forever hereafter professed."[19] Maine's 1819 Constitution acknowledged "the Sovereign ruler of the Universe" and implored "God's Aid and direction." It reiterated the "natural and inalienable right to worship Almighty God" according to the dictates of each person's conscience, and allowed "no preference of any one sect" under the law. Note that once again it was viewed as the *state's* prerogative to determine the extent of religious liberties therein.[20] Maine's statutes in 1911 still called for schools to teach "the fundamental truths of Christianity."[21]

Rhode Island explained in its 1663 charter that the very purpose of its "religious liberties" clause was that the citizens "may be in the better capacity to defend themselves, in their just rights and liberties against all the enemies of the Christian faith."[22] And on and on. The founding documents of every one of the original thirteen colonies reveals them to be awash in the concepts of Christianity and God. *Whatever* the documents intended by "religious freedom," they never in any way, shape, or form intended the state to interfere with Christian religious expression.

It is therefore silly and unsupported to claim, as religious historian Jon Butler tries to do, that "Revolutionary America Wasn't a Christian Nation."[23] Christians played so dominant a role in the American Revolution that Joseph Galloway, a Loyalist, complained that the rebellion was led by "Congregationalists, Presbyterians, and Smugglers."[24]

Of course, it is Thomas Jefferson's single "wall of separation" letter that most secularists leap to cite as evidence of a "secular" Republic. It should go without mentioning that the phrase "separation of church and state" itself never appears in the U.S. Constitution but was extracted from Jefferson's "wall" comment, yet it has been the root cause of innumerable modern problems. Jefferson, certainly no Christian by any acceptable definition, nevertheless wrote the Virginia sabbath law and penned ordinances sanctioning days of prayer and fasting. It was Virginia's incorporation of the Protestant Episcopal Church that caused Baptists and Presbyterians to complain about state ties. By that time, most colonies (then states) had constitutions that established religious liberty (i.e., not regulating *against* the practice of religion). This was a far cry from *prohibitions* against religious activities in public places or with official government sanction.[25] Mark Noll, one of the leading scholars of American religion, acknowledges that "the colonial background of the new states was so overwhelmingly Protestant that it was simply assumed that such things as Sunday legislation, laws prohibiting atheism and promoting public morals, and the regular use of Christian language by government officials were appropriate."[26] The simple fact is that the new United States was so overwhelmingly Christian in its outlook that there was never any consideration given to non-Christian groups such as Muslims, Hindus, or Buddhists in the deliberations about the law or constitutions. Jews, while never numerous enough to attract attention, were quietly allowed to practice their faith and, over time, accepted openly.

How many early Americans attended church was one thing—some suggest only about a third—but what was called "adherence," or "regular participation in religious activities and churchgoing," may have reached three-quarters of the American colonists. The aforementioned Supreme Court justice Joseph Story said in 1812 that the First Amendment allowed Christianity to "receive encouragement from the state, so far as was not incompatible with the private rights of conscience, and freedom of religious worship."[27] Moreover, as Noll explains, "None of the founders interpreted the First Amendment as prohibiting religiously grounded arguments for general public policy."[28] And if America *started* as overwhelmingly Christian and substantially Protestant, it became even more so as the founding generation was replaced by the subsequent citizens who grew up still bothering to read the Constitution. "The line between religion and politics has always been a thin one in America," Noll writes. "In the heyday of 'Evangelical America' [1800–1865] it was virtually nonexistent."[29] Even the U.S. Supreme Court, as late as 1892 (*Church of the Holy Trinity v. United States*), found in a unanimous decision, "Our laws and institutions necessarily are based upon and embody the teachings of the Redeemer of mankind. . . . [In] this sense and to this extent our civilization and our institutions are emphatically Christian. . . . [This] is a Christian nation."[30] And even in 2007, Congress still begins its sessions with prayers; chaplains are still on the payroll of the U.S. military; and presidents still proclaim days of prayer and thanksgiving.

Moreover, virtually every American president publicly acknowledged the Creator, "Divine Providence," or some other euphemism for God—all within the overall Christian context. Polls show that 60 percent of Americans believe their president should be religious, and nearly one-third make adherence to a specific religion the deciding factor in their vote.[31] All forty-three presidents have "been friendly toward organized religion," thirty-two have been church members, and all of them considered themselves to be Christians.[32] Even Jefferson, in a strange way, thought himself a follower of Christian precepts; Theodore Roosevelt "prayed without ceasing"and frequently read the Bible.[33] Roosevelt urged all Christians to work together, but "insisted that Christianity was superior to all other faiths."[34] Woodrow Wilson stated boldly, "The Bible is the word of life," and he prayed unceasingly.[35] To those who knew Franklin Roosevelt, he was a "deeply religious man" who "adorned the doctrine of Christ . . . by a consistent walk and holy life."[36] President Dwight Eisenhower, recalling his time as a general, told Clare Booth Luce in 1952, "Do you think I could have fought my way through this war, ordered thousands of fellows to their deaths, if I couldn't have got down on my knees and talked to God[?] I couldn't live a day of my life without God."[37]

Jimmy Carter ran for the presidency on his image as an evangelical Christian, and his supporters urged people to vote for him based on his religious faith.[38] George W. Bush, amidst a personal crisis, realized that "God sent His Son to die for a sinner like me," whereupon his life became one of marked discipleship.[39]

Some presidents, such as Ronald Reagan and George W. Bush, openly declared their love of Christ. Much of Reagan's Christianity—visible during his life—really only came under scrutiny in his death, at which point his son, Ron Jr., acknowledged that his father was a "deeply, unabashedly religious man."[40] Until Paul Kengor's book *God and Ronald Reagan* came out in 2004, few paid any attention to Reagan's extensive use of scripture, his commitment to prayer, or his own testimonials.[41] Yet in his newly released diaries, Reagan's concern for his dying father-in-law is revealed to be his motivation for setting himself right with the Lord.[42]

The Founders indeed inserted "freedom of religion" clauses into almost all state constitutions, precisely because they were overwhelmingly Christians but were concerned that different denominations might gain the favor of government. "Disestablishment" clauses were strictly intended to *protect* the observance of Christianity and Christian traditions, but in any event, such authority was always considered to be solely the domain of the state. The Founders never dreamed that subsequent generations would seek to take crosses off federal lands, or ban "In God We Trust" from money, or, above all, ban prayer in public schools. Such a perversion of the "freedom of religion" clauses to oppress Christianity would have been abhorrent and fought to the death.

LIE #13

THOMAS JEFFERSON FAVORED "SMALL GOVERNMENT" AND WAS A PACIFIST

[H]e can with some justice be called a "half-way pacifist." . . .
—REGINALD C. STUART, THE HALF-WAY PACIFIST

For the man who ordered America's first "preemptive war," this would seem an odd argument on its face. Nevertheless, it is true that compared to the so-called Federalists (itself a term that turned the actual positions of the pro– and anti–central government factions on their heads), the Sage of Monticello favored less government rather than more—in most cases.[1] Yet this same Jefferson, whom Reginald Stuart called the "half-way pacifist," boldly proclaimed, "The tree of liberty must be refreshed from time to time with the blood of patriots and tyrants."[2]

Even as the Father of Our Country, George Washington, continued to authorize tribute payments to the Barbary pirates, Jefferson subscribed to the popular phrase, "Millions for defense but not one cent for tribute." As secretary of state, Jefferson sought to arrange an alliance of foreign nations that would crush the Tripolitan states, but found no takers. (It seems that many comfortable, civilized states in the 1790s were no more willing to stand up to threats than they were two hundred years later.) He even issued a "Proposal to Use Force against the Barbary States," where he called for tit-for-tat seizures of Algerian ships in which Muslim captives would be sold as slaves![3] He agreed with John Adams that the Barbary incursions constituted "a good occasion to begin a navy."[4] As president, Jefferson took the affront by the bey of Tripoli, who cut down the U.S. flagpole, for what it was—a signal for war—and dispatched two large squadrons, consisting of almost all of America's heavy ships, to end the piracy.[5]

Jefferson did support cutbacks in the "blue water" navy, preferring some two hundred single-cannon gunboats for coastal defense only (virtually all of which were destroyed in the War of 1812). Of course, he didn't hesitate to use the frigates and other heavy ships built by the Federalists once he had a conflict on his hands with the pirates. In other areas of government spending, however, Jefferson started out in the right direction, cutting spending in both real and nominal dollars in his first term, from the last John Adams budget of $10 million down to just over $7 million by 1804. Then spending shot back up, to just under $12 million in real dollars by 1805.[6] Even after adjusted for population growth, spending per person barely fell from the $2 level under Jefferson—it actually plummeted sharply under his successor, James Madison, largely due to the War of 1812, before doubling by the end of Madison's second term.[7] Economist Robert Martin has shown that as per capita income fell during Jefferson's second term due to his embargo (wherein the U.S. government prohibited goods to be sold to the belligerents in the Napoleonic Wars), the increase of government spending as a share of all national spending slightly increased.[8]

In addition to the actual growth, one can glean much from Jefferson's instructions to his secretary of the Treasury, Albert Gallatin, to develop a massive plan of "internal improvements." In the parlance of the day, that meant building roads, clearing harbors and rivers, and building canals. Keep in mind that virtually all of this type of work was funded by the private sector in Jefferson's day—the Lancaster Turnpike Road was started in 1792, and between 1812 and 1840, New England alone saw private companies pour $6 million into road building.[9]

It is therefore surprising to see Jefferson order Gallatin to prepare an extensive report to Congress in 1808 in which he concluded, "The General Government can alone remove these obstacles" to improving transportation.[10] No question Americans faced problems in traveling: when the National Road was undertaken, contractors were permitted to leave "any tree stump less than eighteen inches tall in the roadway[!]" and travelers on almost any stagecoach line in the country expected their vehicle to be overturned at least once during a journey.[11] Gallatin outlined the benefits of a sophisticated internal transportation system, recommending that Congress fund a ten-year, $20 million project in which the federal government would directly construct roads and build canals or provide loans for private companies to do so.[12] He detailed $16 million worth of specific programs, including a canal connecting the Atlantic coast and the Great Lakes. This was at a time when the *entire* federal budget was under $10 million, and the ambitious outlays were some *five times* those of Jefferson's government in the year they were proposed! Jefferson, while agreeing with the proposal, noted that a constitutional amendment might be necessary for such a big-government project. Ultimately, much of Gallatin's plan was funded—by the private sector, without federal aid (although in the case of canals, often with state bond guarantees).

Modern-day Democrats, who still celebrate Jefferson/Jackson Day, might want to familiarize themselves more with Thomas Jefferson's concepts about land, for in this instance Jefferson definitely was of a "small government" mentality. Jefferson strongly endorsed the concept of getting land into the hands of the people—individually, not collectively. The government, he argued, should unload as much land as it could as quickly as was practicable. His influence on the Land Ordinance of 1785, for example, clearly established the principle that people, not the government, should hold the land for whatever purposes they desired. His positions starkly contrast with those of modern-day Democrats who claim their heritage from him, and who routinely seize millions of acres of land ostensibly for the "public good" under eminent domain laws. In his last days in office, for example, President Bill Clinton sealed off millions of acres of land in the West for the government.

Thomas Jefferson was a complex man, a conflicted figure who spoke of liberty in the ideal and who held slaves in reality; who celebrated agrarian farmers (not small, subsistence farming) but whose vision of an interconnected nation ensured the rise of industry and transportation; and who personally fought little armed combat in his life, yet launched America's first preemptive war. He sincerely believed in a true "federalist" model with most power allocated to the states, but he ordered the planning of (though he did not enact) the most comprehensive and sweeping public works project of any American administration prior to the Civil War. While different in many respects from the Federalists whom he despised, Jefferson had more in common with John Adams than he may have thought.

LIE #14

WOMEN HAD NO RIGHTS IN EARLY AMERICA

*The United States had founding mothers . . . but on the whole our history cele-
brates only the white founding fathers. . . .*
—CAROL BERKIN AND MARY BETH NORTON, WOMEN OF AMERICA

*A woman was a legal incompetent, as children, idiots, and criminals under En-
glish law.*
—CAROL BERKIN, FIRST GENERATIONS

Let's get two things straight: (1) being a white woman in colonial America
or the early Republic was no picnic; and (2) it was better than being a
woman in most places on earth, including England then, and better than being a twenty-first-century woman in North Korea or Saudi Arabia! It is also
worth noting that the material status of women depended heavily on the opportunities for men, and since men were rapidly advancing in the English colonies, women's daily lives were better. (Again, the status of slaves and Indians
was much different.)

Although most women in early America had few property rights, and were
not supposed to receive anything in the event of the husband's death except
the lifetime use of the home and one-third of the household goods, in reality
many inherited much of the estate.[1] Pennsylvania provided for a widow to receive one third, the children to receive one-third, and the rest to be disposed of
by the will, meaning the wife could receive up to two-thirds of an estate.[2] One
study has shown that half of the married men gave their wives "a larger share

than they could have expected under intestacy" (i.e., more than what the widows would have received under standing inheritance laws), although there were time limits (i.e., until remarriage or until the children reached legal age).[3] Other historians have found that in New York City, Petersburg, Virginia, and Germantown, Pennsylvania, there was "little discrimination between sons and daughters in allocating shares of the estate."[4] On the whole, women were overrepresented among America's wealthiest individuals, partly because of inheritance.

Under the legal principle of coverture, married women (*femes covertes*) were forbidden from making contracts. However, widows and unmarried women (*femes soles*) could own property. More important, Americans invented the first prenuptial agreements and trusts, which established property rights for women within marriages via contracts.[5] And contracts were sacred in the American colonies. Elizabeth Murray, for example, became a successful Boston businesswoman who made money on her own and inherited still more from two deceased husbands, largely because she had insisted on strong prenuptial agreements.[6] Another largely American concept was the power of attorney, which was widely used by middle-class women to conduct business and sign contracts. Abigail Adams, for example, apparently possessed power of attorney throughout the 1760s, 1770s, and 1780s.

Scholars on inheritance law suggest that one factor determining whether widows received more or less of an estate was the marriage market: in areas where women were scarce, laws tended to favor men who might wed widows.[7] And there was also the ongoing concern for children, whom legislators did not want to see become wards of the state. Hence, most state laws provided something for children that remained out of the control of a widow.

Indeed, while noting that a woman was a "legal incompetent," Carol Berkin concedes that the colonial system was "hierarchical, but it was not autocratic. Marriage was webbed by obligations and duties owed by both husband and wife."[8] "That a married woman lacked a legal identity did not mean," Berkin continued, "that she lacked all legal rights." And, according to Berkin, "we have glimpses of the daily life of Chesapeake wives that suggest that submissive behavior was not the norm."[9] Pennsylvania, for example, in 1718 enacted a *feme sole* act to allow women to take over a business in case of the death of a husband—even in the case of a long absence. Colonial records "indicate that women ran commercial establishments, owned and conveyed land, and frequently represented their husbands in legal matters, suing on contract or tort claims and defending against suits."[10] One woman, the executrix of Maryland governor Leonard Calvert's estate, even demanded a vote in the Assembly to look after the governor's interests better. Her request was denied.[11]

While divorce was extremely difficult (in the South, sometimes a woman needed a majority vote of a colonial legislature!), the laws were more flexible than in Europe. Women were permitted to act as lawyers in some communities. Since divorce was so difficult to obtain, "many colonial couples simply separated by mutual agreement or . . . through the desertion of one of the parties."[12] In fact, however, it was precisely the difficulty of divorce—and the permanence of marriage—that led to extraordinary emphasis on codes of behavior regarding premarital sex and the often-overbearing participation of parents in the process of spouse selection. Consequently, although illegitimate births were not infrequent (about one-third of the women who got married in New England in the 1700s were with child), parents and the community ensured that marriages did take place. As social historian Jack Larkin put it, "Pregnancies usually simply accelerated a marriage that would have taken place in any case, but community and parental pressure worked strongly to assure it."[13] And while New England had "stern" statutes against fornication, they were less effective as a means of ensuring marriage than social control. Gossip was a particularly effective means of persuading men and women to maintain sexual purity.

Women were educated in what were called "dame" schools. As most were expected to be housewives, there was little need for advanced female education. (One of the benefits of working at the Lowell Mills in Massachusetts in the early Republic was that the "Lowell Girls" received an education at company expense.) Girls attending the Young Ladies Academy of Philadelphia in the 1700s received an advanced education, and it "marked a major turning point in women's education in the country . . . [providing] a necessary prelude to the founding of women's colleges in the next century."[14] Real progress in women's education did not occur until the Jacksonian era, when many schools went "co-ed," but a foundation was established with some of these academies. Of course, the Jacksonian-era reforms at the state level removed many of the encumbrances women faced.[15]

Women found the greatest independence in churches—a fact that has continually plagued feminist historians. By the 1770s, Virginia Baptist churches allowed women to vote and serve as exhorters (the "warm-up band" for the preacher).[16] Rev. Ezra Stiles, a famous Baptist minister, concluded in 1771 that based upon "the Principle that there can be no vote unless every Brother consented, the Consent of every Sister may be required."[17] The story of Massachusetts' Anne Hutchinson is well known. Both sides of the liberation debate claim Hutchinson's example supports its own interpretation: either Hutchinson demonstrated the remarkable boundaries women encountered, then crossed, or her banishment to Rhode Island proved the threat posed by "a powerful woman." Hutchinson, however, was not alone in leading prayer groups or even taking on duties that would under other circumstances be considered the domain of the pastor. Sarah Osborn, for example, in Newport, Rhode Island, "pushed her role [in church leadership] to the outer limits" by influencing the selection of new ministers.[18] Of course, the Quakers elevated the status of women long before most other denominations.

One of the problems feminist historians have faced is that they must simultaneously portray women as victims and heroines: for women to be worthy of study as a separate historical topic, women must have done something exceptional or out of the ordinary. Yet as soon as there were examples of women achievers, it challenged the feminist notion of a rigid "classist/sexist" society that held women back.

Take, for example, the problem of interpreting such events as the Industrial Revolution, which replaced the home spinning industry with large-scale textile business. So was this good or bad? Some have suggested it was bad for women because it removed a "vital economic function from the home and thus apparently reduced women's importance in the household." Others argue it was good because it raised the standard of living for all women, provided better cloth that led to reduced disease stemming from cloth-borne parasites, and eliminated boring labor.[19]

When it came to gender "discrimination" at work, scholars have often overlooked the physical demands of various jobs that tended to exclude women. For example, doctors—in an age without anesthesia—had to perform surgery and occasionally amputate limbs while restraining a patient who was protesting to no small degree. It is understandable, therefore, that many male doctors came from the ranks of veterinarians, and vice versa. Smaller and less physically powerful women were at an important disadvantage in such work—but not in being midwives, which was exclusively a female domain.

From Anne Hutchinson to Abigail Adams, there has been no shortage of powerful women and heroines to celebrate, including the legendary Deborah Sampson, a New England infantry "man" who fought in George Washington's Continental Army. A former indentured servant, Sampson eschewed the typical "women's work" at hospitals and, disguising herself, enlisted under the alias of Robert Shurtleff in the Fourth Massachusetts Regiment. Becoming a seasoned combat veteran, Sampson was wounded twice, then tended her own wounds to conceal her sex. Her true identity was not discovered until 1782, when, serving as a general's orderly, she contracted a fever, lost consciousness, and was put under the care of a doctor.

American women, while not yet the political or economic equals of males, had far more protection and rights under Anglo-American law than did the vast majority of females around the world. Many achieved greatness in spite of their legal disadvantages. But few would have voluntarily switched places with any other women in the world.

LIE #15

RESTRICTIONS ON THE RIGHT TO VOTE KEPT VOTER PARTICIPATION LOW

[T]he roaring flood of the new democracy was now foaming perilously near the crest [under Andrew Jackson].
—CHARLES AND MARY BEARD, THE RISE OF AMERICAN CIVILIZATION

Common sense suggests that if more people are eligible to vote, more will participate in the system. But common sense also would say when you start to skid on ice, "turn out of the skid." In both cases, common sense would be wrong.

In the early Republic, Massachusetts, New Hampshire, New Jersey, Maryland, North Carolina, and Georgia all required men to own land or property to vote for their lower house, and ten states had wealth requirements or a "freehold" necessary to vote for the upper house. Nine states established property requirements for voting in their constitutions. More than 70 percent of New Hampshire males met the requirement in 1780, as did 72 percent of Rhode Islanders, 61 percent of Delaware males, and 85 percent of Pennsylvanians. The percentage who voted in elections from 1776 to 1800 in New Hampshire was 66 to 82 percent; in Rhode Island, 59 to 77 percent; and in Pennsylvania, 63 to 88 percent. Voter turnout in the thirteen founding states averaged between 48 and 65 percent between 1776 and 1780. In contrast, the turnout from 1952 to 1960 averaged 85 percent of those who registered. (But only 87 percent of those eligible registered, and of all adults, only 86 percent were eligible.) Put another way, about 64 percent of adults voted, meaning that while it did not happen, it was possible that the winner could become president with about 32 percent of the adult population voting. Since 1960, the numbers have declined. In 2000, 64 percent of the population registered, of whom 83 percent voted, or about half of all Americans, meaning about one-fourth elected the president. Compare that with 1819, where historian Richard McCormick found that 97 percent of those eligible to vote actually cast a ballot in a non-presidential or special election.[1]

Political change came in the early 1800s with a number of state "reforms." First, most states began to drop all property requirements for voting.[2] Second, the parties adopted national nominating conventions instead of allowing state caucuses to determine the nominee.[3] This marked the end of "King Caucus." Most important, it was Congressman Martin Van Buren who conceived of a new political party in the 1820s whose sole purpose was to prevent any national debate over slavery.[4] His party would cement the "New York–Georgia Axis," an alliance of pro-slave Southerners and Northerners willing to ignore slavery in order to maintain power. Although Van Buren's candidate, Andrew Jackson, failed to gain the presidency in 1824, his party organization blossomed, especially through a new partisan press that it developed as a propaganda organ. By 1828, when Jackson won, the new Democratic Party was a well-oiled machine.

Nevertheless, the notion that Jacksonianism unleashed a flood of democracy that "foamed perilously near the crest" is untrue. The first modern campaign of the new two-party system did not occur until 1840, when the Whig candidate, William Henry Harrison, doubled the 1828 vote totals. Harrison, in fact, topped the vote total of Van Buren (who won the presidency in 1836) by more than 60 percent, or "the greatest proportional jump between two consecutive elections in American history."[5]

Reality runs contrary to the narrative of liberal historians, who have sought to make Jackson the heir of Thomas Jefferson and the forerunner of Franklin D. Roosevelt. Coverage of Jackson in the textbooks is fawning: David M. Kennedy's *American Pageant* calls Jackson the "idol of the masses" who "easily defeated the big-money Kentuckian [Henry Clay]."[6] Typically, these narratives portray Jackson's political foes as "the business community and eastern elites."[7] They attempt to portray Jackson as opposing "parasites who grew rich by manipulating credit, prices, paper money and government-bestowed privileges."[8] What universally goes unmentioned is that Van Buren's party system, which produced Jackson's election, was based on patronage and spoils.

Both Jackson's and Van Buren's administrations greatly expanded the scope and power of the federal government, as well as spending by the government, precisely because they had to reward their supporters with party and government jobs.

Rewarding loyalists with party and, later, government jobs guaranteed that both state and federal governments would grow. Inevitably, the federal government grew faster. At the same time, Andrew Jackson, ostensibly "keeping government small," exercised more vetoes than all previous presidents combined—thus expanding the powers of the presidency geometrically. Because Democrats held the presidency for all except two elections from 1828 to 1860, few people noticed the ominous expansion of federal power, especially the growth of executive power. Meanwhile, the tactic of expanding the franchise as a means of encouraging "more democracy" proved ill conceived. People placed an according value on that which was free, and by the year 2000, voter participation rates hovered at only half of the registered electorate. For all the civil rights charlatans who complain about "disenfranchised" voters, the solution seems obvious: restore property requirements to be eligible to vote!

Lie #16

Prohibition Was Unpopular from the Beginning and Failed in All Its Objectives

Many rural Protestant Americans saw Prohibition as a symbolic cultural issue [which allowed them] to control the newcomers in the expanding cities.
—Daniel Goldfield et al., American Journey

Prohibition . . . offered another example of reforming zeal channeled into a drive for moral righteousness and conformity. . . . The Anti-Saloon League [mobilized] Protestant churches behind its single-minded battle to elect "dry" candidates.
—George Brown Tindall and David E. Shi, America: A Narrative History

For decades, the typical "story" of Prohibition was that it was passed through the efforts of a handful of hick, hayseed preachers, and snuck into law because the American public wasn't paying attention. Historians blamed "cultural and class legislation" by Progressive upper classes and Anglo-Saxons who "imposed their Puritanical will on benign but besotted immigrants."[1] According to this story line, it accomplished none of its objectives, but had the unintended consequence of causing the "rise" of organized crime in the United States. We should learn from this "lesson," proponents of this story argue, that "you cannot legislate morality."

Almost every part of that story is wrong. The one part that is correct is that Prohibition failed to end the production and sale of liquor, but even that requires a qualification: "In the early years of national prohibition, liquor was very difficult to obtain. In the later years . . . the supply increased."[2] In fact, though, at the end of Prohibition, slightly less alcohol was consumed by Americans per capita than before, and during the period 1918–19, under wartime prohibition, alcohol consumption was down to half what it was in the prewar years.[3] So by any measure, liquor consumption fell during and even after Prohibition, but it was not completely eliminated.

Attempts to control drunkenness and saloons did not start with Prohibition. Abraham Lincoln ran on a "temperance" platform, and most states had enacted laws well before the Eighteenth Amendment. Social historian John Burnham claims the peak of beer consumption, for example, was reached between 1911 and 1914. Moreover, arrests for drunkenness, hospitalization for alcoholism, and incidents of cirrhosis of the liver declined steadily in the early years of Prohibition, to low points around 1921. "For many years," Burnham notes, "articles on alcoholism literally disappeared from American medical literature."[4] Martha Bensley Bruere conducted a survey of social workers across the country and found that working people drank less than before Prohibition, and that in fact Prohibition had improved the living conditions among low-income workers.[5]

Certainly Protestant churches supported Prohibition, but it was nothing new. Temperance had been a campaign issue since before Lincoln's time, and by the 1900s, the saloon was viewed not as the corner burger-and-beverage sports bar that we have today, nor as the "everybody knows your name" neighborhood bar of the TV series *Cheers,* but as a dingy, depraved center for all of society's ills. Prostitution, gambling, and other crimes emanated from the saloon, and most people (including city and state policy makers) thought venereal disease was directly linked to saloons. Doctors warned of the "syphilis of the innocent," which infected wives and children via husbands' having sex with prostitutes.[6] Saloons were associated with white slavery, brought to public attention in the 1913 play *Damaged.* Following the outcry, Congress passed the Mann Act, which banned interstate transport of females for "immoral purposes."

Not only had most states passed liquor and saloon restrictions prior to Prohibition, but the law itself was an amendment to the U.S. Constitution— hardly an easy thing for proponents to achieve, especially if they represented only "fundamentalist Protestants." As Norman Clark shows, Prohibition had widespread support across social classes, and there was no rural/urban distinction among supporters at first.[7] Indeed, at first both Progressives, who were mostly urban, upper-class elites, and rural Populist Christians were allied in their efforts. But as Clark puts it, "A majority of the people in a majority of the states wanted this truly national effort to influence national morality."[8]

It was only after Prohibition "failed" that the Progressives sought to pin the legislation on the rural religious elements. But why did it fail? There is little question that Prohibition lacked enforcement mechanisms anywhere near what such a law would have required. The federal government provided 1,500 agents to support local law enforcement, while gangs such as Al Capone's could almost match that by themselves. Officers of the Prohibition Bureau were exempted from Civil Service requirements, meaning politicians put in their pals to "enforce" the law, not professionals. A dual set of laws—state and federal—against alcohol meant that neither appropriated enough funds for enforcement, expecting the other to do so, and some states that had enforced their own laws prior to 1919 did not do so afterward.

There were two particularly important detriments to effective enforcement of Prohibition: (1) "there was almost universal public belief that a 'crime wave' existed in the United States," and (2) the elites began to flaunt drinking as a sign of rebellion during the "revolution in manners and morals."[9] The former view lacked any real foundation: criminologists Edwin H. Sutherland and C. H. Gehlke found "no evidence here of a 'crime wave,' but only of a slowly rising level," and that was in urban areas and *not* adjusted for the rise in population.[10] The homicide rate, which rose fairly steadily from 1910 (long before national Prohibition), hit something of a plateau in the late 1920s and did not fall substantially until 1936.[11] As Burnham wrote, "Apparently what happened was that in the 1920's the long existent 'underworld' first became publicized and romanticized," turning the racketeer into a type of folk hero.[12] *But by definition crime had to increase, because liquor-related crimes were not crimes prior to the Volstead Act!* As Norman H. Clark, a critic of the established Prohibition narrative, put it, "There is no reason to suppose that the speakeasy . . . in any quantifiable way, replaced the saloon. In fact . . . most Americans outside the larger cities never knew a bootlegger, never saw a speakeasy, and would not have known where to look for one."[13]

The second factor that ended Prohibition was that it simply became "uncool" and not hip. Liquor became dangerous to obtain and expensive, making it a luxury item available only to the rich. While journalists overwhelmingly reported that "everyone drank," it was true that in their social circles (mostly large cities, where reporters were embraced by the social elites), everyone indeed did drink. One witness who had gone in disguise among the "working classes" reported "very much of a misconception with respect to the liquor problem. . . . [Reporters] have never had any contact with the liquor problem in its earlier pre-prohibition form." Worse, he noted, the problems they reported represented "an extremely small proportion of the population."[14]

Prohibition's repeal began with the press, supported by the "most effective publicity campaigns of modern times," led by the Association Against the Prohibition Amendment, a group funded in the late 1920s by liquor industry money.[15] Playing on journalists' own predilections, the AAPA "developed a virtual monopoly on liquor and prohibition press coverage."[16] Upton Sinclair also noted that much of the leadership of the anti-Prohibition groups came from lawyers, not saloon owners.[17] A final nail in the coffin was revenue: after the start of the Great Depression, both federal and state governments saw the additional revenue of alcohol taxes as irresistible. Once the elites decided drinking was cool, and joined the journalists in their propaganda campaign that "crime was rising" and "enforcement didn't work," Prohibition's days were numbered. Whether it was the proper use of federal laws has, in the modern age, become subsumed by leftists and libertarians who want to use Prohibition as an example that society "cannot legislate morality," when in fact it was a very good example that societies can and do legislate the perceived morality of the majority many times.

SACCO AND VANZETTI WERE INNOCENT AND WRONGLY EXECUTED

The excesses of the fundamentalists, the xenophobes, the Klan, the red-baiters, and the prohibitionists disturbed American intellectuals profoundly. . . . Sacco and Vanzetti were anarchists and Italian immigrants. Their trial was a travesty.
—MARK C. CARNES AND JOHN A. GARRATY, AMERICAN DESTINY

The most notorious case associated with the "Red Scare" began in May 1920 when Nicola Sacco and Bartolomeo Vanzetti . . . were arrested for robbing a shoe company in South Braintree, Massachusetts. . . . The state doctored evidence and witnesses changed testimony, but the judge favored the prosecution.
—JEANNE BOYDSTON ET AL., MAKING A NATION

On April 15, 1920, two anarchists, Nicola Sacco and Bartolomeo Vanzetti, robbed a shoe factory paymaster and a security guard in South Braintree, Massachusetts. In the process of committing the robbery, they killed Alessandro Berardelli, the guard, and Frederick Parmenter, the paymaster. The two men were convicted at Dedham, and Vanzetti was also tried and convicted at Plymouth for a robbery at Bridgewater. It took the Dedham jury only three hours to reach its verdict. Critics claimed that the jurors had rendered a judgment on the two men's political activism, although every juror said anarchism was not a consideration in his decision. While not a major threat today, anarchism was the equivalent of suicide bombers for the 1880–1930 period. Anarchists had nearly killed Henry Clay Frick of Carnegie Steel in his own office and had assassinated President William McKinley. They shot people, made bombs, and blew things up, and were serious about bringing down all government. Sacco and Vanzetti were sentenced to death in the electric chair, and after several appeals, were executed on August 23, 1927.

For the American Left, Sacco and Vanzetti became the most notable cause célèbre until they were replaced by the traitorous Rosenbergs in the 1940s. Future Supreme Court Justice Felix Frankfurter called for a new trial of the men in 1927 with his book *The Case of Sacco and Vanzetti,* which radicals have cited as their "bible" on the case. As late as 2007, Harvard historian Lisa McGirr, investigating the international implications of the case, observed that "other miscarriages of justice . . . failed to attract such an [international outcry]."[1]

Nine eyewitnesses identified Sacco as being at the scene and/or firing at the shooting Berardelli; and four identified Vanzetti. Sacco lied extensively: about his Colt pistol and ammunition; to his employer about his absence on April 15; to the police about his whereabouts on April 15; about never having been in South Braintree (when he worked at a shoe factory there in 1917); and Vanzetti lied about his H. & R. revolver and ammunition. Several different analyses of the firearms evidence have concluded that the bullets came from Sacco's gun. Three experts who conducted the 1983 ballistics test found that the two spent Peters cartridges at the crime scene were made by the same machine that made six of the Peters live cartridges that Sacco had in his pocket when he was arrested. Alibi witnesses for neither Sacco nor Vanzetti proved credible. Guiseppe Adrower, the clerk of the consulate where Sacco claimed to be at the time of the murder, said he did not remember Sacco, then changed his testimony. Thirty years later, one of the eyewitnesses who said he saw Sacco in Boston admitted he perjured himself for a group of Boston anarchists.

Not one to be bound by the findings of a jury or the evidence on which the jury reached its verdict, in 1977, then-Governor Michael Dukakis proclaimed the duo innocent and announced that "any disgrace should be forever removed from their names." Unfortunately for Dukakis, a firearms panel would meet only a few years later and virtually reattach the disgrace to the names of the two murderers.[2]

The case took a strange, but predictable, turn in 1985 when William Young and David Kaiser published *Postmortem: New Evidence in the Case of Sacco and Vanzetti,* where the authors claimed the prosecutor, Frederick Katzmann, had tampered with the evidence—especially Sacco's pistol and the key "Bullet #3."[3] In their "exposé," they claimed the prosecutor substituted a bullet

Sacco (*left*) and Vanzetti (*right*) have been portrayed as innocent or, at the very least, unfortunate victims of nativism or Cold War hysteria. In fact, they were guilty of murder and deserved their punishment.

and shell for the originals taken at the scene. In fact, as James Starrs, a professor of law and forensic sciences, proved in the *Journal of Forensic Sciences,* it was a *defense* expert who switched out the gun barrel, producing the controversy. Interestingly, Professor Starrs informed David Kaiser of the full findings of the 1983 forensics panel, and Kaiser even acknowledged receipt of this material in his notes, although he dismissed it. Starrs, writing in the *Journal of Forensic Sciences* in 1986, described the evidence of the firearms panel as "significant and credible."[4] Starrs summarized the ballistics evidence, in which experts have concluded that Sacco's Colt fired the bullet that killed Berardelli (tests replicated the conclusions of the 1927 ballistics tests), and concluded that "the evidence and the arguments militate against the bullet switching hypothesis" advanced by the defense.[5] This evidence shows beyond a doubt that Sacco was clearly a participant in the murders, whether as the primary shooter (and it was his gun) or as the accomplice, in which case he supplied the gun and stood by.

If the actual evidence were not enough, one of Sacco's early anarchist defenders, Carlo Tresca, in 1941 told former radical-turned-conservative writer Max Eastman that Sacco was guilty but Vanzetti was innocent. Twenty years later, Eastman wrote of the incident in *National Review,* and others confirmed that Tresca had told them the same thing. Other anarchists, such as Ideale Gambera, echoed the notion that Sacco was guilty but Vanzetti innocent. Not only were the other fellow anarchists condemning Sacco and Vanzetti, but so were long-time radical supporters. In 2005, a 1929 letter surfaced from socialist Upton Sinclair to his attorney, John Beardsley. Sinclair, while conducting research for his book *Boston*, learned from Sacco and Vanzetti's attorney, Fred Moore, that the two were indeed guilty. Sinclair met with Moore in a hotel room, and "I begged him to tell me the full truth." Moore told Sinclair the men were guilty, and provided details as to how he "framed a set of alibis for them."[6] An embarrassed Sinclair acknowledged he was "completely naïve about the Sacco-Vanzetti case, having accepted the defense propaganda completely."[7] Sinclair said on his October 1928 visit to Boston that he immediately noticed "something wrong. . . . There was an air of mystery about the Boston anarchists, and I saw they had something to conceal."[8] He began asking "catch questions" (which, of course, should have been asked long before 1929!) and "got the admission from one of the leading defense witnesses that his testimony had been framed." He received the same admission from another witness, before he "begged" Fred Moore, the defense attorney, to "tell me the full truth." Moore first wanted Sinclair to spill the beans on what evidence he had come up with, which he did, saying Sacco and Vanzetti were not "merely terrorists, but that they were guilty of the holdup." Sinclair then went to New York, where he met with Roger Baldwin, an anarchist compatriot of Sacco and Vanzetti, who "told me there was no possible doubt of the guilt" of the two men.

The Sacco-Vanzetti case provided the American Left with some of its most cherished ingredients: poor foreign immigrants wrongly accused of a crime and railroaded to their executions by angry WASPs. There was one small problem: they were guilty, and even their most rabid supporters knew it—except for Upton Sinclair, who chose to believe the lie . . . for a time. Today, historians such as McGirr want us to ignore the evidence and focus on the fantasy.

LIE #18

SENATOR JOSEPH MCCARTHY CONCOCTED THE "RED SCARE,"
AND THERE WAS NOTHING TO FEAR FROM COMMUNIST SUBVERSIVES

*McCarthy never uncovered a single Communist agent in government.... [He
was] the shrewdest and most ruthless exploiter of [anti-Communist] anxieties.*
—GEORGE BROWN TINDALL AND DAVID E. SHI, AMERICA:
A NARRATIVE HISTORY

Is any word more quickly invoked as a means to shut down debate in modern
America than "McCarthyism"? For nearly half a century, the Left has raised
the specter of Senator Joe McCarthy to intimidate people into backing down,
often successfully. What, exactly, was McCarthy's record?

Joseph McCarthy was a relatively insignificant U.S. senator from Wisconsin. A close friend of John F. Kennedy and later Richard Nixon, McCarthy was the godfather to Bobby Kennedy's first child. In turn, Bobby was
McCarthy's devoted staffer. The elder Kennedy, Joseph, stood by McCarthy
long after others had abandoned him, and after a speaker at Harvard de-
nounced both McCarthy and Alger Hiss, John Kennedy exclaimed, "How
dare you couple the name of a great American patriot with that of a traitor?"[1]
In the Senate, McCarthy was placed on the Permanent Subcommittee on Investigations (PSI), which acted as the counterpart to the infamous House
Un-American Activities Committee (HUAC). Both had been established in
the 1930s to deal with Nazi and Communist subversion—the PSI, which
McCarthy chaired, had the specific charge of investigating communism
among federal government employees—and while the former was contained

during World War II, the latter expanded in the administration of Franklin D. Roosevelt.

How did McCarthy, the junior senator from a farm state, become the point man for all anti-Communist rhetoric in the country? With all history, context is crucial. At the time McCarthy burst onto the scene, the United States had witnessed the following in a period of just five years: the Soviet Union had refused to withdraw from all conquered and occupied nations at the end of World War II, despite promises to do so, enslaving millions; China had fallen to Mao Zedong's Communists; the USSR had exploded its own atomic bomb, five years ahead of what Western spies claimed was possible; Soviet spy rings, especially the famous Klaus Fuchs ring, were exposed; other spies, traitors, and informants were uncovered within the U.S. government, including Alger Hiss and Julius and Ethel Rosenberg, who gave the atomic secrets to the Soviets for their bomb; and the American Communists seemed to become more radical and confrontational each day. Hollywood, for example, was rife with Communists, so much so that the incoming president of the Screen Actors Guild, Ronald Reagan, had to simultaneously defend his industry from congressional attacks that led to the blacklisting of the "Hollywood Ten," while at the same time purging Communists from the industry. Against this backdrop of unceasing Communist advances, Joseph McCarthy came to prominence.

It began with a speech for Lincoln's Birthday activities on February 9, 1950, in Wheeling, West Virginia, when reporters said McCarthy claimed to "have here in my hand a list of 205 [active members of the Communist Party and members of a spy ring] that were made known to the Secretary of State . . . and who nevertheless are still working for and shaping policy in the State Department."[2] The infamous list to which McCarthy referred contained 57 names of security risks already given to the House Appropriations Committee whose cases were still pending. Then he cross-referenced that list with another one of 284 security risks given him (of whom 79 had already been dismissed) for 205 original names and 57 still employed at the State Department.[3] McCarthy claimed—and a surviving copy of his speech has "205" crossed out and "57" written in—that he said only 57 were still in government. Regardless, the press immediately ran with the headline STATE DEPARTMENT HAS 205 COMMIES.[4]

Aside from the Rosenbergs, who were out and-out-spies, perhaps no figure was more important to the Soviets than Harry Dexter White, the Harvard economist who in 1941 was appointed assistant to Treasury secretary Henry Morgenthau Jr. He was aided at the Treasury Department by Solomon Adler, Frank Coe, and Harold Glasser, and all played a role in preventing emergency gold from reaching Chiang Kai-shek in China, contributing to the rampant inflation and collapse of the anti-Communist government there. McCarthy—and many other Americans—thought that various individuals inside the U.S. government preferred Mao Zedong the Communist to Chiang, whom they viewed as a "totalitarian." Another New Deal agency, the Agricultural Adjustment Administration, teemed with Communist agents, including, at one time, Alger Hiss. J. Edgar Hoover, director of the FBI, estimated there were 200 to 400 active Soviet spies in the United States, aided and abetted by the 54,000 members of the Communist Party USA.

If anything, McCarthy underestimated the number of active Soviet agents. In addition to White, there was Laurence Duggan at Treasury; Michael Straight at the State Department; and John Abt at Justice. Treasury documents were passed to the Soviets through Nathan Silvermaster and Elizabeth Bentley. Worse, Morgenthau relied so much on White that he made him the Treasury Department's representative to the planning groups that included the American spy organization the Office of Strategic Services (OSS)![5] As the authors of *The Venona Secrets* concluded, "[T]he Soviets believed that White was in a position to advise them on the thinking of high-level U.S. government officials."[6] (White had also possibly extended the war in Germany by leaking a plan rejected by Roosevelt and Churchill that threatened to divide Germany into small provinces.) White died before he could appear on McCarthy's lists, but he was precisely the type of person the Senate and House investigators realized was a problem. When Whittaker Chambers testified before Congress in 1948, he "outed" Communists working in government such as Lee Pressman, Harold Ware, and John Abt (who, in addition to his time in the Justice Department, had also served in the Department of Agriculture), Henry Collins (National Recovery Administration), Charles Kramer (National Labor Relations Board and Office of Price Administration), and Victor Perlo (Office of Price Administration).

Contrary to the notion that McCarthy was out to "expose" individuals, he repeatedly stated, "I do not have all the information about [them]," and that his goal was to "show that there is something radically wrong" with the State Department's investigation program.[7] McCarthy's use of terms was indeed loose and deserved criticism. "Suspected Communists" became "Communist Party members," and "a friend" of a Communist became a "close pal." Yet his overgeneralizations did not distort the essential truth, which was that the State Department had not carefully vetted its employees and that many Communists and, yes, *spies* either had been working in the U.S. government or were still working in the government when McCarthy brought his charges. Dorothy Kenyon, who was appointed to the U. N. Commission on the Status of Women, for example, admitted that she belonged at one time or another to at least a dozen different Communist front organizations.

A more substantial figure in McCarthy's crosshairs was Owen Lattimore, often viewed as his most famous "victim." The editor of *Pacific Affairs*, a pro-Communist journal that excused Stalin's purges, he traveled in China for the Roosevelt administration and sought to swing U.S. policy there toward Mao. In fact, McCarthy never said he was a spy but that he behaved like a Soviet agent. He was employed by Soviet agents and his friends were Soviet agents. Lattimore was even put into his position by . . . a Soviet agent. He lied about not working for the government: Lattimore was a White House liaison to the State Department, where he had an address and where, under oath, he testified that he did not handle Lauchlin Currie's mail (when, in fact, he did). He was indicted for perjury for these lies, for which he was never acquitted. (Charges were dismissed on technical grounds.) The McCarran Committee concluded he was a "willing instrument" of Soviet policy.[8] Moreover, Lattimore was paid by the Office of War Information. He had hardly changed the China policy singlehandedly as McCarthy led people to believe, but neither was he as pure as the wind-driven snow. Lattimore influenced FDR, serving as his personal adviser on China in 1941, and accompanied Vice President Henry Wallace on his trip to China. Upon his return, he claimed the "democratic" Soviet Union's slave labor camps and gulags were akin to "a combination of Hudson's Bay Company and the TVA [Tennessee Valley Authority]"![9] As it turned out, the FBI had kept Lattimore under surveillance since 1949 and noted his close connections to many identified Soviet agents.

On the day that the Tydings Committee, which had been formed to examine suspected Communists in government, announced that the U.S. government was "free of Communist infiltration," the FBI announced the arrest of Julius Rosenberg for espionage. This was shortly after the Communist

North Koreans had invaded South Korea. Yet despite continuing support for McCarthy's basic claims—that the Communist menace was real and that infiltration of the U.S. government and military had actually occurred—the Washington elites were contemptuous of him. Some of that was McCarthy's working-class background and his non–Ivy League education. Many despised his direct appeal to the American public: Dean Acheson called him "the gauleiter and leader of the mob."[10] Richard Rovere called his supporters members of the "zanies and zombies" club.[11] In fact, one-third of all Americans in 1951 had never heard of McCarthy, and in 1953, two-thirds had no opinion at all of the senator.[12] This is hardly the rampant pitchfork-bearing mob led by "zanies and zombies" that some have called "McCarthyism."

To the absurd lie that McCarthy never exposed a real Communist in government, consider Gustavo Duran, Mary Jane Keeney, Edward Posniak, John Carter Vincent—plus Lattimore—and a 1954 article which revealed that every security or loyalty risk McCarthy brought forward in his February 20, 1950, speech had either resigned or been dismissed from government.[13] Other Soviet operatives in the government whom McCarthy named were T. A. Bisson, Cedric Belfrage, Leonard Mins, and William Remington. The latter, Ann Coulter duly notes, was "killed with a bar of soap in prison by a patriotic inmate."[14] Even when it came to the Army—where McCarthy eventually went overboard—he was correct in arguing that several known Communists who were *proven* security risks not only remained in the military but *received promotions.*

If anything, McCarthy was too late. By the time he had identified many of the Communists in government, the FBI had watched them for years (though in many instances they retained their jobs, despite being labeled "security risks"). While in truth much of government had been cleaned up by the time McCarthy gained the public's eye, he nevertheless pushed anticommunism onto the front burner of politics. Many in government, on both sides of the aisle, stood to lose from the exposure of the incompetence (more than complicity) of the federal investigative agencies. But the senator often played into the hands of his enemies with his carelessness and exaggeration. When he began his "who lost China" attacks that ultimately impugned George C. Marshall, his supporters finally deserted him. By the 1980s and 1990s, however, information trickling in from defectors and the former Soviet archives made clear that most of McCarthy's targets were exactly what he said they were: spies, "fellow travelers," and threats to U.S. national security.

Since the first edition of *48 Liberal Lies* came out, M. Stanton Evans's book, *Blacklisted By History: The Untold Story of Senator Joe McCarthy and His Fight Against America's Enemies*, has been published.[15] Among other conclusions, Evans makes a convincing case that the influence of diplomat John Service and his memos to Treasury attaché Solomon Adler played a pivotal role in guaranteeing that the U.S. government only got reports on Chaing Kai Shek that were critical, while ensuring that all reports that reached Washington about the communist leader Mao Tse Tung were favorable. Mao was constantly portrayed as practical, progressive, realistic, democratic, while the pro-American Chaing was relentlessly described in loaded negative terms of incompetence and corruption. All of this proved pivotal in the Treasury Secretary's decision to cut off funds to Chaing. Worse, however, were "policy meetings" in which at times *two* communist agents would be in the room at the same time![16]

Evans's book also proves that the FBI was already suspicious about many of the cast of characters viewed by McCarthy as security risks. Elizabeth Bentley, for example, provided information that the bureau then verified through other means. By 1945, many of those who would be exposed as spies appeared on FBI charts showing their links to still other spies. Bentley filled in the gaps. Outside of McCarthy, the FBI emerges as the *only* institution in government seemingly even concerned with Soviet espionage.

One of the most pervasive lies that Evans's book exposes involves the famous "205" number—supposedly the number of communists in the U.S. government that McCarthy referred to in his Wheeling, West Virginia speech, and the number used by the Tydings committee to try to oust McCarthy from the Senate. In fact that number has never been verified anywhere. Evans found three living witnesses to the speech, of whom none remembered McCarthy saying there were 205 communists in government, only that there were 205 suspects and "55" or "57" communists. (One woman there that day actually wrote down "205" then "57cc." The *Denver Post* and the *Wheeling Intelligencer* articles or editorials written the following day reported "57" or "over fifty," and Evans reproduces the newspapers in his book. In other words, the claim that McCarthy originally stated there were 205 communists, then backtracked to 57, is a lie concocted by the McCarthy-haters in the Senate.

Evans goes on to provide reproductions of actual government documents that without question expose operatives such as Owen Lattimore as communists. Annie Lee Moss, one of the darlings of the Left as a "victim" of McCarthy, is exposed by the Communist Party's own records as a party member![17] This is supported further by an FBI report of 1954 identifying her as a communist in unqualified terms. The case for McCarthy has gotten immeasurably stronger, and the Left, which trots out the mindless phrase of "McCarthyism" to mean "a witch-hunt against the innocent," should be called out at every turn. McCarthy, even with his weaknesses, looks more heroic by the day.

LIE #19

THE ROSENBERGS WERE NOT SPIES AND WERE WRONGFULLY EXECUTED

[Julius] Rosenberg, a former member of the Communist Party, and his wife Ethel
were convicted in a controversial trial on charges of conspiracy to commit espionage
and sentenced to death in April 1951. The Supreme Court refused to hear the
case. . . . The controversy over their guilt has continued to the present day.
　　　　　　　—JEANNE BOYDSTON ET AL., MAKING A NATION

Although they were not major spies and the information they revealed was not
important, the Rosenbergs were executed, to the consternation of many liberals in
the United States and elsewhere.
　　　　　　　—MARK C. CARNES AND JOHN A. GARRATY, AMERICAN DESTINY

The government's case against the Rosenbergs rested on the testimony of their sup-
posed accomplices, some of them secretly coached by the FBI.
　　　　　　　—JOHN MACK FARAGHER ET AL., OUT OF MANY

Has there ever been *any* Communist, anywhere, who was guilty of anything? Reading liberal historians, it would seem not. Certainly to listen
to the modern defenders of Julius and Ethel Rosenberg, they were harmless,
kindhearted people who, no doubt, read to lepers in between building homes
for Habitat for Humanity and working with Haitian AIDS patients.

It's nice to know, isn't it, that historians decide whether "the information
they revealed was not important." In fact, the Rosenbergs potentially could
have condemned millions of Americans to death by atomic firebombs had

their Soviet paymasters not feared U.S. retaliatory strikes that would kill millions in Russia. Nevertheless, the husband-and-wife spy tag team provided Soviet intelligence agents with typed notes and even a sketch of the famous "lens device" of the Nagasaki bomb that experts agreed hastened the development of the USSR's atomic bomb by at least five years. Judge Irving Kaufman, who sentenced them, rightly said, "I consider your crime worse than murder . . . [and by] putting into the hands of the Russians the A-bomb years before our best scientists predicted Russia would perfect the bomb has already caused, in my opinion, the Communist aggression in Korea, with the resultant casualties exceeding 50,000. . . ."[1]

The case against the Rosenbergs began in 1950 when the U.S. government and the United Kingdom unraveled a Communist spy ring built around a Los Alamos physicist, Klaus Fuchs, himself a Soviet spy during the war. Fuchs then led the investigators to Harry Gold. Then, in June of 1950, the trail led from Gold to David Greenglass, then from him to his sister and her husband, Ethel and Julius Rosenberg. Over time, Greenglass's testimony about the involvement of Ethel changed several times. At the trial, he said she typed his notes. Later, he recanted to a reporter, claiming that he had lied to protect his wife, Ruth. He never wavered about the key role of Julius Rosenberg, who not only forwarded the "lens device" sketch to the Soviets, but also actively recruited other agents for the KGB.[2] Greenglass, however, flip-flopped again in interviews with Ron Radosh and Joyce Milton, claiming flawed memory but adamantly stating he had not perjured himself at the trial.[3]

Defenders of the Rosenbergs initially (i.e., in the 1950s, not at the time of their arrest in 1950) marched through a procession resembling that of a terminal cancer patient, from denial to anger to (almost) acceptance. First, they claimed the Rosenbergs were Communists but not spies. Then they admitted Julius was a spy, but Ethel was not. Next they conceded that whatever role Ethel played was unimportant, and that the material supplied by the Rosenbergs was not critical to the Soviets' getting the bomb. The final, "acceptance," stage came when Walter and Miriam Schneir, who kicked off the Rosenbergs' defense with *Invitation to an Inquest* (1965), repudiated their conspiracy theory that the government had framed the Rosenbergs in an August 1995 article in *The Nation,* agreeing with Ronald Radosh and Joyce Milton in their then-controversial condemnation of the Rosenbergs, *The Rosenberg File* (1983).[4]

Just how important was the information the Rosenbergs supplied? Even if the Soviets used none of it, that would not excuse the Rosenbergs one iota. Treason is not the same as murder: the act of aiding and comforting the enemy does not depend on the enemy's being "aided and comforted," only on the *attempt* and *intention* of those committing the treason. If nothing else, giving the Soviets material that was a "dead end" technologically (which this was not) would nevertheless advance Soviet weapons programs by showing them what did not work.

According to ex-premier of the USSR Nikita Khrushchev, who quoted his spymaster Vyacheslav Molotov, the Rosenbergs "provided very significant help in accelerating the production of our atom bomb."[5] Molotov was less specific, saying "I think they were connected with our intelligence effort. . . . Someone helped us mightily with the A-bomb."[6] He then, however, noted that he wouldn't say more, as he might "have use for it in the future." But Richard Rhodes, who studied the documents for his book *Dark Sun: The Making of the Hydrogen Bomb,* compared the dates of the Greenglass/Rosenberg information with that of Soviet physicist Igor Kurchatov and concluded that the Russians were greatly helped by the spies' information.[7]

Initially, even the Left knew that the Rosenbergs were guilty, including the Communist press, which dutifully changed its tune in 1952 when the Soviets began to put on their own show trials in Prague and needed PR cover. Even the left-leaning Wikipedia online encyclopedia admits, "Venona has added significant information to the case of Julius and Ethel Rosenberg, making it clear that Julius was guilty of espionage, but also showing that Ethel was probably no more than an accomplice, if that."[8] Venona, a long-running cryptanalysis project of Soviet intelligence agencies, confirmed that the entire notion that the Rosenbergs were convicted for "merely" being Communists was absurd, and that Soviet sympathizers and agents whipped up the original demonstrations against the verdict to deflect international criticism from their own Czech show trials—most of them against Jews.[9] Hence, the Jewishness of the Rosenbergs became a factor for the first time.

Once the USSR fell, the trickle of information from behind the former Iron Curtain became a flood, and even the Rosenbergs-were-innocent crowd had trouble discrediting the former Communist sources. For example, in October 1995, the Soviet spy Anatoli Yatskov (known to the CIA as "Yakovlev") told the *Washington Post* that the stolen material was of "huge invaluable significance" for Soviet science, enabling the Soviets to "bypass many laborious phases involved in tackling the uranium problem and revealing new scientific and technical ways of solving it."[10] Yatskov also confirmed that Gold was a courier, and he implicated the Rosenbergs directly by confirming that two other American Communists, Morris and Lona Cohen—who were subsequently arrested in London for spying after they fled the United States—had recruited Julius Rosenberg to work for the KGB.

Venona identified Julius, code name "Liberal"; showed that he was an active spy recruiter; and revealed previously unknown parallel spy rings run by Joel Barr and Alfred Sarant. More important, Venona decryptions identified Ethel as equally active in recruiting spies as Julius.[11] After Venona, and the revelations of the other post–Iron Curtain documents, the guilt of the Rosenbergs is no longer in doubt. More troubling, however, is the extent to which the KGB clearly was operating inside the United States. As Radosh and Milton note of the Venona materials, "They reveal a consistent use of the KGB of the Communist Party, U.S.A. [a teenager might well think, "Duh!" here] as well as of its front organizations, such as the Federation of Architects, Engineers, Chemists and Technicians."[12] And it wasn't "just" the atomic bomb materials that the Rosenbergs and their merry band of Communist spies were passing along: they transmitted information on rockets, airplanes, and radar—all areas in which the United States led the Soviet Union.

If all that weren't enough, the Discovery Channel located Julius Rosenberg's KGB supervisor, Aleksandr Feklisov, the officer at the New York Russian consulate from 1940 to 1946. An informant who shared a cell with Rosenberg told investigators that Julius reported to a man named "Alex," and Feklisov's alias showed up in the Venona decryptions as the agent who had been in Rosenberg's apartment.[13] Even Radosh and Milton, considered anathema to the Left after letting the evidence lead them to the conclusion that Julius was certainly guilty, cling to the notion that "the use of the death penalty" for Ethel was "improper and unfair."[14] A sober reading of the horrendous acts of these two spies, however, leads to a much different conclusion, more in line with that of Judge Kaufman: when the Rosenbergs were executed on June 19, 1953, they both deserved every watt they got.

UPDATE: Following publication of the first edition of this book, Morton Sobell, the codefendant in the Rosenbergs' espionage trial, finally admitted that he and his friend, Julius, had both been Soviet agents. That slammed shut the door of speculation, to the point that even the Rosenbergs' son, Michael Meeropol, admitted, "I don't have any reason to doubt Morty."[15] As Ronald Radosh wrote in the *Los Angeles Times*, "With these latest events, the end has arrived for the legions of the American left wing that have argued relentlessly for more than half a century that the Rosenbergs were victims, framed by a hostile, fear-mongering U.S. government."[16] Radosh even mentioned this book in his article and compared my arguments to those of Eric Foner, a Columbia history professor who had claimed that the Rosenberg case was a "witch-hunt." Pardon my boasting, but Radosh actually stated that "Schweikart is right, and Foner is wrong." As a young graduate student, I could never have imagined that comment appearing in a major U.S. newspaper, let alone about a case as important as the Rosenbergs. Maybe, indeed, as Bob Dylan sang, the "times they are a-changin'."

LEE HARVEY OSWALD SHOT JFK BECAUSE HE WAS
A DERANGED MARINE, NOT BECAUSE HE WAS A COMMUNIST

[Oswald was] a troubled former Marine.

—ERIC FONER, GIVE ME LIBERTY

A majority of textbooks identify John F. Kennedy's killer as "a twenty-four-year-old ex-Marine drifter" (Tindall and Shi, *America*), and a "24-year-old misfit [who] had served in the Marines" (Goldfield et al., *American Journey*).[1] Morison, Commager, and Leuchtenberg's *Concise History of the American Republic* noted Oswald "had once expatriated himself to Russia" (note, not the "Soviet Union"). Boydston et al., in *Making a Nation*, describe him as a "quiet former Marine" who "spent time in the Soviet Union. . . ."[2] Harrell et al., in *Unto a Good Land,* added to the typical description of Oswald as a "deeply disturbed former Marine" the key identifying factor—"and self-professed Marxist."[3] Why do you suppose these textbooks eagerly described Oswald as a Marine, but only one mentioned he was a "Marxist," and none correctly identified him as what he was: a self-described Communist? Howard Zinn's *A People's History of the United States,* which does not deal with JFK's death, does not even mention Oswald, possibly because to do so would require acknowledging his Communist sympathies.[4] Likewise, James W. Loewen's *Lies My Teacher Told Me* avoids any mention of Oswald.

In fact, however, as a new book by James Piereson shows, Oswald's communism was the motivating factor in his murder of the president, though leftists (including historians such as Arthur Schlesinger) conveniently omitted any references to Oswald's communism. Piereson notes that "the assassination of a popular president by a communist should have generated a revulsion against everything associated with left-wing doctrines. Yet something very close to the opposite happened."[5] Instead, the historians routinely described Oswald as "emotionally unstable [and one whose] actions were never fully explained. . . ."[6] Not fully explained, unless, of course, you take Oswald's own words at face value.

When conspiracy theories are presented, they almost uniformly are related to the CIA, not Communists. The Warren Commission's "decision to protect CIA secrets," says *American Destiny*, "engendered skepticism toward the [commission]—and the United States government."[7] In other words, while noting that "there is little solid evidence to suggest Oswald was part of a wider conspiracy," the authors go on to suggest that if such a "conspiracy" existed, it certainly must involve "CIA secrets."[8] After warning that "the president was not universally loved and admired. . . . The far right . . . despised him," *These United States* goes on to identify Oswald as "an unstable leftist who had spent years in the Soviet Union and been active in the pro-Castro Fair Play for Cuba organization."[9] The author then plunges into the "toll" of the assassination, which was that "more and more Americans concluded that there was an evil plot afoot, or a conspiracy of them. . . ."[10] In the mother of all cop-outs, *The Enduring Vision* cannot even bring itself to state that Oswald killed Kennedy, instead noting, "Shots rang out. The president slumped. . . . Americans spent the next four days in front of their television sets staring at replays of the murder of accused assassin Lee Harvey Oswald. . . ."[11]

It is astonishing, however, that even among the texts that admit Oswald was a leftist who spent considerable time in the Soviet Union, virtually none of them can take the next step and assume it was *because* of Oswald's Communist sympathies that he killed Kennedy. As Piereson noted, liberal writers in the twentieth century had a monopoly on describing conspiracy theorists as irrational, often right-wing, anti-intellectual bumpkins. This was the thesis of Richard Hofstadter's essay "The Paranoid Style in American Politics."[12] Yet suddenly, as radical leader Todd Gitlin said, the leaders of the New Left were "fascinated by conspiracy theories, impressed by their critiques of the Warren Commission, doubtful of the single-assassin idea. . . ."[13] Quite the contrary, liberal textbook writers had to disassociate Oswald from communism. Following the lead of liberal iconographers such as Arthur Schlesinger Jr., in his *A*

Thousand Days, the new historical narrative was that the "nation" as a whole "killed Kennedy." The Rolling Stones got in on the act with their 1968 song "Sympathy for the Devil," where Mick Jagger sings (for want of a better term), "I shouted out, 'Who killed the Kennedys?' when after all, it was you and me." A shame-based reframing of the Kennedy assassination, where tragedy was an "instrument of punishment" for national sins, trickled into the textbooks.[14]

By the time Robert Kennedy was assassinated, a new, punitive liberalism had replaced the old, John Kennedy–esque muscular liberalism. As Pierson put it, liberals "began to argue that the purpose of national policy was more to punish the nation for its sins than to build a brighter and more secure future for all. The focus of reform was to [compensate] those groups that had suffered as a consequence of cruel policies and customs in the past."[15] It therefore became the purpose of history texts to document those past sins and unjust policies, not to present an honest, balanced story in which the United States overall was a "shining city on a hill"—which is the case. We have Lee Harvey Oswald to blame not only for killing a charismatic president, but also for permanently poisoning the optimism of a generation, a diabolical historical "twofer" that was uniquely destructive.

Historians have not hesitated to accept other presidential assassins at face value. Most texts, for example, identify John Wilkes Booth as a Confederate or Confederate sympathizer.[16] One textbook calls Booth a "disgruntled southern actor," and another a "crazed actor and Confederate zealot."[17] Only a few fail to mention that Booth was a die-hard Confederate.[18] Perhaps it's time to identify John Kennedy's killer as the Communist assassin that he was.

Lie #21

Columbus Was Responsible for Killing Millions of Indians

Estimates of Haiti's pre-Columbian population range as high as 8,000,000 people.... When Christopher Columbus returned to Spain ... [the census] of Indian adults in 1496 [was] 1,100,000.
—James W. Loewen, Lies My Teacher Told Me

When Hernando Cortés and his Spanish army of fewer than a thousand men stormed into Mexico in 1519, the native population numbered about 22 million. By the end of the century, following a series of devastating epidemics, only 2 million people remained.
—Bruce Stutz, Discover magazine, February 21, 2006

For North America alone, estimates of native populations in Columbus's day range from 2 to 18 million. By the end of the 19th century the population had shrunk to about 530,000.
—David J. Meltzer, "How Columbus Sickened the World," The New Scientist, October 10, 1992

Wow. Just, wow. One wonders how any publisher would release such drivel, let alone any writer actually write it. Do you know what the population of Haiti is as of 2007, according to the *CIA World Factbook*? 8.7 million. That's right, more than four hundred years *after* Columbus explored Haiti, when there were supposedly eight million people living there, the population hasn't changed, despite a skyrocketing population growth since 1961.

To think that any premodern civilization could eliminate seven million people in *just over two years* defies all logic, not to mention history. Remember, Columbus's original voyage consisted of only three ships, a carrack, and two caravels. Normally, none of these ships could carry more than one hundred men—when Columbus returned on a second voyage, this time to Haiti, in 1493, he had over one thousand men total. Perhaps a mathematician trained in ergonomics could explain how one thousand men (of course, many died en route, or were sick) could kill *seven million people* in three years!

If one begins with assumptions that such astronomical numbers of Indians or Native Americans existed in the first place, then when somewhat reliable census methods became available and showed a fraction of that, one is left with no other conclusion than the "Columbian exchange" killed most of the natives in the New World. Of course, if one begins with the assumption that the sun is cold, then explaining sunburn will be impossible. Assumptions are important, and when it comes to determining the impact of European diseases and, yes, violence and slavery, on natives in the New World, they are necessary for purposes of measurement. In the past, ridiculous numbers have been thrown about. One author claimed 56 million people died as the result of European exploration in the Americas, but for such numbers to be even remotely true, the starting populations had to be 100 million or more.[1] Most recent research puts the entire native populations on both continents and the islands of the New World at 53 million.[2] But an interesting trend has been that with each new study, the population estimates fall: since 1976, the experts lowered their estimates by four million. More conservative estimates are that there were a total of (on the high side) 8.5 million for *all* of North America, and a low estimate of only 1.8 million.[3] The "European genocide" crowd has more Indians being killed or dying of disease than even existed in all the New World put together!

Furthermore, historians have used unrealistic flexibility in determining when diseases first appeared, and who introduced them. One study of 12,500 skeletons from sixty-five burial sites found that pre-Columbian disease was rampant, and some have speculated that a nonvenereal form of syphilis was involved. Several anthropologists, including Henry Dobyns, now subscribe to the "early epidemic" theory of depopulation—in other words, disease was killing large numbers of natives long before the first Spaniard ever waded ashore.[4] Daniel Reff has argued for a thorough reconsideration of disease as the primary source of depopulation, and does not support the inflated numbers.[5] David Henige correctly labels these fabulously high estimates as "numbers from nowhere."[6]

Some truth is slipping out, however: Rodolfo Acuña-Soto, although accepting the extraordinarily high numbers, attributes the deaths to hemorrhagic fevers transmitted by rodent hosts.[7] Acuña-Soto found that epidemics coincided with many Spanish "invasions" and would look like Europeans "caused" illnesses for which they were not responsible at all. This introduces a remarkable dilemma: On the one hand, James Loewen and others castigate history teachers for ignoring "Afro-Phoenician" voyages (for which almost no evidence exists) by writing, "Unlike the Norse, the Afro-Phoenicians seem to have made a permanent impact on the Americas."[8] If that's true, however, then all of the claims about a "biologically naive" or "virgin soil" spread of European diseases must be completely rejected, as the Afro-Phoenicians infected the Indians first!

Moreover, no one bothered to keep track of how many Indians other Indians killed in warfare. Not only did most Indians not keep records of how many enemy they wiped out, different tribal customs sometimes deliberately overestimated and sometimes deliberately underestimated the actual casualties. It's a reasonable assumption that as many were killed in warfare with each other as in conflicts with Europeans, but it's well known that the Aztecs slaughtered hundreds of thousands in religious ceremonies. Scholars who looked at southwestern regions found entirely abandoned or depopulated areas that are dated to a century before Columbus arrived. Where once scholars dismissed Spaniards' accounts of decaying "great houses" or empty villages, they now are revisiting those observations with an eye toward other explanations. Victor Davis Hanson estimates that the Aztecs alone killed twenty thousand a year, every year, in their ritual sacrifices; and the author of *Aztec Warfare* puts the number killed at a single ceremony in 1487 at between ten thousand and eighty thousand.[9] Perhaps anti-Columbus Indian George P. Horse Capture, who said, "No sensible Indian person can celebrate the arrival of Columbus,"[10] meant, "No sensible Indian other than those who survived the Aztec slaughters!"

LIE #22

THE EARLY COLONIES WERE INTOLERANT AND RACIST

[Puritans] sought to convert the tribes to Christianity. They considered the natives to be wild pagans incapable of fully utilizing nature's bounty.
—GEORGE BROWN TINDALL AND DAVID E. SHI, AMERICA:
A NARRATIVE HISTORY

"Chapter 5: 'Gone with the Wind,' the Invisibility of Racism in American History Textbooks"
—JAMES W. LOEWEN, LIES MY TEACHER TOLD ME

Were American colonies bent on racism and racial slavery when they originated? In fact, there was no original concept of racial slavery when the nation was first settled by Europeans. As Yale historian Edmund S. Morgan points out, blacks often were viewed the same as white indentured servants, and became free as soon as their indenture was up.[1] Until the 1670s, American colonists looked to white indentured servants, not Africans, as their main source of labor. In 1664, some southern colonies declared slavery hereditary, but when they did, they weren't inventing a new way to be racist. They merely had returned *to* a practice that was established throughout the Muslim world and accepted across the entire globe, including in the French and British empires.[2] It must also be remembered that at this point, the Muslim slave trade, mostly of Europeans, dwarfed the slave trade involving black Africans.[3]

Free blacks were common, especially in the North. In 1621, for example, "Antonio the negro" was identified in public records in Virginia, and of the three hundred blacks living in the South up to 1640, many (if not most) had gained freedom simply through the expiration of their indenture contracts. Some became landholders, and even slaveholders. About 10 percent of all blacks were free, 90 percent slave. But there were free blacks in early America. One Marylander, Mathias de Sousa, was an indentured servant who was the first black to vote in America and served in the 1642 legislative assembly. The assembly's proceedings listed him alongside the other members.

Pennsylvania passed a gradual emancipation resolution in 1780, Rhode Island in 1784. The state of New York formed a manumission society in 1785, and New York abolished slavery in 1799—some thirty years before England ended slavery in her empire. Vice President Aaron Burr, who would later shoot former Treasury Secretary Alexander Hamilton in a duel, lobbied for immediate emancipation for all New York slaves right after the Revolution ended.

Free blacks were voting in Massachusetts, Vermont, Rhode Island, Connecticut, and several other states prior to the Civil War. In some cases, despite their relatively small numbers, the community of free blacks who voted swung an election.[4] Indeed, even before they were free, blacks in the Northeast held "'Lection Day" on the day when free white voters would cast their ballots, at which time they elected their own "governors" and spokesmen.[5] While some might ridicule such actions as meaningless gestures, lacking real democracy and power, in fact they showed whites, on the one hand, that blacks could govern themselves in "respectable" European ways, and on the other, gave blacks practice at self-government for when the time came that they would be emancipated.

Interracial marriage was not initially illegal in the colonies and apparently was not entirely uncommon. Maryland, for example, did not ban interracial marriages, but did punish free white women who married slaves.[6] Not until 1717 did Maryland prohibit black/white intermarriage. Most colonies did not originally forbid interracial marriages, and such laws were not passed until the 1660s. Not surprisingly, this is the same time frame in which black slavery started to become hereditary. By 1676, legalized hereditary slavery appeared in Maryland, Virginia, and the Carolinas, and was soon established as an institution in virtually all the American colonies.[7] Yet it is also important to note that while slavery was deeply embedded in the American past—as it was, again, *virtually everywhere else*—Americans were the first to form an Anti-Slavery Society, in 1775, when the Quakers also ingrained the concept of abolition in the national soul. And northern reformers began passing manumission acts in the late 1700s. Saudi Arabia and the Sudan are still awaiting their manumission acts.

Treatment of Indians was far more uneven, given the different cultures of the northern and southern tribes, some with quite "European" ways. There was also the simple reality that until 1763, the English colonists needed Indian allies to ward off the French, and each tribe played its own version of power politics. Many tribes in New England welcomed the English as a counterbalance to the hated Pequots. Until the activist removal of the Cherokee by Andrew Jackson in the 1830s, Indians "lived partially assimilated lives on the margins of the dominant society."[8] Some Indians had already "forgotten their ancient names and nearly all their Indian language."[9] Of course, to the Native American activists, this kind of assimilation was abominable—but it hardly represented "intolerance and racism." The Puritans, while viewing Indians as culturally inferior, embraced no doctrine of racial inferiority when it came to Native Americans. Indeed, some Puritan teachings held that the Indians descended from the Jews.[10]

Certainly the lust for land on the part of white settlers cannot be denied, but as we discussed at length in *A Patriot's History of the United States,* this was as much grounded in a fundamental and unbreachable difference in the very notion of property rights that came with a paper title as it was in pure greed. Plains Indians did not conceive of European-style private property rights—although neither were they Marxist Communists who "shared" everything—and eventually an "irrepressible conflict" was bound to arise between one culture that insisted land could be owned and fenced in, and another that said it could not.[11] New England Indians had extensive land-rights systems, and often eagerly sold land.[12] Some Indians were simply pushed off their lands. Especially as one moved farther west, the concept of property rights became less European.[13] Colonists routinely granted Indians hunting rights on their *own* lands, happy to obtain the furs that the Indians would provide.[14] Over time, it could be argued that once settlers realized that the Indians did not have European concepts of property rights (as embodied in large, fenced-in farms), they developed a "what the heck" attitude and used blunt force to obtain what would inevitably become theirs through the European-based legal system. For the most part, however, in the 1600s, "deeds of sale usually were so specific as to leave little room for misunderstanding.

When disputes arose between Puritans and Indians over land sales, they most often involved questions of boundaries, not privileges."[15] Such an absence of private property rights made conflict inevitable. However, up until the time of Jackson's violent removal of the Cherokee, the U.S. Supreme Court was tending toward recognizing full Indian rights to land regardless of any national interest from the U.S. government. Congress recognized Indian rights of soil in 1786, but simultaneously established treaties to take it away with a cash purchase. Later, however, the presence of these contract rights would help the Indians defend their lands.

In other ways, the colonists were remarkably tolerant of the natives, where virtually any other kingdom or empire—Mongols or Muslims come to mind—would have simply wiped them out or completely subjugated them. Harvard admitted Indian students early in its history; colonists could be tried and put to death for murdering Indians. John Eliot, a missionary to the Algonquins in Massachusetts, learned their language and translated the Bible into Algonquin. The Pequots received a colonial grant from the king of England that acknowledged the political rights of Indians. Some New England courts ruled in favor of Indians who claimed their land had been stolen.

In matters of religion, the very fact that so many different denominations and sects practiced side by side is telling. At a time when England and France had state-sponsored churches, the American colonies had separate Anglican, Catholic, Puritan, Baptist, and Quaker churches, as well as watered-down versions of each. Methodism appeared when George Whitefield arrived in 1641. "New Light" Christianity began to spread, and Presbyterianism arrived. It was a free market of religious ideas—and toleration—unseen in almost any part of the world.[16]

Toleration had its limits. While no Catholic in his right mind would march into Salem or Boston and begin preaching that all Puritans were going to hell, even obnoxious religious zealots—such as Quakers who frequently ventured into Congregational territory—were given multiple warnings before punishment was imposed. This stood in marked contrast to Europe, where the king of France would burn Knights Templars—the organization of crusader knights which had become, essentially, a society of bankers—at the stake for heresy just to get his hands on their money. But in America, by 1800, major seminaries were already educating Unitarians, who denied the divinity of Christ! How's that for "toleration"?

LIE #23

EARLY AMERICA WAS HOME TO FEW GUNS OR GUN OWNERS

[G]un ownership was exceptional in the seventeenth, eighteenth, and early nineteenth centuries. . . .

—MICHAEL BELLESILES, ARMING AMERICA

As whoppers about American history go, this one is fairly new and was refuted in what has to be record time when it comes to academic review processes. It was largely the result of one book, *Arming America: The Origins of a National Gun Culture,*[1] in which author Michael Bellesiles claimed few people owned guns in early America—even on the frontier.[2] The firearms market only developed, he claimed, after industrialization and only then with the help of the government. Most militiamen showed up to fight without weapons, and in fact, Bellesiles argued, the government "failed in [the] task" of arming its citizens. Shame on that incompetent American government!

Of course, the truth is obvious to most ten-year-olds, who know that *no one* went into any frontier area unless armed to the teeth. Boys and girls learned to shoot at early ages, and except for a Bible and skillet, the most commonly found item in any American home, no matter how poor, was always a musket or rifle—often several! James Lindgren, a professor of law at Northwestern University, concluded that "household gun ownership in early America was more widespread than today—in a much poorer world."[3]

Bellesiles used his purported evidence to launch into an attack on the "gun culture," especially controversial positions such as whether automatic weapons should be banned, whether certain ammunition ("cop killer" bullets) was constitutional, and, of course, the widespread availability of guns contributing to high gun violence rates. The dirty little secret is that the international data shows that gun restrictions increase crime and even homicides, or, put another way, when all countries are considered, people are much safer in nations that have fewer gun laws rather than more. This evidence is extensive—in Finland, just as one example, where there are 32 privately owned firearms per 100 people, the firearm homicide rate is lower than in Italy, where only 16 percent of the households have guns.[4] Relying on shopworn myths about lower crime and homicide rates in non-gun-owning nations, Bellesiles opined that "the gun is so central to American identity that the nation's history has been meticulously recontructed to promote the necessity of having a heavily armed American public."[5] For someone who routinely invoked Gordon Wood, R. G. Collingwood, and other historians who caution that sources should be tested against generalizations, Bellesiles needed to add "and against facts." It's also telling that in his chapter-long history of the "European Gun Heritage," Bellesiles does not mention Henry II's famous "Assize of Arms," which laid the groundwork for requiring *every* man—noble or plain freeman—to be armed.[6] The author misrepresented the conclusions of Thomas Esper, who argued that while English longbows were superior in the hands of trained archers, the training took years of practice, whereas a musketeer could be effective within a few weeks of musket practice.[7] Claiming the first settlers were complete buffoons in using firearms, which in his view were nearly useless due to difficulties in loading and firing, he never explained why the Indians were so desperate to acquire these "ineffective" weapons. And on and on.

The errors in this book were obvious early on, and they were multitudinous, so much so that Clayton Cramer wrote a book-length manuscript examining and disproving Bellesiles's endnotes.[8] He also wrote an extensive response to Bellesiles's condensation of his book in article form that appeared in the *Journal of American History.*[9] Astonishingly, Cramer's response, detailing the severe deficiencies in scholarship involved in Bellesiles's article, was not published because, after the *Journal* sat on it for two years, the editors then claimed it was "a bit late" to directly critique the original article.[10] The upshot was that the original article, replete with massive source problems, remained a published article in the most prestigious journal of American history, while editors *declined to publish the piece that would have recorded the accurate history of guns in America*! In 2007, Cramer's rebuttal manuscript became a book, *Armed*

America: The Story of How and Why Guns Became as American as Apple Pie (Nashville: Thomas Nelson, 2007). There were serious errors on almost every page of Bellesiles's book. The notion, for example, that militias' showing up without guns was somehow indicative of the fact that they did not *have* guns was absurd: it showed precisely the opposite, that early Americans treasured their personal firearms and were not going to take them into combat but rather expected the government to furnish a gun. Indeed, after the first days of the Revolution, American militiamen well knew that their hunting rifles—while far better at long range—were nearly useless in close combat because they lacked bayonets, which the government muskets had.

In all of Bellesiles's publications, Cramer argued that the errors were not the result of careless mistakes but rather that Bellesiles engaged in deliberate falsifications. This theme was expanded by Cramer in a journal devoted to exposing plagiarism and fraud, *Plagiary*. What made Cramer's investigation of *Arming America* so exceptional was that unlike other early critics, Cramer was a gun enthusiast and software engineer who worked entirely outside the academy. Or course, antigun critics, such as Jon Wiener in *The Nation*, tried to smear Cramer precisely because of his "amateur" status, only to make an incredible number of errors themselves.[11]

While the battle of the reviews was unfolding, Emory University released its report stating that Bellesiles was "guilty of unprofessional and misleading work," and the panel found "evidence of falsification." Even after confronted with the evidence, it was not clear that Bellesiles "fully understands the magnitude of his own probate research shortcomings." In other words, even after Emory showed him his errors, he was in denial. But long before that, Cramer found:[12]

- When citing the Militia Act of 1792, Bellesiles changed the phrase "every citizen . . . shall within six months . . . provide himself" with a weapon to "shall . . . be constantly provided," then claimed Congress would "provide" that weapon. In fact, individuals were perfectly capable of providing their own.
- Bellesiles quoted George Washington as condemning "the militia" in general as poorly armed when in fact he was criticizing only *specific* units.
- He conflated statistics of state militia weapons and those in the government armories with all weapons in private hands to arrive at a figure of

250,000 guns in America when there were, according to government records, at least 250,000 guns in the hands of state militias *alone.*

When scholars finally smelled the odor and began investigating Bellesiles's archival documents, the stink grew worse. James Lindgren, a probate law expert, notes that while probate evidence appeared in only thirteen pages of the book, that evidence was central to his argument because it was the only data showing consistent change over time.[13] More evidence of fraud surfaced, however, when Bellesiles told Lindgren that he had read some ten thousand microfilm probated inventories at East Point, Georgia's federal archives. In fact, the records had never been processed or microfilmed. The probate records Bellesiles relied on from San Francisco had been destroyed in the 1906 earthquake! When confronted with that tidbit of information, Bellesiles claimed to have "located the documents" and "even sent for them myself."[14] He must have had a time machine to obtain those records. Confronted yet again a year later by Emory University officials, he "completely forgot" which of the archives he had used. One wonders why Detroit cannot turn out a decent time machine anymore.

A reporter for the *Boston Globe* found that Bellesiles's own Web site, which claimed early guns were of poor quality, had coincidentally omitted dozens of guns in estates and had altered the descriptions of guns in Vermont probate records to support his point. Bellesiles claimed his Web site was hacked, perhaps by the same gremlins that damaged his time machine. After trying yet again to make the Vermont records yield a conclusion he liked, Bellesiles introduced a *new* set of probate records that still omitted most of the guns in estates verified by Lindgren, Justin Heather, Randolph Roth, and David Mehegan. Pressed by Emory to respond to critics, Bellesiles offered a statement on the Web site of the Organization of American Historians in November 2001, yet did not answer a single charge that was raised, only new "criticism" he invented. In January 2002, the *William and Mary Quarterly* devoted much of its issue to the debate and allowed Bellesiles to respond, but again he ducked the obvious and most damaging issues.

The ball completely unraveled after that. Columbia University had awarded Bellesiles the Bancroft Prize for works of "distinguished merit and distinction," and no one could argue that *Arming America* wasn't "distinct" in its fallacious logic and some sources that simply appeared to have vanished.

Many of those who had endorsed Bellesiles's book on the jacket and in promotion, including Garry Wills, slowly began to question their support—then withdraw it. The National Endowment for the Humanities removed Bellesiles from the Newberry Library Fellowship in June 2002.

Pressure on Emory University increased after an internal investigation suggested unprofessional practices were present, and the university finally consented to establish a panel of "distinguished scholars" from other universities to review the case. In October 2002, the panel found "evidence of falsification" and "serious failures of and carelessness in gathering and presentation of archival records and the use of quantitative evidence."[15] The report found in one case that of supposed records from thirty-eight jurisdictions, astonishingly few "fragments" of Bellisiles's research actually existed, and "neither he in his subsequently published data nor any other scholar has been able to replicate the low percentages of guns reported" in those tables.[16] Addressing the destroyed San Francisco archives, Bellesiles later claimed they were in Contra Costa, California, and he just mixed up the two. In fact, he didn't even check the San Francisco records until after his research was called into question—and even then, the records he (thanks to his burst of memory) recalled reading in Contra Costa in 1993 were not placed there until 1998! The time machine malfunctions seemed to have gotten worse as the case dragged on. The committee noted that "the records he selected and photocopied from that Contra Costa archive were hardly random, but explicitly chosen because they had the words 'San Francisco' in them, even though they [clearly came from Contra Costa's court]."[17]

In its final report to Emory, the committee could not judge "intentionality," but were "seriously troubled" by Bellesiles's scholarly conduct.[18] Further, the committee found that "the failure to clearly identify his sources" did "move into the realm of 'falsification,' and that he had deliberately omitted data from Alice H. Jones because it contradicted his own."[19] Bellesiles resigned from Emory on the day the report was released, and Columbia University's trustees finally saw the light and rescinded the Bancroft Prize they had awarded to Bellesiles for his "scholarship."[20]

Most telling was the response of those academics who had touted Bellesiles's work, including Garry Wills and Roger Lane. Wills labeled the book a "fraud," and said, "People get taken by very good con men." They do when they are already half in the tank for whatever the con men are selling. As Wills added, Bellesiles "did not have to do it, since he had good evidence for many of his claims."[21] Which claims those were, Wills did not say.

More telling were the comments by Roger Lane, who had first reviewed the book positively in the *Journal of American History:* "He's betrayed us. He's betrayed the cause."[22] The "cause"? I doubt seriously that the "cause" is honest, accurate history. More likely that cause was gun control, itself a topic drenched in poor research and bogus statistics. As with so many of the Left's arguments, the only way to win is to cheat.

LIE #24

ABRAHAM LINCOLN ONLY FREED THE SLAVES
TO BEEF UP HIS TROOP STRENGTH

With the [Emancipation] Proclamation, the Union army was open to blacks. And the more blacks entered the war, the more it appeared a war for their liberation.
— HOWARD ZINN, A PEOPLE'S HISTORY OF THE UNITED STATES

[Abraham Lincoln's] dream, like Jefferson's dream, was a dream of a lily-White America without Negroes, Native Americans, and Martin Luther Kings.
— LERONE BENNETT JR., FORCED INTO GLORY

Another consideration was the potential value of black soldiers. If the North could tap this human reservoir, it could offset the immense losses on the battlefields and the declining zeal of white volunteers.
— IRWIN UNGER, THESE UNITED STATES

As is clear from the quotations, in the wacky world of the New Left, Abraham Lincoln was a racist. According to some, he only issued the Emancipation Proclamation because he needed more bodies for his war machine. Yet for others, such as Bennett, Lincoln was so race-minded that he never intended to use black troops in battle because, according to the Lincoln-as-racist view, black troops were incompetent in his mind. Yet even generally sober treatments such as *The Great Republic* by Bernard Bailyn et al. (whose section on the Civil War was written by the esteemed David Donald) linked emancipation to the military's need for more black troops. Donald's four-page discussion about the Proclamation is built around the premise of military necessity.[1]

For leftist historians, the entire Civil War has always been a problem, because it demonstrated unequivocally that Americans would fight for their ideas. It is absolutely true, as demonstrated in Lie #39, that the Civil War was, ultimately, caused by slavery and little else; that the value of slave property was the "elephant in the room" of antebellum politics; and that some Southerners occasionally admitted as much. It is equally true, however, that the large majority of Southerners did not own slaves and did not particularly care for the elites who did. But they had been born and raised in a culture that emphasized both "states' rights" and constitutional liberties, including (if one chose, and had the money) the right to own a slave.

In the movie *Gettysburg*, when a captured Confederate is asked why he and his comrades were fighting, he replies, "We're fightin' for our rats." The questioner soon realizes he said they were fighting for their *rights*. "Why are you fighting in this war?" Union troops asked a captured soldier. "Because you're down here," he replied.[2] But in fact, the only right at issue was the right to hold other humans as chattel.

It was equally true of Northern soldiers: most believed in the cause of Union, and many wanted to "teach the South a lesson," namely that no state or states could flaunt the Constitution by seceding. But just as Southerners, deep down, knew that the underlying issue was slavery, so too in the North most realized that sooner or later they would have to do something about the slaves. This became obvious immediately, the first time Union soldiers took in former slaves. What were they? Slaves? Freemen? In 1861, when Brig. Gen. Benjamin "Beast" Butler took custody of slaves who had escaped from the next county, he refused to return them, ultimately declaring them "contraband of war." Secretary of the Navy Gideon Welles issued a directive in September 1861 that gave "persons of color, commonly known as contrabands," who were employed by the Union Navy, pay of $10 a month and rations.[3] The Union Army soon followed suit, and again used the term "contrabands." Moreover, the Confiscation Act of 1861 made liable for confiscation any property, including slaves, that the Confederates employed for military use. The 1862 Act Prohibiting the Return of Slaves further cemented the nonslave status of "contraband" blacks.

Already, then, Abraham Lincoln's original war aim of restoring the Union was de facto broadened. While he hoped to start with the loyal border states (e.g., Kentucky, Missouri, and Maryland) and spread emancipation downward, after a July 1862 meeting with border state representatives, he realized he had it backward. Emancipation had to start with the states in rebellion, then spread back northward to the loyalist states. *Never in these discussions with any of the border state representatives or with Lincoln's own cabinet were considerations of black soldiers raised.* For Lincoln, the issue was always about winning, and winning in such a way that a permanent peace and united nation resulted. A day after meeting with the border state representatives, Lincoln took a carriage ride with William Seward, his secretary of state, and Navy Secretary Welles. He told them in an "urgent voice" that the time had passed for an amicable reunion of the warring sections and instead the North needed to focus on the "heart of the rebellion," namely the institution of slavery that had caused secession in the first place.[4]

As Michael Allen and I wrote in *A Patriot's History of the United States*, "[I]t is critical that an understanding of emancipation begin with Lincoln's perception that [slavery] was first and foremost a moral and legal issue, not a military or political one."[5] Lincoln's writings repeatedly cited moral and social—never military—reasons for emancipation. "I never in my life was more certain that I was doing right than in signing [the Emancipation Proclamation]," Lincoln said.[6] More germane to the argument of whether Lincoln merely acted out of the need for more soldiers is the timing. While the North had lost many battles already—indeed, Lincoln could not issue any proclamation about emancipation without a military victory first—Lincoln had already made up his mind on emancipation by the *summer of 1862*! The North had indeed suffered several defeats—first Bull Run and the Battle of the Wilderness—but had yet to experience the truly heavy casualty counts of Antietam, Fredericksburg, or Gettysburg.

Moreover, a little-known fact is that in every major battle of the first two years except Fredericksburg, the South suffered a higher percentage of troop loss as a share of troops committed than did any Union general. Robert E. Lee, for all his purported military genius, suffered 20 percent casualties while inflicting only 15 percent on his enemy, while Grant suffered 18 percent casualties but inflicted 30 percent losses on his foes. (According to Grady McWhiney, the Confederacy lost a higher percentage of men committed to eleven of the first twelve battles or campaigns than did the Union because of its aggressive "attack and die" tactics.)[7]

Far from gaining troops, the Proclamation was almost as likely to *cost* the Union recruits. Illinois regiments, for example, suffered the largest number of desertions immediately after the Proclamation was issued, and one regiment, the 109th, had to be disbanded for disloyalty.[8] A lieutenant in the 86th Illinois regiment found only eight men in his company who approved of the Proclamation. No commentator even mentioned the possibility of blacks replacing whites at the front. Instead, they worried about "the lusts of freed negroes who will overrun our country."[9] (Lerone Bennett, a Lincoln-hater of the first degree, ironically ignored the premise that Lincoln freed the slaves to obtain more soldiers—quite the contrary, Bennett maintained that the Emancipation Proclamation was intended to "re-enslave" blacks. Such fantasies only operate in the nether-universe of über-liberals and black racists.) But this creates a stunning problem: if Northern whites were such blatant racists—as Lerone insists—then it was inconceivable that they would ever use blacks as soldiers. Surprisingly to some, over 100,000 *Southern* supporters of the Union effort fought against the Confederacy, including entire regiments from Mississippi, Alabama, Arkansas, Florida, plus 40,000 Tennesseans.[10]

African Americans made up about 10 percent of the Union Army (179,000), and another 19,000 served in the Navy. In fact, recruitment was slow at first, until Frederick Douglass worked to convince blacks to join the Union forces. It is true that some white officers did not think black soldiers could fight, but they learned differently after African-American units were finally put into combat. Still, the very fact that there was reluctance to use black troops in combat further undercuts the view that emancipation was only a vehicle to get more soldiers.

Many of the earliest black recruits were volunteers from South Carolina and Tennessee. After being relegated to supply and guard details, their constant lobbying for a hand in the fighting finally resulted in black units' being used in combat alongside whites. Far from being an easy choice for Lincoln and his war cabinet, inserting "colored" troops into an all-white corps could easily have eroded large-unit cohesion and even raised the possibility that white troops might not support their black compatriots at critical points on the battlefield. As with anything else they did, blacks had to fight to prove they belonged in the Army. Contrary to the depiction in the film *Glory,* the first use of African-American soldiers in combat came in October 1862 when the 1st Kansas Colored Volunteers beat back Confederate attacks at the Battle of

Island Mound, Missouri. Several months later, black troops advanced across open ground to attack Confederate positions at Port Hudson, Louisiana. Although the assault failed, the courage of the troops convinced white officers and enlisted men alike that blacks would—and could—fight well. Union black troops gained their greatest success at the Battle of New Market Heights in Virginia (September 1864). African-American troops served gallantly, taking forty thousand casualties and earning sixteen Medals of Honor. Not until June of 1864 did Congress finally equalize the pay of U.S. colored troops with that of whites.[11]

A largely forgotten fact of the Civil War is that a large number of free blacks and slaves served in the Confederate Army, with slaves promised their freedom in exchange for service.[12] Some fought because the South was their home, even if as slaves. Most were never permitted to have weapons and were largely confined to physical labor, cooking, and digging. A handful did actually see combat, however.

While the view that the Emancipation Proclamation was *primarily* oriented toward adding black soldiers to the Union Army has receded in recent years—confined mainly to demagogues such as Bennett—it is noteworthy that Bernard Bailyn's textbook, *The Great Republic,* coupled emancipation with the need for black troops.[13] Likewise, to show how such ideas insinuate themselves into even conservative, commonsense teaching, one only has to look at the influential home-school Web site "Family Education," which implies that the Union was running out of men.[14] It is true that more soldiers were being used in guard duty as the North advanced into the Confederacy, but blacks were demanding to be combat soldiers, not guards. Moreover, as normalcy returned to Confederate states long in Union possession (Louisiana, parts of Tennessee), white troops could be rotated out. Although addressing Congress's July 1862 legislation that authorized freedom for any Southern slave who escaped and joined Union forces—not Lincoln's Emancipation Proclamation—the site's author nevertheless argues that Congress "acted not out of ethical considerations, primarily, but from sheer military necessity. The Union needed more troops."[15]

Again, the fact was that the high-casualty battles of Antietam and Fredericksburg had not been fought yet; that the Army of the Potomac, especially, constantly outnumbered the Army of Northern Virginia; and that many were convinced that all the Union Army needed was a general who would fight.

Stating the obvious, in the summer of 1862, when Lincoln had already decided emancipation had to be the "war aim," few in the North thought that the difficulty in defeating the South lay in insufficient troop numbers. Gen. George B. McClellan—who constantly complained about not having a large enough troop advantage—nevertheless always outnumbered Lee, and at Antietam even had Lee's full battle plans. After intercepting Special Order No. 191, McClellan reportedly exclaimed, "Here is a paper with which, if I cannot whip Bobby Lee, I will be willing to go home."[16] While McClellan did not "whip" Robert E. Lee, once again the Union exacted a far higher cost from the Confederates in casualties as a percentage of men committed to the fight than the Union paid. Whether the Union knew it or not, with or without African-American soldiers, the South was losing proportionally more in every exchange than was the North. While black soldiers did contribute to the victory—just as state militias and draftees and countless white volunteers did—it was only a matter of time before the North settled on a general who could fight skillfully and bring the North's industrial dominance to bear. Ultimately, it was Ulysses S. Grant and the overwhelming output of Northern factories, not black troops, that turned the tide of war.

LIE #25

THE SCOPES TRIAL PROVED THAT DARWIN
WAS CORRECT AND CHRISTIANS WERE BACKWARD

Shortly after the trial ended, Bryan died and the movement for anti-evolution laws disintegrated. Fundamentalists retreated for many years from battles over public education. . . .

—ERIC FONER, GIVE ME LIBERTY

The judge found Scopes guilty. . . . But the fundamentalist crusade no longer had the same force.

—SAMUEL ELIOT MORISON ET AL.,
A CONCISE HISTORY OF THE AMERICAN REPUBLIC

After Dayton, the fundamentalists—their fury spent for the moment—went dormant.

—GEORGE BROWN TINDALL AND DAVID E. SHI, AMERICA:
A NARRATIVE HISTORY

It's no surprise that textbook authors cleverly arrange the Scopes trial before, or immediately after, such social maladies as the Ku Klux Klan (Eric Foner) or Al Capone (Tindall and Shi). In Morison and Commager's *A Concise History of the American Republic,* the trial falls under the heading "Nineteenth-Century America's Last Stand." Harrell et al.'s *Unto a Good Land* presents Scopes immediately prior to "Nativist Fears and Immigration Restrictions," and opposite a spooky-looking picture of evangelist Aimee Semple McPherson sporting a Klan-type robe with her hands outstretched and eyes uplifted.[1] Surprisingly, only Daniel Goldfield, whose *American Journey* is reliably leftist on almost all other issues, correctly described the scene in which "Millions of Americans tuned their radios to hear the first trial ever broadcast," and in which the fundamentalists "suffered public ridicule from reporters, including H. L. Mencken, who sneered at the 'hillbillies' and 'yokels' of Dayton [Tennessee]."[2]

To the extent that Americans know anything at all of the Scopes trial, it usually comes from brief descriptions from textbooks as noted in the epigraphs to this chapter, or, more likely, from the famous book and movie *Inherit the Wind,* with Spencer Tracy and a young Gene Kelly.[3] The famous movie scene indeed had drama: lawyer Henry Drummond, played by Tracy in the film, represents the teacher, Bertram Cates (played by Dick York), "unjustly" accused of teaching evolution. Drummond cross-examines Matthew Harrison Brady, played by Fredric March (but representing William Jennings Bryan), exposing him as an ignorant bumpkin. But as historian Burton Folsom Jr. notes, "The problem is that the historians, playwrights, and filmmakers have told the story wrong."[4] Typically, textbooks concluded that "Bryan appeared grossly misinformed about modern science,"[5] yet the trial record showed just the opposite—that he was better read on archaeology and anthropology than was Clarence Darrow!

Scopes's significance in history is that it addressed two central questions of a modern society, namely the origins of man and the propriety of teaching "values" in public schools. It was also a particularly useful target for social critics because the battle lines were so sharply drawn, with Bryan and the hick "Bible-thumpers" on one side and the sophisticated, intellectual elites represented by Darrow on the other. (One text, *Nation of Nations,* described the trial as a "national joke," a characterization neither Darrow nor Bryan would have accepted.)[6] Tennessee state law prohibited the teaching of evolution in public schools (specifically, it should be noted, the teaching of evolution from biology textbooks that presented it as a fact instead of a viable theory). Yet the famous Darrow cross-examination of Bryan was irrelevant to the main points of either attorney, although it was the last major event at the trial. It was natural, then, that writers would make this exchange the climax of their dramas.

Often missed in the cross-examination is why it was necessary in the first place: Darrow was losing. The judge had already ruled that evolution was a theory, and that scientists' opinions were just that—opinions. Darrow also tried to show that evolution was compatible with the Bible, but had to discard that after Bryan's major speech. Instead, Darrow tried to make the trial about Bryan, rather than John Scopes. Both men had reputations for their speaking skills, but Darrow's was in debate, while Bryan's was in stemwinder speeches. Since Bryan already had the case won, he could have declined to appear as a witness for the defense, and he was completely aware that he was leaving his own "home turf" and entering Darrow's domain. Bryan had himself used the "cross-examiner's advantage" many times, to pick apart answers with more questions designed to make the witness contradict himself, so he knew what he faced.

Bryan became overconfident on the basis of his earlier one-on-one victories over Darrow in the case, and he also apparently believed he would have the opportunity to interrogate Darrow, making it even.[7] Up to that time, Bryan had embarrased Darrow, quoting Darwin to Darrow, and even quoting Darrow to Darrow! But Darrow was deceptive, citing the nonexistent "book" of Elijah in the Bible and also, earlier, a nonexistent "book of Buddha." While the movies and books have made great hay out of Bryan's silly line, "I do not think about things I do not think about," they have ignored some of the repartee where Bryan got the best of Darrow. When Bryan said Buddhism is an "agnostic religion," Darrow said, "What do you mean by agnostic?" and Bryan answered, "I don't know." Darrow thought he had Bryan: "You don't know what you mean?" Bryan answered (correctly), "That is what 'agnosticism' is—I don't know."[8]

Darrow also stumbled into a discussion of Confucianism that is routinely ignored, unaware that Bryan had been to China and written two books on Chinese culture and religion. Bryan used Confucianism to show the distinct differences between it and Christianity, forcing Darrow to retreat along different lines. When Darrow tried to expose Bryan as ignorant by asking him how many people were on earth at the beginning of the Christian era, Bryan said he didn't know, then challenged Darrow to provide the information, which he couldn't—because he didn't know it either. When Darrow asked if Bryan had "any idea how old the Egyptian civilization was," Bryan merely answered "no." But he, not Darrow, had been to Egypt, read hieroglyphics, and had traveled the Nile.[9]

In the twelve-day trial that defined the term "media circus," more than one hundred reporters descended on the small Tennessee town. Folsom has argued that "the intellectual community—especially the urban media—did indeed oppose Bryan strongly," and most of the reporters opposed him.[10] Some were honest. Henry Hyde of the *Baltimore Sun* wrote that "the great crowd was plainly sympathetic toward Bryan and roared its approval as he countered the Darrow questions. . . ."[11] As Folsom concluded, Darrow, with "little knowledge of evolution and less of the Bible . . . went up to a celebrated witness and asked him impossible questions that no one could answer, and got away with it."[12] The big-city papers, for the most part, took Darrow's side, even though Scopes lost. Headlines heralded "Tennessee vs. Truth" (*The Nation*), "Tennessee vs. Civilization" (*New Republic*), "Thought: Free or in Chains?" (*School and Society*), "Inquisition in Tennessee" (*Forum*), and "Foreign Amazement in Tennessee" (*Literary Digest*). The *New York Times* praised Darrow's "rationalism, his utterances, and his courage," while *The Nation* called him "an enlightened man."[13] Novels such as *Elmer Gantry* and *Teeftallow* lambasted evangelists as phoneys and antievolutionists as shallow and corrupt. But in a stunning exposé, Burton Folsom discovered that illiteracy was *more correlated* with those who favored evolution teaching![14] Major antievolutionists were well-educated people: half of the North Carolina legislature that voted for an antievolution law had college degrees; all four doctors in the North Carolina House voted against evolution. Many of the famous preachers, including Aimee Semple McPherson, William Bell Riley, and J. Frank Norris, were hardly uneducated country hicks. They all had large, urban congregations.

The case was eventually thrown out in the appeal process on a technicality that the jury, not the judge, should have set Scopes's fine. While movies such as *Inherit the Wind,* and textbooks such as those quoted here, all suggest that the antievolution movement "died" at Dayton, in fact, the leading evolution textbook at issue in the Scopes trial was drastically revised after the trial, and the *Quarterly Journal of Biology,* reviewing two new biology textbooks introduced in 1929, noted, "They have been written with the statutes of Tennessee, [Mississippi], and Arkansas in mind."[15]

What did the trial do to Christianity and fundamentalism? Not nearly as much as the historians claimed. American Christianity has always endured ebbs and flows, from the Great Awakening to the Azuza Street Revival. Having just gone through a period of revival from 1900 to 1913, it was normal for the fires of faith to recede some, just as they had in previous eras. World War

II also intervened, making measurement of religious fervor in the United States more difficult. But immediately after the war, a new wave of fundamentalists and evangelists packed tents and stadiums, led by a powerful young orator named Billy Graham, whose first large revivals in 1949 in Los Angeles were filled to capacity, lasting eight weeks when they were slated for three. *Time* featured Graham on its cover the following year. His mission in New York filled Madison Square Garden for sixteen weeks. Likewise, Oral Roberts established his Evangelistic Association in 1947. The "father of the faith movement," Kenneth Hagin, also began his major ministry efforts in 1949, and the Full Gospel Businessmen's Fellowship International was established in 1951.

By the 1970s, the evolution of, well, evolution had hit some speed bumps. Scientists were less eager to cite evolution as "fact," choosing instead to downplay new theories that were in line with an emerging counterview called "creation science." Several states have sought to have creationism taught as a theory alongside evolution. Creationism was transformed into a broader theory called "intelligent design," to which a considerable number of scientists subscribe.[16] The main difficulty in bringing the debate into classrooms has been that courts label intelligent design as representing a religion, and therefore violating the Establishment Clause of the Constitution, even though creationists argue that atheism is itself a religion.

Neither fundamentalism nor creationism was dealt a permanent blow in the Scopes trial, despite the efforts of reporters and many historians to make it appear so. While nothing can change the now-entrenched view that Bryan "lost" the exchanges in Dayton, some efforts have been made to correct the record. Perhaps if Bryan becomes enough of a victim, someone will eventually produce a remake of *Inherit the Wind* in which he is portrayed sympathetically.

LIE #26

THE 1950S WERE DULL AND BORING AND CREATED A
GENERATION OF CONFORMISTS IN THE WORKPLACE AND HOME

*Increasing conformity in middle-class business and corporate life was mirrored in
the middle-class home. . . . Women were to forget any thoughts of continuing their
own careers. . . .*
—GEORGE BROWN TINDALL AND DAVID E. SHI, AMERICA:
A NARRATIVE HISTORY

*Modern mass society, some writers worried, inevitably produced loneliness and
anxiety, causing mankind to yearn for stability and authority, not freedom.*
—ERIC FONER, GIVE ME LIBERTY

Perhaps Hollywood—and television, in particular—had as much to do as
historians with developing this myth that the 1950s were full of "cookie-
cutter homes" with no tensions and no rebels. Ironically, no television show
had more of an impact on how we viewed the 1950s than a show that was aired
from 1974 to 1984, *Happy Days.* That series, featuring a teenaged Ron Howard as Ritchie Cunningham, a typical 1950s high school student, along with
the token rebel, "The Fonz" (Arthur Fonzarelli, played by Henry Winkler),
portrayed the decade as happy-go-lucky. Problems consisted of little more than
apologizing for toilet-papering a principal's yard, or learning to roller-skate.
Racial issues were almost nonexistent, although the original owner of the diner
that served as the main hangout in the show was Japanese (Pat Morita).
    On a superficial level, the series seemed to confirm the social critics' darker

views of the 1950s: that "corporate America" had created a population of lonely, career-driven, uncaring robots. Such analysts included William Whyte (*The Organization Man,* 1956), Sloan Wilson (*The Man in the Gray Flannel Suit,* 1955), and David Riesman (*The Lonely Crowd,* 1950), along with critics of consumerism such as Vance Packard (*The Hidden Persuaders,* 1957), who argued that advertisers had subtly programmed Americans to purchase what they instructed through marketing.[1] Add to this the views of C. Wright Mills that a "power elite" ran the nation and that ordinary citizens were virtual subjects, and you pretty much have the traditional view of the 1950s.[2]

The real story of the 1950s, however, is different and quite logical. A series of Cold War–related news stories in the late 1940s and early 1950s convinced many Americans that not only was the threat of communism real, it was imminent. The Soviets exploded their own atomic bomb in 1949 and China "went Communist" that same year. Spies such as the Rosenbergs and Klaus Fuchs demonstrated that the U.S. government's most important secrets had been compromised, and congressional investigations (topped by Joseph McCarthy's famous "list") exposed the presence of numerous hard-core Communists inside the U.S. government. Atomic Armageddon seemed a real possibility. North Korea's invasion of South Korea heightened tensions even more. And while foreign policy concerns constituted a serious weight on the minds of Americans, the slow emergence of blacks into mainstream society provided another source of tension. Radical, almost revolutionary forces were already at work in society—a point admitted even by Tindall and Shi, who, after haranguing students with how sexist American society was in the 1950s, concede that "overall the percentage of women working outside the home increased in the 1950s."[3]

In fact, Americans well understood the threats, both to national survival posed by Soviet bombers and to domestic tranquillity posed by a (in their view, probably inevitable and necessary) civil rights movement. These were dynamics of upheaval, and the citizens recognized them as such. Another factor that fostered uncertainty was welcomed by consumers—the automobile. Car production had shot up after World War II, making the United States the most motorized society on earth. Some 60 percent of all American households owned a car, and Detroit's automakers outproduced *every other nation on earth combined* in auto production.[4] In 1955 alone, U.S. carmakers made nine million cars, or more than four times the number turned out by Germany, France,

Italy, and Canada put together.[5] Even before the war, Americans had a ratio of one car to every 4.4 people, compared to one per 137 in Italy. The omnipresence of the automobile introduced a freedom of movement unseen in human history. Not only did people travel to work and local recreations, but for the first time, car vacations and long-term job relocation were feasible. After the 1956 National Highway Act was passed, highway driving rose 400 percent.

As Northerners moved south, Southerners moved west, and Westerners moved east, new cuisines, lifestyles, activities, and above all, surroundings confronted people at every turn. They handled such upheaval, but clearly a demand existed for familiarity and routine. At the very time that McDonald's appeared, offering the same menu anywhere in the country, the nation's eating establishments were diversifying as never before, offering the most varied menus in history. Travel exposed people to "rat holes" and "dives," prompting Kemmons Wilson to create his Holiday Inn chain, with its reputation for sameness and a certain degree of quality. When people moved all around for jobs and excitement, Top 40 radio reassured them with a list of recognizable music. Even Walt Disney, as he developed his famous theme parks, appreciated the need for a "Main Street," where people would instantly feel comfortable, no matter where they were from.

A bubbling upheaval underneath middle-class society was calmed by these conventions and traditions on the surface. Churches became bland, losing most of the evangelical fire that had led to the great revivals of previous centuries. (One major exception was Billy Graham, whose revivals swept the nation.) Denominations grew less contentious, making it easier to live next to people of different faiths. In art, where the critics celebrated the rebellious avant-garde style of Andy Warhol, Americans preferred overwhelmingly the paintings of Norman Rockwell—truly America's artist.

So-called average Americans had witnessed a stunning surge in purchasing power since the Great Depression and the forced savings of World War II. Armed with savings, and new forms of credit, Americans caused a housing and consumer explosion, bringing with it its own anxieties and pressures. The "cookie-cutter" houses of Levittown, New York, so superficially similar and nonthreatening, constituted a massive leap of faith in the American system for millions of homeowners who, for the first time, had substantial debt—but also substantial property. For the first time in the post-"sodbuster" era, where people built their own houses, Americans purchased premade housing by incurring debt. While in many ways the baby boomers born in the 1950s would produce some of our least impressive leaders in government and the arts, the adults of the 1950s included some of the nation's greatest achievers, including Walt Disney, Ronald Reagan, Lee Iacocca, Lyndon Johnson, George H. W. Bush, Bob Hope, John Wayne, Jimmy Stewart, Charles Lindbergh, Billy Graham, Oral Roberts, Joe DiMaggio, Ann Landers, Katharine Hepburn, Sidney Poitier, Walter Cronkite, Ray Kroc, and Kemmons Wilson. Their artistic and literary endeavors included movies such as *Lady and the Tramp* and *Bambi,* television shows such as *The Honeymooners* and *I Love Lucy,* music such as Leonard Bernstein's *West Side Story,* and books such as Herman Wouk's *Caine Mutiny* and Ayn Rand's *Atlas Shrugged.* Affordable airline travel appeared, and the fast-food industries were born during the 1950s; rock and roll changed not only American musical tastes but those throughout the world; and jazz and country music established themselves as two other American-originated mainstream music styles.[6]

The perceived "sameness" and conformity so many historians have noted in the 1950s was a necessary anchor to the phenomenal churning and dynamism of American society. Most Americans understood what was going on in their world, and steadied themselves through the familiar while enabling—and even encouraging—the radical changes under way. The calm waters of 1950s "Happy Days" masked a submerged tsunami that would crash ashore in the next decade.

LIE #27

RICHARD NIXON SENT BURGLARS INTO THE WATERGATE OFFICE COMPLEX

[Through] his approval of the . . . "plumbers" unit, [Nixon] certainly authorized [the break-in].
—DAVID E. HARRELL ET AL., UNTO A GOOD LAND

The [Watergate tapes] also proved that Nixon had not only known about plans to cover up the Watergate break-in but had also ordered it.
—JOHN MACK FARAGHER ET AL., OUT OF MANY

If historians hate Ronald Reagan, their contempt for Richard Nixon is even greater. *A Concise History of the American Republic* begins its section on Nixon by noting that Lyndon Johnson turned over the office to "a successor known neither for his imagination nor his scruples," and that Nixon was "long thought of as a 'born loser.'"[1] *Unto a Good Land,* reasonably fair in its treatment of Nixon, nevertheless informs its readers that he was "crude and shrewd," and "deeply embittered against the accumulated enemies of a lifetime."[2]

It is also accepted as conventional wisdom that Nixon himself orchestrated the May 28 and June 16 burglaries of the Watergate office complex in 1972. But to this day, the objective of the break-ins remains a source of contention. What did Nixon hope to gain by breaking into the Democratic National Committee's headquarters?

The movie *Hoax,* with Richard Gere, centers the break-ins around a diary that was going to reveal substantial (illegal) payments from Howard Hughes to Nixon. According to the film, Nixon ordered the Watergate break-ins to obtain a copy of this nonexistent diary before the Democrats got it.

Little attention, if any, is paid in textbooks to the theory that the burglaries were the brainchild of Nixon's own White House counsel, John Dean, who went on to reinvent himself as a moral critic of Republicans and has made a second career out of writing books bashing conservatives.[3] (Dean denied that he was the mastermind. To vindicate his name, he brought suit against the publisher and authors of *Silent Coup*, an explosive book about Watergate, and against G. Gordon Liddy.)

Under John Mitchell, former attorney general and head of the Committee to Re-elect the President (unfortunately referred to as CREEP), a special investigative group was in place before the Watergate break-ins, staffed by political operatives skilled in "opposition research." One of those operatives was G. Gordon Liddy, who reported to Mitchell. According to sworn testimony given by Liddy in Dean's lawsuit against Liddy, in November 1971, John Dean summoned Liddy and offered him a budget of a "half million [dollars] for openers" to direct a whole range of surveillance activities on the Democrats.[4] Liddy replied that it would take double that amount. Dean, Liddy said, was the "clearinghouse" for the activities.[5] Liddy was introduced to the president's inner circle as the one "in charge of dirty tricks." Liddy proceeded to outline a program called "Gemstone," on January 27, 1972, with Dean and Mitchell present.

At that point, Liddy maintained, the Democratic National Committee (DNC) headquarters was not a target. It was several months later, around the "end of May," 1972, when Jeb Magruder, who managed the CRP, instructed Liddy to gain access to the DNC on "Virginia Avenue Southwest," and find out what was inside the office of the DNC chairman, Larry O'Brien. Liddy "could tell this was not Magruder's idea. He was relaying instructions."[6] Moreover, Liddy said in sworn testimony that he had been "recruited by Mr. Dean to organize and deploy an . . . intelligence capability."[7]

Contrary to the widely believed idea that Liddy's team bugged O'Brien's phone, Liddy claims that the target of the break-in was instead the desk area of R. Spencer Oliver and his secretary, Ida "Maxie" Wells. But why? Oliver was in charge of the Democratic state chairmen. What could be the purpose of investigating him? Liddy testified under oath that "there was no call ever purportedly [made] from Lawrence O'Brien or by Lawrence O'Brien." However, most sources support the conclusion that in fact photos of DNC documents were taken, and that they were handed over to Jeb Magruder.[8] The transmissions were intercepted by a receiver in the Howard Johnson's hotel across the street, and Liddy became even more frustrated that there was little useful political material being generated at all. Nor was he shown the photographs that were taken. E. Howard Hunt, who kept detailed notebooks on the Watergate affair, found when he was being prosecuted that all materials he could have used to construct a defense were missing.

In their book *Silent Coup: The Removal of a President,* published in 1991, Len Colodny and Robert Gettlin argued that the break-in originated with Dean, and involved his personal concerns—not political "dirty tricks."[9] As Liddy testified, that "meant to me that what he [Magruder] wanted was the—whatever there would be of a derogatory nature about us that the Democrats might have. . . ."[10] Therefore, when Jeb Magruder told Liddy he wanted to know what Lawrence O'Brien had in his top drawer (the same place Magruder kept his own political "dirt"), it could have referred to political material, or, if Colodny and Gettlin are right, it could have referred to entirely personal material sought by Dean.

What people generally refer to as the "Watergate break-in" occurred on the night of June 16, 1972, and it was actually the *second* of two break-ins—the one intended to remove or reposition the bugs and to get more photos. When arrested that night, one of the burglars produced a key to Maxie Wells's desk. Since Wells was not even the secretary for O'Brien, but worked in Oliver's area, the objective of the break-in became even more puzzling. Indeed, in his book *Will,* Liddy stated that the purpose of the second break-in was to learn what the Democrats had "of a derogatory nature on us, not for us to get something on [O'Brien] or the Democrats."[11] Both *Silent Coup* and a subsequent investigative report aired on the A&E network alleged that the break-in was a quest for information about a prostitution ring.[12]

Gordon Liddy made the same claims and, as in *Silent Coup,* alleged that John Dean's wife, Maureen, was linked to the ring. The Deans brought a lawsuit against the authors and publisher of *Silent Coup* and against Liddy, which was ultimately settled out of court. In 1996, Liddy offered many days' worth of deposed testimony, in which he recounted his story. This was an important counterbalance to the historians, who had up until that time relied almost exclusively on Dean's version of Watergate, as put forth in his 1976 book, *Blind*

Ambition. But the more important lawsuit involved a $5.1 million action brought by Maxie Wells against Liddy for slander and defamation of character. This was thrown out of court in 1998, but the Fourth U.S. Court of Appeals reinstated it. In 2001, it was again dismissed when a jury could not reach a verdict. Liddy, although celebrating the dismissals as a victory, repeatedly told the press that he craved a trial.

In her suit, Wells claimed that Liddy had defamed her by saying that her desk contained photographs of the call girls. But the jury didn't buy the defamation allegation. One juror wryly noted, "I don't feel you can defame a desk or a phone."[13] When asked, under oath, about Dean, Liddy said, "Sir, as I have said before and I will repeat until my dying day, the man is a serial perjurer."[14]

Even the FBI agreed that John Dean was the "master manipulator of the cover up."[15] But once Howard Hunt's notebooks were destroyed, the main documentary evidence linking him with the burglary was gone. Even after Dean's participation became clear and he turned state's evidence, his exposure as the central figure in the break-in was limited. Dean was sentenced to one to four years in jail but spent only a few months in a special "safe house" facility. When Dean was sentenced, "Hanging Judge" John Sirica adjusted his sentence to time served. Liddy, on the other hand—who refused to "roll over" on his fellow conspirators—was sentenced to twenty years (and served four and a half before President Jimmy Carter commuted the sentence).

The official story, perpetrated by Bob Woodward and Carl Bernstein in *All the President's Men,* and the one basically endorsed by the Democratic-dominated Watergate Committee, was that Nixon, through his aides, had ordered the burglary out of "paranoia" and then tried to cover it up. The reality is quite different.

Nixon claimed his first knowledge of *any* part of the affair came while he was in Florida on June 17. Then he was briefed bit by bit until, on June 20, H. R. "Bob" Haldeman came to him with the news that Liddy had done it. Nixon was told there had been a break-in, but not the nature or purpose of it. In fact, Nixon's response in his memoirs, *RN,* was: "I heard many other theories about the reason for the break-in and bugging of the DNC. . . . I heard so many different stories because I asked the same question so many times: *Why bug the DNC?* [emphasis in original]."[16] On Monday, June 19 (after furious shredding of documents the previous day), Liddy went to the White House, where he was met by Dean. "There is one thing I've got to know right away," Dean said. "Did anybody in the White House—are they aware of what you were doing, that you were going in there?"[17] Objective observers could infer from that question two things: that Dean was genuinely interested in knowing if the president had knowledge of the purposes of the break-in, or just the opposite, that he had known what the purposes were, and wanted to make certain no one else knew. At any rate, Liddy, realizing what he knew could topple Nixon, offered to "go stand on a street corner while somebody shoots me," but according to Liddy, Dean replied, "I don't think we have gotten there *yet* [my emphasis]."[18]

When told, Nixon immediately thought Mitchell was involved, for Liddy worked for Mitchell in the Committee to Re-elect the President. When Dean met with Nixon and Haldeman on June 23, 1972, which produced the famous "smoking gun" tape (incriminating Nixon for knowing about the break-in), Dean had already convinced Haldeman that he had John Mitchell's blessing to use the CIA to block further FBI probing. Nixon told Haldeman to claim that it would impinge on national security and to invoke the CIA to stop the FBI probe. It is clear from Nixon's memoirs that he was amenable to this, and that he did not have to be prodded in the least to "contain" the investigation.

There it was: Nixon conspired to obstruct justice by having the CIA stop the FBI investigation. What was not known at the time—and certainly the Nixon-obsessed Watergate Committee and media then were not going to entertain—was whether the president was set up by Dean, who played on Nixon's paranoia to drag the president into the plot. Nixon was absolutely guilty of conspiracy, but was it after the fact?

Dean's inability—and anyone else's—to challenge Liddy successfully in court is one "scoreboard" on which to tally the veracity of the differing claims. The other is evidence provided by Colodny and Gettlin, evidence that, if true, completely overthrows not only the orthodoxy of "Nixon dreamed up the Watergate burglary," but also lands a crushing blow on the elevated (some would say pompous) position of Woodward and Bernstein and the *Washington Post*.

For his part, Nixon is not excused from any of the crimes he did commit, which were eerily similar to the obstruction of justice charges leveled at Bill Clinton nearly twenty-five years later. In the end, however, Nixon, unlike Clinton, ended up doing the right thing: resigning.

LIE #28

Neither Ronald Reagan's Election nor the "Contract with America" Proved the Triumph of Conservative Ideas

Where had all the voters gone? . . . the 1980 election reflected . . . "the largest mass movement of our time"—nonvoting.
—George Brown Tindall and David E. Shi, America:
A Narrative History

In truth, the favorite candidate of millions of Americans, unhappy with Carter but distrustful of the right-wing ideologue Reagan, was "None of the above."
—Samuel Eliot Morison et al., Concise History
of the American Republic

[The Contract with America was] a political wish list polished by consultants and tested in focus groups.
—Steven M. Gillon and Cathy Matson, The American Experiment

Reagan critics pounced on the low voter turnout in 1980 as an indicator that conservatism "didn't sell." One text claimed, "The election results . . . revealed a new low in voter turnout [and] the new president entered the White House having received a 'landslide' of only 26 percent of the electorate" of 93 million voters.[1] Little consideration is given to the possibility that in the previous decade, the presidents had included one who resigned in disgrace, one voted out for incompetence, and one who told Americans they were to blame for a malaise that had descended over the land. Is it possible that the number of voters was depressed by ten years' worth of cynicism? Nevertheless, in 1980 Reagan won with 26.7 percent of the total voting population (even with a lower turnout), more than did Bill Clinton in 1992 (23.6 percent). Both had third-party candidates in their races as well.

Another tack was to blame Carter for being inept—a truism, but not an explanation. Paul Boyer's *Enduring Vision* added, "Carter himself was a big part of the problem," while "demographics," we learn, "contributed to Rea-

Historians always attach a caption to a picture such as this that mentions how wealthy the Reagans' supporters were, or how they ushered in a decade of greed. But all presidents have had grand inaugural balls, and the 1980s witnessed the greatest boom in the nation's economy for all groups in sixty years, thanks to "Reaganomics."

gan's success."[2] When confronted with ideological change, claim Republicans just had more babies!

When it came to the 1994 election of a Republican House of Representatives for the first time in forty years, *The Enduring Vision* again explained away the change with low voter turnout: "Only 38 percent of eligible voters went to the polls," it reads, although it grudgingly admits, "Still, a significant ideological change seemed underway."[3] As far as the "Contract with America" was concerned, the effort was made to deny that people voted for conservative principles. "Opinion polls," claimed Alan Brinkley's *Unfinished Nation,* "suggested that few voters in 1994 were aware of the 'Contract' at the time they voted."[4] So not only did a very small number of people vote, they didn't know what they were voting for! Or, it seems to have missed the thoughtful academics that while people may not have been aware of the *term* "Contract with America," they were certainly aware of the *principles* (line-item vetoes, for example, had been sought by President Reagan and mentioned in several of his national speeches), and more important, of their local candidates, who championed those principles.

Equally stunning, the same historians either downplayed the anemic popular vote with which Bill Clinton won in 1992 or portrayed his victory as a triumph of liberalism. The election, one text claimed, "reversed 32 years of steady decline in participation," without noting that the high-profile (and slightly goofy) candidacy of Ross Perot accounted for most of the new turnout.[5]

When it came to the Contract with America, authors became downright nasty. Daniel Goldfield's *American Journey* portrayed the success of the Contract as emanating from "personal animosity."[6] Thomas Bailey and his coauthors in *The American Pageant* claimed the Contract constituted an "all-out assault on budget deficits and radical reduction in welfare programs." It only succeeded because Democrats' arguments were "drowned in the right-wing tornado that roared across the land."[7] The question of *why* a "right-wing tornado" would develop in the first place seemed beyond many of the academics. Few of them mentioned, for example, the incredible impact of radio host Rush Limbaugh, who had single-handedly rescued AM radio from oblivion and provided, for the first time in twenty years, a genuine alternative news outlet to the mainstream media. Indeed, the 1994 freshman House members named Limbaugh an honorary member for his influence on the election!

The textbooks could not acknowledge that (a) Americans were dissatisfied with *liberalism,* or (b) the Republicans won because of their ideas. Instead, George Tindall claimed that "many of the Republican freshmen were scornful of compromise and amateurs at the rules of order," without grasping that the voters themselves were "scornful" of the compromises that had led to the abuses of the House Bank (where members were "overdrawing" their checking accounts infinitely), or to the incredible tyranny within the Democratic House leadership (which prohibited Republican measures from even being brought up for a vote, so as not to embarrass Democrats when they voted against the legislation). Likewise, voters were sympathetic to the arguments that perhaps "career politicians" had run Washington for too long, and perhaps it was time to send a few amateurs back to government. As a result, among the freshmen were a former radio disc jockey (J. D. Hayworth), a former wide receiver for a pro football team (Steve Largent), a former television and music pop idol (Sonny Bono), and the black star quarterback of the University of Oklahoma (J. C. Watts—who was denied a place in the black caucus because as a Republican he wasn't "black enough"). These, and many other nonlawyers/first-time candidates won a stunning election in which numerous, heavily favored, and well-entrenched Democrats lost and where virtually *all* of the polls were wrong.

LIE #29

BILL CLINTON WAS IMPEACHED OVER SEX

This is [a] vast right-wing conspiracy that has been conspiring against my husband since the day he announced for president.
—HILLARY CLINTON, JANUARY 27, 1998, ON THE TODAY SHOW.

[Clinton aides] are already starting to whisper [about an] Ellen Rometsch strategy.
—REFERRING TO HOW J. EDGAR HOOVER DEALT WITH CONGRESSMEN INVESTI-
GATING PRESIDENT JOHN KENNEDY'S AFFAIR WITH AN EAST GERMAN SPY,
ABC'S THIS WEEK WITH SAM AND COKIE, FEBRUARY 8, 1998

Given the incivility of American politics by the 1990s and the media's insatiable appetite for scandal, it was apparent Clinton would be forced to defend himself.
—DAVID E. HARRELL ET AL., UNTO A GOOD LAND

Starr and his colleagues came up with very little they could use to legally impugn the president. Now they thought they had finally caught Clinton in an attempt to obstruct justice. . . .
—IRWIN UNGER, THESE UNITED STATES

Bill Clinton had the ignominy of being only the second president ever impeached. As in the impeachment of the first, Andrew Johnson, the Senate
went well outside its constitutional limitations to rule on the "seriousness of the
crime" rather than on whether, indeed, the president had committed the offenses

with which he was charged. In both cases, the Senate knew the president was guilty, and yet decided to render a decision on the nature of the offense and to refuse to convict a sitting president. Make no mistake: Bill Clinton lied repeatedly under oath to federal prosecutors, and he also had his attorney submit a false statement to a federal judge. In Richard Nixon's time, we called this "obstruction of justice," and presidents resigned over such behavior.

Nixon's arch-nemesis, special prosecutor Archibald Cox, noted that there "is a radical difference between what people expect of a president and his aides and what they will cynically tolerate from time to time in municipal aldermen or county commissioners."[1] Clinton's problems arose from his and Hillary's attempt to profit from a land scheme in Arkansas in a development project called Whitewater. Along with their Arkansas friends James and Susan McDougal, the Clintons had invested in Whitewater Development Company, which failed. Subsequently, Arkansas businessman David Hale claimed that then-governor Clinton had pressured him into giving an illegal $300,000 loan to Susan McDougal. Hale had his own problems, which led Clinton supporters to allege he had raised concerns only after his own legal situation became apparent.[2] The Clintons lost money and avoided a Securities and Exchange Commission investigation. Inquiries later concluded there was not sufficient evidence to charge the Clintons in the Whitewater affair.[3]

Nevertheless, the Clintons' role in Whitewater looked more suspicious after the White House deputy counsel, Vince Foster, committed suicide in 1993. Foster had dealt with the Clintons' Whitewater business while he and Hillary were law partners at the Rose Law Firm in Arkansas. Subsequently, Foster's office was cleaned out and the materials secretly held for five days before being turned over to authorities. In addition, in 1978 and 1979, while first lady of Arkansas, Hillary Clinton had turned a $1,000 investment in cattle futures into $100,000. (When an economist reviewed the trades, he concluded there was only a one in 250 million chance that the profits could have been made legally.)[4] The trades seemed to involve payoffs whereby James Blair, her adviser, assumed losses in trades so that she could post profits. Robert "Red" Bone, a commodities broker who had facilitated the trades for Blair through a securities brokerage firm, Refco, admitted that Hillary did not have sufficient funds in her account to cover her activities—in other words, Blair and/or Refco were "covering" Hillary. The question was, in return for what?

Whitewater opened the door for a special investigator. Clinton's attorney general Janet Reno appointed Robert B. Fiske in 1994 to examine the White-water transactions with special focus on Clinton's pressure on David Hale to make substantial loans to Madison Guaranty, and that a bank had concealed transactions related to Clinton's 1990 governor's race. Both Clintons were sub-poenaed. In August 1994, Fiske was replaced by Kenneth Starr, named by a three-judge panel to continue the inquiry. Under Starr, Hale and Susan Mc-Dougal were indicted, as was Webster Hubbell, who pleaded guilty to mail fraud and tax evasion at the Rose Law Firm that was related to Hillary Clinton. The notion that Starr didn't find any wrongdoing in Whitewater was false: three were indicted, and Clinton himself was found guilty of submitting a false statement to a federal court.

Meanwhile, Starr was directed by Attorney General Reno to expand his investigation into an apparently unrelated area, a sexual harassment lawsuit brought by a former Arkansas government employee, Paula Jones. Jones's suit alleged that when Clinton was governor of Arkansas, he asked her to perform oral sex. Jones told no one what happened until *The American Spectator* reported in 1994 that Clinton was using state troopers to procure women for trysts. Clinton, by then president, claimed executive privilege prevented him from appearing in court or testifying. But in 1997, the U.S. Supreme Court ruled against Clinton and the case proceeded. Eventually Judge Susan Webber Wright granted a summary judgment for Clinton, ruling that Paula Jones had not shown she had suffered any damages. Jones appealed, and the Eighth Circuit Court appeared to be more sympathetic to her claims. Consequently, Clinton paid Jones $850,000, without an apology, and Jones agreed to drop the case.[5] (In 2005, Jones took a lie detector test, which indicated she was telling the truth about the affair.)

The "rub" for Clinton—if such is an appropriate term in this case—came when Jones's attorneys deposed Clinton. By that time, a new scandal had surfaced for the president in the form of Monica Lewinsky, a twenty-two-year-old White House intern who had sex with Clinton on many occasions. Matt Drudge's "Drudgereport" Web site broke the news on January 17, 1998, that the press was covering up the Lewinsky affair, virtually forcing the "main-stream media" to report the story. Seeking to prove a pattern of behavior, Jones's lawyers asked Clinton, "Have you ever had sexual relations with Monica Lewinsky?" and Clinton denied it, committing possible perjury. At a re-markable 1998 press conference, Clinton publicly stated, "I did not have sexual relations with that woman, Miss Lewinsky. . . . I have never had sexual relations with [her]. I've never had an affair with her."[6] In the deposition, Jones's attorneys also asked him if he had ever given Lewinsky any gifts, to which he replied, "I don't remember. But I certainly could have."[7]

In fact, Clinton had given Monica a special book, Walt Whitman's *Leaves of Grass,* which he also gave Hillary as a love token. The First Lady was reported to have gasped, "He gave me the same book after our second date!"[8]

During this time, the Clinton spin machine was in full force, its hacks doing everything they could not only to destroy the reputations of Paula Jones and the other women who came forward with allegations of improper sex with Bill Clinton, but also to attack any media person who even suggested there might be any truth to the matter. And Hillary, having perfected Clinton-speak, answered in response to a question at a college speech, "Do you think the charges are false?" answered, "Certainly I believe they are false—absolutely."[9] Here she could "believe" whatever she wanted without having to actually answer a question about whether the charges *were* true. Then she followed up with her standard "vast right-wing conspiracy" response: "There has been a concerted effort to undermine his legitimacy as President, to undo much of what he has been able to accomplish. . . ."[10]

Starr's investigations turned up several other women who claimed to have been targeted by Clinton: Kathleen Willey, who said, "I had a similar thing happen to me in 1993"; and Juanita Broaddrick, who alleged Clinton raped her in 1978 during his campaign for Arkansas governor.[11] These and other serious allegations, especially obstruction of justice and suborning of perjury from witnesses before the grand jury, were included not only in Starr's report but also in the secret material Starr provided to the U.S. House of Representatives and U.S. Senate.[12] Only five congressmen, and no senators, ever looked at the material, and "*not one Democrat saw fit to examine the evidence* [emphasis in original]."[13] The House Judiciary Committee took up the report of the independent counsel and turned out a recommendation to impeach on four counts: two counts of perjury to a grand jury, one of obstruction of justice, and one of abuse of power. When the full House voted, it dropped one of the perjury charges and the abuse of power charge. The House voted 228–206 to impeach on the perjury charge and 221–212 on the obstruction of justice charge.

Getting a conviction in the Senate was nearly impossible, however. During the Watergate era, then-staffer Hillary Clinton had issued a report to her chairman that said if Richard Nixon came to trial, he should not be entitled to legal counsel in the Senate. But as first lady to an impeached president, Hillary wanted Bill to have all the legal protection he could get, and he had a number of lawyers making his case. Thirteen House "managers" acted as prosecutors, but one of their staffers—a Democrat named David Schippers—warned that Democratic senators had told him they would not convict under any circumstances: Senator Pete Domenici (R-NM) flatly stated, "I assure you that you will never get sixty-seven votes to remove the President from office."[14] This comment came *before* the Senate had heard a single word of testimony or reviewed a single shred of evidence. Senator Ted Stevens (R-AK) seemed even more cowardly, telling the leading Republican congressman of the Judicial Committee, Henry Hyde (IL), "Henry, I don't care if you prove he raped a woman and then stood up and shot her dead—you're not going to get sixty votes."[15] Given that the Republicans were in a majority in the Senate, the House managers had reason to think they might act responsibly—a view that was immediately quashed in their meeting with the senators. As Schippers noted after the first meeting between the House managers and Senator Trent Lott, the senators "were *afraid* to ask questions because they were *afraid* to look at the evidence."[16]

In fact, Schippers's team, asked by the House to determine whether there was any "substantial and credible evidence" that Bill Clinton was involved in a conspiracy to obstruct justice (note: nothing about sex in that charge!), came back with *fifteen* separate charges they urged the House to bring. *These were not Republicans, but bipartisan attorneys who examined the evidence that Clinton not only had lied, but had urged—and formulated schemes—to get others to lie and had tampered with witnesses in a federal case!* Schippers concluded that in the context of what Nixon was charged with, Clinton's offenses were far greater. And far from being "partisan" in its operations and attempting to "get Clinton," the House Judiciary Committee went out of its way to give Clinton extra-constitutional consideration in the case. For example, at the impeachment hearing itself, Clinton's defenders were given an astonishing thirty hours to present witnesses or offer evidence, while Schippers's team only had two and a half hours![17] Indeed, throughout the proceedings, the House impeachment attorneys were stunned at how little leeway they were given to present evidence and witnesses—all contrary to not only known law, but previous impeachment precedent. Rather than having to answer questions before the grand jury with the time-tested three options—tell the truth, lie, or plead the Fifth

Amendment—Clinton was given a fourth option, which allowed him to read, then refer to, a statement he had brought with him. Most important, Schippers noted, at no point—ever—did any of Clinton's defenders (either his attorneys or his political defenders in the House and Senate) offer a single piece of exculpatory evidence. Finally, because of "political concerns," the fifteen charges recommended by the attorneys were reduced to only four, and the obstruction of justice charge was completely gutted.

Worse than the partisan restrictions put on the prosecuting team, the Senate ignored its duty and changed the rules in midstream. As with the Andrew Johnson impeachment 130 years earlier, the Senate of the United States exceeded its constitutional charge, which required that the Senate *only* judge guilt or innocence: whether or not the charge rose to the level of an impeachable offense had already been decided by the House impeachment vote. Yet neither the Republican-controlled Senate of 1867 nor the Democrat-controlled Senate of 1998 followed the Constitution. Each also infringed on the House's constitutional mandate by considering whether the offense was serious enough to warrant removal. Five Republicans voted not guilty on the obstruction of justice charge; ten voted not guilty on the perjury charge. No Democrat voted against Clinton on any Senate vote.

Starr had proven beyond a shadow of a doubt that Clinton had lied to a grand jury; and more important, the evidence that *not one* senator looked at showed a pattern of sexual harassment and abuse that was criminal. But Clinton, whose job approval ratings remained in the 60 percent range, was insulated from any chance that any Democrat would defect. Two months after the Senate acquitted him, Clinton was given a contempt of court citation by Judge Susan Webber Wright for submitting a false statement. Clinton had to surrender his Arkansas law license, was suspended from the U.S. Supreme Court bar, and had to pay a $90,000 fine.[18] Once again, Starr—who had been vilified in the popular press as "obsessed with sex"—had been validated in the law. Had Clinton been lying about how much money he had in a bank account, or how many times he met with foreign officials, no one would have questioned that his perjury to a grand jury was also obstruction of justice. But because Starr's evidence involved sexual allegations, Clinton's defenders portrayed the special prosecutor as a Puritan on a crusade to brand Clinton with a scarlet letter. Clinton escaped justice because the Senate subverted the Constitution to render a verdict it thought the voters wanted.

LIE #30

George W. Bush Was Selected, Not Elected, in 2000, and Votes Were Stolen on His Behalf

. . . a statewide recount—could have produced enough votes to tilt the election his [Gore's] way, no matter what standard was chosen to judge voter intent . . .
— THE NEW YORK TIMES, SEPTEMBER 17, 2001

"[Al Gore] thought the court's ruling was wrong and obviously political," [Gore's attorney, David Boies, said]. So he considers the election stolen? [asked a reporter]. "I think he does—and he's right."
— JOHN HEILEMAN, NEW YORK MAGAZINE, MAY 21, 2006

For haters of President George W. Bush, no sin has been greater than that of the perceived "stolen 2000 election." Most of then-vice president Al Gore's political cadre believed the U.S. Supreme Court handed Bush the victory by "shutting down" the recounts of voting in Florida. On December 12, 2000, the Court ruled by a vote of 7–2 that the Florida Supreme Court's scheme for recounting ballots was unconstitutional. It then, in a second vote of 5–4, found no alternative scheme that could be carried out based on the schedule of the Florida legislature, which itself was governed by the requirements of the U.S. Electoral College and the Constitution. Florida secretary of state Katherine Harris's certification of Bush as the winner of Florida's 25 electoral votes based on his final official victory margin of 537 ballots, thus giving him 271 electoral votes and the election, was allowed to stand.

During the vote counting, numerous irregularities had appeared across

Florida. Several television networks proclaimed Gore the winner before the polls had even closed in the western part of the state—the Panhandle—which was in a different time zone. Florida polls closed at 8:00 p.m., Eastern Standard Time, but ten heavily Republican counties were on Central Time. Not only did ABC, CBS, NBC, MSNBC, CNN, and even FOX (later accused of bias *for* Bush) incorrectly announce that all polls in the state had closed at 8:00 Eastern, but CBS issued some eighteen separate comments to the effect that all polls in Florida were closed. Thousands of (likely) Bush voters went home, convinced their vote didn't count and that the election was over. Even Bob Beckel, a Democrat strategist, claimed Bush lost at least 8,000 votes in the Panhandle alone. McLaughlin and Associates, a Republican polling firm, put the number at 11,500 who were dissuaded from casting ballots. Economist John Lott, using estimates that attempted to control for a myriad of factors, concluded Bush lost between 7,500 and 10,000 votes based on previous elections' returns from those counties.[1] Bill Sammon spoke to many voters who turned away upon hearing the news.[2]

The actual impact of the early call of Florida for Gore has actually been *underestimated*. For years, a myth had developed that Gore "won the popular vote" but lost the election. Yet that was not true if the impact of the early call was factored in nationally. Not only would Bush have gained thousands more votes in Florida, but nationwide, untold numbers of people didn't bother to vote because they thought the election was decided. If there were ten thousand votes in Florida that would have gone to Bush, how many nationally did he lose? Enough to in fact give him the popular vote victory as well?

Of course, the recount itself was triggered by Palm Beach residents who claimed they had misunderstood the "butterfly ballot" and marked Pat Buchanan (the Reform Party candidate) instead of Al Gore. The notorious butterfly ballot used in Palm Beach had the names of candidates on one side, with a black arrow in bold pointing across the spine to a corresponding hole to be punched. Moreover, there was a line separating each name. Instructions at the polls told voters, "If you make a mistake, return your ballot card and obtain another," yet according to the claim made by the Gore camp, rather than do that, thousands of voters simply poked a *second* hole in the ballot. Later, they realized what they had done and contacted, not election board officials, but the Democratic Party! About an hour before the polls closed, the Democratic

National Committee (DNC) called a Texas telemarketing firm and hired it to phone thousands of Palm Beach voters. TeleQuest, the firm, called 5,000 voters, 98 percent of whom had already voted, and instructed them to return to the polls "so that this problem can be fixed."[3] Assembling a list of 2,400 voters, TeleQuest gave the names to the Democratic National Committee, which then did something remarkable: nothing.

Since it was not yet known whether the votes would be "needed"—because early calls of Florida had Gore winning—nothing was made public. But by the wee hours of Wednesday morning, when George Bush had amassed a lead, the DNC tracked down the voters and urged them to swear affidavits claiming they had been fooled by the butterfly ballot. However, it was not a semiblind octogenarian who filed the first lawsuit claiming he had been baffled, but a Democratic Party operative named Andre Fladell. Lawyers began drafting their motions for the courts while the shock troops of the Democratic Party, led by Rev. Jesse Jackson, descended on government offices in Palm Beach demanding "Every vote must count!"

By that time, Bush had a lead of about 800 votes, but based on an AP analysis of Florida county-level tallies, it would hold up. Gore's spokespeople claimed that "more than 20,000 voters in Palm Beach County, who in all likelihood thought they were voting for Al Gore, had their votes count for Pat Buchanan. . . ."[4] The Gore camp concluded that the only way to win was to keep counting votes until it produced the desired result. In addition to the "wrongly punched" ballots (for Buchanan instead of Gore), there were more than 19,000 ballots not counted at all because they had two holes—people had voted for more than one candidate. Thus, the Democrats came up with the magic phrase that "20,000 people did not have their votes counted" in Palm Beach. Gore, it was argued, would have won 64 percent of the "overvotes" as well. Gore's camp did not want to hear that the butterfly ballot was *originated* in a Democrat-dominated county; *approved* in that same county; and *administered* by Democrats under Theresa LePore, a Democrat, in the Palm Beach Elections Office. It was also published ahead of time in the papers. Ultimately, Gore knew that the butterfly ballots would come to nothing.

Bush was not about to allow Gore's team to suddenly "discover new votes" that were not there earlier. James A. Baker III, who had worked in the administration of George H. W. Bush, was brought in to watch developments for the

Bush camp. But Gore had succeeded in creating doubt in the mind of the public, and now pinned his hopes on the recount. In one early recount, Bush's lead had slipped to a mere 224 votes in Florida. Gore, who had conceded earlier in the night, now had to "un-concede" and insist on another recount. Florida had already recounted the ballots twice—all six million votes. Now, new tallies could be requested on a county basis for a hand recount, but Gore knew that requesting all sixty-seven counties to conduct hand recounts would not be feasible. For one thing, his own staff couldn't police the recounts to make sure they "came out right." So he settled on demanding hand recounts for Palm Beach, Miami-Dade, Broward, and Volusia counties, which were full of rich liberals and offered Gore the best chance of getting more votes. Gore asked for a recount from canvassing boards by Thursday (as Friday was the observed Veterans Day holiday).

The counts began degenerating into a circus, with board members holding ballots up to the light to determine if voters had actually punched out the chads—the rectangles of paper that showed whether someone had voted for a candidate. (Both Republican and Democratic operatives breathed down the necks of the election board officials to ensure that they were being fair.) Each ballot had to be examined by the entire canvassing board, all under scrutiny of the twenty-four-hour cable news networks. The world learned the difference between a "hanging chad," where the chad was simply not dislodged, which "may be counted as a vote," and an "indented" or "pregnant chad," which "should not be counted as a vote." Each board member had to hold the ballot up to the light to see if light showed through—if so, it was a vote. At that point, Democrat lawyers lobbied to get the members to change their angles to see if any light at all was showing through!

Throughout this process, the election boards changed their own rules repeatedly—itself a violation of Florida voting laws, which already bestowed considerable latitude on the board members, allowing them to "discern the intent of the voter." Now the board members were deciding who the voter "really wanted" to vote for. But after only a few hours, the boards realized they had used shifting standards for all their previous work. Increasingly, it was becoming obvious to even Democratic Party operatives that there simply was not enough time to recount all of the votes by hand—and fight over every single ballot—before Florida law required the secretary of state to certify the election, according to which all county returns had to be received by the secretary's office by 5:00 p.m. on the seventh day after the election. Any missing counties were to be ignored. The Florida Supreme Court (made up of seven Democratic justices) rejected a request by the secretary of state to block all tardy recounts, and thus the "re-recounting" began in earnest. (At the same time Gore's team sought to have 19,000 double-punched ballots viewed as legitimate, it was also working overtime to deny the votes of military men and women who had sent in absentee ballots, eventually disqualifying 149 military ballots.)

By Friday, November 17, Gore had gotten 1,420 absentee ballots disqualified, but new absentee ballots had boosted Bush's lead to 930 votes. But just as it appeared Gore was out of options, the Florida Supreme Court ruled (in complete contradiction to Florida state law) that hand recounts had to be added to the statewide total if completed by Sunday, November 26. Gore had another 115 hours to "find" votes. Unfortunately for Gore, this also allowed the Bush team to revisit the disqualified military ballots, some of which now were reinstated by the canvassing boards, giving Bush another 176 votes. Even so, the canvassing boards were hesitant to begin complete recounts by hand, knowing they could not possibly complete the process in time for the constitutional requirements of certification. And when they did decide to continue—as in the case of Palm Beach County—they waited even longer for the Florida Supreme Court to rule on the process. Then a new problem crept up: some boards had begun "determining the intent" of the voter by counting "pregnant" chads, at which point Republicans now noted that this disqualified hundreds of ballots that had both "hanging" chads and "dimpled" chads.

Although the Miami-Dade board had decided it couldn't possibly recount all 600,000 ballots in time for the Supreme Court deadline of December 12 to certify the electors, the members could recount the 10,750 "undervotes," or ballots that had no selection at all (ignoring the possibility that people actually might have chosen not to vote for a presidential candidate). This was the basis of Republicans' claims that the ballots were not treated equally—if *some* ballots were recounted, then *all* ballots in the state had to be recounted. A series of lawsuits followed, in which the Florida Supreme Court repeatedly tried to defy Florida's laws, and in which appeals to the United States Supreme Court resulted in public chastening. Undeterred, the Florida Supreme Court agreed to hear new arguments on throwing out some 20,000 ballots from Seminole and Martin counties.

On December 11, 2000, the U.S. Supreme Court heard *Bush v. Gore,* in which George Bush's lawyers argued that selective recounting as had already been attempted (and which Gore wanted to continue) was unconstitutional, denying the "one man, one vote" rule. Either the whole state had to be recounted by hand (which Bush was confident would show him the winner, based on the disallowed absentee ballots and gains made in pro-Republican counties) or none of it could be recounted. The United States Supreme Court agreed by a 7–2 (not 5–4) vote.[5] The Supreme Court thus stopped the slipshod recount that was continuing in hiccups in Florida and allowed Harris to certify Bush as the winner. Critics tried to make the important Supreme Court vote the *second* opinion, which was 5–4, which held that since the current recount process was unconstitutional, no alternative scheme could be devised in time to comply with the limits established by the Florida legislature. Indeed, the decision cited the shifting standards used by Palm Beach in departing from its own 1990 rule, then changing the new rule to allow more Gore-friendly ballots.

The Court—particularly the liberal members—Stephen Breyer, David Souter, Ruth Bader Ginsburg, and John Paul Stevens—did a monstrous disservice to the nation with the second opinion. It was obvious to anyone that millions of ballots could not be hand-counted in two days, or in time for the December 12 constitutional requirements to name electors. (The Electoral College didn't actually vote until December 18, which had encouraged Gore's supporters to try to extend the deadline until the 18th). For Justice John Paul Stevens to claim that "preventing the recount from being completed will inevitably cast a cloud on the legitimacy of the election" was correct only if there was a reasonable chance of completing such a full recount. And, issuing a final slapdown to the Florida Supreme Court, the U.S. Supreme Court noted, "When a court orders a statewide remedy, there must be at least some assurance that the rudimentary requirements of equal treatment and fundamental fairness are satisfied." As Justice Antonin Scalia wrote, "Count first, and rule upon legitimacy afterwards, is not a recipe for producing election results that have the public acceptance democratic stability requires."[6] The second (5–4) vote gave the mistaken impression that the Court did not overwhelmingly find constitutional violations of the Florida recounting process. It did. Nevertheless, the press and the Left would forever complain that by a 5–4 vote, the Supreme Court "selected" Bush, when in fact he not only won the Electoral

College fair and square, but without the early call of Florida likely would have won the popular vote as well.

*P*ostscript: In November 2001, the University of Chicago's National Opinion Research Center, with funding from the *Miami Herald,* conducted a comprehensive review of all uncounted machine ballots in the Florida 2000 election and concluded that the only way Gore could have won was by "using counting methods that were never requested, including 'overvotes.'" Yet even this standard could not meet the constitutional test set by the Supreme Court for a statewide hand recount, which the consortium reluctantly agreed Bush would have won.

LIE #31

Muslim Terrorists Are Poor and Uneducated and Hate Us Because We Support Israel

"I have six root causes [for terrorism, and] poverty is THE main factor."
——Bill Cristionson, former CIA director,
in the Washington Post, April 10, 2002

Poverty is a cause of terrorism. . . .
——Bob Carr, New South Wales Iraq Appeal, June 8, 2003

Nineteen hijackers died in the suicide attacks. All were from the Middle East;
twelve were from underdeveloped, highly tribal southwestern provinces of Saudi
Arabia.
——David E. Harrell et al., Unto a Good Land

[They originate because of] the vast global inequities in which terrorism is ulti-
mately rooted.
——Barbara Ehrenreich, Village Voice, October 9, 2001

When Bob Carr, premier of New South Wales, said, "The Al-Qaeda leader, Osama Bin Laden, and others like him get their support because they call on people who are living in poverty in the Gaza strip and elsewhere," and that "people turn to terrorism because they live in despair," he reflected a popular analysis of the root cause of terrorism. Surprisingly, even President George W. Bush said, "We fight against poverty because hope is an answer to terror," and Bill Clinton's economic adviser Laura Tyson said, "We live in a world of unprecedented opulence and remarkable deprivation, a world so interconnected that poverty and despair in a remote region can harbor a network of terrorism. . . ."[1] A Dutch scholar claims "a range of social welfare policies . . . will on balance reduce preferences for terrorism by reducing economic insecurity, religious-political extremism, income inequality, and poverty."[2]

There is a reason so many people want to believe that the Muslim terrorists who attacked the United States on 9/11 and those who have engaged in bombings in Spain, Britain, Indonesia, and elsewhere do so because they are "downtrodden," or uneducated, or frustrated with their material conditions. The reason so many desperately want to believe this is that the alternative is difficult to embrace: that some element in Islam itself is directing these terrorists, and that, in fact, they may really believe that the Koran says they should kill all infidels!

Of course, the truth is that few, if any, of the Islamic terrorists have acted because of their dire material circumstances. The Dutch study excepted, most research has found no evidence of a link between poverty and terrorism. Alberto Abadie, for example, working for the National Bureau of Economic Research, found that the risk of terrorism was not significantly higher for poorer countries, and that a nation's level of political freedom is a more important factor.[3] Alan Krueger and Jitka Maleckova, writing in the *Journal of Economic Perspectives*, concluded "there was little reason for optimism that a reduction in poverty or an increase in educational attainment would meaningfully reduce international terrorism."[4]

When one examines the individual murderers and terrorists, a picture of affluent, educated Middle Easterners emerges. Sayyid Qutb, the generally accepted founder of the radical Islamic movement, "held a comfortable post as supervisor in the ministry of Education" in Egypt, and was "in the mainstream of the vast bureaucratic middle class."[5] Like most of the radical Islamists, he was supremely threatened by sex. His experiences in Greeley, Colorado, at Northern Colorado University in 1949—hardly a time when "women's lib" was in full bloom—terrified him about "sexual mixing." His revulsion peaked when he attended a dance where "naked legs filled the hall, arms draped around waists, chests met chests, lips met lips, and the atmosphere was full of love."[6] God forbid we have an atmosphere of love! His eventual successor in the radical movement, and Osama bin Laden's perpetual sidekick, Ayman al-Zawahiri, likewise "grew up in a quiet middle-class suburb" of Cairo.[7] His father was a doctor who, along with his mother, came from one of the most prominent families in Egypt. Zawahiri was well educated, attending medical school.

Osama bin Laden's background is well known: he came from a wealthy family whose riches came from construction projects obtained through ties to the king of Saudi Arabia. Richard Miniter points out the notion that Osama bin Laden could finance terror entirely out of some "vast fortune" is a myth; it is true that from 1970 to about 1994 he had some $24 million flow through his hands, although much of that was for his father's construction company, with which he worked.[8]

Marc Sageman studied some 400 terrorists and found that an astonishing 75 percent came from the middle class and two-thirds had a college education.[9] Nasra Hassan's study of Palestinian terrorists found similar characteristics: "None of them were uneducated, desperately poor, simple-minded or depressed. Many were middle class. . . . Two were the sons of millionaires."[10] In a recent study of 149 suicide bombers in Iraq, more than 50 came from wealthy Saudi Arabia—more than three times the number who came from Iraq (16); 8 came from Syria, and 7 from Kuwait.[11] One of the few bombers *Newsweek* profiled was a teacher, another a college student. The 2007 plot to detonate multiple car bombs in England was planned and was attempted—until it was foiled—by six doctors, a medical student, and a lab technician. One of them was a neurosurgeon.[12] The London *Times* reported that a senior al-Qaeda figure in Iraq warned a British cleric in April that attacks were on the way, saying "those who cure you will kill you."[13] After studying 350 Latin American, European, and Middle Eastern terrorists, Charles Russell and Bowman Miller observed that two thirds came from "middle or upper classes" and that the "vast majority . . . were quite well educated."[14] Reuven Paz, an Israeli researcher, looked at 154 Arab terrorists killed in Iraq in 2004 and found many were married, had good educations, and came from wealthy Saudi families.[15]

Interestingly, individual wackos such as Unabomber Ted Kaczynski are exceptions to the rule: "While terrorism is a profoundly anti-social activity, from the terrorists' point of view it is also a highly social one. It is carried out by groups—groups that don't tolerate sociopaths. . . ."[16] Far from being "deranged loners," 73 percent of the terrorists are married, and Sageman found that kinship was a factor in some 14 percent of the networks, including the "family" of Khalid Sheikh Mohammed, which helped orchestrate the 9/11 attacks. The Hamburg cell that carried out the 9/11 attacks were all "alienated and friendless until they united."[17] Indeed, Sageman's study found that 88 percent of the terrorists were related, or were connected by marriage or friendship to other terrorists. Michael Bond, surveying the evidence, noted the terrorists were "no worse educated, no poorer and no more religious than anyone else."[18]

The one flaw in the research is that it neglects to show that while most studies correctly note Muslim terrorists as not particularly religious before they became terrorists, one of the main factors causing them to bond was renewed Islamic vigor. Many of the 9/11 hijackers, for example, were attracted to the stricter lifestyle touted by Mohammed Atta, although few, in fact, followed it at all: just days before they hijacked the airplanes and killed thousands of people, they were visiting strip bars in Florida. Whether it is a suppressed sexual anxiety or pure religious fanaticism that drives the terrorists, it is fairly certain at this point that poverty plays no role in their pathology.

LIE #32

THE NEWS MEDIA IS OBJECTIVE, FAIR, AND BALANCED— AND ALWAYS HAS BEEN

"Look Bernie [Bernard Goldberg], of course there's a liberal bias in the news. All the networks tilt left."
—ANDREW HEYWORD, EXECUTIVE PRODUCER, CBS NEWS, IN 1993,
QUOTED IN BERNARD GOLDBERG, BIAS: A CBS INSIDER
EXPOSES HOW THE MEDIA DISTORT THE NEWS

Okay, I admit, there is not a history textbook that flatly says this. But it's a pretty common myth, and one perpetuated by the "mainstream media" every day. Many adult Americans grew up in the age of Huntley and Brinkley, Walter Cronkite, or even Edward R. Murrow, all of whom were viewed as objective or "fair," but none of whom really were. However, the difference between them and the modern television newspeople is that they, at least, were good actors, and concealed their true partisan colors. Certainly, their own views helped shape what was covered, and in the case of Murrow, his famous slime attack against Joseph McCarthy was overt, as was Cronkite's disgust with the Vietnam War.[1] Nevertheless, Americans, by and large, trusted news organizations to provide reasonably accurate, and generally honest, reports of the day's events.

In fact, this approach to fact-based news only dated back to the American Civil War. Prior to that time, *all* news was partisan or motivated solely by the goal of electing a certain party's candidates. It might come as a shock, but almost none of the antebellum papers were interested in making money: there were only a handful of newspapers that depended on circulation to stay alive, such as James Gordon Bennett's *New York Herald* or Joseph Pulitzer's *New York World*.[2] These were by far the exceptions.

From the time of the Revolution until the 1820s, American papers (always with some exceptions) tended to be focused heavily on local news, and were somewhat impartial.[3] Certainly some papers were "Jeffersonian" and others were "Federalist," and their rhetoric could get heated.[4] Parties themselves, however, did not directly fund or control most papers.

That changed drastically when Martin Van Buren conceived of a new political party based on patronage, the Jacksonians or Jacksonian Democrats (later, just Democrats). He knew that getting out the vote was the key to victory at the polls. A number of structural political reforms made this possible—eliminating property requirements for voters, national conventions for candidates, the demise of "King Caucus" (the practice before Andrew Jackson's time of having all candidates selected by small groups of influential citizens in the caucus)—but in the end, propaganda in its purest form was needed. Van Buren intended to supply it. Jacksonians bought newspapers, installed their own men as editors, and the papers became no more than "propaganda agencies," as one historian labeled them.[5] No editor was more loyal to the Democratic cause than Duff Green, with his *United States Telegraph*.[6] Green's *Telegraph* flatly condemned neutrality as an absence of principles, and overall, editors increasingly inserted their points of view into papers.[7] Green obediently repaid his political masters with pro-Jackson editorials, and obligingly turned out a special extra paper during the 1828 election with a circulation of forty thousand.[8]

Green was not alone in his view that objectivity was to be avoided: a Louisville paper criticized an Indiana paper for its neutrality, noting "in this State, people have more respect for an open, independent adversary than for dumb partisans . . . who are too imbecile to form an opinion."[9] One Jacksonian editor stated that "we most of all abhor and detest . . . a neutral paper. It pretends to be all things to all men." This attitude has been confirmed in studies of content, in which the percentage of editorial comment in "news" stories increased, then nearly doubled between 1847 to 1860. Many editors owed their jobs directly and specifically to the Jacksonians, frequently slipping back and forth between editor positions and postmaster jobs. Jackson himself appointed numerous editors to salaried political positions, including many postmasters, while nationally it is estimated that fifty to sixty editors had been given plum political jobs.[10] Gerald Baldasty found that in 1830 the state of Georgia had eleven newspapers, "all of them embroiled in political fights," and the party had at least three patronage papers in each state, with the *Globe* serving as their pilot for editorial policy.[11] By 1850, political bias so dominated the newspaper industry that the U.S. Census estimated nearly 80 percent of American papers were partisan, while other estimates put the number of partisan papers at close to 100 percent![12]

Van Buren's program was devastatingly successful in winning elections, but none of the newspapers could sustain themselves on the basis of their "news." Publishers carried delinquent customers for months, their deficits offset through political contributions, "loans," and subsidies from the U.S. Congress.[13] Richard John, a historian of the postal system, concluded that the subsidization of newspapers through the public mails constituted an important economic bias by favoring the transmission of less thoughtful, considered, and shorter newspapers at the expense of books, which were longer and more costly. By the 1830s, "the news made up roughly 95 percent of the total messages" and equaled the number of letters that passed through an average post office.[14] And since more than half of that news was stridently partisan, one could infer that by the 1830s, partisan propaganda constituted almost half of all postal deliveries.

The Civil War brought radical change. People wanted to know if their sons, brothers, and fathers were fighting, and if they won or lost, and, most important, if they had been killed. Papers published casualty lists, and within the four-year course of the war, most major papers adopted the "inverted pyramid" style of reporting, in which the most important facts (and only facts) were presented first and the least important last. Virtually overnight, editors abandoned the partisan approach to papers and adopted the objective, fact-based approach. "Facts; facts; nothing but facts," said one editor. "So many peas at so much a peck; so much molasses at so much a quart."[15] While the war was the single greatest factor affecting the transformation of the press, business demands played a role. Increasingly papers relied less on party subsidies and had to survive on their own circulations—and that, in turn, brought an unwillingness to alienate up to half of the consumers who might identify with the opposing political party. Comments by editors starkly contrasted with the sentiments offered by Duff Green and other partisan editors. Lawrence

Gobright, the AP's Washington agent, concluded, "My business is merely to communicate facts. My instructions do not allow me to make any comments upon the facts which I communicate. . . . My dispatches are merely dry matters of facts and detail."[16] The share of objective or "nonbiased" papers in circulation rose to more than 66 percent by 1900, while stories labeled by journalism researchers as "biased" declined especially sharply after 1872.[17]

In 1922, the American Society of Newspaper Editors adopted the "Canons of Journalism," which embraced the objective position by stating that the "primary purpose of gathering and distributing news and opinion is to serve the general welfare by informing the people and enabling them to make judgements on the issues." Article IV said that "every effort must be made to assure that the news content is accurate, free from bias and in context, and that all sides are presented fairly."[18] *Editor & Publisher* magazine boasted that the new standards would eliminate the "Typhoid Marys of Journalism."[19] Likewise, the Associated Press's "Managing Editors' Code of Ethics" reflected similar concerns with fairness, accuracy, and truth-telling:

- The good newspaper is fair, accurate, honest, responsible, independent, and decent.
- Truth is its guiding principle.
- It avoids practices that would conflict with the ability to report and present news in a fair, accurate, and unbiased manner.[20]

Veteran reporter Lou Guzzo recalled about the 1950s, "When a reporter on any beat dared fracture the barrier of objective reporting, his copy was tossed back to him for immediate revision."

No city editor he worked for "tolerated even the slightest hint of bias in news reporting," Guzzo noted, and "the newspaper itself espoused so subtle an editorial stance that virtually no one could state with authority that the *Cleveland Plain Dealer* editorial board or the staff was conservative, liberal, or whatever. . . ."[21]

Modern historians and journalists have sneered at the attempt at objectivity, calling the reporters little more than "notetakers," but in fact the papers began to slowly change during the New Deal era.[22] Franklin D. Roosevelt, detested by many editors, was fawned over by reporters, who helped him revise his numerous lies about a "personal friend" in a specific situation (the friend, and the situation, always changed).[23] As Burton Folsom points out, the press overwhelmingly cooperated with FDR. In an effort to portray him as a healthy man, the press never showed him in his wheelchair. Some reporters were even drafted to help design New Deal policy. They also ignored his cheating on Eleanor. He gave reporters and editors private meetings, jobs in his administration, and government loans.[24]

For the most part, the press remained nonpartisan until 1960 when, for a variety of reasons, reporting began to turn rapidly leftward—a shift that occurred well before the Vietnam War. While still maintaining a pretense of objectivity and fairness, reporters, editors, and television news anchors began to steadily slant the news. They repeatedly proclaimed their objectivity, yet survey after survey has shown that the media voted overwhelmingly Democratic in every election since 1970—and the percentages weren't even close. A Roper poll, for example, found that 91 percent of journalists surveyed voted for Bill Clinton in 1992. The public saw the press as liberally biased as well: an October 2003 Gallup poll found that 45 percent of Americans said the news media was too liberal, while only 14 percent said it was too conservative.[25]

Although denied by nearly every influential journalist in the mainstream media, the press is biased, badly slanted to the left. This is not opinion: this is the result of countless scholarly studies in *Journalism History* and *Journalism & Mass Communication Quarterly,* among others. Journalism scholar Jim Kuypers, in 2002, surveying several press treatments of volatile public issues, found "there is a demonstrable liberal bias to the mainstream press in America."[26] As Stuart Garner, CEO of Thomson Newspapers, Inc., candidly admitted, most modern reporters "want to save the world, whether the world wants to be saved or not."[27] Whereas Joseph Pulitzer's motto was "Accuracy! Accuracy! Accuracy!" Jack Fuller, president of the Tribune Publishing Company, observed, "Journalism's unacknowledged shame is how often it fails to live up to Pulitzer's standard even with respect to the most commonplace details."[28] Is it any wonder that a June 2000 Gallup poll, rating the top ten confidence-inspiring institutions, put the military at the top, named by 64 percent of the respondents, followed by the church (56 percent), police (54 percent), the Supreme Court (47 percent), and the presidency (42 percent). Newspapers and television news ranked number nine and ten, respectively, with only 37 percent and 36 percent of respondents saying they had "great" or even "some" confidence in those institutions.[29]

Perhaps the lack of confidence stems from the fact that the major newspapers and television news outlets don't even try to improve. The Media Research Center maintains a Web site documenting bias in the 2004 elections, and coverage of the 2008 primaries suggests nothing has changed.[30]

NATIVE AMERICANS WERE GREAT ENVIRONMENTALISTS, WHILE WHITE SETTLERS DESTROYED THE BUFFALO

The changes they produced in some areas were nearly as cataclysmic as those that occurred during the Ice Age. . . . Having killed off the giant herds, ranchers and farmers quickly shifted to cattle. . . .

—JOHN MACK FARAGHER ET AL., OUT OF MANY

[There] is the assumption that Native Americans were either poor, primitive, starving savages whose numbers were too low to have any impact on the "pristine" landscape . . . or that native peoples were children of nature and original conservationists who were too wise to overuse their environment.

—CHARLES E. KAY, "ABORIGINAL OVERKILL AND NATIVE BURNING" (1995)

Leave it to Hollywood to come up with a classic image that stands history on its head. No one better illustrated the power of the visual image to send a (wrong) message than the "Crying Indian," Iron Eyes Cody, who was featured in Keep America Beautiful's 1979 public service ad, "People Start Pollution, People Can Stop It." Although Earth Day, first observed on March 21, 1971, officially touched off the environmental or ecology movement in the United States, this famous ad firmly ensconced it. In the ad we see an Indian paddle his canoe up a polluted stream as smokestacks belch their black soot into the blue sky. Then he walks to the top of a hill where one expects to see a glorious western landscape, only to find a highway and—the coup de grâce—a car speed by, whereupon the passengers throw a bag of trash out the window that lands at the Indian's feet. The camera pans to his face, at which point a single tear streams down his cheek.

Given Hollywood's affinity for the phony, it was predictable that the tear was glycerine, and the "Indian" was an Italian named Espera De Corti, born in 1904 in Kaplan, Louisiana, to a family of Sicilian immigrants. De Corti became an actor, and while he wasn't an Indian in real life, he played one on television and in the movies, many times, appearing in over a hundred television shows or films.

The "crying Indian" cemented in the minds of many Americans a long-held myth that the Native Americans were somehow superior to all other settlers, particularly Europeans. This myth began with the Thanksgiving story, where the English had to be saved by the Indians, then reached full bloom with the near-destruction of the massive bison herds on the western plains, supposedly all at the hands of the white man.

It is incontestable that white hunters, particularly those gathering meat for the railroads, decimated the buffalo herds. The introduction of the horse by whites changed the life of the Plains Indians, who, up to that time, had largely been farmers. Suddenly mobile, the Plains Indians found that hunting buffalo was relatively easy, and the Plains tribes shifted from a farming/gathering economy to a nomadic lifestyle. As Princeton professor Andrew Isenberg put it, "[T]he nomadic Indians of the western plains abandoned their ecological safety nets in order to concentrate year-round on bison hunting."[1] And although Spaniards had introduced the horse to Mexico, it was other Indian tribes that brought the horse to the Cheyenne and Sioux—two of the foremost buffalo-hunting tribes.

Buffalo herds were vast by almost any account: Thomas Farnham watched a single herd cross his line of sight for three days in 1839, while in 1871, Col. Richard Dodge wrote that the "whole country appeared to be one mass of buffalo."[2] Yet as Isenberg, Brown anthropologist Shepard Krech III, and Dan Flores, a historian at the University of Montana, all note, the Indians had hunted bison, although less effectively, before the horse, using techniques such as surrounding the herds, driving them off cliffs, and setting fire to entire prairie areas to wipe out a whole herd.[3] The French word "brûlé," or "burnt," referred to the Sicangu ("burnt thigh") Sioux division, whose survivors of hunting fires had burns on their legs. Charles McKenzie, traveling the plains in 1804, observed entire herds charred from Indian fires. The "buffalo jump" was a more risky technique that required an Indian dressed in a buffalo skin to lure a herd to a cliff, where he leaped to a small ledge while the animals careened over the side to their deaths.

Espera De Corti, the "Crying Indian," was used in a "Keep America Beautiful" campaign in the 1970s that implied that modern capitalism and industrialism were the cause of pollution and waste; and in contrast, the Indians were great environmentalists. But De Corti was not an Indian, and the Native Americans were already on a path to exterminate the buffalo before white hunters accelerated the process.

Nor were all Indians natural conservationists to the point that they used "all parts of the buffalo." Many travelers reported herds of bison carcasses rotting in the sun, with only a hump or tail removed.

Father Pierre De Smet watched some 3,000 Assiniboin Indians surround a herd of 600, wiping out every one. Some estimates made in the 1850s suggest that Indians harvested about 450,000 animals a year, and some think the number was much higher. The stench permeated the prairie for miles, and many pioneers came across carcasses of buffalo killed by the Indians.[4] But it was not just buffalo: Krech details the Indians' destruction of the white-tailed deer herds, and, ironically, the English government's attempts to protect the herds as early as 1760.[5] Charles Kay has demonstrated that the Indians not only overhunted, but by their actions they drove herds into "long-distance migrations . . . [where they were] able to outdistance most of their human carnivorous predators."[6]

Some scholars have still sought to place the blame on the Europeans.

Charles Kay, Andrew Isenberg, and Dan Flores all reject this view, as does Shepard Krech, who summarizes the leftist position nicely: the Indians "were seduced by new technology and alcohol. Corrupted, [they] were left at the mercy of the boundless greed of the European merchant-capitalists, stripped of free will and agency, transformed into a monolithic forest proletariat. . . ."[7] Of course, using the words "Indians" and "proletariat" in the same paragraph ought to immediately disqualify any professional historian from further publishing! (Krech does not subscribe to the leftist position.)

Let's be clear: there is no doubt, from any quarter, that it was white hunters who polished off most of the buffalo herds—mainly because of their technological lead over the Indians. Armed with long-range, high-caliber hunting rifles, sharpshooters such as Buffalo Bill Cody could take down hundreds of animals in a single day. The commercialization of hides and buffalo meat placed further incentives on killing as many bison as possible. In the 1890s, the leather industry in the United States had grown to an $8.6 million business, with many of the hides coming from buffalo. Buffalo bones, used for fertilizer and pigments, filled five thousand boxcars annually. Tales of the deadly effectiveness of the Plains hunters, such as Cody, are renowned. Working from a stand, in which the lead buffalo were shot at long range so as not to panic the herd, a good hunter could kill ten to fifty animals and skin them in a single morning's work. One warehouse would hold sixty to eighty thousand hides, and the number of hides shipped on the Union Pacific alone exceeded 1.3 million between 1872 and 1874.[8]

If, however, the whites accelerated the destruction of the buffalo, the work of Isenberg, Krech, and others demonstrates without question that the Indians were already on the path to exterminating the bison at a somewhat slower level. When placed in the natural population constraints of fire and other predators, and then measuring the supporting power of the lands on which they existed, the buffalo were doomed eventually no matter what the whites did. Making matters worse, most Indians thought bison had some supernatural origin and were limitless. Some Indians believed the buffalo came from a lake in Canada: "You say they are all gone; but look, they come again and again to us. We cannot kill them all—they are there under that lake."[9] Moreover, in the nineteenth century the Plains Indians' lack of a market economy or system of surplus accumulation made them utterly dependent on trade with the Europeans.[10] No comment more starkly differentiated the Indian and

European concepts of economy than one made by John McDougall, who said of the Blackfeet in 1865, "Without the buffalo they would be helpless, and yet the whole [Blackfoot] nation did not own one."[11] Put another way, Isenberg argues, "Even had they recognized a decline, the inherent instability of the nomadic societies made it difficult always to enforce the mandates against waste."[12] Moreover, as Kay notes, the impact of Indian hunting, burning, and clear-cutting on the forests was significant: "[T]he idea that North America was a 'wilderness' untouched by the hand of man prior to 1492 is a myth. . . ."[13]

Indeed, it was precisely this market-oriented philosophy that *saved* the buffalo. Early government attempts to save the buffalo proved contradictory: one bill, for example, made it unlawful for non-Indians to kill buffalo, while the War Department viewed the removal of the buffalo as necessary for eliminating the hostiles' food source. By 1872, Yellowstone National Park provided the only public refuge for the bison outside of a few zoos. Yet as Andrew Isenberg notes, "This remnant herd and other scattered survivors might eventually have perished as well had it not been for the efforts of a handful of Americans and Canadians. These advocates of preservation were primarily Western ranchers who speculated that ownership of the few remaining bison could be profitable and elite Easterners possessed of a nostalgic urge to recreate . . . the frontier."[14] The American Bison Society, formed in 1905, whose members had almost exclusively come from the Northeast (and many had never seen a buffalo in person), sought to preserve the herds. J. P. Morgan, the banker who saved the railroads, also saved the buffalo by establishing a 20,000-acre tract in Colorado that he stocked with bison. Farmers bred cattle/bison hybrids called "beefalo" and sold the meat. Buffalo Bill's own "Wild West Show" deliberately included mock buffalo hunts to expose the beautiful animals to eastern whites. Touring the United States and Europe from the 1880s to 1913, Cody introduced the buffalo to millions of people, many of whom supported the American Bison Society.

Perhaps the most significant actions, however, came from Western ranchers such as Charles Goodnight, who captured buffalo calves in 1878 and developed his own private bison herd. In the early 1900s, Goodnight shipped almost seven hundred privately raised and protected buffalo to Canada's Wood Buffalo National Park. That herd grew to fourteen thousand by the mid-twentieth century.[15] Ironically, many of the government herds were derived from animals purchased or donated from the private ranchers' herds![16]

Other ranchers raised buffalo for multiple purposes, including hunting. One advertised, "We Supply Buffalo for Zoos, Parks, Circuses, and Barbecues." The American Bison Society even referred customers who wanted to "adopt" a buffalo to ranchers, not the government. One Michigan game reserve was established by purchasing the private herd of Joshua Hill. Virtually all of the Yellowstone herd was rejuvenated in 1902 under the new game warden, Charles Jesse "Buffalo" Jones. It came from two private herds. A government employee, Jones was credited with helping to restore the herds, and did so to a large extent by using the private sector. His "product," he rightly understood, consisted of the herd itself in its natural surroundings. Therefore Jones located his bison corrals near the Mammoth Hot Springs, which was the park's busiest entrance, allowing a private souvenir shop to be set up. After he resigned, the new management wisely kept herds near the Hot Springs.[17]

The private sector saved many other species that would have been doomed under government "protection." California's tule elk, a miniature species of elk, were rescued from extinction by a rancher, Henry Miller. Animals that he shipped from his private reserve to the government did not survive, except for a few that ended up at Yosemite. But Walter Dow, a California businessman, thought the elk would do well in the Owens Valley. Making crates for shipping the elk himself, he personally supervised the transfer in 1933. Ultimately, on government land, the herd dwindled back down to under three hundred, whereas it had thrived and grown in private hands.[18] Equally amazing is the story of the Y.O. Ranch in Texas. Its wildlife hunting catalog includes wildebeest, gazelles, oryx, ibex, sable antelope, kudu, and zebra. More than fifty exotic game species are available to hunt, yet the ranch, whose income partly depends on hunting, ensures the growth and preservation of these animals—so much so that there are "more scimitar-horned oryx on the private game ranches in Texas than in their native territories in Africa, where they are under government protection."[19] It also has more blackbuck antelope than exist in all their native lands in India and Pakistan. Y.O. is, in fact, referred to as "Africa in Texas."

Private herds had powerful advantages over public/government parks. Whereas parks such as Yellowstone struggled to keep poachers out, private reserves enthusiastically welcomed hunters—and their fees. By the twentieth century, hunters created such a demand for buffalo that it became a small industry, and finally public parks acceded to the demand for hunting, allowing shooters to pay $200 each for a buffalo. Yet the market also permitted people to engage in charity. Both the American Bison Society and the Society for the Prevention of Cruelty to Animals (SPCA) ran important education programs to explain the need to the public to replenish the herds. Nevertheless, the buffalo's chief attraction was not its noble beauty but its exotic-tasting meat: by the 1990s, more than 90 percent of the bison in North America were in private hands. Isenberg notes that they were "preserved not for their iconic significance in the interest of biological diversity but simply raised to be slaughtered for their meat."[20] For an animal nearly extinct at one point, it was an amazing turnaround that by the year 2000, more animals were raised on private reserves strictly for their meat than even existed in all the government parks and public zoos put together! When it comes to the bison, left-wing scholars have "buffaloed" American schoolchildren.

LIE #34

THE FIRST THANKSGIVING TOOK PLACE BECAUSE THE INDIANS
SAVED THE PURITANS FROM THEIR OWN INEPTITUDE

*The Wampanoag were actually invited to that Thanksgiving feast for the purpose
of negotiating a treaty that would secure the lands of the Plymouth Plantation for
the Pilgrims. It should also be noted that the INDIANS, possibly out of a sense of
charity toward their hosts, ended up bringing the majority of the food for the
feast.*

—CHUCK LARSON, "INTRODUCTION FOR TEACHERS,"
TACOMA PUBLIC SCHOOLS (1987)

There were, of course, numerous "thanksgivings" even before the Puritans
arrived in America. Spaniards under Francisco Coronado held a thanksgiving feast in 1541 to celebrate finding food and water in Florida, and another
thanksgiving celebration occurred in 1564 among the Huguenot colonists
near modern-day Jacksonville. English thanksgivings had already occurred in
1607 when George Popham and Abenaki Indians along the Kennebec River
had a feast before the English abandoned the fort. Berkeley Plantation in Virginia had a thanksgiving in 1619. The charter of the plantation states, "Wee
ordaine that the day of our ships arrival at the place assigned for plantacon in
the land of Virginia shall be yearly and perpetually keept holy as a day of
thanksgiving to Almighty God."[1] The date of December 4, 1619, was established as the day of thanksgiving. While a "harvest festival" was common in
England at this time of year, what Berkeley Plantation celebrated was strictly a
religious observance to thank God for the settlers' safe passage to the New

World.[2] Subsequent thanksgivings were held in each of the next two years, before the small colony was wiped out.

A much different set of circumstances greeted the *Mayflower*'s Pilgrim settlers. The London investors wanted to control their capital, stipulating that at the end of seven years, everything would be divided equally between the colonists and the merchants. Settlers were to work for the company, although they were allowed to work two days a week on what were called "particular" (private) plots of land. Of course, the merchants realized the Pilgrims would work harder on their own land than for the company. Therefore all wealth was to be put in a common pool. Although the agent for the Pilgrims used arguments "calculated to appeal to Christians . . . in order to justify his acceptance of unpopular terms," the Pilgrims accepted the arrangement because they had little choice.[3] Once they reached the New World, however, the settlers found the communal system only produced want and lack.

It's important to recognize that the colonists arrived *too late* to plant and were already into the colder temperatures when they began to build houses. Of the *Mayflower*'s 102 Pilgrims who arrived at Plymouth Rock, only 46 remained alive by the following spring. Among the dead was Dorothy, the wife of William Bradford, the leader of the Plymouth colony. The following spring they hunted and fished (without any instruction from the Indians) and laid in barely enough provisions. Bradford reviewed the philosophy behind the original communal system: "The experience we had in this common course and condition [was that] by taking away property, and bringing community into a common wealth, [it] would make them happy and flourishing—as if they were wiser than God."[4] Of course, like V. I. Lenin and Mikhail Gorbachev, the Pilgrims found communism didn't work. Bradford described the reality: "For young men that were most able and fit for labor and service did repine that they should spend their time and strength to work for other men's wives and children without any recompense . . . that was thought injustice."[5] Although Bradford recorded "no wante" all summer, and there was a small harvest of corn and other vegetables, plus a "great store" of "wild Turkies" and venison, these stores declined throughout the winter. Still, the Pilgrims depended on supply ships arriving.[6]

Bradford recognized the communal system didn't work: "At length, after much debate of things, the Governor (with the advice of the chiefest amongst them) gave way that they should set corn for every man for his own particular, and in that regard trust to themselves; in all other things to go in the general way as before. And so assigned to every family a parcel of land, according to the proportion of their number."[7] With that, Plymouth was converted to a capitalist system. Bradford assigned individual land for each family to work and manage.

It is true that Squanto, an English-speaking Wampanoag Indian whom the Pilgrims met in 1620, introduced the settlers to North American vegetables and provided other skills, although it is silly to think that the Pilgrims didn't know how to hunt, fish, and build houses. Most of what they received from the Indians came in the form of barter, with the settlers using items brought from their ships to trade. Even in this, leftist historians misrepresent the exchange, making it appear that Indians gave up massive amounts of land for "a few trinkets." But in fact, those "trinkets" were manufactured items that the Indians had never seen, which they obtained for land they thought no one could truly own. Sometime in September 1621, after the abundant crops came in, the Pilgrims decided to thank God (not the Indians), inviting Squanto and Chief Massasoit to bring their immediate families—which amounted to more than eighty people! A three-day feast (not initially called "thanksgiving") ensued, as described by Edward Winslow's December 11, 1621, letter.

Two years later, Bradford issued the first official "thanksgiving" proclamation:

> Inasmuch as the great Father has given us this year an abundant harvest of Indian corn, wheat, peas, beans, squashes, and garden vegetables, and has made the forests to abound with game and the sea with fish and clams, and inasmuch as he has protected us from the ravages of the savages, has spared us from pestilence and disease, has granted us freedom to worship God according to the dictates of our own conscience.
>
> Now I, your magistrate, do proclaim that all ye Pilgrims, with your wives and ye little ones, do gather at ye meeting house, on ye hill, between the hours of 9 and 12 in the day time, on Thursday, November 29th, of the year of our Lord one thousand six hundred and twenty-three and the third year since ye Pilgrims landed on ye Pilgrim Rock, there to

listen to ye pastor and render thanksgiving to ye Almighty
God for all His blessings.[8]

Soon they had a regular surplus—which they used to save the Indians, who
had now suffered from a poor growing season. Again, Bradford set aside a day
of thanksgiving, and again Massasoit and his "family" joined the Pilgrims.

Good Indian-white relations would not last long. King Philip's War pitted
the former Pilgrims against Wampanoags, and, not surprisingly, when the English won, in June 1676 they held another day of thanksgiving to "praise God
for such his Goodness and Favour."

LIE #35

THE "ROBBER BARONS" PILLAGED THE LAND
AND DESTROYED THE ENVIRONMENT

[T]he new corporate mining had disturbing effects. Its impact on the environment was horrendous.

—DAVID GOLDFIELD ET AL., THE AMERICAN JOURNEY (2007)

Contrary to the portrayals of lumberman Frederick Weyerhaeuser (see, for example, the National Park Service Web site) as one who stripped the land, the German immigrant was one of America's greatest environmentalists.[1] By 1885, his firm was processing more than 500 million board feet of lumber from his more than 300,000 acres (he had 900,000 acres by 1900). That is the key: they were *his* acres. He bought them. And once the trees were gone, Weyerhaeuser was out of a gig. Like railroader James J. Hill, who built the Great Northern transcontinental railroad without government aid, Weyerhaeuser recognized that he must conserve and efficiently use his land, not waste it. After learning from inspectors that his lands were not as rich in timber as he thought, Weyerhaeuser devoted considerable resources to reforestation, soil erosion, and fire prevention.

Nature, always held up by environmental radicals as sacred, destroyed American forests through fires. Humans, of course, generally fought forest fires, especially when settlements or crops were nearby. Fire historian and MacArthur Prize winner Stephen Pyne has conducted a detailed investigation of forestry records for the period 1940–1965, and found that in those twenty-five years, lightning started more than 228,000 fires in the United

States, consuming more than one million acres![2] Put another way, "nature" destroyed more fire acreage in twenty-five years than Weyerhaeuser replenished many times over, ending up with far more trees than when he began. Other paper companies followed suit: International Paper established its own nurseries, and by the 1990s was turning out 190 *million* seedlings a year.[3] By the 1920s alone, International Paper produced four million cords of wood a year *more* than it consumed, and eighty years later, the company was planting 48 million trees per year, some five times more than it harvested. Like all paper companies, International Paper and Kimberly-Clark employed armies of professional foresters.[4]

It wasn't just "robber barons" such as Weyerhaeuser: we learn in *Nation of Nations* that "western farmers altered the landscape by reducing the annual fires, often set by Indians, that had kept the prairie free from trees."[5] So when the Indians annihilated entire forests, it was acceptable, while the whites introduced "an artificial ecosystem of animals, woodlots, and crops."[6] Those evil farmers! Shame on them for feeding all those people.

In his rant against American progress, James Loewen (*Lies My Teacher Told Me*) warns, "Today American farming relies on enormous amounts of oil, not only for tractors and trucks and air conditioning, but also for fertilizers and herbicides."[7] One might not know that we use "enormous" amounts of oil *instead of* enormous amounts of coal or wood or even whale oil—previous power sources that have been conserved through more efficient, and cleaner, forms of energy. Indeed, except for the environmental movement and the "antis," the even much cleaner nuclear power might well have replaced some of the oil-based industry.

By the time John D. Rockefeller was finished driving kerosene prices down almost a hundredfold, whale oil was so expensive that the industry had nearly vanished.[8] After kerosene refining was, well, refined, the total value of whale products in the United States fell from $8 million in 1864 to $3 million by 1876. The price of sperm oil was $1.50 per gallon in 1876, compared to an average gallon of kerosene at under $0.50 and falling. Crude oil prices, driven by Rockefeller's obsession with efficiency, plunged to $1 a barrel by 1890. But those were averages, and the lowest-month price was an astounding $0.60 per barrel in 1890—as the real price of a barrel of kerosene dropped to $0.08.[9] Kerosene became six times cheaper than whale oil by the 1890s. Many of these price cuts were engineered by Rockefeller. He saved more than $1.50 per barrel in barrels alone by manufacturing his own kilns and acquiring his own wagons to haul the kerosene. Within just two years of "Rocky" entering the business, prices fell by 50 percent. "We must remember," he told a partner, "we are refining oil for the poor man and he must have it cheap and good."[10]

On the subject of oil, it's ironic that no one single-handedly did more to preserve a species than John D. Rockefeller, the so-called robber baron who dominated kerosene refining. Rockefeller is lambasted in the textbooks. John Garraty's *American Nation* used dark tones to describe Rockefeller's business efficiency: "Rockefeller exploited every possible technical advance and employed fair means and foul to persuade competitors . . . to sell out or join forces. . . ."[11]

Typically, this kind of nonsense ends with the predictable claim that "the average U.S. citizen consumes the same resources as ten average world citizens or twenty-five residents of India."[12] "Economically," wrote James Loewen, "we are the bane, not the hope of the world," and "we can only hope other nations will *never* achieve our standard of living, for if they did, the earth would become a desert." This nonsense comes from the book *Lies My Teacher Told Me*, though considering its utter lack of understanding of real economies, it should be renamed *Lies I Concocted to Make Money*. The fact is, Americans *produce* vastly more than "ten average world citizens," and probably outproduce some fifty residents of India or five hundred residents of Chad. They benefit from our economic progress and their *only* hope is to be more like us in their economic systems.

Poorer nations do not need more foreign aid, they need us to export more capitalism to them. In what is called "Gilder's law," named after futurist George Gilder, a society consumes cheap resources to preserve dear resources. When whales and their oil were cheaper than other forms of energy, people consumed whales. Once kerosene became cheaper, people switched to kerosene; then to electricity. Currently, despite what the environmentalists and the media claim, the most valuable resource is still people, who must operate within the confines of time. People are more valuable than oil, coal, or copper. So naturally our society (and all those who aspire to improve their lot in life) consumes cheaper resources (which have, by the way, never run out—we still have whales, we can still make kerosene) to conserve more valuable resources, namely human activity. Until time travel is perfected and time itself can become a commodity, it remains second only to human intellect and inventiveness as the "ultimate resource."

Federal Regulators Have Protected the Public's Health
by Identifying Harmful Products

The unregulated sale of drugs posed [a] dangerous threat to public health.
—David E. Harrell et al., Unto a Good Land

*These years saw the first sustained campaign against drug abuse. . . . Many easily
obtained medicines . . . contained opium and its derivatives morphine and heroin. . . . Coca-Cola contained cocaine until about 1900.*
—Paul S. Boyer et al., The Enduring Vision

Consumer advocates have often claimed that if not for the Food and Drug
Administration (the FDA, established 1906), unsafe and harmful products would be "kept on the shelves." On the other hand, it is claimed, testing
by the FDA ensures that those products that do come into the marketplace are
safe. Perhaps someone should tell that to pet owners, who in 2007 saw Chinese
products infiltrate most brands of pet food, killing hundreds of cats and dogs,
or the toothpaste makers, who likewise suffered from an "ingredient invasion"
in 2007. One hundred years after it had been established, the FDA was blocking "unapproved" drugs from patient access, including terminally ill patients
who lacked any other hope. Thankfully, the U.S. Court of Appeals for the
District of Columbia, in the *Abigail Alliance v. von Eschenbach* case, ruled that
the U.S. Constitution indeed did protect the rights of terminally ill patients to
use treatments not approved by the FDA.[1]

Historically, how has the FDA done? It may come as a shock that the first big "test case" for the FDA was not a product such as heroin, cocaine, or even tobacco, but that vile, dangerous liquid known as . . . Coca-Cola. The so-called Father of the Pure Food and Drug Act, Dr. Harvey Wiley, a prominent reformer and (of course) a leading Progressive, had established himself as a godlike source of nutritional information for the public. He had worked in the U.S. Department of Agriculture and in 1902 was awarded $5,000 by Congress to study the effect of various food preservatives on twelve human subjects(!). The subjects were "volunteers" who worked in Wiley's office.

These "poison squad" members were fed meals laced with borax, sulfuric acid, sodium benzoate, and formaldehyde.[2] This information is touted on none other than the FDA's *own Web site*. I'm just being picky here, but does it not seem strange that the same agency that refuses to allow dying patients to experiment with nonapproved drugs subjected people to poison tests? Reporters of the day apparently thought so, interviewing the chef through a basement window. Even Wiley's willingness to join the twelve volunteers and eat the meals himself did not reassure the public, which ridiculed the tests in minstrel shows. Eventually, Wiley stopped the experiments, but only after many of his subjects became so ill with vomiting and stomach problems they could not work any longer. Not surprisingly, however, the FDA viewed this as a success for helping Wiley "gain a Congressional hearing, as well as [gain] support for his contention that chemical preservatives had no place in food."[3] The FDA also proudly claims that "although no formal long-term follow-up was done on members of the Poison Squad, anecdotal reports indicate that none were harmed."[4] Certainly that's a criterion that corporate America wishes it were held to!

Wiley's objectivity, however, was in question from the start. He "repeatedly made statements favoring some companies' products over others," determining for example that glucose was bad but sucrose was acceptable.[5] He also supported straight whiskey (which used a distillation of mash and fermented grain at least four years old) over rectified whiskey (a simple mix of alcohol and water), which called into question the whole notion of the "public good," as, according to two recent scholars of the whiskey industry, his efforts were, "if anything, harmful to the consumer, because he endorsed the more poisonous product."[6]

Wiley's campaign against Coca-Cola marked the final phase of a long battle the company had fought with the government over the "secret ingredient," which officials claimed was cocaine. Even before the government trials started, pharmaceutical tests showed that the amount of cocaine in the drink per serving was one-thirtieth of a grain. One historian of Coca-Cola argued that Dr. Asa Candler's process had so diluted the cocaine that "it seemed unlikely that cocaine (or anything else for that matter) could survive."[7] By the time Wiley got the company into the courts, there was no viable evidence that there was any cocaine in the product, so he switched tactics and "initiated a series of charges . . . over the process [the company] used to dilute the cocaine *out* [emphasis in original]."[8] Finally, the obvious silliness of the government's case forced Wiley to shift his ground yet again, now arguing that the product was "misbranded" because it did not contain cocaine!

The 1911 trial in Chattanooga bordered on the surreal. As one historian noted, the government paraded witnesses before the court "whose testimony was designed to horrify the jury and alarm the public." Prosecutors called a laborer to the stand who admitted that "doing hard physical labor next to a steaming hot kettle in a factory in the Deep South in the middle of July, he was *sweating* [emphasis in original]."[9] When Wiley's attorneys could not produce a single "Coca-Cola fiend," the government's case collapsed.

This has not stopped modern Progressives, such as Michael Jacobsen of the anticapitalist Center for Science in the Public Interest, from attempting to bring lawsuits against McDonald's (for "making" teenagers obese), or banning buttered popcorn from movie theaters, or, most recently, targeting ice cream. Allying with the FDA, such "consumer groups" have in fact made litigation a permanent tactic of the nation's health police. Buoyed by their decades-long war against "Big Tobacco," these advocates have found that often merely bringing a charge against a product, medicine, or company is enough to force its removal from the marketplace—without any scientific proof of harm whatsoever.

Nothing illustrates this perverted process more than the Alar scare of the 1980s. Although the public concerns about Alar—a pesticide that contained a "possible" carcinogen for humans called UDMH—were heightened by the CBS TV news show *60 Minutes* in February 1989, the so-called science behind it was based on a single nutritionist's test. Congress called witnesses, including the famous scientist Meryl Streep, whose testimony was widely covered. Peer-reviewed studies showed a correlation between UDMH and lab-animal tumors, but later it was revealed that the lab animals were given levels of

UDMH equal to a boxcar-load of apples *per day*. One study found that the average *daily dose* of UDMH (and we all eat apples daily, right?) was one-tenth that found in tap water, and a tiny fraction found in a normal serving of peanut butter. College students were dismayed to find that an average serving of beer contained almost ten thousand times as much UDMH as Alar-coated apples.

Dr. Richard Adamson, then director of the National Cancer Institute's Division of Cancer Etiology, said, "The risk of eating an apple treated with Alar is less than the risk of eating a peanut butter sandwich or a well-done hamburger," and he has more recently described the cancer risk from eating Alar-treated apples as "nonexistent." The director of the FDA's own toxicological sciences division called the Alar scare "total baloney."[10] Meanwhile, having voluntarily withdrawn Alar in anticipation of public action, apple growers lost millions of dollars.

"Public interest" groups repeatedly see sinister connections between corporations and scientists or regulators in the approval process. If you work for a company as a lobbyist or lawyer, it seems, you aren't just employed—you are a prostitute. Rarely, however, do we get a glimpse of the other side of the coin. In a fight over the sweetener aspartame, a nutritionist who launched some of the earliest charges against it invested money in G. D. Searle—aspartame's manufacturer—with "put" options designed to take advantage of falling stock prices. Woodrow Monte "didn't think there was anything wrong" with producing research that would inevitably cause a company's stock to decline—and making money off it.[11]

So far, most companies have either fought such actions by regulators and consumer groups in the courts or meekly submitted. Yet how many products have come under fire, only to later be shown to be free of their alleged evils? In my lifetime alone, coffee, bacon, and diet soda have all been labeled dangerous or carcinogenic, yet over time, scientists have also discovered correlations (not causes) with health improvements for most of them. Even tobacco has been shown to have positive correlations for some diseases. Nicotine, according to a British study, "can slow down the onset of Parkinson's symptoms" and help with treating schizophrenia and Alzheimer's.[12] According to a 1998 report for the *London Electronic Telegraph*, the World Health Organization even buried a study that showed no link between secondhand smoking and lung cancer and found it might even have a "protective effect."[13] A second study in the *British*

Medical Journal found no increase in the risk of heart disease or lung cancer from "passive smoke."[14] More amazing still, a Vacaville, California, biotechnology company found "positive results" in fighting non-Hodgkin's lymphoma from an experimental cancer drug "manufactured in tobacco plants."[15]

The issue is not whether smoking is harmful—most studies still agree it is—but how many other products are, and will be, banned or driven out of the marketplace because zealots leverage media coverage in such a way as to produce unscientifically grounded hysteria. When the government fought Coca-Cola, Coke won. Next time, we may not be so lucky. Our Ho Hos are at stake!

LIE #37

GLOBAL WARMING IS A FACT, AND
IT'S A MAN-MADE, AMERICAN-DRIVEN PROBLEM

The balance of nature is delicate.... Humans have upset that balance, stripping the land of its green cover, choking the air, poisoning the seas.
MICHAEL SCOTT, THE YOUNG OXFORD BOOK OF ECOLOGY

Starting in 1970, there was a precipitous drop-off in the amount and extent and thickness of the Arctic ice cap.
—AL GORE, AN INCONVENIENT TRUTH (2006)

We know where most heat-trapping gasses come from: power plants and vehicles. And we know how to limit their emissions.
—NATURAL RESOURCES DEFENSE COUNCIL (2003)

The threat of global warming seemed especially urgent.... Heightening global-warming fears, the ten hottest years of the twentieth century all occurred after 1985.
—PAUL S. BOYER ET AL., THE ENDURING VISION

When former vice president Albert Gore beat out many serious luminaries to win the 2007 Nobel Peace Prize for environmental activism, highlighted by his movie *An Inconvenient Truth,* the notion of man-made global warming reached a new pinnacle in the annals of nonscientists hijacking scientific research. Gore did not get away with his distortions entirely, however: in London, the High Court judge signaled that public schools were required to issue a warning before showing Gore's film, because it was "politically biased" and contained serious "scientific inaccuracies" and "sentimental mush."[1] When news of this reached CNN, meteorologist Rob Marciano clapped his hands and exclaimed, "Finally! There are definitely some inaccuracies [in the film]," he said. "The biggest thing I have a problem with is this implication that Katrina was caused by global warming."[2] Even Al Gore's home state of Tennessee is half a degree cooler than when he was a kid![3]

Physicists Henrik Svensmark and Eigil Friis-Christensen, of the Danish National Space Center, released a study on climate change that claimed the "Sun still appears to be the main forcing agent in global climate change."[4] Environmental scientist Fred Singer charges that the misplaced resources going to fight a natural change that is beyond human control "will severely damage national economies, decrease standards of living, and increase poverty. This misdirection will adversely affect human health and welfare in industrialized nations, and even more in developing nations."[5] S. Drobot, J. Maslanik, et al., have theorized that "arctic oscillation" was the most dominant factor affecting Arctic climate, but they found that even after the arctic oscillation index was neutral, other changes associated with arctic oscillation still occurred, leaving them to conclude that a tipping point in warming had already been reached and was receding.[6]

Sami Solanki, of the Max Planck Institute for Solar System Research, began to chip away at the man-caused global warming myth in 2004 when his studies confirmed that "the sun has been at its strongest over the past 60 years and may now be affecting global temperatures."[7] Climatologist Bill Burrows of the Royal Meteorological Society agreed, saying, "Perhaps we are devoting too many resources to correcting human effects on the climate without being sure that we are the major contributor."[8] Solanki's team studied sunspot data going back hundreds of years and concluded that they were correlated with a warming earth. Every time someone produced "evidence" of human-caused global warming, the facts interfered. Yes, Mount Kilimanjaro's snows have retreated—but the retreat started in the nineteenth century, before there were human greenhouse gases. As for Al Gore's dire warnings about seaside cities being swallowed up by the oceans—caused by melting ice—it would take one thousand years for the oceans to rise two inches, and twenty thousand years for them to rise a yard.

The notion of "scientific consensus" on global warming is a political phrase drummed up by hysteria-mongers such as Al Gore. There "is no such consensus," notes Singer.[9] Researcher Benny Peiser examined 1,117 peer-reviewed publications, the contents of which showed that nearly three times as many studies rejected or doubted the notion that humans caused global warming as those that did see humans as the main cause, and two-thirds of studies made no reference to human influence on climate.[10] Even when studies could produce a slight majority saying that human causes were mostly responsible for climate change, 10 percent of the scientists strongly disagreed with the statement, more than those who strongly supported it.[11]

Evidence from balloon-borne radiosondes shows a slight decrease in warming over the equator, nullifying one of the key arguments of the global warming crowd. The federal government's own predictions failed to match reality, as noted in its Climate Change Science Program Report of 2006.[12] As Singer points out, no one has a good model for calculating the impact of water vapor and it's just as likely that water vapor reduces the impact of CO_2. Moreover, the oft-cited "hockey stick" plot showing a skyrocketing trend in warming was shown to have been based on fundamental mathematical flaws.[13] Al Gore cited the breakup of the Larsen Ice Shelf in the Antarctic—but most of Antarctica has been getting colder. And where global warming demagogues worry about the extinction of polar bears, since the 1970s—all while the world was (theoretically) warming—polar bear numbers increased from around 5,000 to as many as 25,000 in 2007.[14]

Dozens of other scientists have challenged the man-made global warming mantra. The part of the Arctic where rising temperature is supposedly endangering polar bears has shown fluctuations since 1940 but no overall temperature rise. Richard Morgan of the World Meteorological Organization noted of the Canadian Arctic that from 1971 to 1981, the ice thickness changed from average to above average, followed by a sharp decrease over two years, followed by another recovery, and so on, to a steady increase to normal conditions since 2001.[15] More astounding is the scientists' observation that the dramatic scenes of ice breaking off and collapsing into the sea is an indicator of the "normal advance of a glacier," that is, of *increasing ice levels*.[16] Morgan pointed out that massive areas of cooling are found all the way from the coasts of South America and the Amazon Valley to the Black Sea and Caucasus. Danish and Swiss researchers discovered from samples taken in Greenland's ice core that a consistent, repeated cycle of warming and cooling occurs every 2,550 years.[17]

Not only have the hysterics on the left misjudged man's role in global warming, they have also ignored the widespread positive effects such a warming trend could have: for example, vast expanses of the earth will, for the first time in centuries, be available for cultivation. Robert O. Mendelsohn, of the Yale School of Forestry and Environmental Studies, suggests the gains in agriculture, in particular, will be greater than the losses. Yet only thirty years ago *Newsweek* ran an article citing "scientific" research claiming the world was entering a period of . . . *global cooling!*[18] When the Copenhagen Consensus, a center for analyzing solutions to the world's biggest challenges, ranked seventeen ways to use its funds, it ranked the Kyoto Protocol (designed to control "global warming") sixteenth, saying that its costs outweighed its benefits.[19]

Fred Singer and Dennis Avery point out in *Unstoppable Global Warming—Every 1,500 Years* that the scare-meisters are hysterical when glaciers retreat, but also when they advance![20] The tactics of the global warming fearmongers led Bjørn Lomborg to publish a book in 2001 called *The Skeptical Environmentalist.* Lomborg challenged all the existing environmentalist boogeymen, including global warming. He concludes that "our [environmental] problems are often getting *smaller* and not bigger."[21]

Unfortunately for Al Gore, almost as many scientific studies have shown *no* global warming—or certainly no human-caused global warming—as have claimed such a warming exists. Consider a Swedish study of air temperatures reconstructed from freshwater pearl mussels, which concluded that "both series do not reveal any significant long-term temperature trends."[22] Or consider the recent comments of nationally known hurricane forecaster William Gray, who says NASA's global warming guru, James Hansen, is 180 degrees off: "In ten years, I expect the globe to be somewhat cooler than it is now."[23] Storms are not getting more severe, and certainly global warming did not "cause" Hurricane Katrina. It is especially important to note that far more powerful hurricanes occurred in the era before the industrial age![24]

A common tactic of the environmentalists is to posit "threats" to the environment without examining what benefits environmental changes bring. Warming climate? More food, fewer hungry people, and less energy consumption to stay warm. More rain? Fewer deserts, and, again, more food. The notion that, as Al Gore suggested, the oceans would rise by twenty feet would

require more than *one thousand years'* worth of heavy ice melts. More significant, the motivation behind most of these environmental scare tactics is to
conceal a deeper assault on free-market capitalism. If it's not harming the
worker, in other words, it must be harming the planet. While some environmentalists (such as Lomborg) are sincere, many more are out-of-work Marxists
who lack a cause now that the Soviet Union is defunct. A good rule of thumb
is, scratch an environmentalist, find an anti-capitalist. The market demands
that humans allocate *scarce* resources, and every time "solutions" are offered
without examining the trade-offs, it is a good bet the market isn't involved
at all.

LIE #38

THE CONSTITUTION WAS THE CREATION OF
"ELITES" PROTECTING THEIR FINANCIAL INTERESTS

The movement for the Constitution . . . was originated and carried through principally by four groups of personal interests which had been adversely affected under the Articles of Confederation: money, public securities, manufacturers, and trade and shipping.
> —CHARLES A. BEARD, AN ECONOMIC INTERPRETATION OF THE
> CONSTITUTION OF THE UNITED STATES

In fact, [the Founding Fathers] did not want a balance, except one which kept things as they were, a balance among the dominant forces at that time.
> —HOWARD ZINN, A PEOPLE'S HISTORY OF THE UNITED STATES

Charles Beard's famous book applying economic determinism to the revolutionary ideas of the U.S. Constitution is something of a dead issue today among most historians, even those on the left. Unfortunately, the "filter down" process of instruction from professors to high school teachers lingers many years after the concepts are outdated. In fairness, Beard himself admitted, "If anywhere I have said or written that 'all history' can be 'explained' in economic terms, I was then suffering from an aberration of the mind."[1] Rejecting the notion that his interpretation sprang from "Marxian theories," Beard nevertheless claimed (rightly) that "whoever leaves economic pressures out of history or out of the discussion of public questions is in mortal peril of substituting mythology for reality. . . ."[2]

As a refresher, Beard examined the economic and financial interests of those members of the Constitutional Convention, finding them to be (surprise!) men of substance. He also examined the ratification conventions and claimed they were similarly the domain of small groups of "propertied" men. Howard Zinn expressed the basic premise with more disgust, but with the same essential economic-determinist verve:

> The Constitution, then, illustrates the complexity of the American system: that it serves the interests of a wealthy elite, but also does enough for small property owners, for middle-income mechanics and farmers, to build a broad base of support. The slightly prosperous people who make up this base of support are buffers against the blacks, the Indians, the very poor whites. They enable the elite to keep control. . . . [3]

The obvious small problem with such silly comments is that (a) Zinn himself has become one of the "wealthy elite" by trashing the Founders; (b) the "American system" (if it was so designed as he and Beard claimed) was so anemic and poorly conceived that critics such as himself obviously evaded its restrictions; and (c) within eighty-five years of its writing, a president, using the Constitution as a guide, liberated the very blacks the document was supposed to keep in their place.

As any good student of history knows, of course, Forrest McDonald has dissected and reversed much of Beard's original study in his book *We the People*.[4] Reassessing Beard's definitions of what constituted "wealth" and property, McDonald found "the details [of Beard's argument] to be incompatible with the broad outlines he sketched," and said the way in which Beard asked the questions was "meaningless."[5] The Philadelphia convention acted neither as a concerted economic group nor as the product of some abstract causes of class struggle. Instead, McDonald found, too many of the interest groups were indifferent to the issues of others and were never aligned toward similar strategies. More significant, the *political* interests of all states were represented, but not the *economic* interests. The Constitution, it had to be concluded, was about ideas, not money.

To anyone except, perhaps, Zinn and Matt Damon's character in *Good*

Will Hunting, this would be obvious, especially considering that economic historians (who would love nothing better than to prove the primacy of economics in everything) have *completely* rejected economic motivations as the main cause of the American Revolution. For the field of economic history, this has been a dead subject for more than two decades, but because of the ongoing economic determinist indoctrination of high school teachers, it is worth a revisit here.

In the movie *Good Will Hunting,* Matt Damon as the heroic Harvard janitor Will overhears Ivy League students discussing Gordon Wood's work (most likely *The Creation of the American Republic*).[6] He pompously informs them that if they want the "real" history of the American Revolution and Constitution, they should read Zinn's book. If they did, they would have missed the better part of scholarship in American economic history for the last twenty years when it came to the causes of the Revolution. As early as 1942, Lawrence Harper began to question the notion that Americans revolted solely against the financial burden of British taxes. He began to look at the impact of the British imperial system on trade.[7] In 1965, Robert Thomas applied the new "econometric" approach to American business life, and discovered that the gross burden on Americans came to $1.24 per person in 1770—not an insignificant amount at a time when a dollar could be equal to a week's wages or more. However, Thomas also saw that the British system did offer some benefits, including the protection of the Royal Navy for American exports, some military protection on the frontier, and certain bounties on American-produced goods. These benefits equaled almost $0.40 per person, making the net loss of belonging to the British imperial system about $1 million total, or less than 1 percent of income.[8] Who goes to war for 1 percent of his income? State and local governments today routinely increase taxes more than that with impunity!

In their survey of American economic history scholarship, Jeremy Atack and Peter Passell concluded, "The British presence was not a serious financial hardship to the colonists."[9] Others, including Peter McClelland, have supported the general findings of Thomas and others that found the Navigation Acts only accounted for, at most, 3 percent of GNP—an amount about equal to the impact of the 1970s oil crisis and substantially less than the burden of the Smoot-Hawley tariff of 1930.[10] Increasingly, historians have come to take the colonists at their word: the taxes themselves were far less important than the process by which they were enacted. When the Americans said "no taxation *without representation*," they meant exactly that—they were willing to be taxed, but wanted a voice in the levying of those taxes. As Bernard Bailyn's *Ideological Origins of the American Revolution* made clear, there were ideas at stake![11]

Some have attempted to rehabilitate Beard using the econometric approach.[12] This has merely led to renewed focus on what is an "interest." In fact, some of the research supposedly supporting Beard showed that slaveholders did not vote for ratification of the Constitution that would supposedly protect their interests. However, along the way, scholars began to adopt a more commonsense, less Marxist view that says when people can, they will obviously seek to advance their interests. This "public choice" approach has viewed legislation as a marketplace in which different bidders affect the desirability (i.e., the political price) of any particular legislation. But when have people not had interests and acted on them?

At issue is whether the Founders placed their economic interests ahead of their fundamental beliefs. They did not. Consider George Washington: no matter how he was damaged by the Navigation Acts, it was nothing compared to the losses he could have suffered by leading the Continental Army. If captured, he was automatically a traitor and subject to be hanged; certainly his plantation could not increase in value during a war. In short, Washington had everything to lose and nothing financially to gain. But he did have an unshakable belief in liberty. So did the other signers of the Declaration of Independence, all of whom were guilty of treason by putting their names to the document. As Rush Limbaugh's father, Rush H. Limbaugh II, pointed out in a classic speech called "Americans Who Risked Everything," almost all of the signers of the Declaration lost money and property, and many lost family, for the cause they cherished. None profited from the Revolution.[13]

People have fought over money in the past. Americans have fought over money. But look deep enough, and in most cases you'll find that the real battle is over ideas, as it was in the ratification of the U.S. Constitution.

NORTHERN CAPITALIST GREED—NOT SLAVERY—DROVE THE CIVIL WAR

[T]he South was fighting against the census returns—census returns that told of accumulating industrial capital, multiplying captains of industry, expanding railway systems, widening acres tilled by free farmers.
                    —CHARLES A. BEARD AND MARY R. BEARD,
                      THE RISE OF AMERICAN CIVILIZATION

It's hard to believe that with all the available evidence, a fusion of Marxists and radical libertarians still want to discount the central place of slavery as *the* causative factor in the Civil War. Charles Beard, the original left-wing historian (along with his wife, Mary), was the first to concoct such an explanation in his *Rise of American Civilization* (1913). It constituted, according to Beard, a "second American Revolution," in which big bad capitalism defeated a feudal southern economy. To someone who subscribes to Karl Marx's dialectic, this was just a step toward full-blown socialism.

Slavery, in fact, was such an overpowering institution in the South that it was absolutely untouchable, in any way, shape, or form. As historian David Lightner contends, "Nowadays most historians have faced up to the fact that the South's preoccupation with states' rights was but a thin veneer over the real issue. The only states' right that was under threat was the right to hold black people in slavery."[1] Slaves were labor, but they were also *capital,* a point that has been downplayed with unfortunate results. While many historians focused solely on the South's loss of labor if emancipation should come, which was significant but not fatal, it was the slave value as capital that constituted the backbone of southern wealth. James Huston has laid the numbers out in stark fashion: in 1859, the slaveholding states in wealth per capita ranked number one through three, and number five through eight.[2] Out of the top seventeen wealthiest states per capita, southern states made up all but *four*! New York, the wealthiest state overall, did not even make the top seventeen when considered per capita. Average per capita income for Southerners was slightly above the national average of all whites in 1860.[3]

Even more astounding, the dollar value of slaves in 1860 stood at approximately $3 billion. Total U.S. national wealth was $16 billion, meaning that slaves alone constituted about 19 percent of American national wealth.[4] Historians have long debated whether economic interests sparked the American Revolution, with the presumption being that the burden of the Navigation Acts and taxes was so severe that the American colonists, to paraphrase Popeye the Sailor, "stood all we could stands, 'cause we can't stands no more!" That debate vanished in the mid-twentieth century when a number of academics found that the total burden of the British taxes was about 1 percent of the American GNP, and common sense tells people that no one will fight over 1 percent (except, perhaps, a New York waiter). The historians concluded that it was the prospect of Britain's passing additional acts, through what the colonists saw as an unjust process, that finally ticked them off.[5] The point is, Americans did not fight the British over 1 percent . . . but close to 20 percent is another matter.

As Huston notes, slaveholding "comprised far more national wealth than railroads and manufacturing *combined;* the $3 billion in slaves was almost 50 percent more than the $2.2 billion invested in railroads and manufacturing."[6] Free laborers well knew they could not compete against slaves, a point made abundantly obvious by the transportation revolution that brought the two systems, for the first time, into direct competition in the 1850s. This competition arose first in the territories, even where slavery did not exist. For example, Charles Calomiris and I discovered that the Panic of 1857 was touched off by a political decision from the U.S. Supreme Court, the Dred Scott decision.[7] East–west railroad bonds crashed immediately after the decision was made public, but those of north–south lines (i.e., lines that did not go to the territories) barely budged. *Dred Scott* threw open the possibility that slavery would be extended into all the western territories—a bleak prospect that the markets well understood.

Modern labor groups decry the practice of outsourcing. Imagine if northern factories had begun "outsourcing" work to southern slave mills! And while the market revolution did not seem likely to change southern slavery in any way, it already had allowed slavery to affect northern market prices, again, especially in western territories where slave labor might directly compete with free labor.

In the debates over the Compromise of 1850, Southerners made clear that *only* slavery, and not the tariff or any other "clash of culture," was at the root of their fears of the national government. Robert Toombs of Georgia, asserting, "I stand upon the great general principle that the South has a right to equal participation in the territories of the United States [and to] *enter them all* with her property and securely enjoy it," proved that Southerners defined their "section" solely by their ability to own slaves (emphasis mine).[8] The territories became the linchpin of the slavery debate because the South, for reasons of political power, had to increase the number of slave states, while the North would not tolerate any new slave states. This is what Huston rightly called the "nationalization of slavery" in property rights: all states, ultimately, had to respect the same property rights, or the definition of property had to be fundamentally changed so as not to include people.[9] Ultimately, if property rights in slaves were beyond the control of Congress, the people of the territories (as Dred Scott claimed), or even the states through Congress, then there was no legal or constitutional means to prohibit slavery even in the North.

As if the sheer burden of the numbers on slave capital were not enough, South Carolina senator John C. Calhoun underscored the point of the necessity of slavery and even went further: "[I]f we have a right to hold our slaves, we have a right to hold them in peace and quiet, and . . . the toleration in non-slaveholding States of the establishment of societies and presses, and the delivery of lectures, with the express intention of calling into question our right to own slaves . . . [is] not only a violation of international laws, but of Federal compact."[10] Then–U.S. senator from Mississippi Jefferson Davis made it rather plain: "What is there in the character of that property [slaves] which excludes it from the general benefit of the principles applied to all other property?"[11]

THE SHERMAN ANTI-TRUST ACT PROTECTED THE "LITTLE GUY" AND REINED IN "BIG BUSINESS" ABUSES

Out of the . . . free frontiersmen, two or three Yankee shopkeepers emerged, a derelict lawyer from the East, a pair of practical Irish miners in collaboration with a pair of Irish saloonkeepers, an English invalid gambler, a land-jobber, a drover and innkeeper from Indiana [who] banded together to form a ruling class [and] have seized all power, all economic control.

—MATTHEW JOSEPHSON, THE ROBBER BARONS

[The oil men] would bring the oil refining to the region where it belonged. . . . But suddenly, at the very heyday of this confidence, a big hand reached out . . . to steal their conquest and throttle their future.

—IDA TARBELL, THE HISTORY OF THE STANDARD OIL COMPANY

A revolutionary new principle had been written into the law books by the Sherman Anti-Trust Act. . . . Private greed must henceforth be subordinated to public need.

—THOMAS A. BAILEY AND DAVID M. KENNEDY, THE AMERICAN PAGEANT

Seldom is national legislation aimed at a single company, much less an individual, but that was the case with the Sherman Anti-Trust Act, which was a response to the new corporate form created by John D. Rockefeller's Standard Oil Company. In July 1890, Congress passed the Sherman Anti-Trust Act with overwhelming support in the Senate (52 to 1) and unanimously in the House. It was a typical government reaction to the public's demand to "do something" when it wasn't clear what the effects of "doing something" would be.

The voting trust, created in 1879 by Rockefeller and S. C. T. Dodd, one of his lawyers, was designed to exchange shares of a new company—the Standard Oil Trust—for those of an existing company. In the process, the larger Standard Oil Trust would acquire 100 percent of the company's stock in exchange for a small percentage of trust certificates. While the monetary values would not immediately change (in theory, the acquired company would benefit greatly as the value of the trust company rose), the acquired company would lose independence. Soon after Standard Oil developed the trust, sugar, whiskey, cottonseed oil, linseed oil, tobacco, lead smelting, paint, and other industries witnessed the formation of their own trusts by the major producers.

At a time when Standard Oil controlled almost 90 percent of the nation's refining capacity, oil and kerosene prices were falling sharply and steadily. It is hard to argue the consumers were worse off. As can be seen in Lie #35, "The 'Robber Barons' Pillaged the Land," prices continually fell in the Rockefeller era. Of course, Ida Tarbell complained that "[Rockefeller] and his colleagues went into their first venture . . . not simply because it was a quick and effective way of putting everybody but themselves out of the refining business, but because . . . they could control the output of oil and its price."[1] To Tarbell, "Rockefeller's one irreconcilable enemy in the oil business has always been the oil producer."[2] In fact, Rockefeller's one irreconcilable enemy was waste and inefficiency: he viewed the producers, at times, as wasteful and inefficient in their operations, and thought he could run a tighter ship. As for the competitors in refining—who naturally screamed bloody murder at Rockefeller's superior efficiency—John McGee, a legal scholar examining the testimony of competitors who said Rockefeller's price cutting had harmed them, found no evidence to support any claims of predatory price cutting.[3] Other scholars recently have started to question the usefulness of the Sherman Act.[4] Indeed, the trust merely represented the latest attempt to organize business so as to stabilize profits. Rockefeller and others had tried "pools," cartels, and a host of other gimmicks to eliminate competition, and all failed, leaving Rockefeller to refer to them as "ropes of sand."[5] But the trust had one quality that made it more vulnerable than the pool or the cartel or other informal agreements: it was a matter of public record. Lawsuits flooded state courts, claiming that the new trusts restrained trade, and in 1892, the Ohio Supreme Court began the process of unraveling the Standard Oil Company.

Sherman has suffered from such broad wording as to render the act virtually unenforceable. Business historian Stuart Bruchey noted that business itself "regarded the Act as impractical, unenforceable, and hence innocuous."[6] The Act read: "Every contract, combination in the form of trust or otherwise, or conspiracy, in restraint of trade or commerce among the several States, or with foreign nations, is declared to be illegal."[7] Defining what was "in restraint of trade" was the difficulty. Did it mean restraining prices? Or entry into the market?

Business, of course, didn't wait for the government to answer those questions. Corporations immediately moved into a less regulated organizational structure called the vertical combination. A "monopoly" is typically understood as a horizontal combination, in which one company seeks to buy out or control all competitors so as to affect price. A vertical combination—already pioneered by the railroads—was now adopted by all major companies. It featured more emphasis on internal controls, especially on cost control through acquiring all parts of the manufacturing and sales process. Standard Oil, for example, would seek to own not only its oil in the ground, but also its own railroads, refining, and sales outlets. Gustavus Swift, with his meatpacking firm, acquired pig farms and cattle ranches, and later, in the twentieth century, his own trucking lines and refrigerated railroad cars, then finally, his own butcher shops and meat stores. Until the 1980s, Kodak Corporation had camera kiosks in most mall parking lots, where customers could drop off and purchase film. By controlling the product top-to-bottom, the new generation of corporate managers could not only predict costs and expenses, but *plan*. Becoming obsessed with planning, these managers grew quite conservative, preferring predictable smaller profits to larger gains that might fluctuate wildly.[8]

More important, however, were the real intentions of the Progressive reformers who passed Sherman. They had hoped to control the power of big business by eliminating the trusts. Yet the vertical combination made businesses far larger, far more powerful than the trusts ever were. The unintended consequence of the Sherman Act was to greatly increase the power and influence of big business in the United States. As Michael Allen and I noted in *A Patriot's History of the United States,* "Thanks to Sherman, American industry embarked on the first great merger wave toward truly giant-sized companies . . . [because] the Sherman Act had slammed shut alternative paths."[9] The first of these was U.S. Steel, the first billion-dollar corporation in the world.

Businesses also—even while adopting the vertical combination—moved into another form of organization called the "holding company," where a company could hold stock in another. While this required special state chartering legislation, New Jersey liberalized its laws in 1889 permitting companies to hold out-of-state companies, initiating a corporate land rush to the Garden State, led by Standard Oil. Eventually, these holding companies would also come under federal fire, as in the E. C. Knight sugar case of 1895, where the Supreme Court declared the regulation of manufacturing a state responsibility. Interstate commerce cases, however, were different, which is the rubric under which the Teddy Roosevelt Justice Department brought the Northern Securities antitrust case. J. P. Morgan, James J. Hill, and E. H. Harriman, along with representatives of the Standard Oil Company, had formed a single holding company worth $400 million (less than half that of U.S. Steel). The government claimed, despite the fact that there were no higher prices at the time, that the formation of such a company signaled a "threat" to create a monopoly, and for the first time the government acted on commerce as a potential threat as opposed to actual behavior, violating the "innocent until proven guilty" premise of American law.[10] Put another way, as big-business historians Louis Galambos and Joseph Pratt noted, "Neither the presidents, the regulatory agencies, nor the courts put forward an effective measure of concentration that could be understood by potential offenders and used as the lynchpin of antitrust policy."[11]

The final, most ironic turn of the Sherman Anti-Trust Act's story comes from research by economist George Bittlingmayer, who examined the effect of the enforcement of the Sherman and Clayton acts on *small* business. Logic would suggest that by punishing the big corporations, the "little guy" would profit, but Bittlingmayer's research found just the opposite: smaller companies were harmed by antitrust attacks on big companies, because profits across the board fell.[12] Applying his theory to Microsoft in the 1990s, Bittlingmayer again found that the competitors of Microsoft—the very companies that supposedly stood to gain from a government "slap upside the head" of the computer giant—saw their stock fall every time the government's case against Bill Gates improved, and rise every time it suffered a setback. Bittlingmayer also found that "low investment of the 1950s and early 1960s was due at least in part to a resurgence of aggressive antitrust and related initiatives interpreted as 'anti-business.' "[13] Indeed, he noted, "one actual effect of antitrust practice may have been to curtail investment."[14] In short, antitrust laws were adopted primarily to stop Standard Oil from lowering its prices to consumers, and have subsequently been employed unevenly and often irrationally against a variety of businesses, usually to the detriment of small business and overall corporate investment. Antitrust laws have worked about like most federal efforts to "fix" a market problem—they made it worse.

LIE #41

THE TRANSCONTINENTAL RAILROADS NEVER
WOULD HAVE BEEN BUILT WITHOUT GOVERNMENT

Government aid . . . took many forms. Without it, the [transcontinental] line could not have been built, quite possibly would not have been started.
—STEPHEN AMBROSE, NOTHING LIKE IT IN THE WORLD

Transcontinental railroad building was so costly and risky as to require government subsidies.
—THOMAS A. BAILEY AND DAVID KENNEDY, THE AMERICAN PAGEANT

. . . some form of public credit was essential [to build the transcontinental railroads].
—JOHN M. BLUM ET AL., THE NATIONAL EXPERIENCE

Though hardly considered a wild-eyed leftist, Stephen Ambrose wittingly or unwittingly reinforced the notion that it takes the government to accomplish great things when, in his best-selling book (later tainted by charges of plagiarism) *Nothing Like It in the World,* he argued that building the transcontinental railroads would have been impossible without the support of the federal government. His views have been the staple of countless U.S. history textbooks, including the widely used *American Pageant* and *National Experience.* Here's a news flash, ladies and gentlemen: James J. Hill built a transcontinental railroad—which was completed in 1893 as far as Seattle—without a cent of federal aid. I guess it didn't require "some form of public credit."

Given the history of railroad building prior to the transcontinentals, under other circumstances it would, in fact, be difficult to imagine how the federal government could even get involved in the first place. Virtually all the interstate railroads constructed before the Civil War were financed by private companies, or, at the very worst, by some sort of state bond guarantee for the securities of the construction firms.[1] Just as private companies had built roads in the early Republic, so too entrepreneurs such as Cornelius Vanderbilt, Erastus Corning, J. Edgar Thompson, and Jay Gould financed most of the nation's large railroads from their own pockets or through the sale of stock. Indeed, this process was so successful, and the number of stockholders grew so large, that a revolution in American business took place in which stockholders (the owners) had to elect professional managers to handle the business for them. Business historians called this the "managerial revolution."[2] The role of stock sales became so important that entrepreneurs separated into two camps based on how they sought to profit from the railroads. One group, called "political entrepreneurs" by historian Burton Folsom, wanted to obtain favors from local and state governments that would increase the value of the roads.[3] The other group, called "market entrepreneurs," usually turned to the market after failing to obtain government aid, but almost without exception proved more successful in their endeavors. Political entrepreneurs, illustrated by the activities of Jay Gould, Jim Fisk, and Daniel Drew, sought to use their political connections to manipulate stock prices, as in the "Harlem Corner" (where the trio bribed aldermen to shift votes on allowing the railroad to build through Harlem) or the "Erie War," where Fisk and Gould watered Erie Railroad stock, against stiff opposition from Vanderbilt. Their counterparts relied on tried and true business methods of building quality systems that provided the consumer with a good product deal at a low price. Because the former group obsessed about stock values in the short term, they tended to undercapitalize their roads or take shortcuts that jeopardized their operations. But the market entrepreneurs had long horizons: Vanderbilt's railroad, the New York Central, ran so safely and efficiently that not a single person died in an accident, compared to twenty-six dead and seventy-two injured on the Erie Railroad under Gould's direction alone.[4] The differences between the political and market entrepreneurs stood out most starkly in the efficiency of the lines: Vanderbilt chopped 13.3 percent from his expenses on the New York Central, increasing profits two hundred times.

Of course, businessmen—especially the railroaders—continued to seek government aid whenever possible, and during the Civil War, when the Union government was desperate to link the coasts to facilitate the shipment eastward of gold, cattle, and horses, the political entrepreneurs found legislators all too eager to listen to their proposals. The result was the Union Pacific and Central Pacific railroads, which in theory were to compete against each other, laying tracks toward some midpoint where they would meet up. In reality, the structure of the government support encouraged them to engage in sloppy and dangerous building and even to avoid connecting at all![5] Even a cursory examination of the land grants to the railroads should have alerted legislators to the incentives for fraud and inefficiency built into the system. Land was given to the companies, along with cash loans, for each mile of road constructed. It was based on a staggered scale in which companies received more money for laying track in hills, and still more ($48,000 per mile) in mountains. This encouraged builders to plot the most mountainous route possible, resulting in "winding, circuitous roads to collect more mileage."[6] Union Pacific's vice president, Thomas Durant, scolded his staff for putting in too much masonry in the supports, instructing them to substitute wooden culverts whenever possible.[7] Paid by the mile of track, the railroads zigzagged to find gold and silver, leading them through the Black Hills and helping initiate the Sioux Wars. Grenville Dodge, the Union Pacific's chief engineer, laid track on ice, which collapsed with the spring thaw. Much of the track laid by both the Union and Central Pacific had to be completely rebuilt just a few years later.

The railroads received nearly $500 million from land sales, and the government benefited greatly from reduced freight prices and mail delivery at reduced rates. But those savings to the government came at the expense of stockholders and bondholders, who bore the brunt of the financial collapse of the roads in the Panic of 1873. Economist Robert Fogel's study of the transcontinental railroads concluded they produced "social savings" of about 5 percent to the United States.[8] Others put the value of the railroads slightly lower when they were in direct competition with canals.[9] Congressmen more directly profited through a series of kickbacks in the Crédit Mobilier scandal, named after one of the construction companies owned by legislators. Crédit Mobilier swelled the costs of construction even above what the already gluttonous and inefficient roads were consuming, lining the pockets of the directors/legislators and driving up the price of the stock.

The waste got to be too much even for Congress, which finally demanded that the Union and Central Pacific link up, which they did in 1869. In 1874, Congress passed the Thurman Law, which required the Union Pacific to pay 25 percent of its earnings back to the government to cover its $28 million debt. Even as the famous "golden spike"—the symbolic spike of gold used to connect the lines in the ceremony (which was eventually removed and replaced with a normal iron spike)—was driven in, managers of both railroads were already planning to rebuild and relocate entire sections of track to cover up their shoddy construction. It took another five years before the Union Pacific fixed the new track it had laid earlier.

When the Panic of 1873 struck, three of the five transcontinentals fell into bankruptcy, which brought banker J. P. Morgan to the forefront. He reorganized many of the failing roads, requiring them to take on professional managers, often trained in his banking system. While these railroads languished in default, James J. Hill's Great Northern slashed costs by 13 percent. Hill, naturally, argued against giving any failing railroad government aid: "[T]he government should not furnish capital to [those] companies, in addition to their enormous land subsidies, to enable them to conduct their business in competition with enterprises that have received no aid from the public treasury."[10]

In contrast to the subsidized Union Pacific and Central Pacific, Hill's Great Northern Railroad showed not only that the private sector could and would build a transcontinental, but that he could beat the subsidized lines in efficiency and operations. A Minnesota railroad that Hill bought in 1878 had previously received federal subsidies and was subject to stock manipulations. Its record was so poor that it was called "Hill's Folly" when the Canadian-born Hill bought the line.[11] He quickly made it profitable, and his success inspired him to keep building. "We want the best possible line, shortest distance, lowest grades and least curvature," he stated, identifying those characteristics that would ensure low costs.[12] With no government land to give away to settlers, Hill actually *paid* $10 to each settler to farm near his railroad route. Hill imported seven thousand cattle from England, giving them away free to pioneers; established experimental farms to develop new, robust seeds and livestock breeds; and promoted crop rotation and fertilizers.[13] One of Hill's competitors was the Northern Pacific, which received 42 million acres of free government land. The Northern Pacific's president, Henry Villard, built lavishly along scenic routes that were outrageously expensive. In contrast, Hill chose the most efficient (if boring) paths, moving his supply depots forward as he built to reduce the time and cost of acquiring materials. Whereas Hill got his coal from supply bases in Iowa, Villard had to move his coal all the way from Indiana, costing him $2 a ton more than the Canadian. Typically, Villard tried to slow down Hill with government obstacles, delaying permits to cross Indian land, all to no avail. When Villard's Northern nearly collapsed in the Panic of 1893 and had to be reorganized with massive loans, Hill simply said of his superior railroad, "[W]e have gone along and met their competition."[14]

James J. Hill proved not only that private financiers would fund a transcontinental railroad, but that he could build one. And he built it so well that it survived when its government-funded competitors all failed. Now there's a lesson in market economics.

LIE #42

THE ROBBER BARONS WERE ONLY ASSUAGING THEIR GUILT
WITH THEIR PHILANTHROPY

Since their wealth was seemingly ill-gained, to purify their earnings, these men
would spend lavishly on their wives and children and donate large sums to show
the world that they were not the selfish people they were portrayed to be.
                                    —KYLE MA, THE INSIDER, AUGUST 30, 2007

[T]his "gospel of wealth" justified the ruthless behavior of entrepreneurs who ac-
cumulated unprecedented wealth and power through shady deals and conspira-
cies.
                                    —JOHN MACK FARAGHER, OUT OF MANY

The central problem with this myth is that it assumes the "robber barons"
felt guilty about their wealth. Of course, according to Ida Tarbell and
Matthew Josephson, these men were without conscience, so it's hard to figure
out where to begin with this. One thing is certain: most of the captains of industry who brought the United States into world preeminence as an economic
goliath believed in the very fiber of their being that they were ethical, responsible, and merely following tested and true business practices. They deserved
their wealth, and gave because they could. But once again, many modern historians are viewing the past through their own affluent lifestyles, and it is *they*
who feel guilt. Researchers have come up with a name for it: "affluenza."[1]
    Part of the confusion (when it is actually innocent confusion and not
ideological bias in historians) has stemmed from the comments of Andrew

Carnegie in his essays, collected in *The Gospel of Wealth* (1889), where he wrote that a wealthy businessman who spent his accumulated wealth on himself and his family was guilty twice: of keeping for himself that which did not belong to him and of depriving society of his talents. Carnegie was only "guilty" if he did not *use* his wealth to aid his fellow man—not because he had more than others. Of course, this was viewed as a subterfuge by leftist historians. Someone like Carnegie was a "despot who underpaid his employees and ruthlessly managed their working conditions."[2] Carnegie "spoke much about the welfare of his workers, but he practiced a hard line," observed the authors of *Unto a Good Land.*[3]

Yet Carnegie and his fellow captains of industry, such as John D. Rockefeller and Andrew Mellon, believed that it was their obligation to give. And did they give: their philanthropy exceeded anything in American history until, perhaps, recent years. Andrew Carnegie, who came to the United States from Scotland at the age of thirteen, worked as a bobbin boy. He then got a job with J. Edgar Thompson's Pennsylvania Railroad. At an early age, Carnegie announced that he wanted to give away the preposterous sum of $350 million in his lifetime. Years later, after founding the Cyclops Iron Company, the Keystone Bridge Company, then, of course, Carnegie Steel, the Scotsman retired a multimillionaire. In 1900, he sold Carnegie Steel to J. P. Morgan, who congratulated him on being "the richest man in the world." Most people know that Carnegie gave away most of his fortune. What most people don't know is that he made a decision to do so some twenty-five years before he retired, whereupon he actually started giving his money away.[4] Ultimately, he gave away close to $400 million, making him per capita probably the biggest single giver in history.

From all angles, the left has taken potshots at the industrialists and their motives. We learn from *The American Pageant* that Vanderbilt was "ill-educated, coarse, and ruthless."[5] Howard Zinn sneers at the establishment of numerous universities by the captains of industry: "The rich, giving part of their enormous earnings in this way, became known as philanthropists. These [men] did not encourage dissent: they trained the middlemen in the American system. . . ."[6] (It is ironic that Zinn, after being educated and teaching in private universities, such as Columbia, Harvard, Spelman, and Boston University, funded by these very philanthropists, claims they didn't "encourage dissent." *Et tu*, Zinn?) In passing, it should also be noted that Zinn spends a grand total of one small paragraph on the remarkable rise of Carnegie, then belabors—literally—the reader with page after page on workers and farmers.

Certainly the story of John D. Rockefeller's career tithing is noteworthy. Rockefeller, a member of the Baptist Church, gave 10 percent of his income from an early age. When he was in his forties, Rockefeller tithed over $100,000 a year. At one point—when a meal cost a quarter and a suit of men's clothes cost $20—Rockefeller gave $1 million per year to his church, in addition to his other philanthropies. He once said that he put God first, his family second, and business third. Here was one of the wealthiest men in the world who put his business third! "From the beginning," he said, "I was trained to work, to save, and to give."[7] Rockefeller gave over $35 million to the University of Chicago alone, and poured millions into black schools, southern schools, and Baptist schools. He donated a small fortune to wiping out the destructive boll weevil in the South.

Likewise, Andrew Mellon determined in mid-career that his great, and growing, collection of art should be available to the public. He decided not only to donate the art itself, but, anticipating the PC threats of future generations, in which liberal trustees gain control of conservative philanthropies, to fund a national gallery to house it and to provide an endowment so the art would always be protected from intrusions by the government. In 1936 he transmitted a letter with this incredibly generous offer to the president— Franklin D. Roosevelt, who had harassed him in the courts and in the newspapers steadily for four years. And, to top it off, Mellon insisted that the National Museum of Art *not* bear his name, because it was the "people's gallery."[8] Reading his most recent biography, which runs more than six hundred pages and mentions virtually every memo or letter Mellon wrote, one never gets the sense that he was in any way "guilty" or "ashamed" of his wealth. Quite the contrary; giving was what rich men did, he thought. While Franklin Roosevelt was insisting, "Americans must forswear that conception of wealth, which, through excessive profits, creates undue private power over private affairs," he nevertheless was all too happy to accept Mellon's fantastic gifts to the public.[9] Even though Roosevelt—having only a short time before referred to Mellon as an "economic royalist"—accepted the gift with enthusiasm and endeavored to see that the necessary legislation was passed, some of his fellow Democrats still wanted to reject a national art museum because it came from a capitalist. Wright Patman called the precedent a "very bad one," and said, "A lasting memorial [in Mellon's] honor should not be constructed in the nation's capital, even at his own expense."[10]

This was typical of many of the New Dealers, who hated ambition, wealth, entrepreneurship, and businessmen more than they cared about the public. Equally typical was Rockefeller's list of priorities, in which God was first, his family was second, and his wealth was third. Even to this day, Americans continue to be blessed by the risks those entrepreneurs took, and the charity they provide.

THE INCOME TAX WAS CREATED TO MAKE THE RICH PAY THEIR FAIR SHARE, AND TAX CUTS ONLY BENEFIT UPPER-INCOME AMERICANS

[Treasury Secretary Andrew] Mellon carried his policies to unreasonable extremes. He proposed eliminating inheritance taxes and reducing the tax on high incomes by two-thirds. . . . Mellon's proposals were too reactionary to win unqualified approval.

— JOHN A. GARRATY, THE AMERICAN NATION

Mellon's spare-the-rich policies thus shifted much of the tax burden from the wealthy to the middle-income groups.

— THOMAS A. BAILEY AND DAVID M. KENNEDY, THE AMERICAN PAGEANT

[President Warren G. Harding] *allowed Secretary of the Treasury Andrew Mellon . . . one of the world's richest men, to pursue "soak-the-poor" policies.*

— IRWIN UNGER, THESE UNITED STATES

The phrase "Nothing is certain but death and taxes" would have puzzled the Founders, as they established the Constitution without *any* direct or income taxes. Instead, they provided for all government revenue to come from two sources: the import tariff (a type of sales tax on imported items, regularly adjusted by Congress) and land sales (which made up a major portion of the government's revenue prior to the Civil War). Even in the Civil War, however, when both the Confederacy and the Union introduced forms of an income tax (with the South's being more oppressive), the assumption was that the income tax was a necessary—and temporary—wartime measure, not an instrument of social change.[1] The U.S. Supreme Court also (correctly) ruled that income taxes, even on corporations, were unconstitutional.[2]

Liberal historians have routinely complained that the income tax was not implemented sooner, and/or used more aggressively. For example, Morton Horowitz argued that the American legal system constructed a scaffold of legalisms that concealed the true costs of public spending by foisting them off on individuals, and that a more redistributionist form of taxation should have been employed.[3] Robert Stanley complained that the 1913 income tax was symbolic, and not genuinely redistributive. Reformers, he lamented, forged a consensus with conservatives to permit only minor taxation as a means to enlist the "lower classes."[4]

Whatever the arguments used in securing passage of the Sixteenth Amendment, the objective was abundantly clear, as a historian of the American income tax wrote: "[S]upport for a radical progressive income tax had far more to do with the search for social justice in an industrializing nation than with the quest for an elastic source of revenue."[5] To obtain enough support for a constitutional amendment, the proponents had to make the income tax incredibly simple (hence what was essentially a one-page income tax return), and the rates were phenomenally low. Passage was greeted with stunningly naive reactions, such as that of a Missouri congressman who said that it marked "the dawn of a brighter day, with more of sunshine, more of the songs of the birds, more of that sweetest music, the laughter of children well fed, well clothed, well housed . . . good, even-handed, wholesome Democracy shall be triumphant."[6]

It didn't take long for the U.S. government itself to dispel such nonsensical arguments, for within six years of the income tax amendment passing, lawmakers, using the excuse of wartime needs, jacked the top tax rate of 6 percent up to an incredible 75 percent. Even the lowest rate, which stood at only 1 percent of those who made over $3,000 but under $20,000 (i.e., the largest number of all taxpayers), skyrocketed to 25 percent. So much for "soaking the rich."

Here was the nation, in 1919, with the lowest rank of taxpayers sending in a hefty 25 percent of their income to the government, while the wealthy were expected to cough up 75 percent! (No wonder one economist, some seventy years later, in a masterful understatement quipped, "The net contribution of the income tax to inducing equality is not obvious.")[7] This should have been a

Progressive's dream, except for one problem: tax revenues dipped steadily with each new tax hike. When Pittsburgh banking and steel magnate Andrew Mellon became secretary of the Treasury, he concluded (to liberals' surprise), that "the result [of higher tax rates] is that sources of taxation are drying up; *wealth is failing to carry its share of the tax burden.* . . . [emphasis added]."[8]

Using Treasury Department statistics, Mellon prepared a chart showing the decline of taxable income from 1916 to 1921. Both the number of returns and the net income resulting from the top wealth holders plunged, with returns falling by four-fifths and income falling from almost $1 billion to $153 million.[9] Mellon found that the rich had been squirreling their money away in tax-exempt bonds, rather than investing in profitable activities. It was a disaster for the nation. As Burton Folsom noted, "[T]he U.S. had more and more large football stadiums and civic centers but fewer and fewer factories where these cityfolks could work long-term jobs."[10]

When Mellon's plan passed Congress, it reduced the top rate to 24 percent, and the lowest rate to 5 percent—far above where the rates initially were in 1913 (and where people expected they would remain), but vastly lower than the stratospheric levels reached in the administration of Woodrow Wilson. The result? The wealthy paid more than ever. In 1921 those earning less than $10,000 paid a total of $155 million in taxes; after the tax cuts "on the rich," the lowest income group paid only $32 million. Those paying over $100,000 had only paid $194 million in 1921, but after the cuts "for the rich," the "rich" paid almost twice as much, or $361 million![11]

Tax cuts always yield more revenue from the wealthiest groups—but they usually yield more revenue overall as well. John F. Kennedy's tax cuts produced more federal revenues than even the White House economists projected. From 1964 to 1967, the cuts always exceeded expectations for federal income, and in 1966, the cuts incredibly produced 11 percent more revenue than projected.[12] And once again, revenue from the wealthy almost doubled, while the taxes paid by the lower income classes fell, even though Kennedy's tax cuts were small compared to those of the Mellon era.[13] As a result of Ronald Reagan's tax cuts, federal income rose by more than 40 percent, and again the rich paid far more, while lower tax brackets paid less. For those obsessed with Reagan-era "deficits," they certainly did not come from the tax cuts.

Since the adoption of the income tax, the combined federal, state, and local tax burden on average Americans has grown immensely. "Tax Freedom

Day"—the day when Americans cease working to pay their taxes and begin to collect income they can keep, according to the Tax Foundation—fell on April 30, 2007, or two days later than in 2006.[14] While George W. Bush steadfastly kept in place the tax cuts he achieved when he took office, when Tax Freedom Day fell to its earliest date since 1984 (April 18), increases at the state and local levels have pushed the overall tax burden back up. The vision of the original backers of the income tax has failed to materialize, however. Repeatedly, both Democratic and Republican presidents have seen that raising taxes on the rich only ensures that the rich will pay less than ever.

LIE #44

BUSINESS FAILURES AND TAX CUTS
COMBINED TO CAUSE THE GREAT DEPRESSION

The income tax cuts proposed by Treasury Secretary Andrew Mellon had increased the volume of money available for speculation.
— PAUL S. BOYER ET AL., THE ENDURING VISION

Like the banks, the investment industry was free from regulation and given to misrepresentation, manipulation of stock prices, and inside deals.
— JEANNE BOYDSTON ET AL., MAKING A NATION

Americans have often blamed the stock market collapse for their plight in the 1930s. The blame is not entirely misplaced . . . the 1920s had been a time of economic growth, but that economic growth depended on an unstable balance of factors. . . . With 50 percent of the nation's income going to only 20 percent of its families, the market . . . was limited.
— IRWIN UNGER, THESE UNITED STATES

What is most astounding about this myth—despite the fact that most major textbooks continue to propagate it—is that *historians* almost all accept the premise that big business and the tax cuts of the 1920s caused the Great Depression, but almost no economists do. If the incredible volume of economic research on the Great Depression in the last forty years has proved anything, it is that business was the least important factor in causing the massive downturn. And the most damaging participant in the whole affair? Government.

One must conclude that most historians still base much of their "economic analysis"—to whatever degree it can be called that—on John Maynard Keynes's *General Theory of Employment, Interest and Money* (1936), or on subsequent Keynesian regurgitations, such as those of John Kenneth Galbraith (e.g., *The Great Crash, 1929,* 1955). Their general story goes like this: The tax cuts recommended by Treasury Secretary Andrew Mellon in the 1920s caused an orgy of speculation in the stock market. That fueled the "disparities in wealth" that already existed because the evil capitalists were again making money after World War I, and thus the "ordinary people" gambled in the stock market as a way to "catch up." (By the way, while the dubious claim that 50 percent of the nation's income went to 20 percent of the families is a standard statistic used in these narratives, they never seem to note that New Deal income tax policies resulted in, as of 2007, some 60 percent of all income taxes being paid by only 10 percent of the taxpayers!)

Anyway, to continue the accepted narrative, "big banks" fed the "speculation" through their "securities affiliates" (brokerage houses), which siphoned off depositor dollars to wager on the market. Business, interested only in short-term gains, ignored the warning signs and continued to erect paper empires, such as Samuel Insull's massive electric utility company. But (for whatever reason—the historians never seem able to say) the "bubble burst," and the stock market crash led to the banking panic. We were doomed until Franklin D. Roosevelt arrived in the nick of time to save the nation by punishing business and providing government jobs that restored full employment. Roosevelt, according to these nostrums, was the savior of capitalism. Since virtually all major college textbooks adopt some version of this, I'll spare the reader a five-page footnote.

It's all baloney, and economists—who, unlike liberal historians, actually have to *prove* things—know it. The first substantial challenge to the Keynesian/ Galbraith model came from Nobel Prize winner Milton Friedman and his associate Anna J. Schwartz in their magisterial *Monetary History of the United States.*[1] They singled out as the main culprit of the Depression the Federal Reserve Board, which was supposedly a private institution but which acted largely as a government agency and which, in the 1920s, was still heavily influenced by administration concerns. From 1929 to 1932, when a crash turned to a recession, then to a depression, the Fed stood by and allowed the money supply to fall by an incredible one-third. They also emphasized the failure of the

Fed to stem the tide of bank collapses, particularly the pivotal Bank of United States in New York, the largest bank in the nation to close up to that point.

Once Friedman and Schwartz opened the door, a trickle of criticism of government policies turned into a flood. What about the claim that Americans were "speculatin' out dere"? Some were; most weren't. Either way, many studies have shown that (1) the "bubble" effect in the market was either nonexistent or minimal; (2) the investments pretty much reflected real values of the companies, both when they went up and when they fell; (3) people were well informed as to what stocks they were buying; (4) those engaging in stock purchases and sales represented a cross section of Americans (28 percent held securities of some type by 1929); and (5) the ultimate cause of the crash was . . . you guessed it, something the government did.[2] Economists, unlike historians, are loath to make absolute statements. Even Eugene White, one of those who has argued for the presence of a bubble, rejects the notion that stock market crashes are the major source of instability—rather it is financial policy, which is the responsibility of the Fed.[3] White also argues that while brokers recognized the oncoming crash, investors did not, although Gene Smiley has found evidence to the contrary. Either way, *many* people, including Charles Merrill, the leading guru of middle-class investors, suspected a correction was in order and warned their investors to pull out long before the crash.[4] As Smiley wrote,

> In the first half of the 1920s common stocks appear to have been underpriced. As firms adopted policies that paid stockholders stable dividends, and as corporate profits rose, common stock prices were bid up. . . . Anticipated corporate profits grew, and investors continued to bid up stock prices. . . . But margin lending alone cannot explain the stock market boom.[5]

As to the notion that there was extreme income inequality, it is true that in *any and all* periods of great economic growth the rich will, proportionately, get richer—temporarily. This is the nature of risk: the few who survive inevitably reap big benefits. Yet while there is little evidence that the tax cuts of the 1920s—strongly associated with Treasury Secretary Andrew Mellon—were funneled into the stock market, there is overwhelming evidence that the tax cuts unleashed the roar of American business. The *average* unemployment rate in the 1920s was under 3.5 percent, and in 1926, unemployment reached the unheard-of low of 1 percent.[6] Typically, however, it has been argued that most income gains in the 1920s went to the top 5 percent.[7] That's fine reasoning if you only go by "wealth" gains and ignore the incredible improvements in daily life produced in the 1920s: real per capita income rose from $522 to $716; consumers' share of GNP rose more than 20 percent, despite the fact that overall prices were falling; three-fourths of nonfarm households acquired electricity; air travel increased tenfold; and more than 11 million families bought homes by the mid-1920s.[8] By 1928, American homes had 15 million irons, 6.8 million vacuum cleaners, 4.5 million toasters, and 750,000 of the new electric refrigerators. Auto production soared an astonishing 255 percent during the decade, and radios became a common household item. Electricity, thanks largely to Samuel Insull and his Rockefeller-like obsession with driving down prices, became so inexpensive that most people could electrify their houses and businesses. Electric power production rose by 300 percent between 1900 and 1929.[9]

Make no mistake: this growth occurred primarily because of business, but it was the tax cuts of Andrew Mellon that released the creative energies of American entrepreneurs. The "rising tide" lifted all boats. When Mellon came in as secretary of the Treasury, tax rates were shockingly high, having risen from a top rate of 5 percent in 1913 to a top rate of 75 percent in 1920! Mellon, who firmly believed the rich should pay most of the taxes, discovered that the best way to ensure they did so was to cut their tax rates. They would then employ their money, pay more taxes, and, in the process, jump-start the economy. And did they pay taxes! The share of taxes paid by those with incomes over $500,000 soared, with "the rich" paying almost 50 percent more than before the tax cut, and the "poor" paying between 40 percent and 70 percent less. Mellon's policies paid off one-third of the national debt in less than a decade. (Imagine, today, with a national debt at over $9 trillion, how a politician would be received who slashed it by a third in less than ten years!)[10]

But this prosperity began to fade some in late 1928. For one thing, Europe's economies were in trouble, and the world economy was already "globalized" far more than people understood. (One exception, ironically, was Benjamin Strong, head of the New York Federal Reserve Bank, who had attempted to design the Fed's policy in such a way as to encourage Britain and the European nations to recover faster.) Another factor that began to work against U.S. economic health was the gold standard, for as nation after nation in Europe left the gold standard, a run on American gold ensued that nearly finished off the reserves of the banks. Perhaps the most important structural weakness was in agriculture, where there were simply too many farmers to maintain profitability. Yet instead of allowing the market to winnow out the unproductive farmers, the government continually sought to artificially prop up prices. Once the farmers began to go under, thousands of farm banks neared bankruptcy. All of this was largely unnoticed in the midst of the phenomenal boom but would react dangerously to any sudden shock.

While no economists can convincingly say what triggered the Great Crash, the Smoot-Hawley tariff has been singled out as the most likely candidate, beginning with Jude Wanniski's 1978 book *The Way the World Works*.[11] Wanniski traced the rises and falls of the stock market to news associated with the Smoot-Hawley tariff, which was massive in its portended effect. Almost every imported good would increase under the tariff, and some raw materials would be taxed significantly higher, causing manufacturers to immediately anticipate higher costs and lower sales. This produced instant investment uncertainty, and shocked prices. The market plunged with each new hurdle in Congress that the tariff crossed.[12] Only recently have economists linked the monetary contraction described by Milton Friedman to the impact of the tariff, with startling results: Douglas Irwin, and Mario Crucini and James Kahn, found that the Smoot-Hawley tariff's deleterious effect on the economy was equal to *5 percent* of GNP! To put that in perspective, the 9/11 attacks were perhaps 3 percent of GNP; Katrina, less than .5 percent.[13]

Once government policy—via Smoot-Hawley—had triggered the Crash, it only remained for the "great engineer," President Herbert Hoover, to mess it up worse with tax increases and more government intrusion. For example, after initially cutting taxes mildly—not enough to offset the monetary contraction—Hoover raised taxes. Congress jumped on the bandwagon by passing a check tax, ensuring that commerce would be further stifled.[14] The Fed allowed the money supply to shrink further by failing to rescue banks that were collapsing, and Hoover steadfastly remained on the gold standard.

In retrospect, if it seems that a single factor, Smoot-Hawley, might have caused the Crash, most economists today agree that remaining on the gold standard was the single most important factor in turning a recession into a depression. As Federal Reserve chairman Ben Bernanke noted, "I do think that the only theory that explains the timing and widespread nature of the

Great Depression has to involve . . . monetary and financial issues which in turn are intimately connected to the gold standard."[15] Once banks began to fail as a result of losing the gold reserves, "contagion" set in, and the obsolete American unit bank system could not transmit information or move cash around fast enough to stop the runs.[16] Hoover's "solutions," such as the Reconstruction Finance Corporation, made matters worse by publicizing the names of borrower banks.

Most of Roosevelt's solutions in reality did little. The public hoopla of "jobs programs" barely dented the unemployment numbers, which still stood at 12.5 percent in 1939, or *ten times* what they had been under Coolidge. Again, modern economists are almost unanimous that the New Deal programs hindered recovery. The NIRA, according to Bernanke, "slowed the recovery by reducing the speed with which wages and prices adjusted."[17] Stephen DeCanio has shown that the minimum wage law slammed the door shut on new hiring by substantially raising the cost of every employee. Suddenly, what was a small, but steady, rise in employment stopped cold.[18] State bank deposit laws, such as the later Federal Deposit Insurance Corporation, actually *contributed* to bank weakness in the 1930s.[19] Most financial economists agree that the Glass-Steagall Act, which separated investment banking (the "securities affiliates") from commercial banking, harmed American banking and made us less competitive than we could be.

Most overlooked by the historians, however, is the fact that the long-term price of New Deal programs has been acknowledged to be steep to the point of bankruptcy, including the portending bailout of Social Security and the complete failure of the Aid to Families with Dependent Children (AFDC), or what modern Americans know as "welfare." (While greatly expanded under Lyndon Johnson, this program was started in the 1930s.) Social Security is on a trajectory for a massive collapse, with no indication that any president other than George W. Bush had any inclination to fix it. In the 1990s, a Republican Congress finally passed "welfare reform," although Bill Clinton vetoed it twice, eliminating the worst parts of AFDC. But as of yet, no one has figured out how to fix the pathology of single-parent homes it created from 1965 to 1994.

Did FDR do anything right? Yes. By taking the United States off the gold standard, he saved what was left of the banking system. But as they say, even a blind squirrel finds a nut once in a while.

LBJ's Great Society Had a Positive Impact on the Poor

Great Society domestic programs cost only a little more than $6 billion between 1964 and 1967. . . . Many of the programs put in place during the sixties remain pillars in the American welfare state. If Johnson's programs fell short of eliminating poverty in the nation, they nevertheless changed many lives for the better.
— David E. Harrell, Unto a Good Land

In 1965 and 1966, the 89th Congress, the most productive since the New Deal, adopted such innovations as . . . rent subsidies, demonstration cities, a teacher corps, regional medical centers . . . and Medicaid to provide medical care for the poor. . . . Lyndon Johnson could take pride in the achievements of the "fabulous 89th" [Congress] which opened up prospects for a new era of reform. . . ."
— Samuel Eliot Morison et al.,
A Concise History of the American Republic

[The Great Society was] the most impressive record of domestic legislation in a single session for 30 years. . . . [It] represented the culmination of New Deal liberalism in its effort to reverse patterns of privation and inequality in American economic life.
— John M. Blum et al., The National Experience

In 1965, Lyndon Johnson proclaimed a "War on Poverty," a never-ending program that could always be extended by simply changing the definitions of poverty. Some of the policies—perhaps all—were well intended, although in retrospect one has to question their function as a vote-getting ploy. But programs such as food stamps, which were often shunned by poor people who still had a modicum of respect, were advertised and hustled, so that eventually a large percentage of those eligible were enrolled. Once a family was dependent on food stamps, the government could dictate their behavior, preventing them from using the stamps for such products as alcohol and tobacco (which everyone agreed was "bad"), but also eventually defining what products constituted "food," reducing individual choice still further. Since government was enmeshed in diets, a controversy erupted in the Reagan administration about whether ketchup, which was nutritious but hardly filling, qualified as "food." If people go to bed hungry, did it require that they receive *filling* food or *nutritious* food?

If the food stamp program revealed some of the difficulties of having the government try to manage individual households' groceries, the Aid to Families with Dependent Children (AFDC) program showed that the law of unintended consequences is always in effect, and therefore essential institutions such as the family cannot be subject to social engineering. Originally, AFDC was a New Deal program intended to provide support to widows who had children. A century earlier, a community or church might have taken over that role, but after the Progressives centralized most charities under state direction for "efficiency" in the late 1800s, many people fell through the cracks. Still, the number of widows with children was relatively small, and thus the program had minimal ill effects. The Great Society legislators, however, expanded the program to include any woman with children in a household where there was no male present. Gone were the requirements that a woman with children had to have been married and then widowed. Now, simply being a "female-headed household" qualified a woman for money for herself and her kids, with a small increase coming for each additional child. In 1950, there were only 651,000 families on AFDC, but by 1970 there were 2.5 million AFDC families, and by 1976 there were 3.5 million families on welfare.[1] Illegitimate births soared 170 percent for blacks and 353 percent for whites (although the total number of black illegitimacies was more than six times higher overall than that of whites).[2]

Ironically, progress against poverty had been rapid from 1960 to 1968, with the largest drop coming after the John Kennedy tax cut. However, in 1968, when the Great Society programs were coming online, progress against poverty ended, and for several years the United States actually had *more* poor people.[3] Spending, however, took off like an Atlas booster rocket: welfare spending per low-income person went from just under $1,000 per person in 1961 to over $8,000 by 1977, with no appreciable change in the poverty levels.[4] Individual states with different welfare policies also found that the fifteen highest-benefit states had more people on welfare and higher unemployment than the U.S. average, and far more than the fifteen lowest-benefit states.[5]

Although by 1980 most people intuitively knew that welfare wasn't working, no book did more to debunk the Great Society welfare programs than Charles Murray's *Losing Ground* (1984).[6] Murray's book systematically destroyed the arguments that a slow economy or other factors could have caused the rise in single-parent households and crime. As a statistician, Murray relied on extensive analytical tables, but no statistics proved his point as well as a few simple comparisons of a fictitious couple, "Harold and Phyllis," and how the new welfare laws presented different options to them. Murray explained that with welfare available to Phyllis, there was no incentive for her and Harold to stay married, or if living together, to get married. Financially, marriage placed a burden on couples because it removed their welfare benefits. By staying unmarried and living together, if Harold had a job, he and Phyllis could "earn" almost double what they could from any other living situation.[7] Moreover, Murray was able to explain why blacks were disproportionately hurt by welfare laws: since the majority lived in urban areas, especially big cities, blacks were easier for government bureaucrats and social workers to identify as "poor" than were rural whites.

AFDC said to any woman who received it, "You don't need a man in the house. You can do better on your own." Since arguments and disagreements were bound to occur in any relationship, the pressures put on women by AFDC to "kick the bum out" proved irresistible. Soon, illegitimacy rates began to skyrocket, to the point that by the early 1990s some two-thirds of all inner-city black children had no father in the home. One study estimated that half of the increase in out-of-wedlock births among black women was directly attributable to additional welfare benefits.[8] Worse, without male role models to identify with, young black males gravitated to the strong male leaders in gangs, which then dragged them into a life of crime. Crime by youths under eighteen more than doubled between 1960 and 1976.[9]

These trends were only accelerated by revisions in divorce laws that introduced "no-fault" divorce. States began changing their laws in the 1970s, at which time usually a full court hearing and some proof of cause was required, to require a simple statement that the parties had "irreconcilable differences." The number of children living in one-parent (mostly single-mother) families rose in the 1970s from 11 percent to 19 percent. By the 1980s, "only 50 percent [of children] could expect to spend their entire childhood in an intact family."[10] This was well down from the 80 percent of children who grew up in a family of two biological parents in the years after World War II. Certainly, no-fault divorce played a part: divorce rates, which stood at 10 per 1,000 in the early 1960s, increased sharply to 23 per 1,000 marriages by 1979, surpassing death as the leading cause of family breakup in 1974.[11]

Despite an assault on the "nuclear family" by leftists, evidence began to surface showing that single-parent households were damaging children, culminating with the comment by Vice President Dan Quayle in 1992 about the television show *Murphy Brown,* which had celebrated the heroine's decision to pursue motherhood without a husband or father present. Quayle said, "It doesn't help matters when prime-time TV has Murphy Brown—a character who supposedly epitomizes today's intelligent, highly paid, professional woman—mocking the importance of fathers, by bearing a child alone, and calling it just another 'lifestyle choice.'" Quayle was ridiculed for his stand.

Within a few years, however, it had become obvious that in fact children were being damaged by family breakup, and that creating a generation of fatherless boys was not in the best interests of either the children or the nation. Barbara Dafoe Whitehead summarized the sociological literature in 1993 in an article called "Dan Quayle Was Right." The social research showed that children from out-of-wedlock or divorced families did worse on almost all measures of well-being. They were more likely to experience poverty; to drop out of high school or get pregnant; to abuse drugs; and to be in trouble with the law. Moreover, children from disrupted families were more likely to suffer from physical or sexual abuse. Those children also had a harder time staying in their own marriages and even holding regular jobs.

By the 1990s—even as Quayle made his comments and faced ridicule—policy makers were reaching a grim consensus that the Great Society programs had been wrong, and that welfare had not worked. It had driven people away from work and into dependency, and it had destroyed families. In 1994, Republicans won both houses of Congress and began crafting a Welfare

Reform Act that limited welfare payments to two years and placed a cap on the total number of years that one could qualify. Although President Bill Clinton vetoed this legislation twice, after consulting the polls, he finally signed it . . . then took credit for it. Despite the dire predictions of the Great Society liberals, most of those who were pushed off welfare found employment. Contrary to predictions that abortion rates would sharply rise, they slightly fell. A part of the damage done by the Great Society had been undone. But what was not undone was the condition of the marriage-less ghetto, in which the overwhelming majority of black women raised families without a husband present. That perpetuated the pathology of young black males associating with gangs and rejecting traditional routes to economic success.

But the sad fact is, no government program has done more to destroy the black family than the Great Society's expansion of Aid to Families with Dependent Children (AFDC). Black economist Walter E. Williams is famous for saying that if he were the "Grand Dragon" of the Ku Klux Klan, he could think of no more destructive program to African Americans than public education. I beg to differ. Some, if not most, of the effects of public education can be overcome with time. The pathologies put in place by AFDC overwhelmingly resulted in black teens being either pregnant or dead. There was no time for them to recover from the program's ill effects. By 1990, 57 percent of all black births were out of wedlock.

The results of welfare reform started coming in a few years later, and while the detrimental effects of welfare were obvious from the results, it was not as clear what else was needed (besides ending welfare) for single mothers to succeed. For example, a Wisconsin study found that the number of women using AFDC plummeted from 96,300 in 1990 to just over 5,000 in 1998. The study also reported that "one out of four women [who] were on AFDC in 1990 were clearly self-supporting" eight years later. Working full-time was necessary, however, to emerge from poverty: "To be successful, you simply had to work four quarters a year."[12] Attitudes toward work, interpersonal skills, and ability to take instruction were also important.

Nationally, 42 percent of black children were living in poverty before welfare reform: seven years later, after welfare reform, barely 32 percent were still in poverty.[13] Similarly, the number of children living in hunger has plummeted since 1992, while the number of families on AFDC was cut by half.[14] But AFDC's damage was long lasting in other ways, especially the demise of the male-headed family. As Wade Horn and Andrew Bush showed in "Fathers, Marriage, and the Next Phase of Welfare Reform," the next step in welfare reform had to be a return to strengthening marriages and especially to getting fathers once again involved in raising their children.[15] In an era when liberals have pushed for normalizing "nontraditional families," that next step will be a big one.

THE DECLINE OF AMERICAN AUTOS AND STEEL WAS CAUSED
BY INSUFFICIENT GOVERNMENT SUPPORT FOR THE INDUSTRIES

*The practical choice is not between government intervention and nonintervention.
[Rather] industrial policies are necessary to ease society's adjustment to structural
changes. . . . Government industrial policies are also appropriate when the public
return on investment is likely to exceed private return.*
—IRA C. MAGAZINER AND ROBERT B. REICH, MINDING AMERICA'S BUSINESS

*American businesses in the 1980s and 1990s embarked on a rigorous downsizing
that resulted in the firing of many skilled and loyal workers.*
—DAVID E. HARRELL ET AL., UNTO A GOOD LAND

How did the U.S. auto industry, which once outproduced and outsold *all*
major foreign competitors by a factor of four, fall on such hard times?
Why did American steel, not only the world leader for decades, but the standard bearer for quality, nearly collapse in the 1970s and 1980s before staging a
recovery? If you listen to liberals such as Ira Magaziner or Robert Reich, you
would have to conclude it was due to government failure—the unwillingness
of (mostly Republican) presidents to "support" Detroit through tariffs or import quotas, or the inability of those same leaders to force the Japanese into
restricting their (superior quality) exports. Magaziner and Reich, for example,
contend that "a minimalist role for government might be appropriate in an
economy that was sheltered from international competition," but, obviously,
not for the modern U.S. economy.[1] A spate of books with titles such as *The*

Deindustrialization of America and *Manufacturing Matters: The Myth of the Postindustrial Economy* heralded a "service" economy that could no longer compete with the Japanese because of insufficient government intervention.[2]

In fact, the only role government played in damaging either industry came through environmental regulations, workplace laws that restricted productivity, and pro-union policies that kept American wages at ridiculously high levels for almost twenty years. But don't get the idea that Detroit's auto executives and the United Auto Workers (UAW) didn't make things much worse: they did. The resulting combination of bad government, bad management, and poor labor policies knocked the world leader in both autos and steel off its pedestal, possibly permanently.

Detroit's problems did not begin in Washington but a century earlier in the boardrooms of the Pennsylvania Railroad and DuPont Chemical, where a new business organization called the "managerial hierarchy" became entrenched. This form of management resulted from large numbers of stockholders—the owners—needing permanent managers who could operate the company. Hence, the arrival of the "professional" managers who were presidents or chief operating officers. Among its many advantages, the managerial hierarchy brought with it a division of management units, in which every unit supervised a single, special area of operations. Sales, legal, research and development, and other units appeared, but by far the most important (although it came under several names) was the finance division. Finance oversaw the raising of capital for future acquisitions, and also imposed budgets on the companies. Within seventy-five years, though, the finance men or "numbers men" dominated most major U.S. corporations, and with their total control of the statistics, they were almost impossible to defeat in boardroom debates. "Production men," or those who had experience in actually making products and building things, were ignored—only because they couldn't make a stronger case with the statistics. Several classic examples of how disastrous this was for Detroit are found in David Halberstam's *The Reckoning,* where plant managers, saddled with excess bumpers or starters, would simply dump them in a local river rather than risk the wrath of their superiors in Detroit, who "knew" how many bumpers or starters they needed. (Halberstam called this the "screw Detroit" game.) In another case, Ford's numbers men, led by future secretary of defense Robert McNamara, were told by the "production men" they needed new, larger paint ovens to accommodate the bigger Ford trucks. Instead, the numbers men suggested painting the trucks in two stages in a single oven, a process that any car owner knew would result in a two-toned truck.[3]

Car designs failed to keep pace with technology or consumer demand. Small "pony cars," such as the Ford Mustang or the Chevrolet Camaro, kept growing and growing, so that after five years they had become the size of a typical 1960s-era family car. Even the famous two-seat Thunderbird was re-made into a large touring luxury sedan. It's not that Detroit didn't have the technology: racing teams had used fuel injectors, blowers, overhead camshafts, electronic ignition, and dozens of other performance and safety technologies for almost a decade. But the Big Three (General Motors, Ford, Chrysler) seemed content to make the auto chassis longer, add more chrome, or change the upholstery inside.

Then came the twin blows of the environmental movement and the consumer movement, highlighted by Ralph Nader's *Unsafe at Any Speed* (1964) and passage of the National Traffic Motor Vehicle Safety Act of 1966.[4] The evidence on the benefits of auto safety regulations is not at all obvious. A 1991 Centers for Disease Control report showed that while the use of auto safety seats for children had risen for eight years, child fatalities had not decreased.[5] Nor has the seat belt regulation pushed by Nader even proven as successful as is widely believed: Hawaii, which had the most rigorously enforced seat belt law and the highest compliance in the nation, "has experienced an increase in traffic fatalities and fatality rates since its law went into effect in December 1985."[6] Sam Peltzman's famous 1975 study showed that the safer cars were made, the more likely drivers were to take risks.[7] Researchers comparing like models of automobiles with, and without, air bags discovered that personal injury claims rose significantly in those with air bags.[8]

By the early 1970s, both the consumer safety and environmental movements had gained their own Kremlin-sized bureaucracies inside the U.S. government, and both bureaucracies had begun churning out rules and regulations to "protect" the environment and the consumer. House and Senate staffs expanded by 55 percent in the 1970s, and the total staff supporting all of Congress grew 68 percent.[9] The federal register of laws grew 424 percent in the decade of the 1960s; the number of lawyers increased by 52 percent; and civil cases rose 134 percent.[10] Some of these regulations were necessary and beneficial. Most were not. Forced to eliminate leaded gasoline, the auto industry introduced the catalytic converter, which reduced gas mileage. When bureaucrats demanded better gas mileage, carmakers replaced metal parts with plastic, hurting the steel industry and making cars less safe. Outright poor designs did not help Detroit's case, and jokes about exploding Pintos became standard late-night fare for comedians.[11]

Clean air regulations, as embodied in the 1965 Motor Vehicle Air Pollution Act, came at an extraordinarily high price—one that has generally been hidden from the American public by environmentalists.[12] One study said the act reduced the gross domestic product by 2.6 percent, or $150 billion in 1970 dollars. Another put the damage done to the economy at a much higher level, about $300 billion, or "about half of the combined federal, state, and local expenditures on education."[13] Few contemplated that the burden of the 1965 act alone was equal to the entire weight that the British Navigation Acts placed on the colonists—resulting in a Revolution! The hidden nature of the laws' impact, magnified by the constant evolution and expansion of original laws, placed a massive drag on American productivity. In 1975 alone, for example, some 177 "new rules appeared, as did 2,865 proposed amendments to existing rules, 309 final rules, and 7,305 final rule amendments" for a total of over 10,600 new rules, proposed rules, and amendments![14]

One study published in the prestigious *Yale Journal on Regulation* looked at 445 manufacturing industries between 1974 and 1986, finding "regulation diverts economic resources and managerial attention away from productivity-enhancing innovation."[15] Another multistate study concluded that from 1972 to 1987 the Clean Air Act alone cost $112 billion and 590,000 lost jobs.[16] It is entirely likely that *no studies* to date have even begun to measure the damage in job losses and diverted investment of the national environmental and health regulations.

Foreign countries, such as Japan, which did not operate under such onerous regulations, were far more productive and soon took the lead in steel and autos. By 1980, Japan produced 11 million automobiles, many shipped to American shores. It represented a stunning achievement for a nation that had only made half a million vehicles in 1960, when Detroit claimed nearly 80 percent of the world market.[17] Unions and auto industry lobbyists whined about "unfair competition" and sought government protection, either in the form of import tariffs or by exercising influence to persuade the Japanese to impose their own export quotas. Likewise, American steel, witnessing spiraling wage costs and regulatory burdens, pleaded for help from the government. In 1968, the U.S. government obliged with the Voluntary Restraint Agreements to reduce steel imports, but rather than restructuring to become competitive, the industry started to rely on such protection. In reality, Japanese companies were obtaining their advantage through labor costs that were only 70 percent of those in the United States.[18] Unions played a key role in the decline of American steel: when American unionized workers made $20 an hour in the early 1980s, their Japanese counterparts earned $3. Mainly, however, environmental concerns and regulations prohibited U.S. steelmakers from opening new, more competitive facilities. Except for Bethlehem Steel, the only truly new facilities built in the 1970s came from the new, radical "mini-mills," such as arc-melting facilities used by Nucor.[19] Japanese assets in steel rose 23 percent between 1966 and 1972, whereas U.S. plant and equipment only rose 4 percent. In just over a decade, from 1974 to 1986, American steel companies shed 337,000 jobs and the industry eliminated 30 percent of its steelmaking capacity. Before it was over, 75 percent of all U.S. steelworkers had lost their jobs.[20]

Steel finally turned the corner in 1987, with American productivity eclipsing that of the Japanese. For the most part, the U.S. government had not intervened—a fact that allowed the steelmakers to get competitive and remain in business. While the United States still trailed Japan in total steel output by 1993, Americans had built their share of the world total back to 11 percent. Companies such as Nucor, with no government assistance, reached world highs in productivity per ton of steel. Likewise, American auto manufacturers staged something of a comeback in the late 1980s, with GM slashing almost two-thirds of its payroll.

And the Japanese? Their government-directed "miracle" began to come apart at the seams in the 1990s. The Ministry of International Trade and Industry (MITI) suddenly looked less than spectacular with its industry "picks." Beginning in 1992, Japan entered a period of severe stagnation, with growth sagging back to "pre-miracle" levels of 1 percent per year.[21] After a decade's worth of praise for Japanese-style management, studies showed that the hype was premature: Japan's high-tech industrial policies and intervention produced neither exceptionally high levels of cooperation nor widespread success. Indeed, as George Gilder pointed out, in all of the areas in which Japan took the lead from the United States, it developed *more* competitors, not fewer.[22] And one of the largest automakers in the world, Honda, had no government sup-port. Quite the contrary: Honda was told by the Japanese government and MITI to stay out of automaking. It became abundantly clear by the end of the 1990s that American policy makers were correct to let the nation's heavy in-dustry sink or swim in global competition, without bailouts, subsidies, or protection.

LIE #47

The Reagan Tax Cuts Caused Massive Deficits and the National Debt

Few doubted . . . that the supply-side formula intensified an ominous fiscal crisis. . . . The national debt grew from $907 billion in 1980 to over $2 trillion in 1986. . . ."

—John Mack Faragher et al., Out of Many

[The Reagan tax cuts resulted in] *slashing rates for the rich. Cutting the government's total income by $747 billion over five years,* [the tax cuts] *meant less money for federal programs. . . .*

—David Goldfield et al., The American Journey

The wanton disregard of facts when it comes to "Reaganomics" constitutes what I call the "pregnancy test" for bias in college textbooks. If you want a quick answer on whether a text is biased, flip to the index under "Reagan" and read that section. Usually, one will quickly find comments such as this: "[I]t was hard to connect so likeable a man to the mean-spirited programs with which he was too often associated. . . ."[1] Or, making it appear that the tax cuts caused the stock market's (temporary) retrenchment of 1987, George Tindall and David Shi wrote darkly that "on October 19, 1987, the bill collector suddenly arrived on the nation's doorstep." Of course, with their great training in economics, they concluded this was attributable to "the nation's spiraling indebtedness and chronically high trade deficits."[2] If any of these historians had ever bothered to consult the most rudimentary facts—such as the government's own tax revenue tables—rather than repeat the talking points of the

Democratic National Committee, they might have achieved some level of accuracy.

According to the U.S. Census data, in 1981—Reagan's first full year in office—federal receipts were $600 billion (and Reagan actually had shrunk the budget by $5 billion from the last Carter budget). In 1989, which was Reagan's last full budget, receipts had shot up to $909 billion. More important, receipts from income taxes after the tax cuts rose from $122 billion in 1980 to $393 billion, or an increase of more than 200 percent! Corporate income tax revenues soared from $64 billion to $106 billion, almost doubling.[3] Keep in mind that this incredible growth was occurring while inflation was being squeezed out of the economy—a stunning accomplishment. There is simply no way any honest analyst can look at the stark reality of these figures and conclude that "tax cuts caused the deficit," in any way, shape, or form.

It is absolutely true, however, that deficits did rise under Reagan, and that the national debt also rose. Overall spending rose from $579 billion under Jimmy Carter to $1.05 trillion by 1989. The culprit? Liberals tried to blame defense spending, and in their two-volume textbook, Tindall and Shi state: "Reaganomics departed from the Coolidge record [which, incidentally, the authors did not particularly care for] mainly in the mounting deficits . . . and in their major cause—growing expenditures for the armed forces."[4] But military spending rose only slightly during the decade, from 22 percent of the U.S. budget in 1980 to 27 percent in 1989, or an increase of under 1 percent of GNP. Food assistance was barely touched, as were "income security" programs (although naturally if employment was surging, as it was, such programs were used far less). But spending on housing and housing assistance rose, as did health care services, and Social Security increased, as did aid to agriculture, science, and recreational resources. Even the least curious person would notice these sound a lot like pork-barrel projects, as indeed they were. What caused the deficits? *The Democratic Congress, with its pork-barrel spending.* Critics claimed Reagan "could have vetoed these budgets," but not without damaging the critical defense outlays that were directly responsible for winning the Cold War. The plain facts are that Reagan's tax cuts worked. Combined with the actions of Federal Reserve chairman Paul Volcker to hold down inflation, the tax cuts generated the most remarkable boom in American history. Even Daniel Yergin, no fan of "the Gipper," noted that the economic boom of the Clinton years "actually began in the Bush administration."[5] In fact, however, both the Bush and Clinton surges continued to spring from the original Reagan tax cuts, which, by 2007, had generated nearly 24 *million* net new jobs, whereas most of Europe (excluding low-tax Ireland) actually lost jobs.

Liberals' deep-seated antipathy to the tax cuts—regardless of the phenomenal record of growth—stems from their approach to taxation. Realize that, as mentioned earlier, the Reagan tax cuts actually *increased* government revenues (as did the Andrew Mellon cuts of the 1920s and the John Kennedy cuts of the 1960s, as well as the George W. Bush cuts of the early 2000s). If the government is receiving more money, what can liberals complain about? The answer is that while more overall money is coming into government with lower tax rates, the politicians' control over individuals via income taxes is diminished. As explained in Lie #43, even the original income tax was not primarily justified on the grounds that government needed more money, but rather that it was simpler than the constant, intricate tariff revisions, and was a means to "soak the rich."

Because of the deep-seated hostility to tax cuts, most textbooks go out of their way to demonize the (incredibly successful) Reagan cuts, and the only possible issue they can use for this purpose is the deficit. As shown, the deficit was entirely the product of congressional pork-barrel spending. Yet textbooks not only misinform by not mentioning that it was Congress, not the president, that caused the deficits, but in my view, they deliberately distort the actual data. No example is more egregious than that of *The American Pageant* by Thomas A. Bailey et al.[6] Long one of the best-selling U.S. history texts on the market, *The American Pageant* in its ninth and tenth editions featured budget deficit and national debt charts that, at face value, suggest Reagan had completely lost control of government spending. The "Federal Budget" chart shows that the deficit exploded from $73.8 billion in 1980 to $212.3 billion in 1985.[7] Something is wrong with the picture, however: the caption at the top of the chart says "Billions of Dollars" (see the chart in *American Pageant*, "The Federal Budget, 1930–1988"). An economist would immediately note that it should read "Billions of *Real* Dollars," and that the numbers have not been adjusted for inflation. Moreover, given that the economy was soaring under Reagan, the nation, in essence, "made more money." What a person (or nation) owes is certainly related to what it "earns," which, in the case of a country, is the GNP. When the numbers used by Bailey and Kennedy for the budget deficits are recalculated in real dollars as a share of GNP, the chart bears no resemblance to the one in the book. Reagan's deficits, while higher than normal, were about where Carter's were when he first took office, and several orders of magnitude less than those of Franklin Roosevelt during World War II. Normally, one would never notice such an error, were it not so egregiously compounded by a *second* chart in the same chapter of the same book. In that chart, "The National Debt, 1930–1990," the dates have been changed from 1988 perhaps because the deficits began to decrease in 1989 and 1990, making the visual image of the first figure less compelling. Second, the "National Debt" chart has headers superimposed on the chart line, in case a student is so thick as to miss its slanted message. Of the six headers, five are events. Only one is a person—Reagan. It reminds one of the *Sesame Street* game: "One of these things is not like the other things, one of these things just doesn't belong." A young viewer will be shown three parakeets and a musk ox, with, one hopes, the appropriate response being that the parakeets are alike! *The American Pageant* wants to make clear that the line that skyrockets upward after 1980 belongs to Reagan (see "The National Debt, 1930–1990" at the top of p. 237).[8] Once again, however, the attentive reader will notice that the data are neither in real dollars nor stated as a share of GNP, which makes all the difference in the world. It does not even seem to be the same chart as the one below it, which I created to reflect the debt in real dollars ("Debt as a Share of GNP, 1930–1990"). The stark visual picture of the bias presented by the two charts is apparent when they are viewed together.

The National Debt, 1930–1990

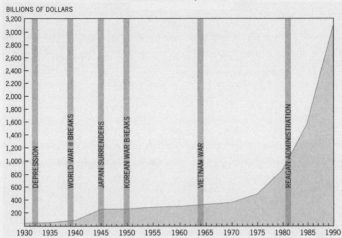

In an attempt to portray the Reagan economy as anything but outstanding, textbooks have distorted coverage to emphasize rising deficits and the national debt. But even then, they have skewed reality: the chart above, from *The American Pageant*, depicts the national debt but doesn't bother to adjust it for "real dollars," giving the impression that the national debt was the worst in the nation's history. It was not—as seen in my own recalculations of the debt numbers in the chart below, which were adjusted for inflation and placed as a share of the GNP. In fact, debt levels under Ronald Reagan were lower than those of the Eisenhower or Truman administrations and were tiny compared to those of Franklin D. Roosevelt. (Note also the *American Pageant* chart features "time bars" to "help" the student, but that every time bar reflects an event . . . except for the last one, for Reagan, which identifies a person, just so the students will properly demonize Reagan!)

Debt as a Share of GNP, 1930-1990

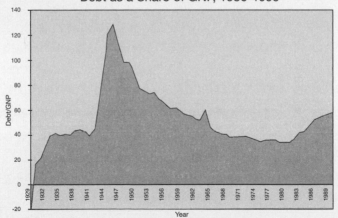

It's one thing for textbooks to slant the language ("Reagan was the candidate of the rich") or the coverage (giving twice as much space to the Iran-Contra scandal as to the soaring economy under Reagan, or his defeat of the Soviet Union). But it's an entirely different matter to manipulate data to present a biased, if not false, picture of the past.

ALGER HISS WAS INNOCENT

Hiss was released two years later, still proclaiming his innocence.
—JOHN MACK FARAGHER, ET. AL., OUT OF MANY

The suave Hiss appeared far more credible than the rumpled Chambers, who was
an admitted perjurer, but Republican Richard Nixon of California forced Hiss to
admit that he had known Chambers under an alias. . . . Hiss was convicted. . . .
While Hiss sat in prison for almost four years, Chambers wrote a bestseller.
—JEANNE BOYDSTON ET. AL., MAKING A NATION

Poor Alger Hiss. He *said* he was innocent. (Of course, so did Nixon, but that is seldom mentioned in any textbook). In modern history books merely proclaiming innocence is good enough for any Communist to get a pass. The "fact" of a conviction is usually noted, but almost uniformly with the addendum that the accused proclaimed his innocence. Poor Hiss "sat in prison for almost four years" while that evil Chambers wrote a bestseller when in fact Hiss was fortunate not to get the same fate as his cronies, the Rosenbergs. Of course, we could turn to that reliable and objective source Wikipedia to sugar coat reality: "Although a variety of evidence has been added to the debate since his conviction, the question of Hiss's guilt or innocence remains controversial. Some reliable sources have suggested that those who believe in Hiss's innocence are in the minority of scholarly opinion."[1] Alger Hiss was, is, and always will be guilty as charged—and not just of perjury, of which he was convicted, but of espionage and treason. The only unfortunate thing about this case isn't that Hiss was sent to prison but that he didn't receive a harsher punishment, like many of his fellow traitors.

Alger Hiss was a state department official whose agency worked on the early machinery of the United Nations. A member of the Yalta delegation (1945), secretary-general of the United Nations Conference on International Organization, and later director of the Carnegie Endowment for International Peace, Hiss had constant access to important levers in the decision-making process during the Cold War. In 1948, he appeared before the House Committee on Un-American Activities when a fellow Communist, Whittaker Chambers, accused him of being a party member. For his testimony, Chambers would bear the brunt of leftist scorn for years but like most of those named by Senator Joseph McCarthy, Hiss had already come up on the FBI's radar as a Communist. Both Elizabeth Bentley, a Soviet spy in the United States who defected in 1945, and Igor Gouzenko, another Soviet defector who had more than one hundred documents with him when he left the Soviet Embassy in Canada in 1945, confirmed that a United States assistant secretary of state was an agent.[2] (Bently even managed to produce the last name—Hiss—although she paired it with a different first name.) At any rate, Hiss appeared before HUAC, stating he did not know Chambers, and Chambers repeated his allegations that Hiss was a Communist on *Meet the Press*. Hiss then sued Chambers for libel, whereupon Chambers doubled down and charged Hiss with espionage, and since both he and Hiss had denied any espionage before the committee, they were both subject to perjury charges. Hiss escaped the more serious espionage charges—of which he certainly would have been convicted—and was instead charged with two counts of perjury and tried twice. During the first trial in 1949, he got a hung jury, but in the second trial, new testimony was introduced that would lead to his conviction. Hiss was convicted in the perjury case on several pieces of evidence, all of which have been laid out in exacting fashion by Allen Weinstein in his book *Perjury*. Out of all of the evidence presented against Hiss, probably nothing was more incriminating than the infamous Woodstock typewriter, on which his wife, Priscilla, typed documents. Tests confirmed that indeed the typewriter was the source of the many pages of copied State Department documents that had been retyped. Of course, defenders then switched gears to claim that the typewriter—which was originally brought in to prove Hiss's innocence—was "remanufactured" by the FBI, and that the documents themselves were forgeries! This introduced the remarkably ludicrous scenario in which the FBI not only forged documents, but then changed a typewriter to match the new false documents![3]

Later, when discussing the role of the typewriter, defenders would argue that Hiss was not a spy because a good spy would know to destroy any documents against him. Even if you buy this speculation, there was still another piece of evidence presented against Hiss that irrefutably proves his guilt (though, of course, not if you're liberal). This is Document 1822, dated March 30, 1945. This was one of the Venona documents, a cable sent from the KGB's Washington station to the Moscow headquarters, which mentioned an American spy (code name ALES) who had been working for the Soviets since 1935. The spy referred to as ALES in the cable had worked in the State Department and had traveled to Yalta, then returned to the United States via Moscow. Only four Americans from the State Department had returned from Yalta via Moscow, among them Alger Hiss. Hiss's lawyer, John Lowenthal, tried to argue that the memo was misread, and it actually exonerated Hiss, arguing in a Clintonesque redefinition of the word "he" that the cable actually referred to Soviet Foreign Minister Vyshinski instead of the spy called ALES. Quickly, two scholars of cryptoanalysis, Eduard Mark and John Schindler, pounced on the Venona intercept and showed beyond a shadow of a doubt that the Russian translation "he" could refer to no one except ALES (i.e., Hiss).[4] Before long, even Lowenthal gave up on trying to use Document 1822 to exonerate his client.

But, just when we thought the case against Hiss was closed for good, a conference on the Cold War, which was held at New York University in April 2007, featured a topic on the Hiss trial in which yet new "evidence" would show once and for all that Hiss was innocent.[5] A contributing editor for *The Nation* and a Russian historian claimed to have evidence that ALES was a formerly unknown official named Wilder Foote, one of the other four men to return from Yalta via Moscow. Foote had worked at the UN, but had never been a Communist; had never been accused of being a Communist; did not appear in any of the Soviet documents naming operatives; was never identified as even a *potential* Communist by the FBI; and, as two authors of the episode note, was "not mentioned in any memoirs or historical accounts; records of the party that are accessible in archives; or as a subject of interest by the various congressional investigating committees."[6] The fact that Foote was not even in Washington at the time Hiss's espionage was committed further complicated the leftists' plans to pull a bait and switch between the two men. But, according to Hiss's supporters, the document proved that Hiss had actually returned earlier than the other men, leaving only two possible identities for ALES— Foote and Edward Stettinius—whom absolutely everyone agreed could not have been an agent. Only Wilder Foote, said one of the Hiss defenders, "Fits the itinerary in every way, and Hiss simply does not."[7] In fact, the "evidence" that Hiss returned to the States early was actually a mistake committed by the Soviet handler who had assumed Hiss was still in Mexico City when he wrote his cable that seemed to provide Hiss's cover.

In yet another vain attempt to exonerate his client, Hiss's lawyer, John Lowenthal, used his connections with a Russian general and archival historian to check the KGB files for the name "Hiss." The general, Dmitri Volkogonov, reported there was no such person in the KGB records, sparking a great deal of celebration among the American Left. That celebration was premature however, as Volkogonov made a U-turn before the champagne corks could land, and issued a follow-up statement just a few weeks after his original comments in which he said that a new search showed that while Hiss was not employed by the KGB, he *was* a spy for the Soviet Ministry of Defense's intelligence agency, the GRU![8]

As Cold War historians John Earl Haynes and Harvey Klehr conclude, "The ALES messages, while important and interesting, are but a few more stones on a large rock pile of evidence. Remove them and little changes *in re Alger Hiss*."[9] One such "rock" is the testimony of Oleg Gordievsky, a KGB agent who defected to the West and later wrote a book in which he spoke of attending a lecture before a KGU audience given by Iskhak Abdulovich Akhmerov, another KGB agent, who identified Hiss as a Soviet agent during World War II, and, for toppers, said that Hiss's code name was ALES.[10] Akhmerov's statement has never been refuted. Moreover, "HISS" was also identified by name in Venona cable #1579, and while it would be unorthodox to name a spy openly, it nevertheless adds another rock on the pile. Another case against Hiss is the testimony of Nathaniel Weyl, who said that Hiss was a member of his Communist cell (or network) in 1933 (Weyl did express reservations about Hiss's guilt as a spy, but not as a fellow cell member, thus confirming Chambers's testimony).[11] KGB officer Vasili Mitrokhin, who published an insider view of the KGB in 1999 with spy writer Christopher Andrew, had no doubt that ALES was Hiss . . .

. . . and even less doubt that Alger Hiss was a spy.

FINAL LIE

History Textbooks Used in Schools Are
Unbiased and Not Politically Correct

It should be evident in these pages, from the extensive examples taken from American history textbooks, that students get a distinctly slanted view of American history—one that portrays the United States as oppressive, imperialistic, and evil. The slant lauds socialistic efforts at wealth redistribution, criticizes American military success, and laments the punishment of anti-American traitors. But there is one last perspective on this issue. In the introduction, a number of ways bias can be inserted into textbooks were reviewed. Which players get treatment? How much? What emphasis do the subjects get?

As noted in the introduction, one means of measuring this is in the pictures—the images of the Ku Klux Klan are more frequently used to portray twentieth-century America than, say, the moon landing, John F. Kennedy, Ronald Reagan, or even the civil rights marches. A picture is worth a thousand words, but words, too, are important.

Recently, I examined the covers of sixteen of the most recent college-level U.S. history textbooks. Several had landscapes or images of nonhuman objects, so I excluded them. Of those that depicted people, only one prominently featured a white male (Lincoln). Every other cover featured African Americans, Hispanics, or women, sometimes showing them in protest marches. If a cover is supposed to represent "what the book is about," then even for a leftist like Howard Zinn, these covers would be misleading, for even Zinn agrees (but laments) that white males have been the dominant force in the nation's past. There is a profound difference between "shaping" our past—which all those groups did—and directing the past (which virtually none of them did, at least not until the mid-twentieth century). Once again, the message? White males were unimportant in American history.

A word count of a number of topics in these American history textbooks—which I have conducted—is revealing. My methodology is somewhat subjective: whether words "counted" toward the individual or not usually was determined by headings and subheadings (whether the topic still included the person or concept in question, for example). Naturally, someone else might perform a word count on these same texts and come away with slightly different numbers—but only slightly. I have used all of the texts referenced throughout this book, but not Howard Zinn's *A People's History of the United States* nor James W. Loewen's *Lies My Teacher Told Me,* as they do not pretend to be textbooks in the traditional sense of the word. Likewise, my choice of people, topics, or concepts was subjective: I chose events or people who could be easily identified and would have minimal "bleed over" into other sections of a book (as opposed, for example, to Franklin Roosevelt or Thomas Jefferson, who could conceivably come up in many chapters, or the Constitution, for the same reason).

I compared, for example, coverage of the Watergate scandal (in which Richard Nixon was not formally impeached, but did resign) to the Clinton impeachment. In *America: A Narrative History,* Watergate got 1,125 words; Clinton's impeachment, 794. *These United States* similarly gave Watergate about 600 more words of coverage than it did the Clinton impeachment, while in *Give Me Liberty* and *Nation of Nations,* the ratio was nearly 2:1. *American Destiny* had a 3:1 ratio of Watergate to Clinton impeachment coverage. Only two of the major texts gave Clinton's impeachment more attention than Watergate (*Out of Many* and *Unto a Good Land*). While one could draw a number of conclusions about this, the obvious message is that Nixon's deeds were far worse than Clinton's. Yet Clinton was punished with only the second impeachment in American history, while Nixon resigned on his own volition (certainly under great pressure).

Critics might contend that a fairer comparison would be the Clinton impeachment and the impeachment of Andrew Johnson, the first impeachment of an American president. *Give Me Liberty* dedicates twice as many words to the Clinton trial as it does to Andrew Johnson's; *American Journey,* almost four times as many words. Only two of the books dedicate more space to Johnson (*America: A Narrative History* and *Making a Nation*—in each case, only a hundred or so). But *Unto a Good Land* has almost 1,450 words on Clinton's troubles, versus 477 for Johnson. "Qualitative" analysis would require more than simple word counts, but having read all these books, I can assure the reader that the treatments of Bill Clinton are overwhelmingly sympathetic, while the tone taken with Andrew Johnson ranges from objective to scornful.

What about famous people and "politically correct" inclusion of women and minorities? No one would argue that Martin Luther King or Booker T. Washington do not deserve extensive coverage. But W.E.B. DuBois? In *These United States* he gets more words than presidential candidate and U.S. senator Barry Goldwater; *Give Me Liberty* dedicates 25 percent more words to DuBois than Goldwater; *Out of Many*, twice as much; and *American Destiny* gives DuBois over 1,000 words, but Goldwater only 116. Indeed, in *Unto a Good Land*, DuBois and Robert E. Lee get almost identical word counts, while in *Making a Nation*, DuBois gets twice as much ink as Lee. Jane Addams gets what appears to be appropriate and proportional treatment (between 100 and 300 words) in most books, although *Unto a Good Land* seemed particularly Addams-obsessed, providing her with almost three full pages.

Finally, the aforementioned Ku Klux Klan appear to be on every historian's mind: every book dedicates at least a page, on average, to the Klan just in the 1920s, not counting more reasonable coverage that fits appropriately in Reconstruction chapters. And, to repeat, almost every textbook adds to the 1920s coverage of the Klan by featuring at least one photo and (usually) an extensive accompanying caption.

Since my first appearance on *Fox & Friends* in September 2008, for what later became a weekly segment called "The Trouble with Textbooks," viewers began sending me more examples of errors and overt political correctness in textbooks. Some of these examples included high school or elementary schoolbooks, such as the lower-level book *American History* by McDougall Littell, which has an astounding seventy mentions of the words "diversity" or "tolerance," yet the words "church, "Christianity," or "Jesus Christ" do not appear once in the index![1] And this bias isn't just present in history books. A recent edition of a literature book used for younger readers, *The Readers' Choice*, dedicates 777 lines of text to environmentalism to 27 mentions of God or the Bible; and has 39 *times* more coverage of pagan religions than Christianity.

This actually represented an *improvement*: earlier versions were even more weighted toward themes of paganism.[2] The Educational Research Analysts, started by Mel and Norma Gabler (who died in 2004 and 2007, respectively), provides a shocking review of high school–level textbook biases and errors.

Mere snippets such as these suggest a seriously flawed, dark, and sinister view of the United States is held by most of those who today write her history. The villains of twentieth-century America are Richard Nixon and William Jennings Bryan, portrayed as a crook and a buffoon, respectively; the image of our nation is the Klan robe and the handcuffed Rosenbergs or Sacco and Vanzetti, not the heroes of Iwo Jima, the firefighters of 9/11, or Billy Graham. When modern textbooks don't slant through coverage, they often mislead by descriptions—Reagan as the candidate of the rich, Roosevelt as the man of the people, Alger Hiss as innocent. Accounts of American military heroism are often missing entirely. (Zinn doesn't even bother covering Civil War battles. After all, they didn't matter—only the draft riots were truly "symbolic" of the conflict.)

If these are the distortions we can spot easily, however, how much more difficult is it to point out to students the utter absence of debates about federalism and the scope of the federal government's power in the twentieth century? How much additional research should teachers have to do to present material about America's religious heritage, and its continued thriving presence after World War II? Where are the explanations about equality of opportunities differing substantially from opportunities of outcome? And when are serious questions about the environment or public health balanced with solid (and sympathetic) information about the damage done to constitutional liberties and personal rights?

Equally disturbing is a special edition of essays from the *Journal of American History*, written by those who write college-level textbooks. One of the comments found in these essays asserts that scholars "need to construct historical interpretations in dialogue with other scholars because the facts do *not* 'speak for themselves.'"[3] The past "was contested all along and continues to be contested," which is code-speak for "We can, and if allowed we will, rewrite history to reflect our liberal views rather than tell what really happened."[4] After insisting that teachers cannot march from election to election, one author in a symposium about textbook writing laments that no one "can assume even the most rudimentary acquaintance with the 'colonial' period, the 'Revolution,' Jacksonian 'democracy,' 'Reconstruction,' or the 'industrial revolution.' . . ."[5] Imagine that: after decades of insisting that military history was not worth studying, that political history was merely "cover" for the "important" history (social history, for example), or that "great men" were unimportant compared to labor movements or minorities, scholars now assert that students can't know about critical political events. Who woulda thunk it? If this keeps up basket weaving will become a more practical discipline than American history!

After fielding questions from hundreds of desperate parents and more than a few concerned educators about what book to use, I still maintain that *A Patriot's History of the United States*, which I cowrote in 2004 with Michael Allen, remains the best alternative. Meanwhile, finding bias in the large number of textbooks that many schools use has actually proven the easy part. But it's only the beginning. For future generations to recognize that they live in the most blessed nation on earth, they need to have an accurate and honest record of America's past, always tempered with the understanding that *because* we remain a "shining city on a hill," the inquiry into the past is always balanced with an appreciation for the liberties that past has provided. The important part of that equation, though, is to realize that *without* American exceptionalism and greatness, addressing the mistakes of the past is a futile and meaningless exercise.

NOTES

INTRODUCTION

1. See, for example, David Goldfield et al., *The American Journey,* combined vol., TLC ed. (Upper Saddle River, NJ: Pearson, 2007); George B. Tindall and David E. Shi, *America: A Narrative History,* brief 6th ed. (New York: Norton, 2004); Samuel Eliot Morison et al., *A Concise History of the American Republic,* 2nd ed. (New York: Oxford University Press, 1983); John Mack Faragher et al., *Out of Many,* combined vol., brief 4th ed., TLC ed. (Upper Saddle River, NJ: Pearson, 2006); John M. Blum et al., *The National Experience: A History of the United States,* 7th ed. (New York: Harcourt Brace, 1989); Bernard Bailyn et al., *The Great Republic: A History of the American People* (Lexington, MA: D. C. Heath, 1985); Paul S. Boyer et al., *The Enduring Vision: A History of the American People,* concise 5th ed. (Boston: Houghton Mifflin, 2006); and Jeanne Boydston et al., *Making a Nation: The United States and Its People* (Upper Saddle River, NJ: Pearson, 2004). Davidson et al. (*Nation of Nations: A Concise Narrative of the American Republic,* 3rd ed., 2 vols [Boston: McGraw-Hill, 2002], 2:695) feature a picture of Tulsa after a race riot with a caption that begins, "As the Ku Klux Klan grew after World War I, race riots erupted. . . ." Irwin Unger's *These United States: The Questions of Our Past,* concise ed., combined vol., 3rd ed. (Upper Saddle River, NJ: Pearson, 2007), is one of the rare exceptions in not including a photograph, but does provide the obligatory page-length treatment.
2. Mark C. Carnes and John A. Garraty, *American Destiny: Narrative of a Nation,* 2nd ed. (New York: Pearson, 2006), 707.
3. Other books examined include Eric Foner, *Give Me Liberty: An American History,* 2 vols. (New York: Norton, 2006); James West Davidson et al., *Nation of Nations: A Concise Narrative of the American Republic,* 4th ed. (Boston: McGraw-Hill, 2006); Alan Brinkley, *The Unfinished Nation: A Concise History of the American People,* 5th ed. (Boston: McGraw-Hill, 2008); David E. Harrell, *Unto a Good Land: A History of the American People* (Grand Rapids, MI: William B. Eerdmans, 2005); and Steven M. Gillon et al., *The American Experiment: A History of the United States* (Boston: Houghton Mifflin, 2002).

4. Michael Kazin, "The Grass-Roots Right: New Histories of U.S. Conservatism in the Twentieth Century," *American Historical Review* 97 (February 1992): 136–54.

5. Edward S. Shapiro, "Liberalism and the College History Textbook: A Case Study," *Continuity* (Fall 1992): 27–45, quotation on 27.

6. Alan Brinkley et al., *American History: A Survey*, 8th ed., 2 vols. (New York: McGraw-Hill, 1992), 2:886–90.

7. Shapiro, "Liberalism and the College History Textbook."

8. Brinkley et al., *American History*, 2:886–90.

9. George B. Tindall and David E. Shi, *America: A Narrative History*, 3rd ed. (New York: Norton, 1992), 1348.

10. John M. Blum et al., *The National Experience: A History of the United States*, 7th ed. (New York: Harcourt Brace, 1989).

11. Ibid., 495–98.

12. Ibid., 418–20.

13. Ibid., 631–32.

14. Ibid., 745–55.

15. Ibid., 755–57.

16. Shapiro, "Liberalism and the College History Textbook," 42.

17. Blum et al., *National Experience*, 810–12, 824–25, 831.

18. Ibid., 421, 432.

19. Burton W. Folsom Jr., *The Myth of the Robber Barons* (Herndon, VA: Young America's Foundation, 1991).

20. Larry Schweikart, "Lessons of Business History: Evaluating Business History Texts," *Continuity*, May 1990, 85–99.

21. C. Joseph Pusateri, *A History of American Business*, 2nd ed. (Arlington Heights, IL: Harlon Davidson, 1988).

22. Bruce J. Schulman, "Out of the Streets and into the Classroom? The New Left and the Counterculture in United States History Textbooks," *Journal of American History* 85 (March 1999): 1527–34.

23. Gary B. Nash, "The Great Multicultural Debate," *Contention* 1 (Spring 1992): 1–28, quotation on 7.

24. Schulman, "Out of the Streets," 1529–30.

25. Ibid., 1530.

26. Robert James Maddox, *The New Left and the Origins of the Cold War* (Princeton, NJ: Princeton University Press, 1973).

27. Peter Collier and David Horowitz, *Destructive Generation: Second Thoughts About the Sixties* (New York: Summit Books, 1989); Roger Kimball, *Tenured Radicals: How Politics Has Corrupted Our Higher Education* (New York: Harper & Row, 1990); John Barron, *MiG Pilot: The Final Escape of Lieutenant Belenko* (New York: Reader's Digest Press, 1980); and Christopher Andrew and Vasili Mitrokhin, *The Sword and the Shield: Mitrokhin Archive and the Secret History of the KGB* (New York: Basic Books, 1999).

28. Schulman, "Out of the Streets," 1530.

29. Ibid., 1531.

30. Ibid., 1532.

31. Jerry Rubin, *Do It: Scenarios of the Revolution* (New York: Simon & Schuster, 1970), 125.

32. David Dalton, "Finally, the Shocking Truth About Woodstock Can Be Told, or Kill It Before It Clones Itself," *The Gadfly*, August 1999, http://gadfly.org/1999-08/toc.asp. Other comments are from the author's discussions with Dalton.

33. Dalton, "Finally, the Shocking Truth."
34. One exception is David Harrell et al., *Unto a Good Land: A History of the American People* (Grand Rapids, MI: William B. Eerdmans, 2005), which dedicates an extensive section to the "counterculture."
35. Alexander Stille, "The Betrayal of History," *New York Review of Books,* June 11, 1998, 15–20.
36. Ibid., 18; James Michener, *This Noble Land: My Vision for America* (New York: Random House, 1996).
37. Joy Hakim, *A History of the United States,* 3rd ed. (New York: Oxford University Press, 2007).
38. Larry Schweikart and Michael Allen, *A Patriot's History of the United States from Columbus's Great Discovery to the War on Terror* (New York: Sentinel [paperback ed.], 2007).
39. Julie Schmidt, "Chegg CEO Rashid Applies Netflix Concept to Textbooks," *USA Today,* January 12, 2009, http://www.usatoday.com/money/companies/management/entre/2009-01-11-chegg-rashid_N.htm.

Lie #1

Epigraphs:
    James West Davidson, *Nation of Nations: A Concise Narrative of the American Republic,* 2 vols., 4th ed. (Boston: McGraw-Hill, 2006).
    James Mack Faragher et al., *Out of Many,* combined vol., 4th ed., TLC ed. (Upper Saddle River, NJ: Pearson, 2006).
    Peter S. Onuf, " 'The Strongest Government on Earth': Jefferson's Republicanism, the Expansion of the Union, and the New Nation's Destiny," paper presented at the Louisiana Purchase Symposium, University of Texas at Austin, February 20–22, 2003, http://www.utexas.edu/law/conferences/lapurchase/Papers/POnuf.doc.

1. Reginald C. Stuart, *The Half-Way Pacifist: Thomas Jefferson's View of War* (Toronto: University of Toronto Press, 1978), 4.
2. George Washington, "Farewell Address," http://www.yale.edu/lawweb/avalon/washing.htm.
3. See William B. Allen, *George Washington: A Collection* (Indianapolis, IN: Liberty Fund, 1988).
4. George Washington to Governor Morris, December 22, 1795, in John C. Fitzpatrick, ed., *The Writings of George Washington from the Original Manuscript Sources, 1745–1799,* vol. 34 (Washington, DC: U.S. Government Printing Office, 1940), 398–403 (quotation on 401).
5. Washington to Charles Carroll, May 1, 1796, in ibid., vol. 35, 29–31 (quotation on 30).
6. http://millercenter.virginia.edu/scripps/digitalarchive/speeches/spe_1796_0917_washington?print.
7. http://memory.loc.gov/ammem/collections/jefferson_papers/mtjprece.html.
8. Larry Schweikart and Michael Allen, *A Patriot's History of the United States, from Columbus's Great Discovery to the War on Terror* (New York: Sentinel, 2007), 168.
9. Joseph Wheelan, *Jefferson's War: America's First War on Terror, 1801–1805* (New York: Carroll & Graf, 2003), 105.
10. William Ray, *Horrors of Slavery, or, The American Tars in Tripoli* (Troy, NY: Oliver Lyon, 1808); Paul Baepler, ed., *White Slaves, African Masters: An Anthology of*

American Barbary Captivity Narratives (Chicago: University of Chicago Press, 1999).

11. Mark S. Longo, "To the Shores of Tripoli," *Military Heritage*, June 2005, 40–49; Donald Barr Chidsey, *The Wars in Barbary: Arab Piracy and the Birth of the United States Navy* (New York: Crown, 1971).

12. Max Boot, *The Savage Wars of Peace: Small Wars and the Rise of American Power* (New York: Basic Books, 2002), 3–29.

13. Frederick C. Leiner, *The End of Barbary Terror: America's 1815 War Against the Pirates of North Africa* (New York: Oxford University Press, 2007).

14. Robert C. Davis, *Christian Slaves, Muslim Masters: White Slavery in the Mediterranean, the Barbary Coast and Italy, 1500–1800* (London: Palgrave, 2004).

15. Also see Larry Schweikart, *America's Victories: Why the U.S. Wins Wars and Will Win the War on Terror* (New York: Sentinel, 2007).

Lie #2

Epigraphs:

Howard Zinn, *A People's History of the United States, 1492–Present* (New York: Harper Perennial, 2007).

Paul S. Boyer et al., *The Enduring Vision: A History of the American People*, concise 5th ed. (Boston: Houghton Mifflin, 2006).

James West Davidson et. al., *Nation of Nations: A Concise Narrative of the American Republic*, 3rd ed., 2 vols. (New York: McGraw-Hill, 2002).

1. Mark C. Carnes and John A. Garraty, *American Destiny: Narrative of a Nation*, 2nd ed. (New York: Pearson, 2006), 655.

2. Davidson et al., 605.

3. Jeanne Boydston et al., *Making a Nation: The United States and Its People*, combined vol. (Upper Saddle River, NJ: Pearson, 2004), 491.

4. "The Teller Amendment, 1898," http://www.etsu.edu/cas/history/docs/teller.htm.

5. "The Treaty of Guadalupe Hidalgo," 1848, http://www.ourdocuments.gov/doc.php?flash=true&doc=26.

6. Paul S. Boyer et al., *The Enduring Vision: A History of the American People*, concise 5th ed. (Boston: Houghton Mifflin, 2006), 266.

7. Mark V. Kwasny, *Washington's Partisan War, 1775–1883* (Kent, OH: Kent State University Press, 1996), 3; Edward M. Coffman, *The Old Army: A Portrait of the American Army in Peacetime, 1784–1898* (New York: Oxford University Press, 1986), 166. See also Larry Schweikart, *America's Victories: Why the U.S. Wins Wars and Will Win the War on Terror* (New York: Sentinel, 2007), ch. 3, passim.

8. Justin H. Smith, *The War with Mexico*, 2 vols. (New York: Macmillan, 1919), 1:105.

9. Ibid., 1:106–7.

10. Ibid., 1:105.

11. Ibid.

12. Irwin Unger, *These United States: The Questions of Our Past*, concise ed., combined vol., 3rd ed. (Upper Saddle River, NJ: Pearson, 2007), 503.

13. Boydston et al., *Making a Nation*, 491.

14. Ibid., 489. It is also worth noting that, again, pictures tell an important story. Boydston and her coauthors show two females (identified indirectly as "missionaries") being carried on the backs of two small Chinese men, with the accompanying cap-

tion, "Thanks to the work of missionaries in China, Mark Twain observed, 'the people who sit in darkness . . . have become suspicious of the blessings of civilization.'" Apparently the modern Chinese, who are racing to embrace such blessings, have no such suspicions, for estimates suggest that at the current rate of growth, by 2010 China will be the most Christianized nation on earth in terms of total numbers!

15. Boyer et al., *Enduring Vision*, 266.

LIE #3

Epigraph:

Robert B. Stinnett, "December 7, 1941, A Setup from the Beginning," *Honolulu Advertiser*, December 7, 2000.

1. Robert B. Stinnett, *Day of Deceit: The Truth About FDR and Pearl Harbor* (New York: Free Press, 2000); George Victor, *The Pearl Harbor Myth: Rethinking the Unthinkable* (Dulles, VA: Potomac Books, 2007).
2. Charles Tansill, *Back Door to War* (Chicago: Regnery, 1952); Walter Millis, *This Is Pearl: The United States and Japan* (New York: William Morrow, 1947); Charles Beard, *President Roosevelt and the Coming of the War* (New Haven, CT: Yale University Press, 1948).
3. John Toland, *Infamy: Pearl Harbor and Its Aftermath* (New York: Doubleday, 1982).
4. John F. Bratzel and Leslie B. Rout Jr., "Research Note: Pearl Harbor, Microdots, and J. Edgar Hoover," *American Historical Review* 87 (December 1982): 1342–51, and their "Once More: Pearl Harbor, Microdots, and J. Edgar Hoover," ibid., 88 (October 1983): 953–60.
5. Dusko Popov, *Spy Counter Spy* (New York: Grosset & Dunlap, 1974).
6. Gordon W. Prange, with Donald M. Goldstein and Katherine V. Dillon, *At Dawn We Slept: The Untold Story of Pearl Harbor* (New York: McGraw-Hill, 1981).
7. Gordon Prange, with Donald M. Goldstein and Katherine V. Dillon, *Pearl Harbor: The Verdict of History* (New York: McGraw-Hill, 1986), 308.
8. James Rusbridger and Eric Nave, *Betrayal at Pearl Harbor: How Churchill Lured Roosevelt into World War II* (New York: Simon & Schuster, 1992).
9. Richard Aldrich, "British and American Policy on Intelligence Archives: Never-Never Land and Wonderland?" *Studies in Intelligence* 38 (1995): 17–26.
10. Larry Schweikart, "Did Roosevelt Anticipate Pearl Harbor?" *Continuity* 26 (Spring 2003): 157–65.
11. David Kahn, "The Intelligence Failure of Pearl Harbor," *Foreign Affairs*, Winter 1991/1992, 136–52; John C. Zimmerman, "Pearl Harbor Revisionism: Robert Stinnett's *Day of Deceit*," *Intelligence and National Security* 17 (Summer 2002): 127–46.
12. "Pearl Harbor Revisited: United States Navy Communications Intelligence, 1924–1941," quoted online at http://www.history.navy.mil/books/comint/ComInt-1.html.
13. Timothy Wilford, *Pearl Harbor Redefined: USN Radio Intelligence in 1941* (Lanham, MD: University Press of America, 2001).
14. Stephen Budiansky, "Closing the Book on Pearl Harbor," *Cryptologia*, April 2000, http://findarticles.com/p/articles/mi_qa3926/is_200004/ai_n8890788/pg_4.
15. Ibid.
16. Philip H. Jacobsen, "Foreknowledge of Pearl Harbor? No!: The Story of the U.S. Navy's Efforts on JN-25B," *Cryptologia* 27 (July 2003): 193–205; Stephen Budian-

sky, *Battle of Wits: The Complete Story of Codebreaking in World War II* (New York: Free Press, 2000), pp. 7–8, 217, and his "Too Late for Pearl Harbor," *Naval Institute Proceedings,* December 1999, 50–51.

17. Jacobsen, "Foreknowledge," quoted online, p. 8.
18. Philip H. Jacobsen's articles include: "Radio Silence and Radio Deception: Secrecy Insurance for the Pearl Harbor Strike Force," *Intelligence and National Security* 19 (Winter 2004): 695–718; "Pearl Harbor: Who Deceived Whom?" *U.S. Naval Institute Proceedings,* December 2003, online at http://www.usni.org/navalhistory/ Articles03/NHjacobsen12.htm; "No RDF on the Japanese Strike Force: No Conspiracy!" *International Journal of Intelligence and Counterintelligence* 18 (2005): 142–49.
19. Budiansky, "Closing the Book on Pearl Harbor."
20. Ibid.
21. These assertions were discredited by Jacobsen, "Radio Silence," passim; and "No RDF on the Japanese Strike Force," passim.

Lie #4

Epigraphs:
Walter LaFeber, *The American Age: United States Foreign Policy at Home and Abroad,* 2nd ed. (New York: Norton, 1994), quoted in Robert James Maddox, "A Visit to Cloudland: Cold War Revisionism in College Texts," *Continuity* 20 (Spring 1996): 1–11 (quotation on 5).

Arnold A. Offner, "Another Such Victory: President Truman, American Foreign Policy, and the Cold War," *Diplomatic History* 23 (Spring 1999): 127–55.

1. Gar Alperovitz, *Atomic Diplomacy: Hiroshima and Potsdam; the Use of the Atomic Bomb and American Confrontation with Soviet Power* (New York: Vintage, 1965).
2. Robert James Maddox, *The New Left and the Origins of the Cold War* (Princeton, NJ: Princeton University Press, 1974). Such nonsense had started passing for "history" in the radical 1960s!
3. Robert J. Maddox, "Give Me That Old Time Revisionism," *Continuity* 26 (Spring 2003): 120–45.
4. Barton J. Bernstein, "The Atomic Bombings Reconsidered," *Foreign Affairs* 74 (1995): 135–52; Michael J. Hogan, ed., *Hiroshima in History and Memory* (New York: Cambridge University Press, 1996).
5. Kai Bird, "The Curators Caved In," *New York Times,* October 9, 1994. Bird, incredibly, claimed "no scholar of the war has ever found archival evidence to substantiate claims that Truman expected anything close to a million casualties, or that such large numbers were conceivable." Here, Bird is partly right: Truman expected *more* than a million casualties, and even then was likely on the low side.
6. John Ray Skates, *The Invasion of Japan: Alternative to the Bomb* (Columbia: University of South Carolina Press, 2000).
7. Richard B. Frank, *Downfall: The End of the Imperial Japanese Empire* (New York: Penguin, 1999), 202–4.
8. Ibid., 137.
9. Eisenhower quoted in D. M. Giangreco, "Casualty Projections for the U.S. Invasions of Japan, 1945–1946: Planning and Policy Implications," *Journal of Military History* 61 (July 1997): 521–58 (quotation on 543).
10. Giangreco, "Casualty Projections," 554.

11. Shockley based his casualty estimates on Quincy Wright's "Historical Study of Casualties," as well as other studies, which he submitted in July 1945. See Giangreco, "Casualty Projections," 568.

12. See "Details of the Campaign Against Japan," June 16, 1945, entire document reprinted in Giangreco, "Casualty Projections," 552–60.

13. Henry L. Stimson, "The Decision to Use the Atomic Bomb," *Harper's Magazine* 194 (February 1947): 97–107 (quotation on 102).

14. For a complete deconstruction of Skates's unsupportable claims, see D. M. Giangreco, "Operation Downfall: The Devil Was in the Details," *Joint Force Quarterly* (Autumn 1995): 86–94, and his more detailed analysis in "Casualty Projections," passim.

15. Giangreco, "Operation Downfall," 92.

16. Sadao Asada, "The Shock of the Atomic Bomb and Japan's Decision to Surrender—a Reconsideration," *Pacific Historical Review* 67 (November 1998): 477–512 (quotation on 505).

17. Nicholas D. Kristof, "The Bomb: An Act That Haunts Japan and America," *New York Times*, August 6, 1995; Sadao Asada, "The Mushroom Cloud and National Psyches: Japanese and American Perceptions of the A-Bomb Decision, 1945–1995," *Journal of American-East Asian Relations* 4 (1995): 95–116.

18. Suzuki noted that he made up his mind *before* the Soviets entered the war the following day. (This is taken from "Interrogations of Japanese Officials on World War II," part of the *Reports of General MacArthur: Japanese Operations in the Southwest Pacific Area*, 2 vols. [Washington, DC: U.S. Government Printing Office, 1966], conducted on May 3, 1949, and quoted in Asada, "Shock of the Atomic Bomb," 489).

19. http://www.trumanlibrary.org/whistlestop/study_collections/bomb/large/documents/index.php?documentdate=1945-08-09&documentid=9&studycollectionid=abomb&pagenumber=1.

Lie #5

Epigraphs:
David Lifton, "Best Evidence: The Video," Rino Studios, 1994. Other comments were made by David Lifton to the author in 1988 and again in 1993.

Barr McClellan, *Blood, Money & Power: How L.B.J. Killed J.F.K* (Fayetteville, AR: Hannover House, 2004). This book got exceptional prerelease publicity because the author was the father of Scott McClellan, the White House press secretary under President George W. Bush.

1. Fletcher L. Prouty and Oliver Stone collaborated in a 2003 book, *JFK: The CIA, Vietnam and the Plot to Assassinate John F. Kennedy* (Yucca Valley, CA: Citadel Publishers, 2003), which was an expanded version of Prouty's *The Secret Team* (New York: Ballantine, 1974). The movie *JFK* also relied heavily on Jim Garrison, *On the Trail of the Assassins: My Investigation and Prosecution of the Murder of President Kennedy* (New York: Sheridan Square Press, 1988). For the most famous of the conspiracy books, see Josiah Thompson, *Six Seconds in Dallas: A Micro-Study of the Kennedy Assassination* (New York: Bernard Geis, 1967); Sylvia Meagher, *Accessories After the Fact: The Warren Commission, the Authorities, and the Report* (New York: Vintage, 1976); Mark Lane, *Rush to Judgment* (New York: Holt, Rinehart, 1966); Edward Jay Epstein, *Inquest: The Warren Commission and the Establishment of Truth* (New York: Viking, 1966); Robert F. Grodin and Peter F. Model, *JFK: The Case for Conspiracy* (New York: Manor, 1976); Harold

Weisberg, *Whitewash,* 4 vols. (Hyattstown-Frederick, MD: H. Weisberg, 1965–1975); David Belin, *Final Disclosure: The Full Truth About the Assassination of President John F. Kennedy* (New York: Scribner's, 1987).

2. William Manchester, *The Death of a President: November 1963* (New York: Harper & Row, 1967); Arthur Schlesinger Jr., *A Thousand Days: John F. Kennedy in the White House* (Boston: Houghton Mifflin, 1965).

3. See Harold G. Moore and Joseph L. Galloway, *We Were Soldiers Once—and Young: Ia Drang, the Battle That Changed the War in Vietnam* (New York: HarperPerennial, 1993).

4. Robert G. Blakey and Richard N. Billings, *Fatal Hour: The Assassination of President Kennedy by Organized Crime* (New York: Berkeley, 1992); John H. Davis, *Mafia Kingfish: Carlos Marcello and the Assassination of John F. Kennedy,* 2nd ed. (New York: Signet, 1989).

5. David Kaiser, *The Road to Dallas* (Cambridge, MA: Harvard University Press, 2008).

6. Robert J. Groden and Harrison Edward Livingstone, *High Treason: The Assassination of President John F. Kennedy, What Really Happened* (Baltimore: Conservatory, 1989); Mark North, *Act of Treason: J. Edgar Hoover and the Assassination of President Kennedy* (New York: Carroll & Graf, 1991).

7. David Lifton, *Best Evidence: Disguise and Deception in the Assassination of John F. Kennedy* (New York: Carroll & Graf, 1992). There is a video Lifton made by the same name.

8. See David R. Wrone, "David Lifton's Body Alteration Theory," http://mcadams.posc.mu.edu/wrone.htm; Ruffis Youngblood, *Twenty Years in the Secret Service: My Life with Five Presidents* (New York: Simon & Schuster, 1973), 129; Godfrey McHugh, "Letter to the Editor," *Time,* February 17, 1981.

9. For discussions of Lifton's thesis, in addition to Wrone, see Gerald Posner, *Case Closed* (New York: Random House, 1993).

10. Aside from Wrone, one of the few historians to actually analyze the evidence has been Michael L. Kurtz, *Crime of the Century: The Kennedy Assassination from a Historian's Perspective,* 2nd ed. (Knoxville: University of Tennessee Press, 1993). Like Wrone, he arrives at the conclusion that "multiple shooters" did it, but cannot identify them.

Lie #6

Epigraphs:

Irwin Unger, *These United States: The Questions of Our Past,* concise ed., combined vol., 3rd ed. (Upper Saddle River, NJ: Pearson, 2007), 720.

Mark C. Carnes and John A. Garraty, *American Destiny: Narrative of a Nation,* 2nd ed. (New York: Pearson, 2006), 845.

1. John P. Roche, "The Demise of Liberal Internationalism," *National Review,* May 3, 1985, 26–44.

2. Ibid., 40.

3. Lawrence S. Wittner, *Cold War America from Hiroshima to Watergate* (New York: Praeger, 1974), 226–27.

4. Vincent H. Demma, "The U.S. Army in Vietnam," in *American Military History* (Washington, DC: United States Army, Center of Military History, 1989), http://www.ibiblio.org/pub/academic/history/marshall/military/vietnam/short.history/chap_28.txt.

5. "President Kennedy's remarks at the Yellowstone County Fairgrounds, Billings, Montana, September 25, 1963," http://www.mtholyoke.edu/acad/intrel/pentagon2/ps40.htm.

6. National Security Action Memorandum No. 263, October 11, 1963, http://www.ratical.org/ratville/JFK/FRUSno194.html.

7. Quoted in Victor Davis Hanson, *Carnage and Cultures: Landmark Battles in Western Culture* (New York: Doubleday, 2001), 404.

8. Robert Leckie, *The Wars of America,* rev. ed. (New York: Harper & Row, 1981), 1006–7.

9. Larry Schweikart and Michael Allen, *A Patriot's History of the United States: From Columbus's Great Discovery to the War on Terror,* paperback ed. (New York: Sentinel, 2007), 713.

Lie #7

Epigraphs:

    Paul S. Boyer et al., *The Enduring Vision: A History of the American People,* concise 5th ed. (Boston: Houghton Mifflin, 2006), 663.

    Jeanne Boydston et al., *Making a Nation: The United States and Its People,* combined vol. (Upper Saddle River, NJ: Pearson, 2004), 729.

    Irwin Unger, *These United States: The Questions of Our Past,* concise ed., combined vol., 3rd ed. (Upper Saddle River, NJ: Pearson, 2007), 756.

1. Unger, *These United States,* 756.

2. Christopher Andrew and Vasili Mitrokhin, *The Sword and the Shield: The Mitrokhin Archive and the Secret History of the KGB* (New York: Basic Books, 1999), 242.

3. Ibid., 242–43.

4. Ibid., 227–28.

5. Ibid., 244–45.

6. Peter Schweizer, *Reagan's War: The Epic Story of His Forty-Year Struggle and Final Triumph over Communism* (New York: Anchor, 2003), 181.

7. Ibid., 181–82.

8. Ibid., 221.

9. Ibid., 226.

10. Tony Judt, *Postwar: A History of Europe Since 1945* (New York: Penguin, 2005), 59.

11. Schweizer, *Reagan's War,* 227.

12. Ronald Reagan, *The Reagan Diaries,* ed. Douglas Brinkley (New York: HarperCollins, 2007), 117.

13. Ibid., 13.

14. Christopher Andrew and Oleg Gordievsky, *KGB: The Inside Story* (New York: HarperPerennial, 1990), 585.

15. Ibid., 590.

16. Unger, *These United States,* 756.

Lie #8

Epigraphs:

    Jeanne Boydston et al., *Making a Nation: The United States and Its People,* combined vol. (Upper Saddle River, NJ: Pearson, 2004), 729.

Paul S. Boyer et al., *The Enduring Vision: A History of the American People,* concise 5th ed. (Boston: Houghton Mifflin, 2006), 664.

James West Davidson et al., *Nation of Nations: A Concise Narrative of the American Republic,* vol. 2, 3rd ed. (New York: McGraw-Hill, 2002), 947.

1. Paul Lettow, *Ronald Reagan and His Quest to Abolish Nuclear Weapons* (New York: Random House, 2005), 21.
2. Ibid., 30.
3. Ibid., ch. 4 passim.
4. Peter Schweizer, *Reagan's War: The Epic Story of His Forty-Year Struggle and Final Triumph over Communism* (New York: Anchor, 2003), 141.
5. Lettow, *Ronald Reagan and His Quest to Abolish Nuclear Weapons,* 90.
6. Ronald Reagan, *The Reagan Diaries,* ed. Douglas Brinkley (New York: HarperCollins, 2007), 140.
7. Ibid., 447.
8. Lettow, *Ronald Reagan and His Quest to Abolish Nuclear Weapons,* 181.
9. Ibid., 173.
10. Reagan, *Reagan Diaries,* 444.
11. Tim Weiner, "Lies and Rigged 'Star Wars' Test Fooled the Kremlin, and Congress," *New York Times,* August 18, 1993.
12. Schweizer, *Reagan's War,* 242.
13. Ibid.
14. Andrew Busch, "Ronald Reagan and the Defeat of the Soviet Empire," *Presidential Studies Quarterly* 27 (Summer 1997): 451–65 (quoted on 462).
15. Ibid., 244.
16. Ibid., 456.
17. "U.S. Military Intercepts Target Ballistic Missile in Hawaii Test," June 22, 2007, http://www.khnl.com/Global/story.asp?S=6699743&nav—enu55_2; Henry J. Holcomb, "Tests of Missile Defense Successful, Lockheed Says," *Philadelphia Inquirer,* June 25, 2007.
18. Jim Wolf, "Pentagon's Flying Raygun Zips Into Budget Battle," June 21, 2007, Yahoo News, http://news.yahoo.com/s/nm/20070621/pl_nm/missile_laser_usa_dc_2.
19. "Modified 747 Completes Key Test," http://www.news.com.au/story/0,23599,22086910-1702,00.html?from=public_rss.
20. "'Star Wars' Indeed," *Investor's Business Daily,* October 3, 2007.
21. Revel quoted in Busch, "Ronald Reagan and the Defeat of the Soviet Empire," 463.

LIE #9

Epigraphs:
James West Davidson et al., *Nation of Nations: A Concise Narrative of the American Republic,* Vol. II: *Since 1865,* 3rd ed. (New York: McGraw-Hill, 2002), 952.

George Brown Tindall and David Emori Shi, *America: A Narrative History,* brief 6th ed. (New York: Norton, 2004), 1196.

David E. Harrell et al., *Unto a Good Land: A History of the American People* (Grand Rapids, MI: William B. Eerdmans, 2005), 1142.

1. Paul Kengor, *The Crusader* (New York: Regan Books, 2006), 219.
2. Ronald Reagan, *The Reagan Diaries,* ed. Douglas Brinkley (New York: HarperCollins, 2007), 2.

3. Peter Schweizer, *Reagan's War* (New York: Anchor, 2003), 141.
4. Ibid.
5. Kengor, *Crusader,* 146.
6. Ibid., 123–25.
7. Ibid., 155.
8. Ibid., 163.
9. Ronald Reagan, *An American Life* (New York: Simon & Schuster, 1990), 267.
10. Reagan, *Reagan Diaries,* 140.
11. Tim Weiner, "Lies and Rigged 'Star Wars' Test Fooled the Kremlin, and Congress," *New York Times,* August 18, 1993.
12. From "Reagan: The American Experience," quoted in Kengor, *Crusader,* 242.
13. Kengor, *Crusader,* 219.
14. John Lewis Gaddis, *The United States and the End of the Cold War* (New York: Oxford University Press, 1992), 225n.
15. Kengor, *Crusader,* 232.
16. Ibid., 233.
17. Ronald Reagan, "It Isn't Only Washington . . . ," *National Journal,* March 8, 1980, 392.
18. John Lewis Gaddis, "Hanging Tough Paid Off," *Bulletin of the Atomic Scientists,* January/February 1989, 11.

Lie #10

Epigraph:
Paul Craig Roberts, "Gullible Americans," August 14, 2006, http://www.informationclearinghouse.info/article14531/htm.

1. Thierry Meyssan, *9/11: The Big Lie* (London: Carnot Publishing, 2002).
2. "Rosie O'Donnell 9/11 Conspiracy Comments: *Popular Mechanics* Responds," March 30, 2007, http://www.popularmechanics.com/blogs/911myths/4213805.html.
3. "Actor Charlie Sheen Questions Official 9/11 Story," March 20, 2006, http://www.prisonplanet.com/articles/march2006/200306charliesheen.htm.
4. "*New York Post* Touts 'Warrior' Hillary Clinton," http://www.newsmax.com/archives/ic/2005/7/31/130028.shtml.
5. David Dunbar and Brad Reagan, eds., *Debunking 9/11 Myths: Why Conspiracy Theories Can't Stand Up to the Facts* (New York: Hearst Books, 2006).
6. Ibid., 38.
7. Steven E. Jones, "Why Indeed Did the WTC Buildings Completely Collapse?" http://wtc7.net/articles/WhyIndeed09.pdf. Jones's own colleagues disavowed his findings, and several actively refuted them. See D. Allan Firmage's letter of April 9, 2006 (http://www.netxnews.net/vnews/display.v/ART/2006/04/09/443801bdadd6e) and other statements at "Debunking 9/11 Conspiracy Theories: Exploding the Myths," http://www.debunking911.com/civil.htm. Ira Fulton, BYU's professor for whom its College of Engineering is named, issued his own response challenging Jones, "Fulton College Response to Professor Steven Jones's Statements Regarding Collapse of World Trade Center," available from BYU.
8. See Peter Meyer, "The World Trade Center Demolition and the So-Called War on Terrorism," http://www.serendipity.li/wtc.htm#later.

LIE #11

Epigraphs:
Frank Rich, "Dishonest, Reprehensible, Corrupt," *New York Times,* November 27, 2005.
David Goldfield et al., *The American Journey,* brief 4th ed., combined vol., TLC ed. (Upper Saddle River, NJ: Pearson, 2007), 938–39.
Irwin Unger, *These United States: Questions of Our Past,* concise ed., combined vol., 3rd ed. (Upper Saddle River, NJ: Pearson, 2007), 820.

1. Tommy Franks with Malcolm McConnell, *American Soldier* (New York: Regan Books, 2004), 418–19.
2. Richard Miniter, *Disinformation: 22 Media Myths That Undermine the War on Terror* (Washington, DC: Regnery, 2005), 100.
3. Adrian al-Haideri, 2001, worked on secret WMD sites, three hundred of which were being used to conceal all WMD programs. See *Insight Magazine,* September 30, 2002. Another defector was quoted in Reuters with similar information: Reuters, December 22, 2001. On the biological agents, see Miniter, *Disinformation,* 101.
4. "The Saddam Tapes," Intelligence Summit, February 18, 2006, ISGQ-2003-M0007379, copies in author's possession.
5. *World Tribune,* August 12, 2002.
6. Ryan Mauro, "WMD: Believe Iraq or Believe the Evidence?" http://www.worldthreats.com/middle_east/Iraq-WMD.htm#_edn10.
7. London *Sunday Telegraph,* August 5, 2003.
8. *Washington Times,* March 30, 2003.
9. "Tarmiya," Federation of American Scientists, http://www.fas.org/nuke/guide/iraq/facility/tarmiya.htm.
10. "A Nation at War: Chemical Agents; American Soldiers Find Drums Possibly Storing Chemical Agents," *New York Times,* April 8, 2003.
11. "Text of David Kay's Unclassified Statement," http://www.cnn.com/2003/ALLPOLITICS/10/02/kay.report/.
12. Georges Sada, *Saddam's Secrets: How an Iraqi General Defied and Survived Saddam Hussein* (Brentwood, TN: Integrity Publishers, 2006), 1–2.
13. Ibid., 252.
14. "Experts: Iraq Has Tons of Chemical Weapons," cnn.com, September 4, 2002.
15. Sada, *Saddam's Secrets,* 254.
16. Ibid., 264.
17. "President Bush Outlines Iraq Threat," http://www.whitehouse.gov/news/releases/2002/10/20021007-8.html.
18. Jim A. Kuypers, *Bush's War: Media Bias and Justifications for War in a Terrorist Age* (Lanham, MD: Rowman & Littlefield, 2006), 58.
19. Ibid., 51–73; Tom Shales, "A Few Rounds of Applause for George W. Bush," *Washington Post,* January 30, 2002.
20. *CBS Morning News,* January 31, 2002.
21. Kuypers, *Bush's War,* 72.
22. Quoted in Stephen F. Hayes, *The Connection: How al Qaeda's Collaboration with Saddam Hussein Has Endangered America* (New York: HarperCollins, 2004), xiv.
23. Ibid., 27.
24. http://www.regimeofterror.com/.

25. Hayes, *The Connection*, 27.
26. George Tenet, *At the Center of the Storm: My Years at the CIA* (New York: Harper-Collins, 2007).
27. Christina Shelton, "Iraq, al-Qaeda and Tenet's Equivocation," *Washington Post*, June 30, 2007.
28. Ibid.
29. Ibid.
30. Quoted in Hayes, *The Connection*, xi.
31. Laurie Mylroie, "Bin Ladin and Iraq," January 27, 1999, Federation of Atomic Scientists, http://www.fas.org/irp/news/1999/01/990127-in.htm.
32. http://www.fas.org/irp/news/1998/11/indict1.pdf.
33. Hayes, *The Connection*, 103.
34. http://www.janes.com/security/international_security/news/fr/fr010919_1_n.shtml.
35. Miniter, *Disinformation*, 112.
36. Gwynne Roberts, "Militia Defector Claims Baghdad Trained Al-Qaeda Fighters in Chemical Warfare," London *Sunday Times*, July 14, 2002.
37. Hayes, *The Connection*, 87.
38. "Lawsuit: Iraq Involved in 9/11 Conspiracy," September 5, 2002, http://www.cbsnews.com/stories/2002/09/05/september11/main520874.shtml.
39. "Spain Links Suspect in 9/11 Plot to Baghdad," March 16, 2003, http://observer.guardian.co.uk/international/story/0,6903,915142,00.html.
40. The digital link at the *Independent* no longer works. Paper copy in author's possession.
41. Michah Morrison, "The Iraq Connection," *Wall Street Journal* online, September 5, 2002, http://opinionjournal.com/extra/?id=110002217.
42. Hayes, *The Connection*, 130.
43. Ibid., 50.
44. *Newsweek*, July 4, 1994, cited in Hayes, *The Connection*, 51.
45. "Al-Qaeda Video Reflects Group's Troubles," http://usatoday.com/news/world/2007-07-05-al-qaeda-video_N.htm.
46. Ibid.
47. "About that 500 Tons of Yellowcake . . . ." *American Thinker*, July 20, 2005.

Lie #12

Epigraph:
Mark Weldon Whitten, *The Myth of Christian America* (Macon, GA: Smyth & Helwys, 1999), 2–4.

1. Whitten, *The Myth of Christian America*, 2–4.
2. Joseph Story, *Commentaries on the Constitution of the United States,* quoted in William J. Federer, *The Original 13* (St. Louis: Ameriresearch, 2007), 15.
3. Bouvier quoted in ibid., 16–17.
4. Quoted in Gary Scott Smith, *Faith & the Presidency: From George Washington to George W. Bush* (New York: Oxford University Press, 2006), 4.
5. Ibid., 33–34.
6. Ibid., 36.
7. Claudia L. Bushman, Harold B. Hancock, and Elizabeth Moyne Homsey, eds., *Proceedings of the Assembly of the Lower Counties of on the Delaware 1770–1776, of*

the Constitutional Convention of 1776, and of the House of Assembly of the Delaware State 1776–1781 (Newark: University of Delaware Press, 1986), 209.

8. George Washington, "Thanksgiving Proclamation," October 3, 1789, in John C. Fitzpatrick, ed., *The Writings of George Washington from the Original Manuscript Sources, 1745–1799, Series 8a, Correspondence and Miscellaneous Notes, 1773–1799,* vol. 30 (Washington, DC: U.S. Government Printing Office, 1940), 217.

9. "Constitution of Maryland," November 11, 1776, http://www.yale.edu/lawweb/avalon/states/ma02.htm.

10. *Journals of the Continental Congress, 1774–1789* (Washington, DC: U.S. Government Printing Office, 1928), November 1, 1777.

11. Jonathan Elliot, *The Debates in the Several State Conventions on the Adoption of the Federal Constitution* (Washington, DC: U.S. Government Printing Office, 1845), 5:253-54, http://memory.loc.gov/cgi-bin/ampage?collId=lled&fileName=005/lled005.db&recNum=275&itemLink=r%3Fammem%2Fhlaw%3A%40field%28DOCID%2B%40lit%28ed0053%29%29%230050005&linkText=1.

12. George Washington, "Thanksgiving Proclamation," 217.

13. Ibid., 59–60.

14. Ibid., 62.

15. Ibid., 89.

16. Ibid., 92.

17. Ibid.

18. Ibid., 93.

19. Ibid., 119.

20. Ibid., 120.

21. Ibid., 124.

22. Ibid., 199.

23. Jon Butler, "Why Revolutionary America Wasn't a Christian Nation," in James Hutson, ed., *Religion and the New Republic: Faith in the Founding of America* (New York: Norton, 1996); R. Laurence Moore and Isaac Krammick also argue this point in *The Godless Constitution: The Case Against Religious Correctness* (Lanham, MD: Rowman & Littlefield, 2006).

24. Mark A. Noll, *A History of Christianity in the United States and Canada* (Grand Rapids, MI: William B. Eerdmans, 1992), 122.

25. Larry Schweikart and Michael Allen, *A Patriot's History of the United States: From Columbus's Great Discovery to the War on Terror,* paperback ed. (New York: Sentinel, 2007), 96–98.

26. Noll, *History of Christianity in the United States,* 145.

27. Ibid., 147.

28. Ibid., 148.

29. Ibid., 243.

30. Smith, *Faith & the Presidency,* 13. Also see Norman De Jong, "The First Amendment: A Comparison of Nineteenth and Twentieth Century Supreme Court Interpretations," *Journal of Political Science* 16 (Spring 1988): 69.

31. Ethan Cole, "Poll: American Voters Want a Religious President," *Christian Post,* June 15, 2007, http://www.christianpost.com/article/20070615/27995_Poll:American_Voters_Want_a_Religious_President.htm.

32. Smith, *Faith & the Presidency,* 5.

33. Ibid., 134.

34. Ibid., 136.

35. Ibid., 164.

36. Ibid., 193.
37. Ibid., 227.
38. Ibid., 301.
39. Ibid., 368.
40. Quoted in ibid., 7.
41. Paul Kengor, *God and Ronald Reagan: A Spiritual Life* (New York: ReganBooks, 2004).
42. Ronald Reagan, *The Reagan Diaries*, Alan Brinkley, ed. (New York: HarperCollins, 2007), 85; Kengor, *God and Ronald Reagan*, passim.

LIE #13

Epigraph:
Regemaid C. Stuart, *The Half-Way Pacifist: Thomas Jefferson's View of War* (Toronto: University of Toronto, 1978).

1. For the inversion of these terms, see Larry Schweikart and Michael Allen, *A Patriot's History of the United States: From Columbus's Great Discovery to the War on Terror* (New York: Sentinel, 2007), 116–26.
2. Stuart, *The Half-Way Pacifist*, 4; Thomas Jefferson to William Stephens Smith, November 13, 1787, in Julian P. Boyd., ed., *The Papers of Thomas Jefferson*, vol. 12 (Princeton, NJ: Princeton University Press, 1955), 356.
3. Wheelan, *Jefferson's War: America's First War on Terror, 1801–1805* (New York: Carroll & Graf, 2003).
4. Ibid., 80.
5. Wheelan, *Jefferson's War*, passim.
6. *Historical Statistics of the United States: Colonial Times to 1970* (White Plains, NY: U.S. Department of Commerce, Bureau of the Census, 1989), 1:211. Real figures were compiled using 1800 as a base year. Special thanks to Tiarr Martin for his paper, "The Growth of Government During the 'Age of Jefferson and Jackson,'" 1989, in author's possession.
7. Martin, "Growth of Government," graph D.
8. Robert F. Martin, *National Income in the United States, 1799–1938,* National Industrial Conference Board Study #241 (NICB, 19390). See also Paul David, "The Growth of Real Product in the United States Before 1840: New Evidence, Controlled Conjectures," *Journal of Economic History* (June 1967): 151–97; Richard Easterlin, "Regional Income Trends, 1840–1950," in S. E. Harris, ed. (New York: McGraw-Hill, 1961), 525–47; and Jeremy Atack and Peter W. Passell, *New Economic View of American History,* 2nd ed. (New York: Norton, 1994).
9. Larry Schweikart, *The Entrepreneurial Adventure: A History of Business in the United States* (Fort Worth, TX: Harcourt, 2000), 97.
10. Albert Gallatin, "Reports on Roads and Canals," document no. 250, 10th Cong., 1st Sess., in *New American State Papers—Transportation,* vol. 1 (Wilmington, DE: Scholarly Resources, 1972).
11. Mansel G. Blackford and K. Austin Kerr, *Business Enterprise in American History,* 2nd ed. (Boston: Houghton Mifflin, 1990), 82; Paul Johnson, *The Birth of the Modern: World Society, 1815–1840* (New York: HarperPerennial, 1991), 174.
12. Schweikart, *Entrepreneurial Adventure,* 96.

LIE #14

Epigraphs:
Carol Berkin and Mary Beth Norton, *Women of America: A History* (Boston: Houghton Mifflin, 1979), 3.
Carol Berkin, *First Generations: Women in Colonial America* (New York: Hill & Wang, 1996), 14.

1. Alice Hanson Jones, *American Colonial Wealth: Documents and Methods*, 2nd ed., vol. 1 (New York: Arno Press, 1977), passim.
2. Carole Shammas, Marylynn Salmon, and Michel Dahlin, *Inheritance in America from Colonial Times to the Present* (New Brunswick, NJ: Rutgers University Press, 1987), 30.
3. Ibid., 52.
4. Ibid., 57; David Evan Narrett, "Patterns of Inheritance in Colonial New York City, 1664–1775: A Study in the History of the Family," Ph.D. dissertation, Cornell University, 1981; Stephanie Grauman Wolf, *Urban Village: Population, Community, and Family Structure in Germantown, Pennsylvania, 1683–1800* (Princeton, NJ: Princeton University Press, 1976); Suzanne Dee Lebsock, "Women and Economics in Virginia: Petersburg, 1784–1820," Ph.D. dissertation, University of Virginia, 1977.
5. Melvin I. Urofsky, *A March of Liberty: A Constitutional History of the United States* (New York: Knopf, 1988), 23.
6. Mary Beth North, "A Cherished Spirit of Independence: The Life of an Eighteenth-Century Boston Businesswoman," in Carol Berkin and Mary Beth Norton, *Women of America: A History* (Boston: Houghton Mifflin, 1979), 48–67.
7. Shammas et al., *Inheritance in America*, 36.
8. Ibid., 14.
9. Berkin, *First Generations*, 9.
10. Urofsky, *March of Liberty*, 23–24.
11. Ibid., 24.
12. Mary Beth Norton, *Liberty's Daughters: The Revolutionary Experience of American Women, 1750–1800* (Boston: Little, Brown, 1980), 47.
13. Jack Larkin, *The Reshaping of Everyday Life, 1790–1840* (New York: HarperPerennial, 1989), 194.
14. Berkin and Norton, *Women of America*, 47.
15. Urofsky, *March of Liberty*, 300–3.
16. Norton, *Liberty's Daughters*, 128.
17. Ibid., 128–29.
18. Ibid., 132.
19. Berkin and Norton, *Women of America*, 8.

LIE #15

Epigraph:
Charles A. Beard and Mary R. Beard, *The Rise of American Civilization* (New York: Macmillan, 1994), 550.

1. Richard P. McCormick, "New Perspectives on Jacksonian Politics," *American Historical Review* 65 (October 1959–July 1960): 288–301.

2. Richard P. McCormick, "Political Development and the Second Party System," in William Nisbet Chambers and Walter Dean Burnham, eds., *The American Party Systems: Stages of Political Development* (London: Oxford University Press, 1967), 90–116, and his book, *The Second American Party System: Party Formation in the Jacksonian Era* (New York: Norton, 1966).

3. James Stanton Chase, "Jacksonian Democracy and the Rise of the Nominating Convention," *Mid-America* 45 (1963): 229–49.

4. Robert V. Remini, *Martin Van Buren and the Making of the Democratic Party* (New York: Columbia University Press, 1959), 12–23.

5. Paul S. Boyer et al., *The Enduring Vision: A History of the American People* (Lexington, KY: D. C. Heath, 1993), 279.

6. David M. Kennedy, *The American Pageant,* 12th ed. (New York: Houghton Mifflin, 2002), 271.

7. David Goldfield et al., *The American Journey: A History of the United States,* combined ed. (Upper Saddle River, NJ: Prentice-Hall, 1998), 301.

8. John Murrin et al., *Liberty, Equality, Power: A History of the American People,* 3rd ed. (Fort Worth, TX: Harcourt Brace, 2002), 442.

LIE #16

Epigraphs:
Daniel Goldfield et al., *The American Journey,* brief 4th ed., combined volume, TLC edition (Upper Saddle River, NJ: Pearson, 2007), 712.

George Brown Tindall and David E. Shi, *America: A Narrative History,* brief 6th ed. (New York: Norton, 2004), 852–53.

1. James West Davidson et al., *Nation of Nations: A Narrative History of the American Republic,* 2 vols., 3rd ed. (New York: McGraw-Hill, 2001), 2:795; Steven M. Gillon and Cathy D. Matson, *The American Experiment: A History of the United States* (Boston: Houghton Mifflin, 2002), 820; Alan Brinkley, *American History: A Survey,* 2 vols., 9th ed. (New York: McGraw-Hill, 1999), 2:827.

2. J. C. Burnham, "New Perspectives on the Prohibition 'Experiment' of the 1920s," *Journal of Social History* 2 (1968): 51–68 (quotation on 59).

3. Ibid., 59, based on figures from Clark Warburton, *The Economic Results of Prohibition* (New York: Columbia University Press, 1932). As Burnham notes, some argue that even these figures were too high.

4. Ibid., 60.

5. Martha Bensley Bruere, *Does Prohibition Work? A Study of the Operation of the Eighteenth Amendment Made by the National Federation of Settlements, Assisted by Social Workers in Different Part of the United States* (New York: Harper & Brothers, 1927). Norman H. Clark, *The Dry Years: Prohibition and Social Change in Washington* (Seattle: University of Washington Press, 1965), 136, 144–45, notes that as workers benefited from the prosperity of the 1920s, they had less need for alcohol and the saloon.

6. See J. C. Burnham, "The Progressive Era Revolution in American Attitudes Toward Sex," *Journal of American History* 59 (March 1973): 885–908; Prince A. Morrow, "Report of the Committee of Seven on the Prophylaxis of Venereal Disease in New York City," *Medical News* 79 (December 21, 1901): 961–70; and Allan M. Brandt, *No Magic Bullet: A Social History of Venereal Disease in the United States Since 1880,* exp. ed. (New York: Oxford University Press, 1987).

7. Norman H. Clark, *Deliver Us from Evil: An Interpretation of Prohibition* (New York: Norton, 1976), 10, 83.

8. Ibid., 9.

9. Burnham, "New Perspectives," 61, 63.

10. Edwin H. Sutherland and C. H. Gehlke, "Crime and Punishment," in *Recent Social Trends in the United States, Report of the President's Research Committee on Social Trends* (New York: McGraw-Hill, 1933), 2:1128.

11. U.S. Bureau of the Census, *Historical Statistics of the United States, Colonial Times to 1970* (Washington, DC: U.S. Government Printing Office, 1975), 1:414.

12. Burnham, "New Perspectives," 61.

13. Clark, *Deliver Us from Evil,* 146–47.

14. Whiting Williams, quoted in Commission on Law Observance and Enforcement, *Enforcement of Prohibition Laws, Official Records of the National Commission on Law Observance and Enforcement Pertaining to Its Investigation of Facts as to Enforcement, Benefits and Abuses under Prohibition Laws, Both Before and Since Adoption of the Eighteenth Amendment to the Constitution* (Washington, DC: U.S. Government Printing Office, 1931), 3:183–84.

15. Burnham, "New Perspectives," 66.

16. Ibid. See Dayton E. Heckman, "Prohibition Passes: The Story of the Association Against the Prohibition Amendment," Ph.D. dissertation, Ohio State University, 1939.

17. Upton Sinclair, *Prohibition: The Era of Excess* (Boston: Little, Brown, 1962), 226–30, 339.

Lie #17

Epigraphs:

Mark C. Carnes and John A. Garraty, *American Destiny: Narrative of a Nation,* 2nd ed. (New York: Pearson, 2006), 707.

Jeanne Boydston et. al., *Making a Nation: The United States and Its People,* combined vol. (Upper Saddle River, NJ: Pearson, 2004), 542.

1. Lisa McGirr, "The Passion of Sacco and Vanzetti: A Global History," *Journal of American History* (March 2007): 1085–1115 (quotation on 1087). Richard Newby, *Kill Now, Talk Forever: Debating Sacco and Vanzetti* (Bloomington, IN: Author House, 2007), tried to inform McGirr directly (she did not respond), and published corrections in *The Journal of American History*. McGirr dismissed the central fact of the episode with the stunning phrase "The focus on the guilt or innocence of Sacco and Vanzetti has caused us to neglect the international movement in their support" (1087). In other words, the fact that they were *guilty* should not stop us from treating them as though they were innocent!

2. Henry C. Lee et al., "Examination of Firearm Related Evidence: The Nicola Sacco and Bartolomeo Vanzetti Case," *AFTE Journal* 17 (July 1985).

3. William Young and David E. Kaiser, *Postmortem: New Evidence in the Case of Sacco and Vanzetti* (Amherst: University of Massachusetts Press, 1985); and an excellent Web site that provides an overview, http://www.law.umkc.edu/faculty/projects/ftrials/SaccoV/s&vevidence.html.

4. James E. Starrs, "Once More into the Breech: The Firearms Evidence in the Sacco and Vanzetti Case Revisited: Part I," *Journal of Forensic Sciences* 31 (April 1986): 630–54, and "Part II" (July 1986): 1050–78, quotation in "Part II," on 1074.

5. Starrs, "Once More into the Breach," 1050.
6. "Novelist's Book About Murder Trial Called Into Question," http://www.cbc.ca/arts/story/2006/01/28/uptonsinclair-boston.html.
7. Upton Sinclair to John Beardsley, August 29, 1929, copy in author's possession, reprinted in Newby, *Kill Now, Talk Forever,* 2007 ed., 634–35.
8. Ibid.

LIE #18

Epigraph:
George Brown Tindall and David E. Shi, *America: A Narrative History,* brief 6th ed. (New York: Norton, 2004), 1041.

1. Arthur Herman, *Joseph McCarthy* (New York: Free Press, 2000), 10.
2. Ibid., 99.
3. Ibid., 98.
4. *Nashville Tennessean,* quoted in Edwin R. Bayley, *Joe McCarthy and the Press* (Madison: University of Wisconsin Press, 1981), 18.
5. Herbert Romerstein and Eric Breindel, *The Venona Secrets: Exposing Soviet Espionage and America's Traitors* (Washington, DC: Regnery, 2000), 46.
6. Ibid., 46.
7. Herman, *Joseph McCarthy,* 115.
8. M. Stanton Evans, *Blacklisted by History: The Untold Story of Senator Joe McCarthy* (New York: Crown, 2007), 385–98.
9. Herman, *Joseph McCarthy,* 123.
10. Ibid., 146.
11. Richard H. Rovere, *Senator Joe McCarthy* (Cleveland: Meridian Book, 1960), 20–21.
12. Herman, *Joseph McCarthy,* 160.
13. Lord Varney Harold, "What Has Joe McCarthy Accomplished?" *The American Mercury,* May 1954.
14. Ann Coulter, *Treason: Liberal Treachery from the Cold War to the War on Terrorism* (New York: Crown Forum, 2003), 60.
15. M. Stanton Evans, *Blacklisted by History: The Untold Story of Senator Joe McCarthy and His Fight Against America's Enemies* (New York: Crown, 2007).
16. Ibid., 106.
17. Ibid., 529–535.

LIE #19

Epigraphs:
Jeanne Boydston et al., *Making a Nation: The United States and Its People,* combined ed. (Upper Saddle River, NJ: Pearson, 2004), 635–36.
Mark C. Carnes and John A. Garraty, *American Destiny: Narrative of a Nation,* 2nd ed. (New York: Pearson, 2006), 814.
John Mack Faragher et al., *Out of Many,* combined vol., 4th ed., TLC ed. (Upper Saddle River, NJ: Pearson, 2006), 720.

1. "Judge Kaufman's Statement upon Sentencing the Rosenbergs," http://www.law.umkc.edu/faculty/projects/ftrials/rosenb/ROS_SENT.HTM.

2. Aleksandr Feklisov and Sergei Kostin, *The Man Behind the Rosenbergs* (New York: Enigma Books, 2005).

3. Ronald Radosh and Joyce Milton, *The Rosenberg File,* 2nd ed. (New York: Holt, Rinehart, 1997), xxii.

4. Walter and Miriam Schneir, *Invitation to an Inquest: A New Look at the Rosenberg-Sobell Case* (New York: Doubleday, 1965), and their retraction, "Cryptic Answers," *The Nation,* August 14–21, 1995, 152–53; Radosh and Milton, *Rosenberg File,* xiv.

5. Nikita Khruschev, *Khruschev Remembers: The Glasnost Tapes,* trans. and ed. Jerrold L. Schecter, with Vyacheslav V. Luchkov (New York: Little, Brown, 1990); Robert D. McFadden, "Khruschev on the Rosenbergs: Stoking Old Embers," *New York Times,* September 25, 1990.

6. *Molotov Remembers: Inside Kremlin Politics* (Conversations with Felix Chuev), ed. Albert Resis (Chicago: Ivan R. Dee, 1993), 6.

7. Richard Rhodes, *Dark Sun: The Making of the Hydrogen Bomb* (New York: Simon & Schuster, 1995), 144, 158.

8. http://en.wikipedia.org/wiki/VENONA.

9. Herbert Romerstein and Eric Breindel, *The Venona Secrets: Exposing Soviet Espionage and America's Traitors* (Washington, DC: Regnery, 2000), 251–52.

10. Michael Dobbs, "How Soviets Stole U.S. Atom Secrets: Ex-Kremlin Agent Reveals Unknown Spy in the '40s Effort," *Washington Post,* October 4, 1992.

11. Romerstein and Briendel, *Venona Secrets,* 234.

12. Radosh and Milton, *Rosenberg File,* xvi.

13. Ibid., xxiv.

14. Ibid., xxii.

15. Ronald Radosh, "Case Closed: The Rosenbergs Were Soviet Spies," *Los Angeles Times,* September 17, 2008.

16. Ibid.

Lie #20

Epigraph:
   Eric Foner, *Give Me Liberty: An American History,* vol. 2 (New York: Norton, 2006), 289.

1. George B. Tindall and David E. Shi, *America: A Narrative History,* brief 6th ed. (New York: Norton, 2004), 1111; David Goldfield et al., *The American Journey,* combined vol., TLC ed. (Upper Saddle River, NJ: Pearson, 2007), 835.

2. Samuel Eliot Morison et al., *A Concise History of the American Republic,* 2nd ed. (New York: Oxford University Press, 1983), 727; Jeanne Boydston et al., *Making a Nation: The United States and Its People* (Upper Saddle River, NJ: Pearson, 2004), 669–70.

3. David E. Harrell, *Unto a Good Land: A History of the American People* (Grand Rapids, MI: William B. Eerdmans, 2005), 1093.

4. Howard Zinn, *A People's History of the United States* (New York: HarperPerennial, 2002); James W. Loewen, *Lies My Teacher Told Me* (New York: Touchstone, 1995).

5. James Piereson, *Camelot and the Cultural Revolution: How the Assassination of John F. Kennedy Shattered American Liberalism* (New York: Encounter Books, 2007), x.

6. James West Davidson et al., *Nation of Nations: A Concise Narrative of the American*

Republic, 4th ed. (Boston: McGraw-Hill, 2006), 865. The text does concede that Oswald "spent several years in the Soviet Union."

7. Mark C. Carnes and John A. Garraty, *American Destiny: Narrative of a Nation,* 2nd ed. (New York: Pearson, 2006), 835.
8. Ibid., 835.
9. Irwin Unger, *These United States: The Questions of Our Past,* concise ed., combined vol., 3rd ed. (Upper Saddle River, NJ: 2007*),* 690.
10. Ibid., 690.
11. Paul S. Boyer et al., *The Enduring Vision: A History of the American People,* concise 5th ed. (Boston: Houghton Mifflin, 2006), 608.
12. Richard Hofstadter, "The Paranoid Style in American Politics," in his book, *The Paranoid Style in American Politics and Other Essays* (Cambridge, MA: Harvard University Press, 1965).
13. Todd Gitlin, *The Sixties: Years of Hope, Days of Rage* (New York: Bantam Books, 1993), 313.
14. Piereson, *Camelot and the Cultural Revolution,* 206–7.
15. Ibid., 209.
16. John Mack Faragher et al., *Out of Many,* combined vol., brief 4th ed. (New York: Norton, 2004), 426; Boyer et al., *Enduring Vision,* 317; Unger, *These United States,* 351, for example, flatly identify Booth's connections to the Confederacy, while Morison, Commager, and Leuchtenberg, *Concise History,* strongly imply it through context (333).
17. Boydston et al., *Making a Nation,* 368; Tindall and Shi, *America: A Narrative History,* 569.
18. Carnes and Garraty, *American Destiny,* 447; Eric Foner, *Give Me Liberty: An American History,* 2 vols. (New York: Norton, 2006), 1:473.

LIE #21

Epigraphs:
James W. Loewen, *Lies My Teacher Told Me* (New York: Touchstone, 1995), 63.
Bruce Stutz, "Megadeath in Mexico," *Discover Magazine,* February 21, 2006, 1.
David J. Meltzer, "How Columbus Sickened the World," *The New Scientist* 136 (October 10): 1992, 38–41.

1. The best-known propagandist for European "genocide" is Alfred W. Crosby Jr., *Ecological Imperialism: The Biological Expansion of Europe, 900–1900* (New York: Cambridge University Press, 1986).
2. John D. Daniels, "The Indian Population of North America in 1492," *William & Mary Quarterly* (April 1999): 298–320.
3. Douglas Ubelaker, "North American Indian Population Size, A.D. 1500–1985," *American Journal of Physical Anthropology* 77 (1988): 289–94; David Cook, *Demographic Collapse: Indian Peru, 1520–1660* (Cambridge, MA: Cambridge University Press, 1981); Betty Meggers, "Prehistoric Population Density in the Amazon Basin," in John W. Verano and Douglas H. Ubelaker, *Disease and Demography in the Americas* (Washington, DC: Smithsonian Press, 1992).
4. Henry F. Dobyns, *American Historical Demography* (Bloomington: Indiana University Press, 1976). Dobyns is one of those who, after beginning with an estimate of Indian population of 40 million, has revised his numbers downward. See also William H. MacLeish, *The Day Before America* (Boston: Houghton Mifflin, 1994).

5. Daniel T. Reff, *Disease, Depopulation, and Culture Change in Northwestern New Spain, 1518–1764* (Salt Lake City: University of Utah Press, 1991).
6. David Henige, *Numbers from Nowhere: The American Indian Contact Population Debate* (Norman: University of Oklahoma Press, 1998).
7. Rodolfo Acuna-Soto et al., "Megadrought and Megadeath in 16th Century Mexico," Centers for Disease Control 8 (2002), http://origin.cdc.gov/ncidod/EID/vol8no4/01-0175.htm.
8. Loewen, *Lies My Teacher Told Me*, 50.
9. Victor Davis Hanson, *Carnage and Culture: Landmark Battles in the Rise to Western Power* (New York: Anchor, 2002); Ross Hassing, "El sacrificio y las guerras floridas," *Arqueología Mexicana* 11 (2003): 46–51, and his *Aztec Warfare: Imperial Expansion and Political Control* (Norman: University of Oklahoma Press, 1988).
10. Quoted in Loewen, *Lies My Teacher Told Me*, 70.

Lie #22

Epigraphs:

George Brown Tindall and David E. Shi, *America: A Narrative History*, brief 6th ed. (New York: Norton, 2004), 45.

James W. Loewen, *Lies My Teacher Told Me* (New York: Touchstone, 1995), 45.

1. Edmund S. Morgan, *American Slavery, American Freedom: The Ordeal of Colonial Virginia* (New York: Norton, 1975), passim.
2. Larry Schweikart and Michael Allen, *A Patriot's History of the United States: From Columbus's Great Discovery to the War on Terror*, paperback ed. (New York: Sentinel, 2007), 19.
3. Robert C. Davis, *Christian Slaves, Muslim Masters* (London: Palgrave, 2002).
4. James Oliver Horton, "Weevils in the Wheat: Free Blacks and the Constitution, 1787–1860," http://www.apsanet.org/imgtest/FreeBlacksConstitution.pdf, 4.
5. Lee Lawrence, "Chronicling Black Lives in Colonial New England," *Christian Science Monitor*, http://www.csmonitor.com/durable/1997/10/29/feat/feat.1.html.
6. *Proceedings and Acts of the General Assembly*, September 1664, vol. 1, pp. 533–34, http://www.msa.md.gov/megafile/msa/speccol/sc2900/sc2908/000001/000001/html/am1—533.html.
7. Jack P. Greene, *Imperatives, Behaviors, and Identities: Essays in Early American Cultural History* (Charlottesville: University of Virginia Press, 1992); Winthrop Jordan, *White over Black: American Attitudes Toward the Negro, 1550–1812* (Chapel Hill: University of North Carolina Press, 1968).
8. Jack Larkin, *The Reshaping of Everyday Life, 1790–1840* (New York: HarperCollins, 1988), 4.
9. Ibid., 5.
10. Thomas Torowgood, *Jewes in America, or Probabilities That the Americans Are of That Race*, cited in Alden T. Vaughan, *New England Frontier: Puritans and Indians, 1620–1675* (Norman: University of Oklahoma Press, 1995), 20.
11. Schweikart and Allen, *A Patriot's History of the United States*, 60.
12. Vaughan, *New England Frontier*, 106–7.
13. Even pro-Indian historian Richard White admits that the exchange was more complex than a simple "whites-took-Indian-land" explanation. See his *The Middle Ground: Indians, Empires, and Republics in the Great Lakes Region, 1760–1815* (New York: Cambridge University Press, 1991).

14. Vaughan, *New England Frontier,* 108–9.
15. Ibid., 109.
16. See Paul Johnson, "God and the Americans," *Commentary* (January 1995): 25–34; Clifton E. Olmstead, *History of Religion in the United States* (Englewood Cliffs, NJ: Prentice-Hall, 1960); Jon Butler, *Awash in a Sea of Faith: Christianizing the American People* (Cambridge, MA: Harvard University Press, 1990); Edwin S. Gaustad, *The Great Awakening in New England* (Chicago: Quadrangle, 1968); Patricia U. Bonomi, *Under the Cope of Heaven: Religion, Society, and Politics in Colonial America* (New York: Oxford University Press, 2003).

LIE #23

Epigraph:
   Michael Bellesiles, *Arming America: The Origins of a National Gun Culture* (New York: Knopf, 2000), 5.

1. Bellesiles, *Arming America.*
2. Ibid.
3. James T. Lindgren, "Fall from Grace: Arming America and the Bellesiles Scandal," *Yale Law Journal* 111 (2002): 2195, 2002, quoted online at http://papers.ssrn.com/sol3/papers.cfm?abstract_id=692421.
4. David B. Kopel, *Gun Control in Great Britain: Saving Lives or Constricting Liberties?* (Huntsville, TX: Office of International Criminal Justice, 1992); Gary Kleck and Don B. Kates, *Armed: New Perspectives on Gun Control* (Amherst, NY: Prometheus Books, 2001); John R. Lott Jr., *More Guns, Less Crime* (Chicago: University of Chicago Press, 1998); http://www.guncite.com/gun_control_gcgvinco.html; Martin Killias, John van Kesteren, and Martin Rindlisbacher, "Guns, Violent Crime, and Suicide in 21 Countries," *Canadian Journal of Criminology* 43 (October 2001): 1721–25; Don B. Kates and Gary Mauser, "Would Banning Firearms Reduce Murder and Suicide: A Review of International Evidence," *Harvard Journal of Law and Public Policy* 30 (Spring 2007): 651–94.
5. Bellesiles, *Arming America,* 9.
6. Stephen P. Halbrook, *That Every Man Be Armed* (Oakland, CA: Independent Institute, 1994), 38–39.
7. Thomas Esper, "The Replacement of the Longbow by Firearms in the English Army," *Technology and Culture* 6 (1965): 382–93.
8. Clayton Cramer, "Firearms Ownership & Manufacturing in Early America," 2001, Web site, http://www.claytoncramer.com/ArmingAmericaLong.pdf.
9. Michael Bellesiles, "The Origins of Gun Culture in the United States, 1760–1865," *Journal of American History* 83 (September 1996): 425–55.
10. See Cramer's review of this process under "Arming America," http://www.claytoncramer.com/unpublished.htm.
11. Jerome Sternstein, "Shooting the Messenger: Jon Wiener on *Arming America,*" HistoryNewsNetwork.com, October 28, 2002, http://hnn.us/articles/1074.html.
12. These and fabrications far too numerous to recount here are in Clayton Cramer's "Fraud in Michael Bellesiles's *Arming America,*" and a more detailed version exists here: http://www.ggnra.org/cramer/ArmingAmericaLong.pdf.
13. Lindgren, "Fall from Grace." See also James Lindgren and Justin L. Heather, "Counting Guns in Early America," *William and Mary Law Review* 43 (2002): 1777–1842.

14. Elizabeth Farrell, "Historian's Book on Colonial-Era Gun Ownership Is Challenged," *Chronicle of Higher Education* (September 21, 2001), http://chronicle.com/free/v48/i04/04a01801.htm.
15. "The Bancroft and Bellesiles," http://hnn.us/articles/1157.html.
16. http://www.news.emory.edu/Releases/Final_Report.pdf, 8.
17. Ibid., 15.
18. Ibid., 16.
19. Ibid., 18.
20. "The Bancroft and Bellesiles," http://hnn.us/articles/1157.html.
21. Quoted from C-SPAN in "Arming America, The Origins of a National Gun Culture," Wikipedia, http://en.wikipedia.org/wiki/Arming_America,_The_Origins_of_a_National_Gun_Culture.
22. Quoted in Sternstein, "Shooting the Messenger."

LIE #24

Epigraphs:
Howard Zinn, *A People's History of the United States* (New York: HarperPerennial, 2002), 192.
Lerone Bennett Jr., *Forced into Glory: Abraham Lincoln's White Dream* (Chicago: Johnson Publishing, 2007), 147.
Irwin Unger, *These United States: The Questions of Our Past,* concise ed., combined vol. (Upper Saddle River, NJ: Pearson, 2007), 344.

1. Bernard Bailyn et al., *The Great Republic: A History of the American People* (Lexington, MA: D. C. Heath, 1985), 470–74.
2. Shelby Foote telling a story of a Rebel prisoner in Ken Burns's PBS series *The Civil War,* VHS, 9 vols., Alexandria, VA: Florentine Films, 1989, vol. 1.
3. *Official Records of the Union and Confederate Navies in the War of the Rebellion,* Series 1, 689.
4. Stephen B. Oates, *With Malice Toward None: The Life of Abraham Lincoln* (New York: Mentor, 1977), 334.
5. Larry Schweikart and Michael Allen, *A Patriot's History of the United States: From Columbus's Great Discovery to the War on Terror* (New York: Sentinel, 2007), 328.
6. Frederick Seward, *Recollected Words of Abraham Lincoln,* ed. Don and Virginia Fehrenbacher (Stanford, CA: Stanford University Press, 1996), 397.
7. Grady McWhiney, *Attack and Die: Civil War Military Tactics and the Southern Heritage* (Tuscaloosa: University of Alabama Press, 1984).
8. Allen C. Guelzo, "Defending Emancipation: Abraham Lincoln and the Conkling Letter, 1863," *Civil War History* 48 (2002): 313–37.
9. Ibid., 320.
10. Larry Schweikart, *America's Victories: Why the United States Wins Wars and Will Win the War on Terror* (New York: Sentinel, 2007), 72.
11. Charles H. Wesley, "The Employment of Negroes as Soldiers in the Confederate Army," *Journal of Negro History* 4 (July 1919): 239–53; Elsie Freeman, Wynell Burroughs Schamel, and Jean West, "The Fight for Equal Rights: A Recruiting Poster for Black Soldiers in the Civil War," *Social Education* 56 (February 1992): 118–20.
12. Ervin L. Jordan Jr., *Black Confederates and Afro-Yankees in Civil War Virginia* (Charlottesville: University of Virginia Press, 1995).

13 Bailyn et al., *The Great Republic*.
14. "The Emancipation Proclamation," http://school.familyeducation.com/african-american-history/slavery-us/47036.html?page=2&detoured=1.
15. Ibid.
16. "Special Orders, No. 191," September 9, 1862, http://www.nps.gov/archive/anti/ordr_191.htm.

LIE #25

Epigraphs:
Eric Foner, *Give Me Liberty: An American History*, 2nd ed., vol. 2 (New York: Norton, 2006), 681.

Samuel Eliot Morison, Henry Steele Commager, and William E. Leuchtenberg, *A Concise History of the American Republic*, 2nd ed. (New York: Oxford University Press, 1983), 589.

George Brown Tindall and David E. Shi, *America: A Narrative History*, brief 6th ed. (New York: Norton, 2004), 852.

1. David E. Harrell et al., *Unto a Good Land: A History of the American People* (Grand Rapids, MI: William E. Eerdmans, 2005), 871–73.
2. Daniel Goldfield et al., *The American Journey*, brief 4th ed., combined vol., TLC ed. (Upper Saddle River, NJ: Pearson, 2007), 713.
3. Jerome Lawence and Robert E. Lee, *Inherit the Wind* (New York: Ballantine Books, 2007); Ray Ginger, *Six Days or Forever?* (Boston: Beacon Press, 1958); Paolo Coletta, *William Jennings Bryan: Political Puritan, 1915–1925* (Lincoln: University of Nebraska Press, 1969); *Inherit the Wind*, directed by Stanley Kramer, 1960.
4. Burton W. Folsom Jr., "The Scopes Trial Reconsidered," *Continuity* 12 (Fall 1988): 103–27, and his "An Urban-Rural Dimension of the Scopes Trial," in Joseph F. Rishel, *American Cities and Towns: Historical Perspectives* (Pittsburgh: Duquesne University Press, 1992), 109–22.
5. Irwin Unger, *These United States: The Questions of Our Past*, concise ed., combined vol., 3rd ed. (Upper Saddle River, NJ: Pearson, 2006), 586.
6. James West Davidson et al., *Nation of Nations: A Concise Narrative of the American Republic*, 3rd ed., 2 vols. (Boston: McGraw-Hill, 2002), 2:697.
7. Folsom, "Scopes Trial," 107.
8. Ibid., 113.
9. William Jennings Bryan, *The Old World and Its Ways Describing a Tour Around the World and Journeys Through Europe* (St. Louis: Thompson Publishing, 2007).
10. Folsom, "Urban-Rural Dimension of the Scopes Trial," 109.
11. *Baltimore Sun*, July 21, 1925, quoted in Folsom, "Scopes Trial," 123.
12. Folsom, "Scopes Trial," 124.
13. Folsom, "Urban-Rural Dimension," 110.
14. Ibid., 115.
15. Quoted in ibid., 118.
16. See "Does Intelligent Design Postulate a 'Supernatural Creator?'," http://www.discovery.org/scripts/viewDB/filesDB-download.php?command=download&id=565. Among the scientists who subscribe to creation theory are Jon Sarfati (chemistry), A. E. Wilder-Smith (chemistry), Terry Mortenson (geology), Ariel A. Roth (biology), Henry M. Morris (hydraulic engineering), Fazale Rana (chemistry), Hugh

Ross (astronomy), and many others. Although it would be premature to call Michael Behe a "creationist," his book *Darwin's Black Box: The Biochemical Challenge to Evolution* (New York: Free Press, 2006) is a powerful challenge to the Darwinian orthodoxy. On the other hand, Stephen Jay Gould, a passionate evolutionist, acknowledged the "extreme rarity" of transitional animals that might prove evolution. (Quoted in Ann Coulter, *Godless* [New York: Crown, 2006], 219.)

Lie #26

Epigraphs:
George Brown Tindall and David E Shi, *America: A Narrative History,* brief 6th ed. (New York: Norton, 2004), 1056.
Eric Foner, *Give Me Liberty: An American History,* vol. 2 (New York: Norton, [Seagull ed.], 2006), 831. By ascribing their own views to "critics" or "some said," historians cleverly attempt to avoid charges of bias. Yet in Foner's case, a full eighteen pages of his thirty-five-page chapter on the 1950s and early 1960s are dedicated to such "social critics," discussions of segregation and/or racism, perceived setbacks to the feminist movement, or veiled diatribes against WASPs. One could easily substitute "Foner said" in every case where he used the term "critics said" or "some said."

1. William Whyte, *The Organization Man* (New York: Doubleday/Anchor, 1957); David Riesman, *The Lonely Crowd* (New Haven, CT: Yale University Press, 1950); Sloan Wilson, *The Man in the Gray Flannel Suit* (New York: Simon & Schuster, 1955); and Vance Packard, *The Hidden Persuaders* (New York: D. McKay, 1957).
2. C. Wright Mills, *The Power Elite* (New York: Oxford University Press, 1956).
3. Tindall and Shi, *America,* 1056.
4. John B. Rae, *American Automobile Industry* (Boston: Twayne, 1984), see chart on 174.
5. Larry Schweikart, *The Entrepreneurial Adventure: A History of Business in the United States* (Fort Worth, TX: Harcourt, 2000), 386; Rae, *American Automobile Industry,* chart on 174.
6. See, for example, William Strauss and Neil Howe, *Generations: The History of America's Future, 1584–2069* (New York: William Morrow, 1991).

Lie #27

Epigraphs:
David E. Harrell et al., *Unto a Good Land: A History of the American People* (Grand Rapids, MI: William B. Eerdmans, 2005), 11.
John Mack Faragher et al., *Out of Many,* combined vol., 4th ed., TLC ed. (Upper Saddle River, NJ: Pearson, 2006), 82.

1. Samuel Eliot Morison, Henry Steele Commager, and William E. Leuchtenburg, *A Concise History of the American Republic,* 2nd ed. (New York: Oxford University Press, 1983), 745.
2. Harrell et al., *Unto a Good Land,* 1112, 1124.
3. Len Colodny and Robert Gettlin, *Silent Coup: The Removal of a President* (New York: St. Martin's, 1991), 109–10.
4. *Maureen K. Dean and John Dean v. St. Martin's Press, Inc., Len Colodny, Robert Get-*

tlin, G. Gordon Liddy, and Phillip Mackin Bailley (1996). http://www.nixonera
.com/media/transcripts/liddy.pdf.

5. Ibid., 40.
6. Ibid., 80.
7. Ibid., 83.
8. *Judiciary Committee Impeachment Hearings, 93rd Congress, Book I, Events Prior to the Watergate Break-in* (Washington, DC: U.S. Government Printing Office, 1974).
9. *Dean v. St. Martin's*, 97; Colodny and Gettlin, *Silent Coup*, passim.
10. *Dean v. St. Martin's*, 97.
11. G. Gordon Liddy, *Will: The Autobiography of G. Gordon Liddy* (New York: St. Martin's, 1980), 237.
12. Barbara Newman, *Key to Watergate*, A&E, 1992, http://www.nixonera.com/media/audio/key.ram.
13. "Liddy Hangs Tough on Watergate Theory," CBS News, February 2, 2001, http://www.cbsnews.com/stories/2001/02/02/national/main269091.shtml.
14. "Liddy Case Dismissed," CBS News, February 1, 2001, http://www.cbsnews.com/stories/2001/01/29/national/main267968.shtml.
15. Federal Bureau of Investigation, Office of Planning and Evaluation. FBI Watergate Investigation: OPE Analysis. July 5, 1974. File Number 139-4089, 11.
16. Richard Nixon, *RN: The Memoirs of Richard Nixon* (New York: Grosset & Dunlap, 1978), 632.
17. *Dean v. St. Martin's*, 119.
18. Ibid., 123.

Lie #28

Epigraphs:
    George Brown Tindall and David E. Shi, *America: A Narrative History,* brief 6th ed. (New York: Norton, 2004), 1176.
    Samuel Eliot Morison, Henry Steele Commager, and William E. Leuchtenburg, *A Concise History of the American Republic,* 2nd ed. (New York: Oxford University Press, 1983), 761.
    Steven M. Gillon and Cathy D. Matson, *The American Experiment: A History of the United States* (Boston: Houghton Mifflin, 2002), 1276.

1. Winthrop D. Jordan and Leon F. Litwack, *The United States: Combined Edition,* 7th ed. (Englewood Cliffs, NJ: Prentice-Hall, 1991), 866.
2. Paul S. Boyer et al., *The Enduring Vision: A History of the American People, from 1865,* vol. 2, 5th ed. (New York: Houghton Mifflin, 2004), 951–52.
3. Ibid., 976.
4. Alan Brinkley, *The Unfinished Nation: A Concise History of the American People,* 3rd ed. (Boston: McGraw-Hill, 2000), 1015.
5. John M. Murrin et al., *Liberty, Equality, Power: A History of the American People,* 3rd ed. (Fort Worth, TX: Harcourt Brace, 2002), 1103.
6. Daniel Goldfield et al., *The American Journey: A History of the United States,* combined ed. (Upper Saddle River, NJ: Prentice-Hall, 1998), 1001.
7. Thomas A. Bailey et al., *The American Pageant,* vol. 2, 11th ed. (Boston: Houghton Mifflin, 1998), 1002.

LIE #29

Epigraphs:
   David E. Harrell et al., *Unto a Good Land: A History of the American People* (Grand Rapids, MI: William Eerdmans, 2005, 1177.
   Irwin Unger, *These United States: The Questions of Our Past,* concise ed., combined vol., 3rd ed. (Upper Saddle River, NJ: Pearson, 2007), 802.

1. Peter Goldman, "Was Justice Finally Done?" *Newsweek,* January 13, 1975; Ann Coulter, *High Crimes and Misdemeanors* (Washington, DC: Regnery, 1998), 15.
2. Jeff Gerth, "Clintons Joined S.&L. Operator in an Ozark Real-Estate Venture," *New York Times,* March 8, 1992.
3. "Ray: Insufficient Evidence to Prosecute Clintons in Whitewater Probe," CNN .com, September 20, 2000, http://archives.cnn.com/2000/ALLPOLITICS/stories/09/20/whitewater/.
4. Roger Morris, *Partners in Power: The Clintons and Their America* (New York: Henry Holt, 1996), 233.
5. Peter Baker, "Clinton Settles Paula Jones Lawsuit for $850,000," *Washington Post,* http://www.washingtonpost.com/wp-srv/politics/special/clinton/stories/jones111498.htm.
6. "What Clinton Said," *Washington Post,* http://www.washingtonpost.com/wp-srv/politics/special/clinton/stories/whatclintonsaid.htm.
7. Coulter, *High Crimes and Misdemeanors,* 44.
8. Matthew Campbell, "Hillary in Retreat," London *Sunday Times,* March 8, 1998.
9. Hillary Rodham Clinton, *Living History* (New York: Simon & Schuster, 2003), 443.
10. Ibid.
11. Michael Isikoff, "A Twist in *Jones v. Clinton*," *Newsweek,* August 11, 1997.
12. *The Starr Report: The Official Report of the Independent Counsel's Investigation of the President* (Rocklin, CA: Forum, 1998).
13. David Schippers, *Sellout: The Inside Story of the Clinton Impeachment* (Washington, DC: Regnery, 2000), 254.
14. Ibid., 14.
15. Ibid., 23.
16. Ibid., 13.
17. Ibid., 164–65.
18. "Clinton Found in Civil Contempt for Jones Testimony," http://www.cnn.com/ALLPOLITICS/stories/1999/04/12/clinton.contempt/.

LIE #30

Epigraph:
   John Heileman, "The Comback Kid," *New York Magazine,* May 21, 2006.

1. John R. Lott Jr., "Documenting Unusual Declines in Republican Voting Rates in Florida's Western Panhandle Counties in 2000," May 8, 2001, working paper for Social Science Research Network, http://papers.ssrn.com/sol3/papers.cfm?abstract_id=276278.
2. Bill Sammon, *At Any Cost: How Al Gore Tried to Steal the 2000 Election* (Washington, DC: Regnery, 2001).

3. Ibid., 78.
4. Ibid., 82.
5. *Bush v. Gore*, 531 U.S. 98 (2000).
6. Sammon, *At Any Cost*, 243–45.

LIE #31

Epigraphs:
http://foi.missouri.edu/terrorbkgd/rootcauses.html.
http://www.catholicweekly.com.au/03/jun/8/04.html.
David E. Harrell et. al., *Unto a Good Land: A History of the American People* (Grand Rapids, MI: William Eerdmans, 2005), 1185.
Barbara Ehrenreich, "The Empire Strikes Back," *Village Voice*, October 9, 2001.

1. George W. Bush, March 22, 2002, http://whitehouse.gov/news/releases/2002/03/200203221.html; Tyson quoted from "It's Time to Step Up the Global War on Poverty,"*BusinessWeek*, 2001, in Richard Miniter, *Disinformation: 22 Media Myths That Undermine the War on Terror* (Washington, DC: Regnery, 2005), 125.
2. Brian Burgoon, "On Welfare and Terror: Social Welfare Policies and Political-economic Roots of Terrorism," Amsterdam School for Social Science Research Working Paper No. 04/07, 2.
3. Alberto Abadie, "Poverty, Political Education, and the Roots of Terrorism," National Bureau of Economic Research Working Paper No. 10859.
4. Alan B. Krueger and Jitka Maleckova, "Education, Poverty and Terrorism: Is There a Causal Connection?" *The Journal of Economic Perspectives* 17 (Autumn 2003): 119–44 (quotation on 119).
5. Lawrence Wright, *The Looming Tower: Al-Qaeda and the Road to 9/11* (New York: Knopf, 2006), 7.
6. Qutb quoted in ibid., 22.
7. Ibid., 32.
8. Miniter, *Disinformation*, 26.
9. Marc Sageman, *Understanding Terror Networks* (Philadelphia: University of Pennsylvania Press, 2004), and his paper "Understanding Terror Networks," Foreign Policy Research Institute, November 1, 2004.
10. Nasra Hassan, "An Arsenal of Believers," *New Yorker*, November 19, 2001.
11. "Profiles in Killing," and "The Bombers: A Breakdown," *Newsweek*, August 14, 2007, http://www.msnbc.msn.com/id/20123887/site/newsweek/page/3/.
12. Mitch Potter, "U.K. Doctor Plot Thickens," Toronto *Star*, July 4, 2007, http://www.thestar.com/article/232270.
13. Ibid.
14. Charles Russell and Bowman Miller, "Profile of a Terrorist," *Perspectives on Terrorism* (Wilmington, DE: Scholarly Resources, 1983), 45–60.
15. Susan B. Glasser, "Martyrs in Iraq Mostly Saudis," *Washington Post*, May 15, 2005.
16. Sageman, "Understanding Terror Networks," 78.
17. Miniter, *Disinformation*, 132. See also John Miller and Michael Stone, *The Cell* (New York: Hyperion, 2002), passim.
18. Michael Bond, "The Making of a Suicide Bomber," *New Scientist*, May 15, 2004, http://www.newscientist.com/article/mg18224475.900-the-making-of-a-suicide-bomber.html.

LIE #32

Epigraph:

Andrew Heyword, quoted in Bernard Goldberg, *Bias: A CBS Insider Exposes How the Media Distort the News* (Washington, DC: Regnery, 2002), 43.

1. Edwin R. Bayley, *McCarthy and the Press* (Madison: University of Wisconsin Press, 1981); Rodger Streitmatter, *Mightier Than the Sword* (Boulder, CO: Westview Press, 1997), 150–69.
2. Gerald Baldasty, *The Commercialization of the News in the Nineteenth Century* (Madison: University of Wisconsin Press, 1992); Thomas C. Leonard, *News for All: America's Coming of Age with the Press* (New York: Oxford University Press, 1995).
3. James L. Moses, "Journalistic Impartiality on the Eve of Revolution: The *Boston Evening Post,* 1770–1775," *Journalism History* 20 (Autumn–Winter 1994): 125–30; Bernard Bailyn and John Hench, eds., *The Press and the American Revolution* (Boston: Northeastern University Press, 1981).
4. Michael Lienesch, "Thomas Jefferson and the American Democratic Experience: The Origins of the Partisan Press, Popular Political Parties, and Public Opinion," in Peter Onuf, ed., *Jeffersonian Legacies* (Charlottesville: University of Virginia Press, 1993), 316–39. One newspaperman, James Callender, was called "Jefferson's Matt Drudge" in a recent review of William Safire's book *Scandalmonger* (New York: Simon & Schuster, 2000), quoted online at http://www.cjr.org/year/00/1/cornog.asp.
5. Erik McKinley Eriksson, "President Jackson's Propaganda Agencies," *Pacific Historical Review* 7 (January 1937): 47–57.
6. Gretchen Garst Eweing, "Duff Green, Independent Editor of a Party Press," *Journalism Quarterly* 54 (Winter 1977): 733–39; Culver H. Smith, "Propaganda Technique in the Jackson Campaign of 1828," *East Tennessee Historical Society Publications* 6 (1934): 53. See also M. Green, "Duff Green, Militant Journalist of the Old School," *American Historical Review* 52 (January 1947): 247–64.
7. Washington, DC, *U.S. Telegraph,* October 7, 1828.
8. Robert V. Remini, *The Election of Andrew Jackson* (Philadelphia: J. B. Lippincott, 1963), 49.
9. *Louisville Public Advertiser,* July 9, 1828.
10. New York *Lyons Western Argus,* August 1, 1832.
11. Baldasty, *Commercialization of News,* 7.
12. See Gerald J. Baldasty's dissertation, for example: "The Political Press in the Second American Party System: The 1832 Election," Ph.D. dissertation, University of Washington, 1978, 140–70. He performed a content analysis of five metropolitan newspapers and four non-metropolitan newspapers, in which he found that in the city papers, political topics made up more than one-half of all stories, and in the non-metropolitan publications, nearly 70 percent (Baldasty, *Commercialization of News,* Table 1.1., 23).
13. Richard B. Lielbowicz, *News in the Mail: The Press, Post Office and Public Information* (New York: Greenwood Press, 1989).
14. Richard R. John, *Spreading the News: The American Postal System from Franklin to Morse* (Cambridge, MA: Harvard University Press, 1995), 49, and chapter 2, passim. Leonard, *News for All,* 13, 43.
15. Michael Schudson, *Discovering the News* (New York: Basic Books, 1978), 78, 86.
16. Gobight quoted in David T. Z. Mindich, *Just the Facts* (New York: New York University Press, 1998), 109.

17. Harlan S. Stensaas, "Development of the Objectivity Ethic in U.S. Daily Newspapers," *Journal of Mass Media Ethics* 2 (Fall/Winter 1986–1987): 50–60; and Donald L. Shaw, "At the Crossroads: Change and Continuity in American Press News, 1820–1860," *Journalism History* 8 (Summer 1981): 38–50.

18. "Code of Ethics," Society for Professional Journalists, http://spj.org/ethics/code/htm.

19. Bruce J. Evensen, "Journalism's Struggle over Ethics and Professionalism During America's Jazz Age," *Journalism History* 16 (Autumn–Winter 1989): 54–63 (quotation on 54).

20. "Associated Press, Code of Ethics," http://www.asne.org/ideas/codes/apme.htm.

21. Lou Guzzo to the author, January 27, 2001, via e-mail.

22. James L. Baughman, *The Republic of Mass Culture: Journalism, Filmmaking, and Broadcasting in America Since 1991* (Baltimore: Johns Hopkins University Press, 1992), 14–21; James Boylan, "Declarations of Independence: A Historian Reflects on an Era in Which Reporters Rose Up to Challenge—and Change—the Rules of the Game," *Columbia Journalism Review* (November/December 1986): 29–45.

23. See, for example, James Farley, *Jim Farley's Story* (New York: Whittlesey House, 1948); Betty H. Winfield, *FDR and the News Media* (Urbana: University of Illinois Press, 1990).

24. Burton W. Folsom, "The Myth of Franklin Roosevelt and the New Deal," 2007, manuscript in author's possession.

25. Frank Newport and Joseph Carroll, "Are the News Media Too Liberal?" October 8, 2003, http://www.gallup.com. The Roper poll is mentioned in Steve Bell, "The Media and Politics: It's More Than the News," March 2001, and the poll is in the author's possession. For numerous wordings of questions exploring the liberal bias, see Rich Noyes, "The Liberal Media: Every Poll Shows Journalists Are More Liberal Than the American Public—and the Public Knows It," June 30, 2004, http://www.mediaresearch.org/SpecialReports/2004/report063004_p2.asp.

26. Jim A. Kuypers, *Press Bias and Politics* (New York: Praeger, 2002), 202.

27. Quoted in Tim Jones, "A Simple Formula: Writing What People Will Read," *Chicago Tribune,* November 15, 1999.

28. Jack Fuller, *News Values* (Chicago: University of Chicago Press, 1996), 11.

29. "Top Ten Confidence-Inspiring Institutions in 2000," *The American Enterprise,* October/November 2000.

30. Media Research Center, "Rise and Shine on Democrats: How the ABC, CBS, and NBC Morning Shows Are Favoring the Democrats on the Road to the White House, 2008," August 2007, http://www.mrc.org/SpeciaReports/2007/Riseandshine/Campaign2008.pdf.

Lie #33

Epigraphs:

John Mack Faragher, *Out of Many,* TLC ed., combined vol., 4th ed. (Upper Saddle River, NJ: Pearson, 2006).

Charles E. Kay, "Aboriginal Overkill and Native Burning: Implications for Modern Ecosystem Management," *Western Journal of Applied Forestry* (October 1995): 121–26, referring to the works of P. C. Jobes, "The Greater Yellowstone Social System," *Conservation Biology* 5, 387–94, and M. S. Alvard, "Testing the 'Ecologically Noble Savage' Hypothesis: Interspecific Prey Choice by Piro Hunters of Amazonian Peru," *Human Ecology* 21, 355–87.

1. Andrew C. Isenberg, *The Destruction of the Bison* (Cambridge, MA: Cambridge University Press, 2000), 39.
2. Larry Schweikart and Michael Allen, *A Patriot's History of the United States: From Columbus's Great Discovery to the War on Terror* (New York: Sentinel, 2006), 404.
3. Shepard Krech III, *The Ecological Indian: Myth and History* (New York: Norton, 1999), 123–49; Dan Flores, "Bison Ecology and Bison Diplomacy: The Southern Plains from 1800 to 1850," in Helen Wheatley, ed., *Agriculture, Resource Exploitation, and Environmental Change* (Brookfield, VT: Variorum, 1997), 47–68.
4. Larry Schweikart, "Buffaloed: The Myth and Reality of Bison in America," *The Freeman: Ideas on Liberty* 52 (December 2002), online at http://www.fee.org/publications/the-freeman/article.asp?aid=4525.
5. Krech, *Ecological Indian*, 161–63.
6. Kay, "Aboriginal Overkill," 123, and his "Aboriginal Overkill: The Role of Native Americans in Structuring Western Ecosystems," *Human Nature* 5, 359–98.
7. Ibid., 152. This is not Krech's view. He summarizes the positions of Harold Hickerson, "Fur Trade Colonialism and the North American Indians," *Journal of Ethnic Studies* I (1975): 15–44; Richard White, *The Roots of Dependency: Subsistence, Environment, and Social Change Among the Choctaws, Pawnees, and Navajos* (Lincoln: University of Nebraska Press, 1983); Daniel H. Usner Jr., *Indians, Settlers, & Slaves in a Frontier Exchange Economy: The Lower Mississippi Valley Before 1783* (Chapel Hill: University of North Carolina Press, 1992); and Kathryn E. Holland Braund, *Deerskins and Duffels: The Creek Indian Trade with Anglo-America, 1685–1815* (Lincoln: University of Nebraska Press, 1993).
8. Schweikart, "Buffaloed," passim.
9. Frank Gilbert Roe, *The North American Buffalo: A Critical Study of the Species in Its Wild State* (Toronto: University of Toronto Press, 1951), 643–44, quoted in Krech, *Ecological Indian*, 149.
10. Edward Thompson Denig, *Five Indian Tribes of the Upper Missouri: Sioux, Arikaras, Assiniboines, Crees, Crows,* in John C. Dwers, ed.(Norman: University of Oklahoma Press, 1961), 79.
11. Roe, *North American Buffalo*, 609.
12. Isenberg, *Destruction of the Bison*, 84.
13. Kay, "Aboriginal Overkill," 125. Kay, it should be noted, nevertheless wants to return to the "biological diversity" of the pre-Columbian era.
14. Isenberg, *Destruction of the Bison*, 164.
15. Edmund Contoski, *Makers and Takers: How Wealth and Progress Are Made and How They Are Taken Away or Prevented* (Minneapolis: American Liberty Publishers, 1997), 289.
16. Ibid., 176.
17. Schweikart, "Buffaloed," passim.
18. Contoski, *Makers and Takers*, 289–91.
19. See the Y.O. Ranch's history and homepage, http://www.yoranch.com/YORanch.html, including its hunting links; Contoski, *Makers and Takers*, 297.
20. Isenberg, *Destruction of the Bison*, 189.

LIE #34

Note: The epigraph was written for Tacoma Public Schools in 1987 (http://www.manataka.org/page269.html), along with Susan Bates, "The REAL Story of Thanksgiving," which, referring to the Pequot War, tells students that Squanto "taught [the British] to grow corn and fish," but that the English weren't satisfied and invaded the Indians' "paradise," capturing or killing the Pequot Nation. Note how this conflates the Pequot War with events that happened sixteen years earlier. Bates reprinted this rant in "The Real Story of Thanksgiving," *Alternative Press Review,* November 23, 2005, http://www .altpr.org/modules.php?op—odload&name–ews&file=article&sid=530&mode–ocomments&order=0&thold=0.

1. "The First Thanksgiving Was Celebrated in Virginia," http://www.virginia.org/site/features.asp?FeatureID=50.
2. Contrast with New England. See W. DeLoss Love, *The Fast and Thanksgiving Days of New England* (New York: Houghton Mifflin, 1895).
3. Tom Bethell, "How Private Property Saved the Pilgrims," *Hoover Digest,* 1999, http://www.hoover.org/publications/digest/3507051.html.
4. Modern History Sourcebook: William Bradford, from *History of Plymouth Plantation,* c. 1650. http://www.fordham.edu/halsall/mod/1650bradford.html.
5. William Bradford, *Of Plymouth Plantation* (New York: Capricorn Books, 1962), 90.
6. Ibid., 80.
7. Ibid., 90.
8. http://www.juntosociety.com/thanksgiving/thanksgiving7.htm; Bradford, quoted in William J. Federer, *America's God and Country Encyclopedia of Quotations* (St. Louis: Amerisearch, 1994), 66.

LIE #35

Epigraph:
David Goldfield et al., *The American Journey,* combined ed. (Upper Saddle River, NJ: Pearson, 2007)

1. Derrick Jensen, George Draffam, John Osborn, and Inland Empire Public Lands Council, *Railroads and Clearcuts* (Sandpoint, ID: Keokee Publishing, 1995). A source dealing with the "destruction of the American wilderness" that strongly implies, though it does not flatly state, that the earlier timbermen raped the land, is Jack Shepherd, *The Forest Killers: The Destruction of the American Wilderness* (New York: Weybright & Talley, 1975).
2. Stephen J. Pyne, *Fire in America: A Cultural History of Wildland and Rural Fire* (Princeton, NJ: Princeton University Press, 1982), 11–26.
3. W. E. Haskell, *The International Paper Company, 1898–1924: Its Origin and Growth in a Quarter of a Century with a Brief Description of the Manufacture of Paper from the Harvesting of Pulpwood to the Finished Roll* (New York: International Paper, 1924), 8–9.
4. Clinton Woods, *Ideas That Became Big Business* (Baltimore: Founders, 1959), 110, 313–14.
5. James West Davidson et al., *Nation of Nations: A Concise Narrative of the American Republic,* vol. 1, 4th ed. (New York: McGraw-Hill, 2006), 402.
6. Ibid.
7. James W. Loewen, *Lies My Teacher Told Me* (New York: Touchstone, 1995), 261.
8. Alexander Starbuck, *History of the American Whale Fishery* (Secaucus, NJ: Castle Books, 1899); David Moment, "The Business of Whaling in America in the 1850's," *Business History Review* 31 (Autumn 1957): 261–91; and Teresa D. Hutchins, "The

American Whale Fishery, 1815–1900: An Economic Analysis," Ph.D. dissertation, University of North Carolina, 1988.

9. Hutchins, *The American Whale Fishery, 1815–1900: An Economic Analysis,* table VI-5. For oil prices, see Harold F. Williamson and Arnold R. Daum, *The American Petroleum Industry, 1859–1899* (Evanston, IL: Northwestern University Press, 1959), 118, 372–73.

10. Allan Nevins, *Study in Power: John D. Rockefeller,* 2 vols. (New York: Scribner's, 1953), 1:672; Burton W. Folsom Jr., *The Myth of the Robber Barons: A New Look at the Rise of Big Business in America* (Herndon, VA: Young America's Foundation, 1991), 83–100.

11. John A. Garraty, *The American Nation,* 5th ed. (New York: Harper & Row, 1983), 456–58.

12. Loewen, *Lies My Teacher Told Me,* 262.

LIE #36

Epigraphs:
David E. Harrell et al., *Unto a Good Land: A History of the American People* (Grand Rapids, MI: William B. Eerdmans, 2005), 800.

Paul S. Boyer et al. *The Enduring Vision: A History of the American People,* concise 5th ed. (Boston: Houghton Mifflin, 2006), 444.

1. *"Abigail Alliance v. von Eschenbach,"* http://en.wikipedia.org/wiki/Abigail_Alliance_v._von_Eschenbach. The FDA has appealed the case as of 2007.

2. Carol Lewis, "The 'Poison Squad' and the Advent of Food and Drug Regulation," 2002, http://www.fda.gov/FDAC/features/2002/602_squad.html.

3. Ibid.

4. Ibid.

5. Jack High and Clayton A. Coppin, "Wiley and the Whiskey Industry: Strategic Behavior in the Passage of the Pure Food Act," *Business History Review* 62 (Summer 1988): 286–309 (quotation on 294).

6. Ibid., 307.

7. See Frederick Allen, *Secret Formula* (New York: HarperBusiness, 1994), 28–66.

8. Larry Schweikart, *The Entrepreneurial Adventure: A History of Business in the United States* (Fort Worth, TX: Harcourt, 2000), 274.

9. Allen, *Secret Formula,* 58–59. See also Mark Pendergast, *For God, Country and Coca-Cola: The Unauthorized History of the Great American Soft Drink and the Company That Makes It* (New York: Collier, 1993).

10. In 1989, the British government found "no risk to health" from Alar or UDMH; a UN panel and the World Health Organization concluded Alar was "not oncogenic in mice" and that concern was unwarranted; in February 1992, the American Medical Association issued a statement saying, "The Alar scare of three years ago shows what can happen when science is taken out of context or the risks of a product are blown out of proportion. When used in the approved, regulated fashion, as it was, Alar does not pose a risk to the public's health." These and other comments are found on the American Council on Science and Health Web site. See Kenneth Smith and Jack Raso, "An Unhappy Anniversary: The Alar 'Scare' Ten Years Later," February 1, 1999, http://www.acsh.org/publications/pubID.865/pub_detail.asp.

11. "Preapproval 'Research' & History of Aspartame," http://www.holisticmed.com/aspartame/history.faq and cited in Gregory Gordon, "NutraSweet: Questions Swirl,"

October 12, 1987, reprinted in U.S. Senate Committee on Labor and Human Resources, November 3, 1987, regarding "NutraSweet Health and Safety Concerns," Document # Y 4.L 11/4:S.HR6.100, 483–510 (quotation on 508).

12. Robin McKie, "Warning: Nicotine Seriously Improves Health," *UK Observer,* July 18, 2004.

13. Victoria Macdonald, "Passive Smoking Doesn't Cause Cancer—Official," *London Electronic Telegraph,* March 8, 1998, http://www.telegraph.co.uk/htmlContent.jhtml ?html=/archive/1998/03/08/wtob08.html.

14. Sarah Boseley, "Claim That Passive Smoking Does No Harm Lights Up Tobacco Row," *UK Guardian,* May 16, 2003.

15. Associated Press, "Vacaville Company Trying to Fight Cancer with Tobacco," August 7, 2002.

LIE #37

Epigraphs:
Michael Scott, *The Young Oxford Book of Ecology* (Oxford: Oxford University Press, 1994), 137.
Natural Resources Defense Council, http://www.nrdc.org/globalWarming/ (May 27, 2003).
Paul S. Boyer et al., *The Enduring Vision: A History of the American People,* concise 5th ed. (Boston: Houghton Mifflin, 2006), 703.

1. "Schools Must Warn of Climate Film Bias," http://www.dailymail.co.uk/pages/ live/articles/news/worldnews.html?in_article_id=485336&in_page_id=1811.

2. "CNN Meteorologist: 'Definitely Some Inaccuracies' in Gore Film," http://news-busters.org/blogs/paul-detrick/2007.

3. H. Sterling Burnett, "The Truth About Al Gore's Film: An Inconvenient Truth," National Center for Policy Analysis, June 28, 2006, http://eteam.ncpa.org/com-mentaries/the-truth-about-al-gores-film-an-inconvenient-truth.

4. H. Svensmark and E. Friis-Christensen, "Reply to Lockwood & Fröhlich—the Persistent Role of the Sun in Climate Forcing," March 2007. http://www.space center.dk/publications/scientific-report-series/Scient_No._3.pdf/view.

5. S. Fred Singer, "Global Warming: Man-Made or Natural?" *Imprimis* 36 (August 2007): 1.

6. S. Drobot, J. Maslanik et al., "On the Arctic Climate Paradox and the Continuing Role of Atmospheric Circulation in Affecting Sea Ice Conditions," *Geophysical Research Letters* 34 (October 29, 2006).

7. Michael Leidig, "Hotter-Burning Sun Warming the Planet," London *Sunday Telegraph,* July 19, 2004, reprinted in the *Washington Times,* July 19, 2004; Lawrence Solomon, *The Deniers* (Minneapolis, MN: Richard Vigilante Books, 2008).

8. Ibid.

9. Singer, "Global Warming," 2.

10. Burnett, "The Truth About Al Gore's Film: An Inconvenient Truth."

11. Ibid.

12. "Climate Change Science Program Report 1.1," 2006, http://www.climatescience .gov/Library/sap/sap1-1/finalreport/default.htm.

13. Richard Muller, "Global Warming Bombshell," *Technology Review,* October 15, 2004, http://www.technologyreview.com/Energy/13830/.

14. H. Sterling Burnett, "Polar Bears on Thin Ice, Not Really!" National Center for Policy Analysis, January 25, 2007, http://eteam.ncpa.org/commentaries/polar-bears -on-thin-ice-not-really.
15. Tom Harris, "Scientists Respond to Gore's Warnings of Climate Catastrophe," June 12, 2006, http://www.canadafreepress.com/2006/harris061206.htm.
16. Boris Winterhalter, quoted in ibid.
17. W. Dansgaard et al., "North Atlantic Climatic Oscillations Revealed by Deep Greenland Ice Cores," in F. E. Hansen and T. Takahashi, *Climate Processes and Climate Sensitivity* (Washington, DC: American Geophysical Union, 1984), 288–98.
18. Peter Gwynne, "The Cooling World," *Newsweek*, April 28, 1975, 64.
19. S. Fred Singer and Dennis T. Avery, *Unstoppable Global Warming—Every 1,500 Years* (Lanham, MD: Rowman & Littlefield, 2007), 15.
20. Ibid., 135–136.
21. Bjørn Lomborg, *The Skeptical Environmentalist* (Cambridge, MA: Cambridge University Press, 2001), 5.
22. B. R. Schone et al., "A 217-Year Record of Summer Air Temperature Reconstructed from Freshwater Pearl Mussels," *Quaternary Science Reviews* 23 (November 2003): 1803–16.
23. Jeff Poor, "Famed Hurricane Forecaster William Gray Predicts Global Cooling in Ten Years," Business and Media Institute, March 4, 2008, http://www .businessandmedia.org/articles/2008/20080304113132.aspx.
24. See the testimony of John Christy, Professor of Atmospheric Science, University of Alabama/Huntsville before the House of Representatives, May 13, 2003, in Singer and Avery, *Unstoppable Global Warming*, 164–71.

LIE #38

Epigraphs:
    Charles A. Beard, *An Economic Interpretation of the Constitution of the United States* (New York: Macmillan, 1935), 324.
    Howard Zinn, *A People's History of the United States, 1492–Present* (New York: Perennial, 2003), 101.

1. Beard, *An Economic Interpretation of the Constitution*, xiii.
2. Ibid., xvii.
3. Zinn, *People's History of the United States*, 99.
4. Forrest McDonald, *We the People: The Economic Origins of the Constitution* (Chicago: University of Chicago Press, 1958).
5. Ibid., 400.
6. Gordon S. Wood, *The Creation of the American Republic, 1776–1787* (Chapel Hill: University of North Carolina Press, 1998).
7. Lawrence Harper, "Mercantilism and the American Revolution," *Canadian Historical Review* 23 (1942): 1–15.
8. Robert P. Thomas, "A Quantitative Approach to the Study of the Effects of British Imperial Policy on Colonial Welfare," *Journal of Economic History* 25 (1965): 615–38.
9. Jeremy Atack and Peter Passell, *A New Economic View of American History*, 2nd ed. (New York: Norton, 1994), 62.
10. Peter McClelland, "The Cost to America of British Imperial Policy," *American Economic Review* 59 (1969): 370–81.

11. Bernard Bailyn, *Ideological Origins of the American Revolution* (Cambridge, MA: Belknap, 1992).
12. Robert A. McGuire and Robert L. Ohsfeldt, "Economic Interests and the American Constitution: A Quantitative Rehabilitation of Charles A. Beard," *Journal of Economic History* 44 (June 1984): 509–19.
13. Rush H. Limbaugh II, "Americans Who Risked Everything," http://www.rush limbaugh.com/home/folder/american_who_risked_everything_1.LogIn.html.

LIE #39

Epigraph:
    Charles A. Beard and Mary R. Beard, *The Rise of American Civilization* (New York: Macmillan, 1927), 54.

1. David Lightner, *Slavery and the Commerce Power: How the Struggle Against the Interstate Slave Trade Led to the Civil War* (New Haven, CT: Yale University Press, 2006), 140. In fact, however, Lightner's book is misnamed, as most of the evidence he presents suggests just the opposite—that the interstate commerce clauses were never viewed as mechanisms with which to eliminate slavery, except by a handful of people, and that the courts never applied the commerce clause to slavery.
2. James L. Huston, *Calculating the Value of the Union: Slavery, Property Rights, and the Economic Origins of the Civil War* (Chapel Hill: University of North Carolina Press, 2003), 29–30.
3. Ibid., 32.
4. Ibid., 27.
5. Lawrence Harper, "Mercantilism and the American Revolution," *Canadian Historical Review* 23 (1942): 1–15; Robert P. Thomas, "A Quantitative Approach to the Study of the Effects of British Imperial Policy on Colonial Welfare," *Journal of Economic History* 25 (1965): 615–38; and Peter McClelland, "The Cost to America of British Imperial Policy," *American Economic Review* 59 (1969): 370–81; and Jeremy Atack and Peter Passell, *A New Economic View of American History*, 2nd ed. (New York: Norton, 1994).
6. Huston, *Calculating the Value of the Union*, 27.
7. Charles Calomiris and Larry Schweikart, "The Panic of 1857: Origins, Transmission, and Containment," *Journal of Economic History* 51 (December 1991): 807–34.
8. Ulrich Bonnell Phillips, *The Life of Robert Toombs* (New York: Macmillan, 1913), 81–82.
9. Huston, *Calculating the Value of the Union*, 143.
10. John C. Calhoun to Percy Walker, October 23, 1847, in Robert L. Meriweather et al., eds., 25 vols. *The Papers of John C. Calhoun* (Columbia: University of South Carolina Press, 1959), 24:617.
11. Jefferson Davis, Speech in the Senate, February 13, 14, 1850, in Rowland Dunbar, ed., *Jefferson Davis, Constitutionalist: His Letters, Papers, and Speeches*, 10 vols. (Jackson: Mississippi Department of Archives and History, 1923), 1:279, 283.

LIE #40

Epigraphs:
Matthew Josephson, *The Robber Barons: The Great American Capitalists, 1861–1901* (New York: Harcourt, Brace, 1934), 28.
Ida M. Tarbell, *The History of the Standard Oil Company,* brief ed. (New York: Norton, 1966), 21.
Thomas Bailey and David M. Kennedy, *The American Pageant,* 8th ed. (Lexington, MA: D. C. Heath, 1987), 509.

1. Tarbell, *History of the Standard Oil Company,* 184.
2. Ibid., 166.
3. John S. McGee, "Predatory Price-cutting: The Standard Oil (N.J.) Case," *Journal of Law and Economics,* October 1958, 137–69.
4. For example, James Langefeld and David Scheffman, "Evolution or Revolution: What Is the Future of Antitrust?" *Antitrust Bulletin* 31 (Summer 1986): 287–99; Robert H. Bork, *The Antitrust Paradox: A Policy at War with Itself* (New York: Basic Books, 1978); Harold Demsetz, "Barriers to Entry," *American Economic Review* (March 1982): 47–57: Yale Brozen, "Concentration and Profits: Does Concentration Matter?" *Antitrust Bulletin* 19 (1974): 381–99; Dominick T. Armentano, *Antitrust and Monopoly: Anatomy of a Policy Failure,* 2nd ed. (New York: Holmes & Meier, 1990).
5. Larry Schweikart, *The Entrepreneurial Adventure: A History of Business in the United States* (Fort Worth, TX: Harcourt, 2000), 256.
6. Stuart Bruchey, *The Wealth of the Nation: An Economic History of the United States* (New York: Harper & Row, 1988), 132.
7. U.S. Code 15:1, http://www.law.cornell.edu/uscode/html/uscode15/usc_sec_15 _00000001—-000-.html.
8. All of this is relayed in Alfred D. Chandler, *Visible Hand: The Managerial Revolution in American Business* (Cambridge, MA: Belknap, 1977).
9. Larry Schweikart and Michael Allen, *A Patriot's History of the United States: From Columbus's Great Discovery to the War on Terror,* paperback ed. (New York: Sentinel, 2007), 452. On the mergers, see Naomi Lamoreaux, *The Great Merger Movement in American Business, 1895–1904* (Cambridge, MA: Cambridge University Press, 1985); and Louis Galambos and Joseph C. Pratt, *The Rise of the Corporate Commonwealth: U.S. Business and Public Policy in the Twentieth Century* (New York: Basic Books, 1988).
10. Schweikart, *Entrepreneurial Adventure,* 257–58.
11. Galambos and Pratt, *Rise of the Corporate Commonwealth,* 62.
12. George Bittlingmayer, "Antitrust and Business Activity: The First Quarter Century," *Business History Review* (Autumn 1996): 363–401; "The Stock Market and Early Antitrust Enforcement," *Journal of Law and Economics* 36 (April 1993): 1–32; "Output and Stock Prices When Antitrust Is Suspended: Experience under the NIRA," in Fred S. McChesney and William Shughart II, eds., *The Causes and Consequences of Antitrust: A Public Choice Perspective* (Chicago: University of Chicago Press, 1995); and with Thomas W. Hazlett, "DOS Kapital: Has Antitrust Action Against Microsoft Created Value in the Computer Industry?" *Journal of Financial Economics* 55 (March 2000): 329–59.
13. George Bittlingmayer, "Regulatory Uncertainty and Investment: Evidence from Antitrust Enforcement," *CATO Journal* 20 (Winter 2001): 295–324 (quotation on 321–22).
14. Ibid., 322.

LIE #41

Epigraphs:
Stephen E. Ambrose, *Nothing Like It in the World* (New York: Simon & Schuster, 2000), 19.
Thomas A. Bailey and David M. Kennedy, *The American Pageant*, 8th ed. (Lexington, MA: D. C. Heath, 1987), 504–5.
John Morton Blum et al., *The National Experience: A History of the United States*, 7th ed. (New York: Harcourt, Brace, 1989), 418–20.

1. Larry Schweikart, *The Entrepreneurial Adventure: A History of Business in the United States* (Fort Worth, TX: Harcourt, 2000), chapter 5, passim.
2. Alfred D. Chandler, *Visible Hand: The Managerial Revolution in American Business* (Cambridge, MA: Belknap, 1977).
3. Burton Folsom Jr., *The Myth of the Robber Barons* (Herndon, VA: Young America's Foundation, 1991).
4. Schweikart, *Entrepreneurial Adventure*, 148.
5. Building the Union Pacific: From Wyoming Tales and Trails, http://www.wyomingtalesandtrails.com/pac2.html
6. Folsom, *Myth of the Robber Barons*, 18.
7. Ibid.
8. Robert W. Fogel, *Railroads and American Economic Growth: Essays in Econometric History* (Baltimore: Johns Hopkins University Press, 1960).
9. Albert Fishlow, for example, put it at 4 percent in *Railroads and the Transformation of the Antebellum Economy* (Cambridge, MA: Harvard, 1960).
10. Albro Martin, *James J. Hill and the Opening of the Northwest* (New York: Oxford University Press, 1976), 410–11.
11. Schweikart, *Entrepreneurial Adventure*, 152.
12. Stewart Holbrook, *James J. Hill: A Great Life in Brief* (New York: Knopf, 1955), 93; Martin, *James J. Hill*, 366; Folsom, *Myth of the Robber Barons*, 26–27.
13. Schweikart, *Entrepreneurial Adventure*, 153.
14. Ibid.

LIE #42

Epigraph:
John Mack Faragher et al., *Out of Many*, combined vol., 4th ed., TLC ed. (Upper Saddle River, NJ: Pearson, 2006), 509.

1. See Ronit Lami's articles, "Affluenza and Its Effect on the Family," (London) *Family Business Magazine*, 2003, and "'Affluenza,' A Wealth of Solutions," http://www.affluenza-and-wealth.com/AFF_articles.html.
2. Faragher, *Out of Many*, 509.
3. David E. Harrell et al., *Unto a Good Land: A History of the American People* (Grand Rapids, MI: William Eerdmans, 2005), 605.
4. "Prenuptual Reveals Carnegie's True Plan," http://findarticles.com/p/articles/mi_qn4156/is_20050501/ai_n14609494.
5. Thomas Bailey and David M. Kennedy, *The American Pageant*, 8th ed. (Lexington, MA: D. C. Heath, 1987), 509.

6. Howard Zinn, *A People's History of the United States, 1492–Present* (New York: Perennial Classics, 2003), 262–63.
7. Quoted in Burton W. Folsom Jr., *Myth of the Robber Barons: A New Look at the Rise of Big Business in America* (Herndon, VA: Young America's Foundation, 1991), 83.
8. David Cannadine, *Mellon: An American Life* (New York: Knopf, 2006).
9. Ibid., 520.
10. Ibid., 563.

Lie #43

Epigraphs:
  John A. Garraty, *The American Nation*, 5th ed. (New York: Harper & Row, 1983), 638, 666.

  Thomas A. Bailey and David M. Kennedy, *The American Pageant*, 9th ed. (Lexington, MA: D. C. Heath, 1991), 755.

  This version comes from the 4th ed. of Irwin Unger's *These United States: The Questions of Our Past* (Boston: Little, Brown, 1989), 676. The concise combined volume, 3rd ed. (2007), notes only "Between 1920 and 1929 Mellon won further victories for his drive to shift more of the tax burden from high-income earners to the middle and wage-earning classes" (569), which means he is still wrong.

1. For a comparison of the North and South's tax regimes during the Civil War, see Richard Bensel, *Yankee Leviathan: The Origins of Central State Authority in America, 1859–1877* (Ithaca, NY: Cornell University Press, 1990).
2. See Burton W. Folsom's discussion in *Myth of the Robber Barons: A New Look at the Rise of Big Business in America* (Herndon, VA: Young America's Foundation, 1991), 106–7.
3. Morton Horowitz, *The Transformation of American Law* (Cambridge, MA: Harvard University Press, 1979).
4. Robert Stanley, *Dimensions of Law in the Service of Order: Origins of the Federal Income Tax, 1861–1913* (New York: Oxford University Press, 1993).
5. W. Elliot Brownlee, *Federal Taxation in America: A Short History*, new ed. (Cambridge, MA: Cambridge University Press, 2004), 45.
6. Stanley Lebergott, *The Americans: An Economic Record* (New York: Norton, 1984), 407–8; Edwin Seligman, *The Income Tax* (New York: Macmillan, 1911), 420; Gerald Eggert, "Richard Olney and the Income Tax," *Mississippi Valley Historical Review* (June 1961): 24–25.
7. Lebergott, *The Americans*, 408.
8. Mellon quoted in Folsom, *Myth of the Robber Barons*, 108.
9. Andrew Mellon, *Taxation: The People's Business* (New York: Macmillan, 1924), 74.
10. Folsom, *Myth of the Robber Barons*, 109.
11. James Gwartney, "Tax Cuts: Who Shoulders the Burden?" Federal Reserve Bank of Atlanta, *Economic Review*, March 1982, Table 5.
12. Congressional Budget Office, *A Review of the Accuracy of Treasury Revenue Forecasts, 1963–1978* (Washington, DC: U.S. Government Printing Office, February 1981), 4.
13. Bruce Bartlett, "The Futility of Raising Tax Rates," CATO Institute *Policy Analysis*, April 8, 1993, http://www.cato.org/pubs/pas/pa-192.html.
14. "America Celebrates Tax Freedom Day," http://www.taxfoundation.org/tax-freedomday/.

LIE #44

Epigraphs:
Paul S. Boyer et al., *The Enduring Vision: A History of the American People, from 1865,* vol. 2, 5th ed. (New York: Houghton Mifflin, 2004), 744, 745.

Jeanne Boydston et al., *Making a Nation: The United States and Its People,* combined vol. (Upper Saddle River, NJ: Pearson, 2004), 570. To their credit, the authors admit, "No single factor explains the onset and persistence of the Great Depression. . . . Today most scholars believe that numerous flaws in the national and international economic structure, along with ill-conceived government policies, bear a large degree of responsibility for the catastrophe" (569–70). However, the *only* "misguided policies" they highlight are "those of the Republican administrations of the 1920s . . . committed to reducing the interference of government in the economy, lowering taxes on the wealthy, and reducing government spending." They strongly imply that Federal Deposit Insurance saved the banking system, *not* (as virtually all economic historians agree) abandoning the gold standard. They do not mention Roosevelt's astonishing tax increases, nor his suggestion to tax wealthy Americans at 100 percent!

Irwin Unger, *These United States: Questions of Our Past,* concise ed., combined vol., 3rd ed. (Upper Saddle River, NJ: Pearson, 2007), 591.

1. Milton Friedman and Anna J. Schwartz, *A Monetary History of the United States, 1867–1960* (Princeton, NJ: Princeton University Press, 1963).
2. On the "bubble," a significant debate remains as to which was the central factor in the crash, a mania/bubble or business/market fundamentals. The point is, it is a debate, and even those who argue for a "mania" greatly qualify their conclusions. These are but a sampling of the recent scholarship that rejects such a notion as the *main* causative factor of the Crash: Gary Santoni and Gerald Dwyer, "Bubbles vs. Fundamentals: New Evidence from the Great Bull Markets," in Eugene White, *Crises and Panics: The Lessons of History* (Homewood, IL: Dow/Jones Irwin, 1990); Eugene White, "The Stock Market Boom and Crash of 1929 Revisited," *Journal of Economic Perspectives* 4 (Spring 1990): 67–83; Frederic S. Mishkin and Eugene N. White, "U.S. Stock Market Crashes and Their Aftermath: Implications for Monetary Policy," in William C. Hunter, George G. Kaufman, and Michael Pomerleano, *Asset Price Bubbles: The Implications for Monetary, Regulatory, and International Policies* (Cambridge, MA: MIT Press, 2003), 53–79; Peter Rappoport and Eugene N. White, "Was There a Bubble in the 1929 Stock Market?" *Journal of Economic History* 53 (September 1993): 549–74; Gerald Sirkin, "The Stock Market of 1929 Revisited: A Note," *Business History Review* 49 (Summer 1975): 223–41; J. Bradford De Long and Andrei Shleifer, "The Stock Market Bubble of 1929: Evidence from Closed-end Mutual Funds," *Journal of Economic History* 52 (September 1991): 675–700; R. Glen Donaldson and Mark Kamstra, "A New Dividend Forecasting Procedure That Rejects Bubbles in Asset Prices: The Case of 1929's Stock Crash," *Review of Financial Studies* 9 (Summer 1996): 333–83. On what Americans knew about stocks, see Peter Rappoport and Eugene N. White, "Was the Crash of 1929 Expected?" *American Economic Review* 84 (March 1994): 271; Gene Smiley, *The American Economy in the Twentieth Century* (Cincinnati: South-Western Publishing, 1994), ch. 6; Jeremy Atack and Peter W. Passell, *A New Economic View of American History,* 2nd ed. (New York: Norton, 1994), 606–7.
3. Mishkin and White, "U.S. Stock Market Crashes," passim.

4. Eugene White, "Anticipating the Stock Market Crash of 1929: The View from the Floor of the Stock Exchange," NBER Working Papers 12661, National Bureau of Economic Research, 2006; Edwin J. Perkins, *Wall Street to Main Street: Charles Merrill and Middle-Class Investors* (Cambridge, MA: Cambridge University Press, 2006).

5. Gene Smiley, *Rethinking the Great Depression* (Chicago: Ivan R. Dee, 2002), from uncorrected advance proof, 10–11.

6. Larry Schweikart, *The Entrepreneurial Adventure: A History of Business in the United States* (Fort Worth, TX: Harcourt, 2000), ch. 9.

7. See, for example, Charles Holt, "Who Benefited from the Prosperity of the Twenties?," *Explorations in Economic History* 14 (July 1977): 277–89.

8. Schweikart, *Entrepreneurial Adventure*, 335.

9. Ibid., 332–33.

10. Andrew Mellon, *Taxation: The People's Business* (New York: Macmillan, 1924), laid out his arguments for cutting taxes. For the impact, see Gene Smiley and Richard H. Keehn, "Federal Personal Income Tax Policy in the 1920s," *Journal of Economic History* 55 (June 1995): 285–303; James Gwartney and Richard Stroup, "Tax Cuts: Who Shoulders the Burden," *Economic Review* (March 1982): 19–27.

11. Jude Wanniski, *The Way the World Works: How Economies Fail—and Succeed* (New York: Basic Books, 1978).

12. Robert B. Archibald and David H. Feldman, "Investment During the Great Depression: Uncertainty and the Role of the Smoot-Hawley Tariff," *Southern Economic Review* 64 (1998): 857–79; Douglas Irwin, "The Smoot-Hawley Tariff: A Quantitative Assessment," *Review of Economics and Statistics* 80 (May 1998): 326–34; and his "Changes in U.S. Tariffs: The Role of Import Prices and Commercial Policies," *American Economic Review* 88 (September 1998): 1015–26.

13. In addition to Irwin's articles, noted above, see his "From Smoot-Hawley to Reciprocal Trade Agreements: Changing the Course of U.S. Trade Policy in the 1930s," in Michael Bordo et al., *The Defining Moment: The Great Depression and the American Economy in the Twentieth Century* (Chicago: University of Chicago Press, 1998), 325–52; Mario J. Crucini and James Kahn, "Tariffs and Aggregate Economic Activity: Lessons from the Great Depression," *Journal of Monetary Economics* 38 (1996): 427–67; and Crucini's "Sources of Variation in Real Tariff Rates: The United States, 1900–1940," *American Economic Review* 84 (June 1994): 732–43.

14. William D. Lastrapes and George Selgin, "The Check Tax: Fiscal Folly and the Great Monetary Contraction," *Journal of Economic History* 57 (December 1997): 859–78.

15. Randall E. Parker, *The Economics of the Great Depression: A Twenty-first Century Look Back at the Economics of the Interwar Era* (Cheltenham, UK: Edward Elgar, 2007), 54; Barry Eichengreen, *Golden Fetters* (New York: Oxford University Press, 1992); Peter Temin, *Lessons from the Great Depression* (Cambridge, MA: MIT Press, 1989).

16. Charles Calomiris, "Financial Factors of the Great Depression," *Journal of Economic Perspectives* 7 (Spring 1993): 61–85; Charles Calomiris and Joseph Mason, "'Contagion' and Bank Failures During the Great Depression: The June 1932 Chicago Banking Panic," *American Economic Review* 87 (December 1997): 863–84, and their "Consequences of U.S. Bank Distress During the Depression," ibid., 93 (June 2003): 937–47; "Fundamentals, Panics, and Bank Distress During the Depression," ibid., 93 (December 2003): 1615–47.

17. Parker, *Economics of the Great Depression*, 54–55.

18. Stephen J. DeCanio, "Expectations and Business Confidence During the Great Depression," in Barry N. Siegel, ed., *Money in Crisis: The Federal Reserve, the Economy, and Monetary Reform* (San Francisco: Pacific Institute, 1984).
19. Charles Calomiris and Gary Gorton, "The Origins of Banking Panics: Models, Facts, and Bank Regulation," in Glenn R. Hubbard, ed., *Financial Markets and Market Crises* (Chicago: University of Chicago Press, 1991); Douglas Diamond and Philip Dybvig, "Bank Runs, Deposit Insurance, and Liquidity," *Journal of Political Economy* 91 (June 1983): 401–18.

LIE #45

Epigraphs:
David Edwin Harrell et al., *Unto a Good Land: A History of the American People* (Grand Rapids, MI: William B. Eerdmans, 2005), 1098.

Samuel Eliot Morison, Henry Steele Commager, and William E. Leuchtenburg, *A Concise History of the American Republic*, 2nd ed. (New York: Oxford University Press, 1983), 734.

John Morton Blum et al., *The National Experience: A History of the United States*, 7th ed. (New York: Harcourt, Brace, 1989), 755–57.

1. Warren Brookes, *The Economy in Mind* (New York: Universe Publishers, 1982), Table 7:3.
2. Ibid.
3. Ibid., Table 7-A; Michael Tanner, *The End of Welfare* (Washington, DC: CATO Institute, 1996), 70.
4. Robert Rector and William Lauber, *America's Failed $5.4 Trillion War on Poverty* (Washington: Heritage Foundation, 1995), 92–95.
5. Brookes, *Economy in Mind*, Table 7–5.
6. Charles Murray, *Losing Ground: American Social Policy, 1950–1980* (New York: Basic Books, 1984).
7. Ibid., 160–61.
8. Wade Horn and Andrew Bush, "Fathers, Marriage, and the Next Phase of Welfare Reform," Acton Institute Policyforum, Spring 2003, no. 3, 7.
9. Brookes, *Economy in Mind*, Table 7:3.
10. Barbara Dafoe Whitehead, "Dan Quayle Was Right," *The Atlantic*, April 1993, reprinted at http://www.franks.org/fr01222.htm, 1.
11. Ibid., 5.
12. Sammis White and Lori A. Geddes, "Income Success Among Former Wisconsin Welfare Recipients: Work Matters," Wisconsin Policy Research Institute, September 2002, 15, quotation in "Note from the President."
13. Robert E. Rector and Patrick F. Fagan, "The Good News About Welfare Reform," Heritage Foundation "Backgrounder," #1468, September 5, 2001, chart 2.
14. Ibid., charts 3 and 4.
15. Horn and Bush, "Fathers, Marriage, and the Next Phase of Welfare Reform," passim.

Lie #46

Epigraphs:
Ira C. Magaziner and Robert B. Reich, *Minding America's Business: The Decline and Rise of the American Economy* (New York: Vintage, 1983), 6, 7.
David Edwin Harrell Jr. et al., *Unto a Good Land: A History of the American People* (Grand Rapids, MI: William B. Eerdmans, 2005), 1152.

1. Magaziner and Reich, *Minding America's Business*, 331. See also Barry Bluestone and Bennett Harrison, *The Deindustrialization of America: Plant Closings, Community Abandonment, and the Dismantling of Basic Industry* (New York: Basic Books, 1984); Martin and Susan Tolchin, *Selling Our Security: The Erosion of America's Assets* (New York: Knopf, 1992).
2. Chalmers Johnson, *MITI and the Japanese Miracle* (Stanford, CA: Stanford University Press, 1982); Otis L. Graham, *Losing Time: The Industrial Policy Debate* (Cambridge, MA: Harvard University Press, 1992); Stephen Cohen and John Zysman, *Manufacturing Matters: The Myth of the Post-Industrial Economy* (New York: Basic Books, 1987).
3. David Halberstam, *The Reckoning* (New York: Avon, 1987). See also James J. Flink, *The Car Culture* (Cambridge, MA: MIT Press, 1975).
4. Ralph Nader, *Unsafe at Any Speed* (New York: Grossman, 1965).
5. Edmond J. Contoski, *Makers and Takers: How Wealth and Progress Are Made and How They Are Taken Away or Prevented* (Minneapolis: American Liberty Publishers, 1997), 98.
6. Ibid.
7. Sam Peltzman, "The Effects of Automobile Safety Regulation," *Journal of Political Economy* (August 1975): 677–725.
8. Contoski, *Makers and Takers*, 99.
9. Warren Brookes, *The Economy in Mind* (New York: Universe Books, 1982), 112.
10. Ibid., 111.
11. Larry Schweikart, *The Entrepreneurial Adventure: A History of Business in the United States* (Fort Worth, TX: Harcourt, 2000), 416–17.
12. Peter Asch, *Consumer Safety Regulations: Putting a Price on Life and Limb* (New York: Oxford University Press, 1988).
13. Robert Crandall, *Why Is the Cost of Environmental Regulations So High?* (St. Louis: Center for the Study of American Business, Washington University, February 1992), 3.
14. Gene Smiley, *The American Economy in the Twentieth Century* (Cincinnati: South-Western Educational Publishing, 1993), 381.
15. James C. Robinson, "The Impact of Environmental and Occupational Health Regulation on Productivity Growth in U.S. Manufacturing," *Yale Journal on Regulation* 12 (1995): 388–434 (quotation on 388).
16. Michael Greenstone, "The Impacts of Environmental Regulations on Industrial Activity: Evidence from the 1970 and 1977 Clean Air Act Amendments and the Census of Manufacturers," *Journal of Political Economy* 110 (2002): 1175–1219 (quotation on 1176).
17. Schweikart, *Entrepreneurial Adventure*, 418.
18. See Hans G. Mueller, "The Steel Industry," in J. Michael Finger and Thomas D. Willett, eds., *The Internationalization of the American Economy, The Annals of the American Academy of Political and Social Science* 460 (March 1982): 73–82; Robert

E. Baldwin, Barry Eichengreen, and Hans van der Den, "U.S. Antidumping Policies: The Case of Steel," in Anne O. Kreuger, ed., *The Structure and Evolution of Recent U.S. Trade Policy* (Chicago: University of Chicago Press for National Bureau of Economic Research, 1984), 67–103; Mansel G. Blackford and K. Austin Kerr, *Business Enterprise in American History*, 2nd ed. (Boston: Houghton Mifflin, 1990), 430–31.

19. Larry Schweikart, interview with Ken Iverson, President, Nucor Steel, June 8, 1995.

20. John P. Hoerr, *And the Wolf Finally Came: The Decline of the American Steel Industry* (Pittsburgh: University of Pittsburgh Press, 1988), 606–7; Richard Preston, *American Steel* (New York: Prentice-Hall, 1991), 80–81.

21. Scott Callon, *Divided Sun: MITI and the Breakdown of Japanese High-Tech Industrial Policy, 1975–1993* (Stanford, CA: Stanford University Press, 1997).

22. George Gilder, *Recapturing the Spirit of Enterprise* (Oakland, CA: ICS Press, 1992).

Lie #47

Epigraphs:

John Mack Faragher et al., *Out of Many*, combined vol., 4th ed., TLC ed. (Upper Saddle River, NJ: Pearson, 2006), 851.

David Goldfield et al., *The American Journey*, brief 4th ed., combined ed., TLC ed. (Upper Saddle River, NJ: Pearson, 2007), 885.

1. Samuel Eliot Morison, Henry Steele Commager, and William E. Leuchtenburg, *A Concise History of the American Republic*, 2nd ed. (New York: Oxford University Press, 1983), 763.

2. George Brown Tindall and David E. Shi, *America: A Narrative History*, brief 6th ed. (New York: Norton, 2007), 1188.

3. See the appropriate years in the U.S. Census, under "Federal Government," http://www.census.gov/prod/www/abs/statab1951-1994.htm.

4. George Brown Tindall and David E. Shi, *America: A Narrative History*, 5th ed., 2 vols. (New York: Norton, 1999), 2:1612.

5. Daniel Yergin and Joseph Stanislaw, *The Commanding Heights: The Battle for the World Economy* (New York: Touchstone, 2002), 351.

6. Thomas A. Bailey et al., *The American Pageant*, 11th ed. (Boston: Houghton Mifflin, 1998).

7. Thomas A. Bailey and David Kennedy, *The American Pageant*, 9th ed. (Boston: Houghton Mifflin, 1991), 845.

8. Ibid., 848.

Lie #48

Epigraphs:

John Mack Faragher, et al., *Out of Many*, combined vol., 4th ed. (Upper Saddle River, NJ: Pearson, 2006), 719.

Jeanne Boydston et al., *Making a Nation*, combined vol. (Upper Saddle River, NJ: Pearson, 2004), 635.

1. Victor Navsky, "Hiss in History," *The Nation*, April 12, 2007, cited in Wikipedia, "Alger Hiss," http://en.wikipedia.org/wiki/Alger_Hiss#cite_note-1

2. Allen Weinstein, *Perjury: The Hiss-Chambers Case* (New York: Afred A. Knopf, 1978), 356; Sam Tanenhaus, Whittaker Chambers: A Biography (New York: Random House, 1997). There is also evidence from behind the former Iron Curtain: Maria Schmidt, "Noel Field—The American Communist at the Center of Stalin's East European Purge: From the Hungarian Archives," *American Communist History* 3 (December 2004).
3. Weinstein, *Perjury*, Appendix: "Forgery by Typewriter," 577–81.
4. Eduard Mark, "Who Was VENONA's ALES? Cryptanalysis and the Hiss Case," *I&NS* 18, Autumn 2003; John R. Schindler, "Hiss in VENONA: The Continuing Controversy," paper presented at a Center for Cryptologic History Symposium, October 27, 2005, Laurel, Maryland.
5. Lynne Duke, "Stepping Out of the Shadows," *Washington Post*, April 5, 2007.
6. John Earl Haynes and Harvey Klehr, "Hiss Was Guilty," HistoryNewsNetwork, April 16, 2007, http://hnn.us/articles/37456.html.
7. Richard Pyle, "Scholars Restudy Alger Hiss Spy Case," washingtonpost.com, April 5, 2007.
8 "Russian General Retreats on Hiss," *New York Times*, December 17, 1992.
9. Haynes and Klehr, "Hiss Was Guilty."
10. Christopher Andrew and Oleg Gordievsky, *KGB: The Inside Story of Its Foreign Operations from Lenin to Gorbachev* (New York: HarperCollins, 1990), 287.
11. Nathaniel Weyl, *Treason: The Story of Disloyalty and Betrayal in American History* (Washington: Public Affairs Press, 1950).

FINAL LIE

1. *American History: Beginnings Through Reconstruction* (Evanston, IL: McDougall Littell, 2008). "Consultants" for this book included Robert Dallek, a liberal biographer of Lyndon Johnson.
2. See the annual commentary at Educational Research Analysts, http://www.textbookreviews.org.
3. Gary J. Kornblith and Carol Lasser, eds., *Teaching American History: Essays Adapted from the* Journal of American History, *2001–2007* (New York: Bedford St. Martin's, 2009), 3. Anyone interested in the number of instructors/courses using a particular textbook, pages 69–70.
4. Ibid., 8.
5. Ibid., 15.

INDEX

Page numbers in *italics* refer to illustrations.